LUMINESCENCE

Katherine Road U.M. Church, Forest Gate

The first of these pictures is of one of the main churches Fred Barrett pastored, Katherine Road Methodist, which is in Essex. The second picture is of a preaching wagon used by Fred Barrett as an evangelist for Wesleyan Home Missions. And the third picture is of Fred doing what all good Methodist preachers are tempted to do when they go to Epworth where John Wesley was born and raised—namely, preach from the tomb of Samuel Wesley, as John once did when he was forbidden to enter his father's former church and preach there, but could not be denied preaching from his father's tomb, which technically belonged to the Wesley family. The last of these pictures is of C. K. Barrett as a young pastor and scholar with his parents.

"It was rather daunting to be C.K. Barrett's successor. Our local church in Nottingham had been Methodist and so it was appropriate for another Methodist to succeed Barrett in a Theology Department whose other professors had traditionally been Anglicans and Canons of the Cathedral next door to the Department. Initially my wife and I bypassed our nearest Methodist chapel in North Road on Sundays because two New Testament Professors in the congregation might be somewhat intimidating for local (lay) preachers. But we soon realized that we need have no concerns on that front, since Kingsley was away every Sunday preaching elsewhere in the region, with local stewards more than willing to come and pick him up each time, since he didn't drive. In my own preaching round Methodist chapels in the region, a typical warmly appreciative remark would refer to Mr. Barrett who taught somewhere in 'the college in Durham.' One of my favourite memories was of an exceptional occasion when he took the service in North Road and began by holding up a piece of mechanism, which, he explained, came from his wife Margaret's washing machine. He wryly noted Margaret's comment that 'We need a little man' (to mend the machine), and added, 'Apparently I was not "a little man."' No indeed! He was a great man, the leading New Testament scholar in the United Kingdom, and high within the top ten in the world. Daunting, yes; but what an honour!"

—JAMES D. G. DUNN
Emeritus Lightfoot Professor of Divinity, Department of Theology, University of Durham

"C. Kingsley Barrett is widely known as an outstanding and great scholar in New Testament studies. It may be less known, however, that he served as a preacher in nearby communities, in chapels, churches and, at times, in cathedrals, radio broadcasts, and even in the open air. It is therefore of great importance that his sermons now are published and made accessible to readers in general. Barrett drew closely on the Biblical text. He selected central themes and concepts and made them to come alive, also citing hymns—in particular hymns written by Charles Wesley—and referring to literature and sports, as well as to historical persons and events. In his piety and theology he was rooted in the Methodist-Wesleyan tradition and managed at the same time to communicate to a wide range of auditors. Thus his sermons were both educational and led the listeners to a life-changing response characterized by dedication and service. With his sonorous voice and his systematic form of presentation he established excellent contact with the congregation. The reader will personally benefit greatly by reading the sermons, as well as in various ways drawing on them in groups and in worship services."

—PEDER BORGEN PHD
Professor Emeritus, Department of Religious Studies,
Norwegian University of Science and Technology, Trondheim, Norway

"At a time when a great gulf exists between serious biblical scholarship and most preaching, the sermons of C. K. Barrett—arguably the most significant New Testament scholar of the twentieth century—offer an instructive and rewarding corrective. Barrett had a gift for drawing out the theological significance of passages so as to stimulate the intellect of the most sophisticated thinkers and at the same time to make the biblical truths interesting, understandable, and relevant to ordinary Christians. These sermons are pure gold."

—DAVID BAUER
Ralph Waldo Beeson Professor of Inductive Bible Studies,
Dean of the School of Biblical Interpretation, Asbury Theological Seminary

"Some readers of the luminaries of New Testament commentaries have often pondered how that scholar might preach a New Testament text, how they might apply the text, and how they might work this exacting exegesis out for lay folks. In a former era most of those New Testament scholars could be heard in their local churches preaching, but in the last generation an increasing number of our luminaries have faded from the church scene. It is nothing but a delight and spiritually forming experience to read the sermons of C.K. Barrett, a scholar I have treasured my entire academic life. I now admire his spiritual formation as visible in every one of these sermons."

—SCOT MCKNIGHT
Julius R. Mantey Professor of New Testament, Northern Seminary, Lombard, IL

"Like many others, I first encountered C.K. Barrett as a great New Testament scholar. But the sermons published here reveal another Barrett—Barrett the preacher. He was a preacher who knew how to unravel a biblical text and put it back together again, a preacher whose sermons sounded like a summons from the God of eternity. It is wonderful to have this treasury of Barrett's pulpit work to inspire a new generation of Christ's heralds today."

—TIMOTHY GEORGE
founding dean, Beeson Divinity School, Samford University;
general editor of the *Reformation Commentary on Scripture*

"Sermons that are to be significant beyond their original delivery need to have a clear-eyed grasp of the subject matter of Scripture, of the realities of our world, and of the nature of discipleship. They also need to be engaging and accessible. These sermons by Kingsley Barrett have all these qualities in spades."

—WALTER MOBERLY
Durham University

LUMINESCENCE

The Sermons of C. K. and Fred Barrett

∽

—Volume Three—

Edited by
BEN WITHERINGTON, III

CASCADE *Books* • Eugene, Oregon

LUMINESCENCE
The Sermons of C. K. and Fred Barrett

Volume Three

Copyright © 2018 Ben Witherington III. All rights reserved. Except for brief quotations in critical publications or reviews, no part of this book may be reproduced in any manner without prior written permission from the publisher. Write: Permissions, Wipf and Stock Publishers, 199 W. 8th Ave., Suite 3, Eugene, OR 97401.

Cascade Books
An Imprint of Wipf and Stock Publishers
199 W. 8th Ave., Suite 3
Eugene, OR 97401

www.wipfandstock.com

PAPERBACK ISBN: 978-1-5326-3249-5
HARDCOVER ISBN: 978-1-5326-3251-8
EBOOK ISBN: 978-1-5326-3250-1

Cataloging-in-Publication data:

Names: Barrett, C. K. (Charles Kingsley) | Barrett, Fred | Witherington, Ben, III (editor)

Title: Luminescence : the sermons of C.K. and Fred Barrett, volume three / edited by Ben Witherington III.

Description: Eugene, OR : Cascade Books, 2018 | Includes bibliographical references.

Identifiers: ISBN 978-1-5326-3249-5 (paperback) | ISBN 978-1-5326-3251-8 (hardcover) | ISBN 978-1-5326-3250-1 (ebook)

Subjects: LCSH: Barrett, C. K. (Charles Kingsley), 1917–2011 | Barrett, Fred. | Sermons, English—20th century.

Classification: LCC BS491.5 B5 2018 (print) | LCC BS491.5 (ebook)

Manufactured in the U.S.A   05/03/2018

CONTENTS

Preface | xi
Introduction | xv

SERMONS FROM THE OLD TESTAMENT

"WALKING WITH GOD"—Genesis 5.24; Hebrews 11.5 | 3

"THE RECONSECRATIONS OF LIFE"—Genesis 13.1–4 | 7

"MOUNT MORIAH, THE HILL OF TESTING"—Genesis 22.2 | 11

"THE GLORY OF GOD IN THE FACE OF MAN"—Genesis 33.10 | 15

"THE GOD OF DIFFERENT PERSONALITIES"—Exodus 3.6 | 19

"THE CRIMES OF THE CARELESS"—Exodus 22.6 | 23

"THE CHRISTMAS FAITH AND THE CHRISTMAS FEAST"—Exodus 24.11 | 27

"THE FIRST SANCTUARY AND ITS FURNITURE"—Exodus 25.21, 22 | 30

"THE DAY OF DAYS"—Deuteronomy 16.3 | 35

"MOUNT PISGAH—THE HILL OF VISION"—Deuteronomy 34.1–4 | 38

"THE CALL TO THE CAPABLE"—Judges 9.7 | 42

"SAMSON—A CHARACTER STUDY"—Judges 16.20 | 47

"GOD AND BREAD"—Ruth 1.6 | 51

"DAVID HARPING BEFORE SAUL"—1 Samuel 16.17, 23 | 54

"THE GREEN EYE OF THE YELLOW GOD"—1 Samuel 18.9 | 58

"STRENGTHENING A MAN'S HAND IN GOD"—1 Samuel 23.16 | 62

"THE GRACE OF HUMILITY"—2 Samuel 7.18 | 66

"CONCERNING THE SAFETY OF YOUNG PEOPLE"—2 Samuel 18.29 | 69

"RELIGION AS LOYALTY"—1 Kings 2.4 | 72

"UNACCOMPLISHED AIMS"—1 Kings 8.17–19 | 77

"CAN RELIGION BE MADE EASY?"—1 Kings 12.28 | 80

"MOUNT CARMEL—THE HILL OF DECISION"—1 Kings 18.20, 21 | 83

"THE BROKEN ALTAR"—1 Kings 18.30 | 87

"LISTENING IN AND LISTENING OUT"—1 Kings 19.11 | 91

"A RELIGION THAT COSTS"—1 Chronicles 21.23, 24 | 95

"GOD'S GOODNESS AND MAN'S RESPONSE"—1 Chronicles 22.14-16 | 99

"A CHARGE TO KEEP"—Ezra 8.29 | 103

"RIDICULE AND REBUILDING"—Nehemiah 4.2-3 | 107

"THE HERITAGE OF YOUTH"—Psalm 16.6 | 111

"THE FEAST IN THE PRESENCE OF FOES"—Psalm 23.5 | 115

"WORSHIP IN THE BEAUTY OF HOLINESS"—Psalm 29.2 | 118

"KNOWN IN ADVERSITIES"—Psalm 31.7 | 121

"THE AUSTERITIES OF THE HILLS"—Psalm 84.5 | 124

"THE SOUL'S STRONGHOLD"—Psalm 91.1 | 128

"SETTING THE LAW TO MUSIC"—Psalm 119.54 | 131

"DISTANT AND NEAR"—Proverbs 17.24 | 134

"THE HEARTH OF GOD"—Isaiah 31.9 | 138

"THE UNDISCOURAGED SERVANT"—Isaiah 42.4 | 142

"BLIND TO HIS BEAUTY"—Isaiah 53.2 | 145

"THE FOOL AND HIS PENKNIFE"—Jeremiah 36.23 | 149

"THE LIKENESS OF MAN ON THE THRONE OF GOD"—Ezekiel 1.26 | 153

"PUT YOURSELF IN HIS PLACE"—Ezekiel 3.15 | 157

"SHOWERS OF BLESSING"—Ezekiel 34.26 | 161

"THE CHURCH AS BENEFACTOR"—Micah 5.7 | 164

"TO THE WORK! TO THE WORK!"—Haggai 2.4 | 168

"A WHITSUNTIDE ASSURANCE"—Haggai 2.5 | 172

"WOUNDED IN THE HOUSE OF FRIENDS"—Zechariah 13.6 | 175

"THINKING UPON GOD'S NAME"—Malachi 3.16 | 179

SERMONS FROM THE NEW TESTAMENT

"THE UNWANTED CHRIST"—Matthew 8.34 | 185

"THE SERVANT'S TEMPER AND METHOD"—Matthew 12.19, 20 | 189

"LOVE'S LABOR NOT LOST"—Matthew 26.8 | 192

"DARKNESS AND DAWN"—Matthew 28.1 | 196

"EMPHASIZE YOUR FAITH"—Mark 4.24 | 199

"CHRIST AND GOOD YOUNG PEOPLE"—Mark 5.21, 22 | 203

"THE DAYSPRING FROM ON HIGH"—Luke 1.78, 79 | 207

"THE SIGN TO THE SHEPHERDS"—Luke 2.12 | 210

"THE PILGRIMAGE TO BETHLEHEM"—Luke 2.15 | 212

"THE DOCTRINE OF THE DEPARTING ANGEL"—Luke 2.15; Acts 7.10 | 214

"LAUNCH OUT"—Luke 5.4, 5 | 217

"RELIGION ON THE DOORSTEP"—Luke 5.9 | 221

"THE GOSPEL OF A TOUCH"—Luke 5.13; 8.46 | 224

"WHERE IT IS GOOD TO BE"—Luke 9.33 | 228

"WHAT SETS ANGELS SINGING"—Luke 15.10 | 230

"THE GRACE OF GRATITUDE"—Luke 17.17 | 234

"CHRIST LIFTED UP"—John 12.32 | 237

"HIS MISSION AND OURS"—John 17.18; 20.21 | 241

"THE GARDEN BY THE CROSS"—John 19.41 | 245

"THE MAN WHO MISSED THE MEETING"—John 20.24 | 248

"FROM BAD TO WORSE"—Acts 12.2, 3 | 252

"MIDNIGHT MUSIC"—Acts 16.25 | 255

"THE GRACE OF CONTINUANCE"—Acts 26.22 | 259

"A GREAT TRIAL SCENE"—Acts 26.29 | 263

"CHRIST CRUCIFIED AND RISEN"—Romans 8.34 | 266

"THE FULL-ORBED GOSPEL"—Romans 15.29 | 269

"RUFUS—A CHOICE CHRISTIAN"—Romans 16.13 | 272

"THE CHRISTIAN OPTIMIST"—1 Corinthians 1.4 | 275

"CHRIST'S FAITH IN US"—1 Corinthians 13.7 | 278

"CHRIST'S CAPTIVE"—2 Corinthians 2.14 | 282

"GRACE ABOUNDING"—2 Corinthians 9.8 | 286

"GOD'S UNSPEAKABLE GIFT"—2 Corinthians 9.15 | 289

"SERMON ON THE MOTTO FOR 1937"—2 Corinthians 13.11 | 293

"THE CHRISTIAN'S CREDENTIALS"—Galatians 6.17 | 296

"THE UNSEARCHABLE RICHES"—Ephesians 3.8 | 300

"THE MIND OF CHRIST"—Philippians 2.5 | 303

"THE GRACE OF CONTENTMENT"—Philippians 4.11–13 | 307

"THE PREACHER'S PLEA FOR THE PEOPLE'S PRAYERS"
—2 Thessalonians 3.1 | 310

"OUR ENJOYMENT OF GOD'S GIFTS"—1 Timothy 6.17 | 313

"THE SPIRIT'S THREEFOLD GIFT"—2 Timothy 1.7 | 316

"THE SECOND CHANCE"—2 Timothy 4.11 | 320

"THE STORY OF A SLAVE"—Philemon 10, 11 | 324

"THE SACRIFICE OF PRAISE"—Hebrews 13.15 | 327

"GOD WILLING"—James 4.15 | 331

"THE GRACE OF CHARITY"—1 Peter 4.8 | 334

"THE ADDITIONS OF GRACE"—2 Peter 1.5 | 337

"THE WAY OF BALAAM"—2 Peter 2.15 | 340

"FELLOWSHIP WITH GOD"—1 John 1.3 | 343

"THE GRACE OF PATIENCE"—Revelation 1.9 | 346

"CHRIST AT THE DOOR"—Revelation 3.20 | 350

"KNIGHTS OF THE CROSS"—Revelation 14.4, 5 | 354

"NO MORE SEA"—Revelation 21.1 | 359

PREFACE

THIS VOLUME IS DIFFERENT from the previous two in this series in several respects. In the first place, Penelope and I must thank Jordan Stanley, one of Asbury's doctoral students, for his help with the transcribing of the one hundred sermons in this volume which show that Fred Barrett was prepared to preach throughout the canon of both the Old Testament and the New Testament.[1] I am responsible for the final editing and annotations of this volume, as with the previous two, but as you will notice in what follows, Penelope Barrett Hyslop has provided a fine introduction to this volume, giving us a sense of the relationship between Kingsley and his father, and the influence of the latter on the former, not least in regard to preaching.

My task in what follows in this preface, and in the footnotes, is to present these sermons in clear English, annotate them where references can be found, and provide the occasional comparative comment in light of the previous two volumes in this series. We can say at the outset that the geographical scope of Fred Barrett's ministry may have been more narrow than Kingsley's (he did not, I think, travel abroad and minister in foreign countries), and he may have preached in fewer places in England than did Kingsley (e.g., he did not preach in universities and cathedrals as Kingsley not infrequently did), but we should not underestimate the impact Fred Barrett had in his various pastoral tenures at Katherine Road Methodist Church, or at Spring Head Mission, or at Bishop St., and elsewhere, including in many open-air services and revivals. The sheer list of chapels preached in does not tell the whole tale of the depth and impact of a person's ministry.

In terms of homiletical form, Kingsley follows rather closely the practice of his father. Sermons usually have three points, quotes from hymns are regularly cited, and the sentence that ends one section of the sermon leads to the next heading for the next point. In other words, the sermons are carefully crafted. But that is not all.

Kingsley uses some of the same illustrations as his father, perhaps because he heard his father use them, or perhaps because he read the same sources, but probably it involves some of both. For example, the illustration Fred Barrett cites from Harold Begbie's book in the sermon entitled "The Reconsecrations of Life" is also cited, more

---

1. It is interesting that he did not share the reluctance of his son to deal with either the apocalyptic in the book of Revelation, or purple passages like Isaiah 53.

than once in Kingsley's sermons. Or again, in the sermon entitled "Mount Moriah, the Hill of Testing," Fred tells a bit of the story of the missionary Sam Pollard, who went to China, or alternately the story of David Livingstone in Africa. Kingsley also uses the same stories several times.

Kingsley, it will be remembered, said of his father that he was one of the greatest preachers he had ever heard. Now it might be possible to take that as the natural utterance of a loving son who was proud of his father, except that when you read these sermons you realize they are often powerful and not infrequently eloquent. Fred Barrett had a way with words, and though he may not have been the scholar his son was, he was also no country preacher. This is all the more remarkable in view of the fact that he had no formal education beyond the age of thirteen or fourteen. He was nonetheless thoughtful, with a good grasp of theology and ethics, not to mention a very considerable knowledge and understanding of the Bible. And one notable difference from his son's preaching style is that Fred not merely loved poetry, and quoted it frequently, he had a penchant for looking for the poetic or "mystical" phrase in the text to preach on, and this sometimes led to something that bordered on allegory. Consider for example his exposition on dawn in his sermon on Matthew 28, entitled "Darkness and Dawn." Kingsley does not go down that road.

Fred gives a clue about how he went about composing his sermons in the sermon on 2 Peter 1:5, called "The Additions of Grace." He says he has one Bible for his devotions, but uses a different Bible to compose his sermons. He adds, "It is very, very seldom that I use my personal devotional reading for sermonic purposes. Long ago I learned from Dr. Jowett the value of a preacher having literally a Bible never used for homiletical purposes, but reserved for the culture of his own soul." This is not to say that his sermons don't have devotional aspects and value to them. They do. But they focus on proclamation not devotional practices such as *lectio divina*.

One of the significant differences in the preaching of Kingsley and Fred, as revealed in these sermons, is that while time and again Kingsley focuses on "Christ and him crucified" in his preaching, both during the Easter season and at other times, Fred wants to place at least equal if not more emphasis on the resurrection of Christ. It must be remembered that Kingsley owed much to the German theological tradition which indeed, from Luther right through to the twentieth century with scholars like Bultmann and Kasemann, focused on "Christ and him crucified" and saw this as the heart of the gospel. It would be hard to imagine Kingsley placing the same emphasis where his father does, in what we hear Fred Barrett say in his sermon "Christ Crucified and Risen" (Rom 8:34):

"One asks if there is not a real point in Michelangelo's indignant protest to his fellow painters, "Why do you keep filling gallery after gallery with endless pictures of the one ever reiterated theme, of Christ in weakness, Christ dying, most of all of Christ hanging dead?" The symbol of our faith is not a crucifix, and certainly not one with a dead man on it. Paul's Christ, cried Michelangelo, is not dead but risen. Paint

PREFACE

him as the conqueror of death! Paint him as the Lord of life! Paint him as what he is, the irresistible Victor, who, tested to the uttermost, has proved himself in very deed mighty to save.

There is a real danger in our failure to remember that Easter follows Good Friday and in making the crucifix our symbol. Gazing at the cross alone and too long tends to kindle a queer inferiority complex in our minds that often leads to shrinking from the powers that are arrayed against us as against him, and that breeds a cowardice in which we lose heart and fling away our weapons. Bring in the upper thought that he conquered in death and we gain courage and become sure of the triumph of the good and true.

In some cases, and with some types of piety, continued meditation on the cross has led only to the luxury of grief, to vapid, lachrymose sentimentalism. By all means remember that he died for you and that will bring you to your knees in grief and gratitude. Remember that he rose again and is abroad in the world, then you will get up from your knees and follow his footsteps as he goes forth to seek and save. You will keep coming back to the cross for inspiration, but you will not "seek the living among the dead."

In his following sermon, Fred adds that the phrase "Christ and him crucified" should not be seen as a limitation but rather a concentration for good preaching, but he emphasizes that the word Christ means "the risen Christ." The death and resurrection must both be emphasized, but since life rather than death has the last word in the gospel, perhaps the resurrection should have preeminence.

As with Kingsley's sermons there are various literary allusions in Fred's sermons (e.g., a reference to Milton's "Samson Agonistes," and to Tennyson's "Sir Galahad" in the "Samson" sermon), but what we seldom find is allusions or quotes from twentieth-century theologians or biblical scholars (there is a reference to George Adam Smith or F. J. Foakes-Jackson and a few others occasionally), or for that matter early Reformers such as Luther, both of which things occur quite regularly in Kingsley's sermons.[2] Fred does not go down that road.

Two other things stand out. Fred references many nineteenth-century hymns, often revival hymns, and somewhat less frequently refers to the hymns of Charles Wesley or Isaac Watts, unlike his son. And then there is this surprise—he overwhelmingly chooses lines from hymns by nineteenth-century female hymn writers such as Fanny Crosby or Elizabeth Clephane, and many others. Indeed, I can find only two references to any hymns written in the twentieth century, even though Fred ministered into the middle of the twentieth century. He stuck to the eighteenth- and nineteenth-century hymns that populated the Methodist and Revivalist hymnbooks. Further, his sermons often read more like revival sermons "preaching for a verdict" in a hurry to get to the application and get the audience to change their lives, or increase their devotion, or

---

2. Luther is cited once in these sermons, and none of the old catechisms are cited, unlike in some of his son's sermons.

fully live out the faith. That is to say, Fred's sermons have more of a regular ethical focus or thrust, whereas the sermons of Kingsley are often more theological and even philosophical in character.

For example, Fred Barrett's preaching of the Old Testament mostly focused on its ethical content, and indeed, he does more justice to the ethics of the Old Testament than his son, not only because he focused more on it, but also because he plumbed its depths to a greater degree. For example, consider these remarks about some of the Mosaic Law in Exodus:

> Here is a pretty problem in ethics for you. Is a man morally responsible, not only for what he does, but for what results from his action? Must he be held accountable for consequences he did not intend resulting from his conduct? In my judgment, there are consequences of our actions, or of our failure to act, at a given moment which are altogether unexpected; by no knowledge accessible to us could we foresee them. For these consequences, it seems to me, we are not guilty. But there are cases in which we might have known that certain results would follow our action or our neglect. In such cases, we are not guiltless though there was no ill intent in our minds. We might have known that evil would follow a certain course of conduct and we ought to have found out. The text [Exod 22:6, about a fire which damages a neighbor's property] presents the case of a man who did not intend to cause damage. The law held him guilty because he was careless of consequences and did not take necessary precautions.

These sermons were preached from 1922 to 1952, and interestingly one of them was preached at both the first and the last of these dates. Fred, however, dates his ministry from 1906 according to the sermon "The Full-Orbed Gospel." This means that the sermons in this volume do not reflect his earliest efforts but come from during the time he was already an experienced pastor and evangelist. Like his son, Fred Barrett recycled his sermons, and some he preached as many as thirty times. But there is no evidence he preached as many times over as long a period as Kingsley. And it is to be noted that while Kingsley seems to have been often the especially chosen preacher for the high holy days in the calendar (and so there are many more Christmas and Easter and Watchnight and Pentecost sermons from him than from his father), one is hard pressed to find a lot of "high holy day" sermons from the pen of Fred Barrett, though there are some. I attribute this to Fred being a parish minister primarily throughout his ministry, while Kingsley was often a special days preacher, as well as a regular circuit preacher during his academic tenure between 1945 and the early 1980s.

Two tendencies also characterize the preaching of both father and son. Neither did expository preaching, going verse by verse through a text. Both would take a key idea, or a memorable phrase or thought and milk it for all it was worth. And both had a penchant for finishing a sermon with a line or lines from a favorite hymn. They knew their Methodist audiences would know the source of most of those quotes or

PREFACE

allusions. It is, however, right to ask the question how many of these sermons Kingsley actually heard, since the bulk of them seem to have been preached in the 1930s and '40s, when he also was on the Methodist circuit, and not sitting in a congregation listening to his father. As for the sermons from the '20s, he likely heard many of those before he went off to school at Shebbear. In any case, Fred Barrett was a remarkable preacher, and I trust you will find his sermons interesting, challenging, and edifying and not infrequently eloquent and even poetical.

INTRODUCTION

By Penelope Barrett Hyslop

My grandfather, Fred Barrett, spent the last couple of years or so living with us in Durham. As I was only twelve when he died, my personal memories of his life and preaching in particular are limited. I remember him as a very jolly grandpa and I know my mother much appreciated his skill in arranging party games for children's parties. She was able to concentrate on the catering of party food while Grandpa kept us all thoroughly amused. I also remember that he never seemed as quiet as he perhaps should have been when he was a member of a congregation. We could always hear him rattling the change in his pocket during the sermons! I do also have some memories of him in the pulpit. He never wore a dog collar but always had a white tie. In retrospect, it is clear that he had a real evangelical zeal and a good connection with his congregation.

Luckily, in order to be able to give a fuller picture of my grandfather I have found some pages that he wrote about his life. He was born in 1880 in Leeds, the second child of five. His father was a fellmonger (a dealer in hides and skins) and he praises his parents for the fun that he remembered from his childhood. He says his parents made sure that they were kept tidy and fed and brought up to be respectable and honest.

My grandfather only attended one school and left school at the age of thirteen. He recalls how he used to recite at school concerts and states how this helped him later because he was used to facing an audience and also trained his memory. My father did exactly the same thing while he was at Shebbear (a Bible Christian Methodist boarding school.) My father took parts in school productions of Shakespeare. Although my grandfather had the chance of a scholarship to continue his education, he needed to get a job to contribute to the family income. He started his working life as an errand boy and he remembers bringing home with pride his first week's wages—three shillings and four pence. Later he became an apprentice for a firm in York. It was at this time that he started going to James Street Methodist Free Church in York.[3] Here my grandfather committed himself to a life of service to God. He started by helping run the Sunday School and joined a mission and Temperance Brass Band. He and a

---

3. As so many chapels it has now been closed for years, but I do remember going there with my parents, as father preached there quite frequently.

INTRODUCTION

group of others also conducted open-air services in the poorest areas of York. This was invaluable experience for my grandfather. I find it amazing that this was a group of teenagers who were committed to these activities on a regular basis.

My grandfather's next task was to become recognized as a preacher. He became, first of all, a fully accredited local preacher. He continued with his job, but I feel sure that what he really wanted to do was become a full-time evangelist. Through a meeting with the Rev Thomas Cook he became a full-time Gospel Car Evangelist (see the picture above). Despite the obvious cares and concerns of his family, because in his own words "he was leaving a certainty for an uncertainty," he gave in his notice and took on a precarious lifestyle. This was a calling with no salary at all. He started at Cleethorpes but soon was sent to Lingdale with the Gospel Car Florence.[4] He preached all over the Cleveland, Middlesbrough, Redcar and Saltburn, and Danby circuits. Later my father often preached at many of these small chapels where Grandpa had surprised his superiors by his ability to preach and to convert people to Christianity.[5]

After about eighteen months out on the road with Florence, my grandfather, while still doing a lot of mission work, found time to do the necessary studying to become a Methodist minister, and he started his ministry in the Walton and Felixstowe circuit in 1905. In 1907 Grandpa moved to Katherine Road, Forest Gate, in London. This was a huge church with seating for 1250 people. The church was usually full to capacity on a Sunday night, including extra chairs in the aisles. In 1947, he returned to celebrate the fortieth anniversary of the beginning of his work in London. In his own words: "We had great crowds and I came away humble and yet exalted that, after 40 years, so many people kept a place in their hearts for this now elderly man who had gone to them as a young minister."

In 1916, Grandpa married Clara Seed (she had been a deaconess at Katherine Road) and they moved to Salford to a large downtown church. He describes it as one of the dirtiest and dreariest districts he had ever known. This was where my father was born. However, after five years they were ready to move. They went back to London—this time Fentiman Road in the Brixton circuit.

Fentiman Road, by all accounts, was the jolliest of Grandpa's churches. Grandpa found he had a group of young and inexperienced stewards who were taken aback by his ideas of how to develop the church's life but they committed themselves fully to helping run the church. Grandpa issued a *Monthly Messenger* and for eight years they sent out two thousand copies. I still have some of these copies. They started Saturday Popular Concerts and the crowds came. Grandpa and my father must have sung duets at these concerts and I remember father singing them with me in my childhood. In

---

4. Florence was a horse-drawn caravan. It consisted of a single room and cannot have had any modern amenities. My grandfather had to rely on the friendliness, hospitality, and goodwill of the local people to provide for both him and the horse.

5. As a child my favorite chapel was always Lingdale because we got a fabulous homemade faith tea after the service. Much later on I became very fond of visits to Skinningrove; I used to drive my parents there after mother wasn't so keen on driving too far.

INTRODUCTION

short, Fentiman Road prospered, and Grandpa says, "It was a sheer joy to watch the joy of the people at the church." While he was there, he was also released to conduct missions in Newcastle, Sheffield, Rochdale, Huddersfield, Leeds, Bideford, Exeter, Bury, and Norwich.

In 1930 Grandpa went back to Katherine Road. The church had fallen on hard times. The congregation was much depleted and there was a deficit on the church current account. He doesn't say much about his second stay at Katherine Road, except to say that they cleared the deficit and that this is where my father was accepted as a local preacher.

Grandpa's next church was in Wednesbury (1936–1944) where he became the superintendent of the Spring Head Mission. He enjoyed the fact that the mission stood for a great deal in the municipal life of the town. He must have relished all the extra commitments this brought as well as always producing new ideas to keep the church work appealing. His final appointment was to Bishop Street, Central Hall, Leicester.

I have great admiration for my grandfather. I find it impossible to imagine what my life would have been like if I had left full-time education at thirteen. It seems that he must always have been driven to seek his goals in circumstances that any teenager of the twenty-first century would find at the very least daunting.

He was undoubtedly a product of the times in which he lived. From the mission work that he started as a teenager, to becoming an itinerant evangelist preaching against the evils of the time, and then a Methodist minister, where he relished every aspect of church life and was never afraid of being innovative.

Ben has given a good comparison of the sermons of both men, but perhaps I may just add a few comments of my own. My grandfather exhorted his congregations to follow a better and Christian life. He was perhaps flamboyant in the pulpit, but also a very caring minister of his flock, and in this he was ably helped by his wife. She was by comparison quiet, but always a good listener and always concerned for others rather than herself. In Grandpa's notes about his life he quotes the last words she said in their house. The ambulance had come to take her to hospital late at night and she said, "I am so sorry to have brought you out so late." I guess these words sum up the sort of person she was.

Among all the paperwork I have inherited I found a cutting from the Methodist Recorder. Unfortunately, I do not know the date but I am guessing it is probably from the 1930s. I quote: "There is probably no man in the United Methodist ministry who has conducted so many evangelical missions as the Rev. Fred Barrett." After a list of various places where he conducted missions, the article continues: "Combining culture with a keen sense of humor and extraordinary powers of mimicry, Mr. Barrett has the zeal and consuming passion for souls of an old-time hot gospeller."

A further testament to his impact on the lives of those he met is in the letters my father received after Grandpa's death. There are probably one hundred or so letters, which came from all parts of the country. Virtually all of them describe him in

INTRODUCTION

the most glowing way and how he affected their lives for the better. However, rather than choosing to quote from these letters I have chosen to include something that my grandfather wrote in his very last monthly bulletin (July/August 1951).

> As I write my heart is full of gratitude to my many friends and of praise of God. I close my letter with a word of witness. When I was a lad of thirteen, God called me and saved me. It is of grace divine that I have been kept. To my amazement and my joy God counted me worthy and called me to preach the Gospel. For over fifty years, as local preacher and minister, it has been the joy of my life to proclaim salvation by grace through faith.

How deeply my father felt about his parents is best summed up in his own words. This is what he wrote in the copy of his first book:[6]

> The first copy of this book: and it is of course for you. For whom else could it be?—unless indeed one could have happily written Mother's name with yours. It is a fragment of a debt I shall never pay, for apart from you—both of you—the book would never have been. Nor do I mean by that simply that it was your love and faith in me that sent me to Cambridge, though for that I shall never cease to be grateful. But my first grounding in Biblical Theology was your preaching, and still I learn from every conversation with you. What I have of scholarship, as of much else, I owe to you. All this in gratitude, love and what cannot be translated—*pietas*.

Both men were deep thinkers and had a real thirst for learning with a total commitment to preaching. They both read extensively: among my grandfather's favorite authors were Charles Kingsley, Charles Dickens, and Jonathan Swift. My father loved reading detective stories and read a lot of history books. He also read literature that I had to teach at school and was always interested in discussing these texts with me.

Whereas my grandfather was at least on the surface an extrovert, and I suspect enjoyed the more administrative aspects of the role of minister, my father was often described as shy. He certainly never particularly enjoyed most of the administrative duties he took on at the university. We shall never know, but I wonder whether the apparent difference in their personalities was in some part due to their wives. By all accounts my grandmother was quiet and reserved, and my mother was certainly never lost for words and provided wonderful hospitality for all who visited my parents.

I don't think I ever saw my father as shy and he certainly wasn't in the pulpit. Ben has already given a very good idea of how my father preached. As a child, I used to accompany him to services and read lessons for him. I must have had to practice with him, but I have no recollection of this. It was a fun thing to do except for the church I put on a blacklist. I had been invited to sit with the children in the choir stalls but nobody warned me that they would leave before the sermon. I felt very isolated but on

---

6. *The Holy Spirit and the Gospel Tradition*. This was first published in the 1940s by SPCK, with a revised 2nd edition in 1966. It has fortunately been reprinted recently by Wipf and Stock, in 2011.

INTRODUCTION

show, and cried. My father, despite the fact that he always checked through his sermon at some point during the hymn before the sermon, came to my rescue and took me to sit with him in the pulpit. An honor indeed!

My father and I had much in common—a love of history, languages, etymology, and music. When I was little he used to read to me and I used to like the story of Scott's journey to the South Pole. Even as a child I found it very moving. However, I knew that father could never finish it—that was always read by my mother. He was a man of many hidden emotions.

I have read in Grandpa's notes how both he and my father had harvest festival services to take on the Sunday following the cremation of my grandmother. They both went out to preach. Some sixteen years later when Grandpa died on Christmas Day, my father went out to preach as planned, we had Christmas lunch and opened our presents. Only then were my brother and I told that Grandpa had died. As a twelve-year-old, I showed some unhappiness that I had not been able to share this with my parents earlier that day. But, in later life, I understand the commitment of both men, and indeed it has helped me when I was confronted with similar situations.

These three volumes present the reader with sermons covering a century. Because of the way both men constructed their sermons with quotations, anecdotes, and a vivid eye for detail, as well as a Christian purpose, they seem remarkably fresh. They certainly provide me with much to think about.

All that remains is to say that it has been a privilege to be part of this project. Thanks to Jordan Stanley for typing my grandfather's sermons. I didn't envy him that job because I find his writing difficult to read. I must thank Ben again for all his work. He must have spent many hours typing, reading, and selecting these sermons. Without him this material would never have seen publication. It is difficult to express what this has meant to me. Thank you, Ben.

Easter 2018

SERMONS FROM THE OLD TESTAMENT

"WALKING WITH GOD"
—Genesis 5.24; Hebrews 11.5

(Preached twice at Spring Head Mission and Bishop Street, dates not recorded)

Genesis 5.24 "Enoch walked with God: and he was not, for God took him."

Hebrews 11.5 "Before his translation he had this testimony, that he pleased God."

"Enoch walked with God." That was a favorite text of old preachers of an earlier generation, and what a useful and helpful text it is. It is seldom nowadays that one hears a sermon on walking with God. I can only guess that the cause lies in the fact that we know so little of that great experience. I shall return to that presently, but I want to begin with the second of the scriptures I have read to you.

THE MAN WHO SATISFIED GOD

Enoch, says the writer of the Epistle to the Hebrews, "had this testimony, that he pleased God." Moffatt translated that, "the record was that he had satisfied God." That made me sit up and it gave me my subject—the man who satisfied God. The idea behind it is that of a servant who has given satisfaction to his master.

That record is very remarkable when you remember the height of the divine standards. Everywhere in the Bible it is made clear that God is not unreasonable. He makes allowances for the blundering efforts of his children. He sees and reads their hearts and judges according to what is there. He is equally clear that for His own the high ideals are set, and high standards are held. Jesus is more than our pattern, but he is our pattern, and in him God has given us an example. His standards demand whole-hearted endeavors and sustained effort. "It does not take much brains to be a Christian," sneered a skeptic to Samuel Chadwick. "No," was the reply, "but it takes all there is." And it takes more than brains. It takes all there is of man and his spiritual energy, and that's a high order. The problem is that so many of us are unable to pass when judged in light of the ideal. Well, here was a man who, when judged by divine standards, had the testimony that he "satisfied" God.

LUMINESCENCE

THE LIFE THAT SATISFIED GOD

What was the life that satisfied God? And where is the record of it? Come back to the first text. "Enoch walked with God." That is all that is said about this primitive saint. His is the briefest biography in the Bible. It must have deeply impressed the chronicler. In a chapter that reads more like a record of births, marriages, and deaths than a page from the inspired Word of God, the name of Enoch is twice mentioned in a way that suggests the joy of the chronicler at coming to the name of a man of whom more can be said than that he lived, had children, and died. He began not one, but two, sentences with "Enoch walked with God." No more than this. Enoch's name is immortalized, not because he did anything grand in this world's estimation, he did not wield a sword like Lamech or play instruments like Jubal, but because he made an impression on his age of the high known quality.

The Bible is the only book in the world which proclaims uniformly the supremacy of moral and religious qualities. It keeps eulogies for the good rather than the great. All we know is that he lived a life of truth and great godliness, and that the Bible gives him a prominent place in the pantheon of workers, and a name to be remembered forever as a man who walked with God. Which means that he sought God's company and had no desire for anything but what lay in God's path. His was a life of fellowship and progress, an anticipation of the New Testament; walking in the light with God. Such a life is the life that satisfies God. If such high honors are given to such a life, it is worth your while to ponder—

WHAT WALKING WITH GOD MEANS FOR US

It means substantially the same in every age—a vivid eagerness for God's presence and the habit of daily communing with Him. You will not walk with God in any vital sense unless you have deliberately chosen to meet and walk with Him. The prophet Amos said, "Can two walk together unless they be agreed?" The meaning of the question is, unless they have made an appointment, you do not meet God carnally. No, we should have a meeting place where spirits meet and blend, where heaven comes down, our souls to greet. If we walk with God, it will be because we would rather go His way than travel any road dictated by personal desire, love of ease, or love of gain. Our song will be, "I'd rather walk in the dark with God than go alone in the light."

Look at it from the opposite side. Where is our walk with God, brothers, when we turn aside because the way we are going seems rough and steep and some other way seems easier and offers pleasures and treasures that appeal to us? William Cowper had that in mind when he wrote: "The dearest idol I have known, whate'er that idol be, help me to tear it from Thy throne, and worship only Thee."[1]

---

1. He is quoting a line from the hymn "O for a Closer Walk with God."

"WALKING WITH GOD"—GENESIS 5.24; HEBREWS 11.5

Whatever else it means, walking with God means walking in the light, and it means making religion the everyday business of life. God is always with us, but we are only near Him if we recognize and feel His presence in us. God is barely ever in our thoughts except in seasons of trouble. We are not walking with God if we only pray once weekly or even daily. He means not only praying to Him in the morning, but realizing His presence all through the day, so that you can call on him at any time, seeking his guidance, finding his help, learning his will. I once heard a preacher preach on the text of Zechariah 10.12: "and they shall walk up and down in the name of the Lord." *That is it*, having God as our constant companion, walking beside us all the way and all the days.

Walking with God means a life of progress. Our meaning of the word "walk" is "to go on." The man who walks with God is not content with any experience of the past. He will ever be moving on to higher ground, growing in grace and increasing in knowledge. One of my friends (T. J. Cot) said, "Religion is walking and talking with God, and the quality of religion depends on who does most of the talking." Notice another thing about Enoch—

WHERE WE FIND EXCUSES, ENOCH FOUND OPPORTUNITIES

We excuse ourselves on the ground that with such unpropitious and evil company as surrounds us, walking with God is impossible. But Enoch had the same kind of environment. Our writer says that he was a contemporary of that godless heathen, Lamech. That says a great deal. In the Epistle of Jude, we are told that Enoch had to lift up his voice in protest against the evils around him. Things were not easy for him, but he walked with God. And the fact that we are placed in a godless environment is no excuse for turning from God, but a reason for maintaining a closer walk.

We make family cares and duties an excuse for neglecting religious exercises. Of Enoch it is expressly stated that he walked with God after the birth of his son, Methuselah. Whatever he had done before, when a child came to his house, he knew he had to ponder the path of his feet. I have known homes where the coming of a baby made a break in the religious habits of a home. And yet if anything should lead us to a closer walk with God, it is the fact that we need the grace which comes from such a walk and that little children will be likely to follow in our example.

IS GOD SATISFIED WITH ME?

Those who have walked most closely with God will bear most emphatic witness that they are satisfied with Him. The questions we ought to ask is, "Is God satisfied with us?" Enoch's record was that he satisfied God. Have we a like record? That is a question not easily answered. Certainly, no person who walks closely with God will himself answer in the affirmative. He will call himself an unprofitable servant, and not in much modesty. The person who, of all persons, might have claimed that he had met God's highest demands was the Apostle Paul, but he said he was the "least of all." He was forever following after the ideal.

We shall never get beyond the need of God's grace and we shall always know ourselves as sinners saved by grace. We shall never get to the point where there is no more room for growth and progress. What I can see and want to urge is that God must be dissatisfied with many of us. Our progress has been so slow, our walk with Him so hesitant. But I have known some people who were modern Enochs. In the spirit of their humility I know that God takes joy in them and that the Savior saw the travail of their road and was satisfied. We are sure for them are the words, "well done."

Why should we not be following those who in their lives satisfy God? At least we know the things that grieve Him. Let us not rehearse them. Let us instead pray for and seek after a closer walk with God. That is the ideal Christian life. Not so much work we do for Him as what we suffer Him to be to us and for us. It was Mary, who sat at Jesus' feet, who chose the better part. It was Enoch who satisfied God. In one of the simple songs of salvation, Dora Greenwell has a word for us: "And oh, that He fulfilled may see, the travail of His soul in me, and with His work contented be, as I with my dear Saviour."

～

"THE RECONSECRATIONS OF LIFE"
—Genesis 13.1–4

(Preached four times from Spring Head Mission 6/7/42 to Pleck 1/16/44)

Genesis 13.1–4 "And Abram went up out of Egypt . . . into the place of the altar which he had made there at the first: and there Abram called on the name of the LORD."

ABRAM WENT UP OUT of Egypt. Perhaps he never ought to have gone down into Egypt. Certainly, he ought not to have acted as he did there. At the call of God, he had gone out from home and kindred. The call of God was accompanied by the promise that Abram should be made a great nation and that the Land of Canaan should be given to him and his children. When he got to the promised land instead of finding a fortune he found a famine. Instead of trusting the Lord, of whom he said later, "The Lord will provide," the patriarch felt that he must rely on his own resources. That is why he went down into Egypt. While there, he felt that to keep himself and his dependents alive, he must have recourse to craft and dishonesty. He had to learn that God fulfills His word and needs not man's crafty devices. Abram was humbled in the sight of God and the Egyptians. He came away thinking very meanly of himself. His return to the altar at Bethel seems to be the acknowledgment that he had been wrong, that he should have remained in dependence on God.

RETURN AND REPENTANCE

His return was the expression of his repentance. Its candor and courage we can appreciate. It was his frank admission that he had erred. To repair, as far as possible, the error, he returned to the old place, the old practice. We have not always the courage to do that, though we are aware that the only hope lies in candid and straightforward repentance, in an open return to the things which should never have been abandoned. It is not surprising that Abram's repentance took the form of return to the place of the altar. He "expressed his inward passion in the building of an altar." The building of an altar had a definite meaning. It was the token and medium of his covenant with God, his confession of faith, the correction of his life. When he went back to the altar, after doubt and sin, we may say he was repenting of his sin, renewing his covenant, and reconsecrating his life. And that brings us to our subject, *The Reconsecration of Life*. There are times when we need to return to what the altar symbolizes, times that we reconsecrate ourselves to God.

Let us frankly begin at the beginning and confess that there is need for reconsecration after a fall. Abram had sinned. We must not minimize that fact, but the real question is how a person behaves after he has fallen. Abram went straight back to the old altar and knelt there in penitence and reconsecration. That is the only way of salvation. Too often, after one falls, through shame, or self-will, or pride, or fear, we do not return. That is when a fall leads to further sins. The way of repentance and confession is hard, but it leads to life.

David sinned grievously, but he sobbed out the contrition of his broken heart, and the joy of salvation was restored to him. Peter denied his Lord with oaths and curses, but he "went out and wept bitterly," and Christ restored him. The other day I took up and reread Harold Begbie's book *Broken Earthenware*. The Puncher, converted from the lowest depths of degradation, had a relapse. It was cold, his vitality was low, and a friend urged him to have a drink. Then the old demon of drink had him by the throat and he staggered through the streets drunk. The people did not mark or jeer, they were sorry he had fallen. But the door of his home opened and the Puncher came out. He had taken off his coat and put on his Army red jersey. He went straight to the Salvation Army Hall, knelt in the penitent form, and gave himself afresh to God.

Probably by the mercy of God we have been spared the need for a return like that, but for most of us there is need for reconsecration to the enthusiasm of earlier years. We look back to the zeal of our youth. The heart was young and leapt in chivalrous ambition. Maybe we were crude, but we were keen. We were in love with Christ and love cares little for the smiles and sneers of others. The kingdom came first with us and no sacrifice was too great to make for it. And now? We are inclined to smile rather cynically at the enthusiasm of our own youth and the youth around us. We are older now, and wiser, we think. We take things more calmly and let others, if they like, put passion and zeal into the work of the kingdom.

I could, if I wanted, make a parable of Abram's experience. In Egypt, he had come into touch with an older and higher culture that would astonish him and make his own simple ways seem old fashioned and out of date. How crude and mean his altar would seem after the elaborate Egyptian temples. And we too have traveled and come into contact with more elaborate schemes of life and worship. We have elaborated our theology into philosophy and really you cannot expect educated men and women to believe the things that are sufficient for ignorant men and women. We want something weightier, more elaborate in ritual, more exquisite in music. Even the old chapel with its old enthusiasm does not now attract us.

"THE RECONSECRATIONS OF LIFE"—GENESIS 13.1-4

Or it may be that just a mood of sloth and indifference has settled down on us. It did the old monks and they called it accidie.[1] We cannot explain it any more than they could. We only know that in utter contrast to the happy and abounding zest of earlier days we are like physical invalids who don't know what is the matter, but they have no appetite and no strength, no joy in life. I cannot put the clock back, I do not want to try to. I thank God for the riches of knowledge, the wider experience, and the new methods. But if the new knowledge lacks the old passions, if what you call a broad religion has become very thin, there is only one thing to do, and that is to go back to the old altar and lay yourself and your gifts upon it.

RECONSECRATION AMID THE VARYING EXPERIENCES OF LIFE

Very often when we ought to make a special pilgrimage to the altar, we forget God. Life brings us not only expansion of thought, but enrichment of life. Some new joy comes to us as God's gift. Love comes into life and someone is prepared to take us for better or for worse, for richer or poorer, until death do us part. That is a wonderful experience and ought to lead us to another altar besides the marriage altar. Too often falling in love is the beginning of neglect of the house and the service of God. God lays a little child in our arms and that brings wonderful joy. That ought to make us raise our Ebenezer and kneel in reconsecration, but often in our enjoyment of the gift we pass by the altar. It may be that to us, as to Abram, success and wealth come and it gives opportunity for a happier life. Abram rebuilt the altar, but we all know men whose spiritual degeneration began when they began to increase in the world's goods. It need not be so, it ought not to be so. It will not be so if you take your wealth to the altar.

Sometimes the experience is of another color. Pain, bereavement, sorrow come into our lives. Often, they lead only to repining and retirement. We nurse our griefs in silent mercy. Bring your griefs to the altar and find consolation through reconsecration. That is the way into peace. When John Bright was left sad and lonely by the death of the wife who had gladdened his life for two brief years he dedicated his life to the repealing of the laws through whose operation wives, mothers, and little children were starving. Anna Waring did a similar thing. She received the sentence that she must spend her few remaining years in seclusion from the interests and happy activities of life. Retiring to her room, she came out next morning with the poem that is one of our favorite hymns. "Father, I know that all my life is portioned out for me, and the changes that are now to come I do not ask to see, but I ask Thee for a present mind

---

1. This is the Middle English spelling of the Latin word *acedia* and ultimately it is a transliteration of the Greek word that means "negligence." The spelling here is actually the Anglo-French spelling and goes back to the Medieval Latin form of the word.

intent on pleasing Thee."[2] And if the circumstances of our life are less dramatic, let us make each new experience the occasion of a new consecration.

NEED FOR RECONSECRATION AS WE FACE NEW TASKS

New ways of life bring new temptations and fresh opportunities. It is a great and altogether helpful thing to kneel before God as you face untrodden ways and new duties. A new life at a new school, starting out in business, joining the forces, bring us to a parting of ways and reconsecration is our duty and our safeguard. When God calls us to some new task in the church, to some new service, to some fresh adventure for the kingdom, let us give ourselves afresh to Him. Apart from Him we can do nothing, but all things are possible to dedicated men and women. You can put a sublime meaning into the simple words, "Consecrate me now to Thy service, Lord."

Here is our great and gracious opportunity. Before us are the symbols of our Lord's unchanging love. Here is the reminder of the cross where we first saw the light and the burden rolled away. Let the Communion Table stand for the altar and before it let us kneel in adoring love, singing gratitude, and utter consecration to our Lord.

∼

---

2. This is a line from the hymn "Father I Know That All My Life" that Anna Waring wrote.

"MOUNT MORIAH, THE HILL OF TESTING"
—Genesis 22.2

(Preached twice at Spring Head Mission 3/7/37 and Bishop Street 3/7/48)

Genesis 22.2 "Take now thy son, thine only son Isaac, whom thou lovest, and get thee into the land of Moriah, and offer him there for a burnt offering upon one of the mountains which I will tell thee of."

OF ALL THE HILLS of God, with but one exception, Mount Moriah is the setting of the most poignant scene. The one exception is "The Green Hill Far Away." Few, certainly no parent, can read the trial on Moriah without being deeply and harmfully marred in spirit. Probably, at first, we are moved to call this a hill of the devil. We shall badly miss our way unless, through careful study, we allow this scene to move us to admiration, faith, and love. Let us begin by facing—

TWO PERPLEXING QUESTIONS

The question of temptation. We are troubled, at the outset, by the words "God did tempt Abraham." In modern English the word "tempt" has acquired the meaning of "enticing in the direction of evil." The difficulty is easily averted if we substitute, as the Revised Version does, the word "prove." "God did prove Abraham." Or taken still with Moffatt's translation, "God did put Abraham to the test."

There is the question of the morality of the test. This is a more difficult question to answer. As we read the story we feel that the test was not fair, that it ought not to have been asked. Read through the text slowly, "take now thine only son, whom thou lovest." Think not only of the love, but of the promise centered on Isaac. What of a God who would be the one to say, "Take the son of your love and promise, and slay him as a sacrifice?" There is nothing irreverent in asking such a question. Indeed, it ought to be asked and faced lest we libel God, as we do when we suggest that those we dearly love, we love more than Him. Is there an answer to the second question?

I think that there is. For one thing, let us read to the end of the story. "All is well that ends well," we say. Reading on to the end we find that this is not the story of a human sacrifice, but the story of the arresting of a human sacrifice. Now our judgment is that God never intended that Isaac should be slain. But that is not a final answer. Abraham thought his son was to be offered on the altar.

THERE WAS NOTHING IN THE CUSTOMS OR CONSCIENCE OF THE TIME AGAINST SUCH AN OFFERING

This story must be read in light of the times in which it is set. In our day, if a man slew his son he would be hanged. He would avail nothing to say in his defense that the deed had been done at the bidding of a verse or vision. But in Abraham's day a man had the absolute right of life and death over his son. It was a common custom to offer one's firstborn as a sacrifice to one's god. There would have been no conscience against the act and Abraham would have been commended for it. It is probable that the Patriarch's intended act was suggested by the local customs. Maybe Abraham thought that he ought now to do for his God what his neighbors did for their idols. But we must go further still. It seems to me that the greatest fact to consider is that—

ON MORIAH THE OFFERING OF HUMAN SACRIFICES IN THE NAME OF GOD RECEIVED ITS DEATH BLOW

You never read again of any man of God feeling that he ought to slay and offer to God his son or daughter. God finished this inhumane business there. And how? By teaching Abraham that he intended him to offer his son, not as an outward act, but in the realm of the spirit and the will. On the platform of the knowledge and morality he had attained, God met him and taught him and his descendants that the sacrifice of sons and daughters in the material sense was not required. God did move him to offer Isaac to Him in order to show at the conclusion that Isaac belonged more truly to God than to his earthly father. For all time men knew, or ought to know, that what God requires is a living sacrifice in the realm of the spirit, a living body consecrated and not a dead body consumed. Now that we have moved into the realm of the spirit and the will, we can—

LEARN A LESSON IN OBEDIENCE OF FAITH FROM ABRAHAM

What a story of absolute trust and obedience this is! We frequently sing "Trust and Obey," but think of what it meant to Abraham—so trusting and obeying God that he was willing to surrender what was his dearest and best. Your Moriah is the height to which you climb when you are willing to surrender to God what you hold most dear at the call of God. Now that is not, as already suggested, in the course and material sense, but in the realm of the spirit and the will. God may be asking you to sacrifice your cherished, secret ambition. He may be asking you to give up the child you wanted to keep at your side to comfort your old age or to succeed you in the business you have brought up.

Some years ago, there was a missionary play, "Farley Goes Out." Mr. Farley, a well-to-do tradesman, thought it was one thing to know a missionary and to collect money to send somebody as a missionary, but when his own son said, "I must go out, Father," it was another matter. Following that thought we ought to—

LEARN A LESSON FROM ISAAC ON MOUNT MORIAH

We are in danger of forgetting that Isaac was not a child, but a young man able to carry the wood and help build the altar. Abraham kept from him, as long as possible, the fact that he was not to sacrifice but to be sacrificed. At last the truth had to be told him and he did not resist or turn away. He suffered himself to be stretched on the altar and saw the knife. He was a willing sacrifice. And there are times still when God asks, not for something we use, but for ourselves: all that we have and are. God asks us to give ourselves completely over to Him. Can you truly sing: "Ready for all thy perfect will, my acts of faith and love repeat, till death thy endless mercies seal, and make the sacrifice complete?"[1]

AN ILLUSTRATION THAT GATHERS UP THE TWO LESSONS

In the closing hours of the year 1885, a young man with his prospects in the Civil Service attended a watchnight service in Clapham, London. He was Sam Pollard and he knelt in that service and pledged his life to Christ for service in China. There was one obstacle left: his mother would not give him up. In the selfsame hour, she was kneeling with her husband in a church service at St. Just in Cornwall. These moments were filled with thanksgiving and confession, with the surrender of wills and the dedication of lives. The mother learned through her agony. "At last," she says, "as the old year was leaving and the new year entering, I said 'Lord, I am willing.'"

That was a modern Moriah. For the mother, it meant giving a mother's all. For the son, it meant toil far from home among the Miao people in faraway China and a grave in the Shimenkan Mountains. When we come to our Moriah may God give us the grace to be as willing and obedient. I began by saying that there is one more poignant hill of God than Moriah. Let us turn there now.

---

1. This is the rarest of all Methodist hymns. The title is "O Thou Who Camest from Above" and the lyrics are by Charles Wesley, but the tune is by his grandson Samuel S. Wesley.

MOUNT MORIAH AND MOUNT CALVARY

Side by side, does not one foreshadow the other? Can you think of Abraham offering up Isaac and saying, "God so loved the world that he gave His only begotten Son"? God did what he asked of Abraham. Calvary finishes Moriah. When they stretched Jesus on the cross, no angel intervened. When they drove the nails in his hands no hand stayed the hammer. There was no substitute. Jesus was the Lamb of God—slain. When you come to your Moriah and are asked to sacrifice your dearest and best, or to give yourself, remember what God gave and Jesus offered. I beseech you brethren, by the mercies of God that ye present yourselves a living sacrifice, holy, acceptable to God which is your reasonable service.

"THE GLORY OF GOD IN THE FACE OF MAN"
—Genesis 33.10

(Preached forty-seven times, including James St, York 6/13/34, Pleck 8/1/37, and Nottingham 9/7/42)

Genesis 33.10 "I have seen thy face as though I had seen the face of God."

UNLESS THAT IS SIMPLY a prettily phrased compliment with a good deal of flattery, it is one of the most staggering and sublime utterances that ever fell from the lips of one mortal man about another. That any man should see the glory of God is a wonder. If we think of that honor being granted at all, we think of it as the high honor which is the privilege of a few saintly souls of surprising holiness, and granted to them only in honor of deep meditation and rapt adoration. But that Jacob, the supplanter, should see God, and see Him in the face of Esau, the "profane person"—well, here is a marvel of marvels.

And everything about the incident suggests that the expression was not merely a piece of fulsome flattery, but the truth leaping from a surprised soul. It is too swift and unpremeditated to be anything less than the lip's utterance of the heart's feeling.

RECALL THE FACTS OF THE CASE

If they do not carry conviction, no argument will. Jacob had deceived his father and deeply wronged his brother. Esau had been deprived of birthright and blessing by a miserable trick. The twin brothers had parted with anger and the lust of vengeance in the heart of Esau and a great fear in the heart of Jacob. The years had sped away. In a hard school, Jacob had learned that what a man sows he reaps. The supplanter had been supplanted. Now he was returning a wiser and better man, a rich and prosperous man too. He had reached the borders of the old homeland. His return might have been a triumph but for the sudden appearance of Esau and his warlike band. That turned the triumph into terror. Here were the consequences of his deception and treachery meeting him with a vengeance. He had made his peace with God, but he still had to face the brother he had so cruelly wronged.

Now comes a miracle of grace. In fear and trembling Jacob went forward expecting the worst and knowing he deserved it. But God had touched Esau's heart. He looked upon his brother, something went soft within him, his lips quivered, his eyes shone with strange, tender light. There was no form of hate, but a look of love on his face. Instead of a clinched fist or an upraised weapon there were outstretched arms. Jacob found pity where he expected vengeance, saw compassion where he looked for anger, discovered love and forgiveness where he deserved wrath and punishment. It is written, "Esau ran to meet him, and embraced him, and fell on his neck and kissed him." Why, those are the very words Jesus used to tell of the father's welcome of the prodigal. Esau was doing a divine thing, a God-like action and it transfigured his face. Jacob saw it and summed it up in a genuine, poetic, inspired flash—"I have seen thy face as though I had seen the face of God."

THE DIVINE GLORY CAN BE SEEN ON A HUMAN FACE

It has perhaps been one of the weaknesses of our theology that we have fixed too wide and deep a gulf between humanity and God. We have been anxious to emphasize the transcendence of God and have missed His immanence. It ought always to have been clear that the Divine dwells in the human as revealed through it. The great figures under which men thought and spoke of God are entirely human. He is the Good Shepherd, the Gracious Guide, the enduring friend. He comforts like a mother and pities and forgives like a father. When we go back to the sources of our personal knowledge of God we have to confess that the light of the knowledge of God shone for us is a human face—the face of a godly man, and saintly woman, or a lovely child.

And what ought to have left us in no doubt at all is the fact that, when God was pleased to fully reveal His glory He did it through a human life. The glory of God was seen in the face of Jesus Christ. Men saw God full of grace and truth in the Word made flesh. Reverently one asks, "How else could God reveal Himself to men except in a man, to persons except through personality?" The human heart craves such a revelation and cannot be satisfied with less. God meets and satisfies such craving.

As Browning makes David say to poor, tortured Saul, "It shall be a face like my face that receives thee, a man like to me thou shalt love and be loved forever, a hand like this hand shall open the gates of new life to thee! See the Christ stand!" On the side of a privilege we accept that and most of us thank God that He has revealed Himself to us through human lives. What we do not always realize is that now—

GOD WANTS TO REVEAL HIMSELF TO OTHERS THROUGH US

It seems too much to expect. We are so conscious of defect and weakness. But we must not hesitate to accept the responsibility which is a further privilege too. We are not simply to be the recipients of a Divine revelation, we are to be the medium of it. It is

"THE GLORY OF GOD IN THE FACE OF MAN"—GENESIS 33.10

for us as St. Paul says to "mirror the glory of the Lord with face unveiled" (2 Cor 3.18, Moffatt). God wants it and the world needs it. Men and women around us are blind to many forms in which the glory of God is set. They do not see the glory that fills God's House for they do not come, and they are blind to the glory of God revealed in nature. Only through Godlike men and women, filled with the constraining love of Christ, manifesting the spirit of the gospel in their consecrated lives, will they come face to face with God.

If the beauty of Jesus is not seen in us it will not be seen at all by many. They must see the Divine brightness, benignity, compassion on our faces or they will miss it. For them, God's light must shine in human eyes, His love irradiates human faces. They must say of us what Jacob said of Esau—"I have seen thy face as though I had seen the face of God." In his book *Margaret Ogilvy*, J. M. Barrie has a tender and beautiful chapter on, "How my mother got her soft face."[1] We are getting to the heart of our subject when we seek for—

THE SECRET OF THE CELESTIAL LOOK

It cannot be put on. A man who tries to look important generally ends by looking ridiculous. We do not deceive when we try to look pleased at unwelcome visitors. Any man who says in effect, "Now I'm going to look like God," will spoil the whole effect. Moses "wist not that his face shone." Consciousness would have taken the shine off. Shining is the outshining of the heart's transformation. The man who looks most like God is least conscious of it.

Love lights up the face. It is almost sacrilege to intrude, but watch the face of a mother as she bends over her baby, or the face of a man as he turns to the woman he loves. Take note of the homely face of a genuine lover of God as with his heart expanded and warmed he says, "Bless Him. I love Him." Communion with God transfigures the face. It was from the mount when he had talked with God that Moses came down with a shiny face. The seraphim are the "burning ones." Standing near God they have become like Him. Because they were like their master men took knowledge of the disciples that they had been with Jesus. Some of us are so little like God because we are so seldom with Him.

But the way I want specially to emphasize is the way in which Esau revealed God. He did the Divine thing. That is what you must do. People try you, irritate you, annoy you—don't lose your temper, keep your patience. Someone has wronged you, deeply and grievously, the natural thing would be to harbor revenge and try to get your own back. Don't do it. Forgive and prove forgiveness by returning good for evil. To angry words, give soft answers. Do good to them that hate you and pray for those who despitefully use you. Give a helping hand to men who are down through their own folly

---

1. This book was first published in 1925. Barrie was best known for creating the character Peter Pan.

and sin. Go on with your good work though you are laughed at or scorned. It's not natural, you say. I know, that is my point, it is supernatural, it is Divine. By doing such acts you prove yourselves sons and daughters of the Highest and you will carry the family likeness on your face.

In Esau's case, it was just a flash of the Divine that lit up his face. But the heavenly look should be permanent on our faces. The secret of it is to act like the God Jesus revealed, and keep on so acting. Every Divine act reacts in the soul and the countenance. It has been said that you never see a coarse face under a Salvation Army bonnet. The exceptions are so few as to prove the rule. Some of the faces are homely and plain, but the years of fellowship with God and of Divine service have made homely faces glow with Divine light.

THE POWER OF THE REVELATION

We all know that that is the real winsomeness. We can recall men and women, some of them passed on, who held the Real Presence in their eyes. We did not need telling they were Christian. They did not talk much about religion, they lived it. Everything about them was gracious, attractive, heavenly. Do not be content to admire and praise them, emulate them. "Let your light so shine before men," and "seeing your good works" they will think of God and glorify the father.

Deliberately I finish with an abrupt question. About most of us, men see a good deal that is human and sometimes something that is devilish. We are continually attributing animal qualities to one another. We say, "He is as cunning as a fox, as cross as a bear, as stubborn as a donkey, as silly as a sheep." Does any man ever say to you or think of you, "I have seen thy face as though I had seen the face of God"?

"THE GOD OF DIFFERENT PERSONALITIES"
—Exodus 3.6

(Preached seven times from Fentiman Road 9/22/29 to Bishop St. 10/29/50)

Exodus 3.6 "I am the God of thy Father, the God of Abraham, the God of Isaac, the God of Jacob."

WE HAVE THE VERY highest authority for lifting this text out of its setting and letting its truth stand alone. Our Lord Himself, when speaking of the resurrection, quoted this great saying (see Matt 22.32). So, we are abundantly justified in stating the text and saying at once that the idea to be emphasized is that our God is—

THE GOD OF DIFFERENT PERSONALITIES

There is room in His thought and His love for different types of human nature. The Three men mentioned are amongst the best known of Bible characters and are as different as three men well could be. Yet God was the God of each. Look at the three men. Abraham was a spiritual adventurer, a pioneer of faith. He went out from home and friends not knowing whither he went, but only knowing that an imperative voice called him to seek a better country.

Isaac was Abraham's son, but a greater contrast than that between father and son can hardly be imagined. Abraham was an adventurer, the man who went out. Isaac was a man of quiet, meditative ways. He was content to let others go out while he stayed at home. It is no injustice to him to say that he was commonplace, lacking initiative. For part of his life he was his mother's son and for the rest his wife's husband.

Jacob was a different man altogether. A strange mixture this man, the man with a double name—Jacob/Israel—and a double nature. The man who chose the blessing and yet stooped to deceit to win it, the man who could be worldly and devout, crafty and pious, the supplanter and the spiritual. For some things, we love him and for others we loathe him.

The point is that God was the God of Abraham, Isaac, and Jacob. The God of the princely pioneer, the commonplace stay-at-home, and of the sinning and repenting double dealer. And He is the same today. Neither the years nor His nature change. That ought to be of immense comfort to us for it means that there is room in His mind and heart for us all. For how we differ! You might say we are all included in these three types. There are still those who are driven by a divine discontent, urged by inner impulses, called by a holy voice, to be pilgrims in the region of faith, adventurers for the kingdom, ever seeking a fuller, finer, purer religion than that of their fathers and friends. So, too, there are those whose lives are as commonplace and uneventful as Isaac's, people who are content to let others lead while they follow and to be just ordinary folk. Perhaps most of us see ourselves in Jacob for we are strange mixtures, sometimes roaring on wings of faith and love, but sometimes trailing our wings in the mud. We are princes with God who sometimes forget and act like children of the devil.

Or, you may make the distinction broader and say that we differ in other ways. Some of us are mystics and some are practical men and women, some put the emphasis on prayer and worship, others are philanthropic and social services, some love to be up and doing and others love to stand and wait, some of us are of a choleric temperament, some phlegmatic, some sanguine, some of us are bright and gay and others somber and sad. And God is the God of all because He is the God of each. There is a place for each in His love and care. The love of God is broader than the measures of our mind and the heart of the Eternal large enough to take us all in. The text is reinforced by a very gracious word concerning our Master—"Jesus loved Martha and her sister Mary, and Lazarus." The busy, bustling housewife, the contemplative listener, and the commonplace brother. Do not try to monopolize God for yourself and your own type, do not excommunicate those who differ from you. Just remember that He is the God of Abraham, Isaac, and Jacob. Pass on to another thought—

GOD IS EVER THE SAME BUT MEN OF DIFFERENT TEMPERAMENT AND CHARACTER CALL HIM DIFFERENT NAMES

They apprehend and emphasize different aspects of His character. To Abraham, amidst the perils and disappointments of his spiritual pilgrimage, God was "a shield and exceeding great reward." Isaac's name for God was "The fear of Isaac." God was to Jacob the "Rock"—the rock against which he dashed himself in vain and which came ultimately to be the foundation of his life and hope.

God never changes, but still men see Him through the eyes of their own temperament, experience, and bias. He seems to change to meet our need. He is always Love, but love coming to us according to our need. In childhood, He comes as the Good Shepherd, in youth, as the Captain of our salvation, in middle life He is the Giver of rest and strength, in old age, the One who bears and carries. Different conceptions will be stated in different terms and different needs will apprehend different aspect. Sorrow will name Him the Comforter, sin will rejoice in Him as a pardoning

God, weakness will lay hold in His strength. Some will speak of His justice, some by His love, and some of His holiness. Some will think of Him as the Judge and some as the Father. So long as men are sincere, earnest, devoted in their worship let us allow them latitude and room. For the God and Father of our Lord Jesus Christ is the God of different personalities. It follows inevitably that—

GOD HAS DIFFERENT WAYS OF EDUCATING DIFFERENT PERSONALITIES

You cannot read the stories of these three men without realizing that God trained them in different schools and disciplined them in different experiences. Abraham was educated and perfected through many a disappointment and the postponed fulfillment of many a hope. Isaac's school was his family life, his quiet nature was cultured among quiet scenes. Jacob's sins came home to roost and through them he learned life's great lessons.

The God of different personalities still sends different men to different schools. One bears through the failure of earthly things to seek a Heavenly City. Another sees in quiet, peaceful, homely scenes the goodness and the love of God. Another learns in the hard school of experiences the folly and futility of sin. Adversity is the university of one and success the school of another. If you ask me why, I can only answer because you are you and he is he. God does not deal with us in batches and in crowds. He knows us as individuals and sends us to the school He sees fit. Do not let us murmur and fret, covet or envy, rather let us trust and praise the heart that places, the hand that guides, and the love that has room for us all. There is another thought and I have only time to mention it, but I dare not omit it. It is this—

GOD IS THE GOD OF SUCCEEDING GENERATIONS

The God of Abraham, of Abraham's son Isaac, and of Isaac's son Jacob, and of their succeeding race. Honesty demands the admission that that is the main and first thought of the text. God was calling Moses to undertake a particularly difficult task, and telling him to undertake it in the name and strength of his fathers' God. There is something inexpressibly beautiful in that truth. You and I have to do, not with an unknown and unrevealed God, but with the God of our fathers known of old and who revealed Himself to men and women of other days. And this God is our God and will be our guide and our educator. We can both lengthen and strengthen the list. The God of Abraham, Isaac, Jacob, and the God of Paul, Augustine, Luther, Wesley. "We came unto our Fathers' God, their Rock is our salvation." And He will be the God over our children after us. We shall see Him in clearer light and see new revelations of His power, and our children may, and please God, will, advance upon our knowledge. He leads us on. But He will always be the God of Abraham, Isaac, and Jacob, our fathers'

LUMINESCENCE

God, and with adoring, wondering, and deepening gratitude we shall come to know Him better and love and trust Him more and as we see Him in Christ Jesus we shall each for himself or herself look up into His face and say, "My Lord, and my God."

"THE CRIMES OF THE CARELESS"
—Exodus 22.6

(Preached at Fentiman Road, undated, and Spring Head Mission 7/28/40)

Exodus 22.6 "If fire break out, and catch in thorns, so that the stacks of corn, or the standing corn, or the field, be consumed therewith; he that kindled the fire shall surely make restitution."

THIS TEXT IS TAKEN from a section of the book of Exodus which commentaries call "The Lesser Law." That is to distinguish it from the section in "the Law" which includes the Ten Commandments. This "Lesser Law" includes a brief code of laws of deep moral interest affecting the life of the nation. The application of the penalties described here would work something little short of a revolution in the life of today. Take, for example—

THE LAW GIVEN IN OUR TEXT

It is simple enough but by no means unimportant. Outwardly it meant more to the people who first received it than it can mean to us. They lived in a hot, dry country where the danger of fires was ever present. The law enjoined that if a farmer wanted to burn over his stubble field, or set fire to a heap of rubbish, it was part of his responsibility to see that the wind was in the right direction and that every precaution was taken to protect his neighbor's property. If he neglected to take precautionary measures, and his neighbor's crop was damaged, the man who kindled the fire was held liable and had to pay for the damage done. As I say, the particular application means little to us. Though I have heard my wife say strong things when a neighbor kindled a fire in the garden just after the washing was hung out! The point is that the underlying principle is sound and of manifold application.

The question raised concerns our liability for the consequences of our action or our neglect. Here is a pretty problem in ethics for you. Is a man morally responsible, not only for what he does, but for what results from his action? Must he be held accountable for consequences he did not intend resulting from his conduct? In my judgment, there are consequences of our actions, or of our failure to act, at a given moment which are altogether unexpected; by no knowledge accessible to us could we foresee them. For these consequences, it seems to me, we are not guilty.

But there are cases in which we might have known that certain results would follow our action or our neglect. In such cases, we are not guiltless though there was no ill intent in our minds. We might have known that evil would follow a certain course of conduct and we ought to have found out. The text presents the case of a man who did not intend to cause damage. The law held him guilty because he was careless of consequences and did not take necessary precautions. In this sermon, we will keep to such cases because they give us our subject.

THE CRIMES OF THE CARELESS

That is not too strong a phrase to use. Not least among the tragedies of life are those wrought by "want of thought," rather than "want of heart." We know the man who has a kind heart and means well, but who does untold injury because his morality does not include judgment of knowledge as well as sentiment. He relies on his good intention and does not trouble to consider consequences. We often let him off lightly because he is such a good fellow, means so well and apologizes so profusely when he has failed. But he needs the stern reminder that he is responsible for finding out the likely consequences of his actions. The utilitarian school of ethics has done us great service in calling attention to the fact that the results of actions are as liable to moral judgment as the motives are. That will become clearer as we apply the principle to some modern situations.

Let me put in here the illustration that made the sermon. Mr. Thomas Holmes, Police Court missionary, in his *Pictures and Problems from London Police Courts*, tells the story.[1] The lady had no ill intent. Indeed, Mr. Holmes says, "doubtless it was kindly meant." We should not do anything like that, but consider some of the ways in which we are guilty.

Inclinations and obligations begin with a very simple thing, for it is in the simple things we oftenest fail. There is a letter to write, and engagement to keep, some work to be done. But we simply don't feel inclined to fulfill our obligation. Suppose the engagement is to take our Sunday School class. Our neglect means the disorder of the school and maybe some scholar saying, "Well, teacher doesn't care, why should I?" If that scholar is lost to the school, and lost to the kingdom, can the teacher elude responsibility?

Take another small, but not unimportant, matter: *careless chatter*. Our tongues are small members but they can light hell's fires. Yet how careless we are in utterances we have not verified. In some of our practical jokes we only mean to amuse ourselves

---

1. This book was published by Edward Arnold in about 1908.

but often we are playing with fire. The care of the gossips and slanderers is more serious. He means no harm, only likes to be thought of as "in the know," but he soils the fair name of another. There may be no willful malignity, but there is moral inattention. He who kindles the fire, must bear the blame. But we must go further and deeper and discuss—

LIGHTING FIRES WHICH CONSUME SOULS

We talk about the folly of playing with fire, but who lights the fires? Into your shop or office comes an innocent youth or maiden. They blush at some of the things they hear, but get accustomed to them if their purity is stained and their souls scorched with evil, who is to blame? And what of those who by their criticism, or by their inconsistencies, destroy the faith of another or lead him away from his church allegiance? Take the following as an authentic case. It is taken not from a temperance speech, but from an article in a daily paper.

A young man from over in one of the colonies was present at an English house party. He was asked to have a drink, he declined. But his host persisted and the young man yielded. That young colonial was just struggling back to sobriety and that one glass rekindled the old fire. Can you exonerate his host? Is it going too far to speak of the crimes of the careless? Is it a sufficient excuse to say that we meant no harm?

THE BIBLE HOLDS THE INCENDIARY RESPONSIBLE

We have to answer for our well-meaning but careless actions. In the old Law, the man who started the fire had to make reparation and pay for the damage done. You can do that when you are dealing with fields and corn stacks. You cannot when you are dealing with life and character. If a fire breaks out at my house, the insurance company can make good some of the damage, but some things can never be replaced. If a man's reputation has been destroyed, if he has been robbed of his faith, if fires of passion have been started in his soul, what reparation can be made? What compensation is sufficient? I will not say there is no forgiveness. I believe there is forgiveness for every sin repented of. But you will find it hard to forgive yourself. "O God," prayed a young man, "bury my influence with me."

AN INADMISSIBLE PLEA

It is not enough to plead that it is our nature to be careless. Nature is but the raw material out of which character is shaped. It is useless to say that you can't help being careless. You can and you must. To help you in your need the way of prayer is open. Go to the one you have wronged and make such reparations as are feasible. Go to God and seek His forgiveness. Claim the grace that pardons and purifies. If any man be in

LUMINESCENCE

Christ he is a new creature. Instead of lighting the fires that destroy, you may, by the grace of God, kindle faith, hope, and love in the hearts of your fellows.

∼

"THE CHRISTMAS FAITH AND THE CHRISTMAS FEAST"
—Exodus 24.11

(Preached once at Fentiman Road, Christmas 1936)

Exodus 24.11 "And they saw God, and did eat and drink."

THAT STRIKES US AS odd and incongruous. We expected to be told more of those who "beheld their God." Instead, we are told that they set down to a feast. The two clauses of the text seem to clash. It would sound better if we read, "They saw God, and did fear, and tremble, and worship." But what is written is written for our learning.

We need to remember that there was, and there is, a widespread belief that a vision of God was a harbinger of death. The seventy elders who with Moses ascended Mount Sinai, the mount of blackness and darkness, were terror stricken. They feared they would die. But "upon the nobles of the Children of Israel Jehovah laid not His hands." God did not smite them. They did not die, they lived. The anticipation of the revelation filled them with dread, the realization made them rejoice. They saw God, and did eat and drink.

SERMONS AND SANDWICHES

Ought we to be nurtured at the interpretation of these two clauses? The faith and the feast stand close together in our own religious life. One of our most prolific evangelists (FWB, in *The Luggage of Life*) took part in a church anniversary.[1] He tells that on the Sunday there were "special sermons, solemn praise, and stately anthems." On the Monday, there were "sandwiches, cream puffs, and jam tarts." And he raises the question, what is the philosophical connection between the sermons of yesterday and the sandwiches of today? What relation exists between singing and scones? What fellowship hath religion with revelry? There's a pretty problem for you. You think it strange when you read the text and yet you do the same thing.

---

1. He is referring to F. W. Boreham, a British Baptist evangelist, and his book *The Luggage of Life*, published in 1912.

LUMINESCENCE

THE CHRISTMAS FAITH AND THE CHRISTMAS FEAST

Never do religion and revelry go together more than at the present season. Indeed, the text, as well as any I know, sums up a modern Christmas. "They saw God"—"veiled in flesh the Godhead see, hail the Incarnate Deity!"[2] That is the Christmas vision of faith. You look onto the face of the Babe of Bethlehem and "behold your God." Then away you go to the feasting and revelry, the good cheer and the good fellowship. You are called to "awake and salute the happy morn." You pay your tribute to the Savior of the world who is come, and then you turn to the turkey and the plum pudding in the home decked with holly and mistletoe. The faith and the feast, the doctrine and the dinner, the carol and the carnival, stand side by side.

THERE IS NO CONDEMNATION

No word of condemnation was passed on these elders. And if a negative commendation in an obscure language is not sufficient, let us make a more general survey. What were the seasons of spiritual enlightenment and elevation among the Jews? Pentecost—Tabernacles—Passover—Dedication. Solemn, heart-rending, soul-stirring seasons these were. And they were called "feasts," and were, in fact, occasions of family reunions of domestic and natural rejoicing.

Turn to the New Testament, to the life of the Master. There is a tradition that, though our Lord wept often, He was never seen to smile. I do not believe it. The Savior who watched children playing in the marketplace and took babies in his arms must often have smiled. The Man of Sorrows was unsurpassed with the mirth of gladness among his fellows. He wrought the first miracle and magnified His glory at a marriage feast. He went out to dine with Zacchaeus and Matthew. Some things He said I can only understand as I picture Him with a twinkle in his eye. He has set more people singing for sheer joy than any one on earth.

At our sacred service of Holy Communion we sing, "Here, O Lord, I see Thee face to face," and we do eat and drink of the "feast of love."[3] There we softly sing of those who have passed from the sight of our eyes and who "see Him as He is," who "sat down at the marriage supper of the Lamb." So, I dare to attest that . . .

NOTHING IN THE FAITH FORBIDS THE FEAST

The vision of God is consistent with and consecration of the engagements of life. Religion is not the grave of joy, but its satisfaction. In God's presence, there is fullness

---

2. A line from Charles Wesley's Hymn "Hark the Herald Angels Sing." There is a humorous story in regard to the title. Charles had originally had the first line as "hark how the welkins ring" (a welkin is a bell). Fellow Methodist George Whitefield didn't think that rang any bells, and so he suggested the change to the first line we now all know.

3. A hymn of the same title by Horatius Bonar (1855).

"THE CHRISTMAS FAITH AND THE CHRISTMAS FEAST"—*Exodus 24.11*

of joy and at His right hand are pleasures for evermore. Break forth unto joy and song together for the Lord hath comforted His people. Behold your God regards your lowly estate and is coming to save the fallen and cheer the faint. It is good that we should make merry and rejoice. And a minister can say, "God bless you and your happy homes." And He will.

Only remember the right order. The revelry follows the revelation. The vision of God comes first. You have not kept Christmas if you have not beheld His glory. First of all, "O come let us adore Him." If you follow that order the revelation will sanctify the rejoicing. Let me say bluntly what I mean. No man who really sees God this Christmas will get drunk. Of course not! But selfishness and greed and grudges, just as much, must not take place. When we see God, we know that pride and prejudice, unforgiveness and uncharity, have no place in His presence. When we truly see Him, we become like Him and enter into the joy of our Lord.

∼

"THE FIRST SANCTUARY AND ITS FURNITURE"
—Exodus 25.21, 22

(Preached twenty-three times from West Burton to Sileby, dated from Hadley 7/13/38 to Caledon St, Pleck 11/1/42)

Exodus 25.21, 22 "And thou shalt put the mercy seat above upon the ark; and in the ark thou shalt put the testimony; that I shall give thee. And there I will meet with thee, and I will commune with thee from above the mercy seat."

AT FIRST GLANCE, IT may seem unnecessary, a waste of your time and the preacher's strength, to prepare and deliver a sermon on the erection and furnishing of Israel's first sanctuary. At best, it was only a tent temple to be superseded when the Jews were settled in their own land. Though the ark was transferred to Solomon's Temple, it was lost and all traces of it disappeared during the Great Captivity. Besides, it belonged to a dispensation long since over, while we have entered into a new covenant. To us has come the higher, clearer revelation of the way God tabernacles with men. The Temple has given way to the church, and there is open to all believers a new and living way into the true Holy of Holies. I am not likely to forget these things. Gladly I admit them. The primitive sanctuary, its ritual, and its furniture these all belong to that which is "in part," and when "that which is perfect" is come, that which is in part is done away. Men who know the living way will never rebuild the old temple or restore its ritual.

But we shall greatly err, and to our own impoverishment, if we fail to see here the eternal behind the ephemeral, the essential behind the transient, and the spirit behind the form. Here at least is the first intimation that God will in very deed dwell with men and find His rest in the sanctuaries they consecrate to Him. He is not far from anyone of us, but will have His tent pitched by the side of ours. There begins here that which found its consummation when "the Word became flesh and tabernacled among us." From the consecration of His first sanctuary comes the most comforting and inspiring truth that God is with us, "familiar, patient, condescending, and free."

There is more than an interesting and suggestive beginning. The very material furniture speaks to us of something that is essential in the nature of intercourse between God and trusting souls. It states the first and last terms in which God and men may live in communion. These primitive and outworn articles suggested to the devout Jew what should be in our minds every time we come up to the House of the Lord. They suggest something that our churches should stand for in this and every age. From this point of view, it will be no waste of time or strength to see the significance of the first sanctuary and its furniture through the eyes of a spiritually minded Jewish worshipper.

THE ARK AND THE TESTIMONY

First of all, let us note that an ark, or coffer, of acacia wood was to be given a central place in the sanctuary. There was nothing unusual in that. Sacred chests were often placed in Egyptian temples. They usually contained emblems or images of some deity. But the primary object of this ark was to enclose the tablets of stone on which was inscribed the Law of God. "Thou shalt put into the ark the testimony that I shall give thee."

The first step, then, in the preparation of a shrine for God on earth was the enshrining of His will. The supreme thing to be proclaimed was the supremacy of the Divine will. That is what the Law expressed. And at every service, though he did not actually enter the holy place, the devout Jew would be reminded of a will higher than his own, of a Law that was to be a standard of living. You can see the spirit behind that form, the truth that is greater than the symbol.

One of the great services that our modern sanctuaries have to render is to remind men of God's will and of the Law which contains the laws of life. In the world, it is so fatally easy to magnify our own will and depend on our own judgment, to accept the world's standards, conform to its fashions and live according to its laws. More than a few of us have yielded and taken the easy way.

The tablets of stone gave place to the scroll of the law, the scroll has given way to the printed and preached word, but the fact abides. The sermon may be dense and the service poor, but ever there stands the Law of the Lord—Thou shalt have none other Gods before me—Thou shalt not steal, bear false witness, commit adultery, or covet thy neighbor's possessions. The sanctuary stands for the creation and recreation of the Divine standard, it rebukes our sins and calls us to obedience. It is a continual reminder of the Divine Law which it is our duty and our life to keep.

THE CALL ON GRATITUDE

Then the ark, according to Hebrews 9, was to hold Aaron's rod and a golden pot filled with manna. Those were the relics and reminder of the deliverance and mercies by which God claimed obedience. No Israelites could be reminded of the deliverance from bondage and the guidance on the way to the promised land without realizing the depth of his obligation and the reasonableness of obedience.

Here, too, is part of the service the modern sanctuary has to render. Outside, the Law may seem stern and forbidding and religion an exacting and unreasonable service. Inside, there are tokens and reminders of the love which is the other side of Law and which turns statutes into songs and duty into delight. Some can point to the very place where kneeling the light broke into their minds and the peace of pardon came into their hearts. There is the place where you stood and plighted your troth in the comradeship that has been one of God's best gifts to you. Yonder the seat you occupied when God comforted your soul in sorrow. You can people the pews with those godly folk who for Christ's sake, provided the restraints and imposed the constraints which have kept you straight.

If we come reverently to the House of God what thoughts are stirred by hymns and psalms? They tell of the goodness and mercy, the grace and the patience, which have followed us all our days. As individuals, as a church, as a nation, what wondrous blessings and marvelous loving kindness we have to acknowledge. If we attend the church's most sacred service of remembrance, the broken bread and the wine speak to us of the body that was broken and the blood shed for us and for our salvation. So, in the sanctuary, with all its memories and suggestions of redeeming love we realize that it is no unreasonable demand that we should obey God's commands and make His will the law of our life. The "mercies of God" make the sacrifice of obedience a "reasonable service."

CONSCIENCE AT WORK

It is not difficult to imagine what would happen when an Israelite stood before those symbols. There was the Law he ought to have kept—there the reminder of his obligation. By the Law was the knowledge of sin and in the light of God's goodness was the revelation of his ingratitude. While he worshipped, conscience would get to work, and what outside had seemed trivial would stand condemned as the shame of his life.

That is not the least service the sanctuary renders still. We live at such a place and are immersed in so many things that conscience gets little chance. Many outside are careless and heedless. We can go on hugging ourselves in our pride and saying to our souls the flattering unction that we are as good as most and better than many. That way lies ruin. Our salvation does not begin until we are conscious of our need for it.

When we came into the sanctuary it becomes not a question of how we compare with others, but how we stand when judged by the Law and Lord of Life. We are faced with the responsibility of our privileges and obligation imposed by mercies, conscience is quickened, shame is awakened, penitence is born. In the eternal Light, we know ourselves to be "sons of ignorance and night." Like Israel and Peter, we know ourselves unworthy and undone. There has been no substitute for the sanctuary ever suggested in this matter. Without the Sanctuary Light and revealing love, righteousness will not seem reasonable and sin will not seem worthwhile bothering about. Now let us turn to the last and golden value of what is signified in the sanctuary furniture.

THE MERCY SEAT

"And thou shalt put the mercy seat above upon the ark . . . and there will I meet with thee." The conscience-stricken, humbled, penitent Israelite turned to meet the God whose Law he had broken and whose love he had so ill requited. Then would he fear in his heart lest God should visit his disobedience with distinction and his ingratitude with vengeance. Yet as in fear he looked he found God sending forgiveness from a seat of mercy. There above the ark of the testimony was the symbol and revelation, not only of the Law which demands and deserves obedience, but of the love which forgives and saves.

Here is the central and unique message of God's House. Here is the gospel of grace which the church holds in trust. Nowhere else is it proclaimed. And what stands for such a gospel can never be dispensed with. Though men have forgotten their covenant, failed to keep the Law, and sinned against love, God meets them in mercy and brings them peace and joy. "There is a place where Jesus sheds the oil of gladness on our heads, a place than all beside more sweet—it is the bloodstained mercy seat."[1] I am not now attempting to state why or how. Those golden cherubs, in the attitude of devotion, with outstretched wings covering the mercy-seat, their faces turned towards it, may well remind us of that there are things the angels desire to look into and even "they cannot search the mystery, the length, breadth, and height." For as Charles Wesley goes on, "God only knows the love of God." Enough that God has found the way and offers peace and pardon as the free gift of His love.

It is a wonderful message and I do not fear for the church while it has such a gospel to proclaim. When I first sat down to write the message my heart failed and my pen halted. Who am I and what are my gifts that I should speak of things so sacred and proclaim such wonderful tidings? Yet my heart was singing for gladness, though the words that came were the words of a simple, old, and almost forgotten hymns. "I have long withstood His grace, long provoked Him to His face, would not hearken to His calls, and grieved Him by a thousand falls." And yet, "There for me the Saviour stands, shews His wounds and spreads His hands." And I wanted to shout in ecstasy, "God is love, I know I feel Jesus weeps and loves me still."[2]

So, the first sanctuary and its furniture reminds us of what all sanctuaries must stand for, the revealing of Law and love, the call to obedience and the call on gratitude. And when conscience reproves us and in penitence we know ourselves lost and

---

1. This is a line from stanza 2 of the hymn "From Every Stormy Wind That Blows," written by Hugh Stowell in the nineteenth century.

2. These are lines from Charles Wesley's hymn "Depths of Mercy."

undone, then must ever be the glorious proclamation that we may, "Come boldly to the Throne of Grace that we may obtain mercy and find grace to help in every time of need."

~

"THE DAY OF DAYS"
—Deuteronomy 16.3

(Preached once at Spring Head Mission 11/10/40)

Deuteronomy 16.3 "Remember the day when thou camest forth out of the land of Egypt."

You would have thought they never could forget that day. What a day it was! It marked the end of their bondage, the beginning of individual freedom, and the inauguration of their national life. It was clearly a day which the Lord made. Their deliverance was the Lord's doing and it was, at the time, marvelous in their eyes. But the reiterated "remember" of the book of Deuteronomy reveals the fact that their memories were no better than ours.

The text calls the Israelites to concentrate their minds upon a definite point of time and definite experience of God's goodness to them. They are not simply asked to amble through their past history selecting this incident or that according to their fancy, but to remember, in all its intensity and detail, the great day when, with high hand and outstretched arm, God brought them out of the land of bondage and into the experience of freedmen. They were to remember that particular day, and not casually or hurriedly, but patiently and deliberately. They were to surround themselves with things that would arrest their memory. The food they ate was to be of the plainest, to remind them of the food their fathers were glad to eat in the great day of escape.

We can all realize the good that would come to the people through the deliberate attempt to recall that day. It would be a reminder of the goodness and power of God and of the journey they had made. It would help to keep faith and love alive within them. It would cure them of those tendencies they sometimes had to return to Egypt. And therein lies the value of making certain anniversaries, days of specific remembrance. We all need them, for our memories are short and great experiences are in danger of fading into the commonplace. So, let us give heed to the call of the text and set ourselves to the definite observing of certain days.

LUMINESCENCE

A DAY TO REMEMBER

You will all realize that tomorrow is the anniversary of November 11, 1918. Some of you are old enough to recall it. Those of you who are not ought to be told of it. What a day it was! Through four long years we alternated between hope and despair. We had not the alarms that now startle us but we had casualty lists as the result of trench warfare that filled us with dismay and sorrow. Hardly a home but was darkened by loss. How we prayed! Then suddenly the end, a victorious end for us loomed in sight. Through the weekend we wondered and waited, there was no wireless then to give us news. Even the Monday morning found us uncertain. Then the sirens sounded and we knew that the end of the agony had come. We all laughed and wept at the same time.

I was in Manchester at the time and shall never forget the scenes. Train-drivers and conductors left their trains in the lines and joined in the celebrations. It was the anniversary at my church. Someone passed a note with the words, "What about we sing outside?" We went and the crowd stopped all the traffic. Thanksgiving services were held and the people joined in singing, "Now thank we all our God."[1] We ought to remember that day. Remembrance will recall gratitude and the vows we made. It should rekindle faith and renew consecration.

It is easy to pass from that great day of deliverance to great days in our spiritual experience that ought not to be forgotten. Here is the value of the observance of days in the Christian year. And there is one great act of love and mercy those of us who are free in spirit ought never to forget and an act of worship that ought not to be omitted.

"THIS DO IN REMEMBRANCE OF ME"

Thus said Jesus on the eve of His death. And he broke bread and gave it to the disciples. Then He went out and on the cross gave His life for the sins of men. I am not now thinking of any theory of the atonement, or of any special way of observing the sacrament of the Lord's Supper. I am only saying that there was an expression of Divine love, a Divine act of deliverance that ought not to be forgotten. And I know how soon and how eagerly we forget. Though I am little of an ecclesiastic and nothing of a ritualist, I am sure that we cannot, as Christians, afford to forget that "Jesus Christ died for our sins according to the Scriptures." I need the reminder there is in the Communion Service that "He loves me, and gave Himself for me." To remember the day is to be sure of His love and to acknowledge our debt.

Now to come to more personal experience, all of us who are Christians in any real sense have behind us a day, a special signal, which stands out above all other days. It is the day which, in a simple song, we hail as the *"happy day when Jesus washed my sins away."* The day when one greater than Moses led us out of a bondage greater than

---

1. This is a translation from a German hymn, "Nun Danket Alle Gott," by Martin Rinkart, written in 1636.

that of Egypt. The day when we were "translated out of the kingdom of darkness into the kingdom of God's love." Some of us can fix the date on the calendar, others cannot. But if we cannot fix a precise date, we are sure of the personal experience. Though we cannot put our hand on the moment we are in no doubt of the fact. The power and love of the Lord broke the power of canceled sin and set us free, our chains fell off, our hearts were free, and we went forth and followed our Lord.

Perhaps there are people who speak too much of the past and have too much in it. Maybe we get a bit tired of hearing those who are continually telling us of their confessions. I am convinced that many of us are on the other side. We allow time to blur what used to be so distinct and to trivialize what used to be so precious. We ought always to remember and sometimes to tell what the Lord hath done for our souls. It would remind and assure us of God's wonderful love, it would recall the glow of our faith and renew our love. We are all inclined to forget and as we grow older the danger is of our losing our heart—our heart for loving and serving. Remember the day you came out of Egypt and you will set your face with a fresh zeal to the promised land.

"MOUNT PISGAH—THE HILL OF VISION"
—Deuteronomy 34.1–4

(Preached at Bishop Street 3/7/1948)

Deuteronomy 34.1–4 "And Moses went up from the plains of Moab unto the mountain of Nebo to the top of Pisgah . . . and the LORD shewed unto him all the land . . . and the LORD said unto him . . . I have caused thee to see it with thine eyes, but thou shalt not go over thither."

THERE ARE SOME PICTURES which, once seen, are never forgotten. By their beauty or awfulness they lay hold of the imagination and forever retain their place in the memory. You can recall, here and there, great pictures from the Bible Gallery. David waiting for tidings of his rebellious but loved son Absalom. Daniel kneeling at his open window. Judas kissing his master in the garden. Paul before Agrippa. Jesus praying in the garden of Gethsemane.

The text set before us is one of the most beautiful pictures in the Old Testament Gallery—Moses on Mount Nebo. He is looking down on the land, not far away, that he has been trying to reach and which his feet are never to tread. The land which for forty years he has looked forward prayerfully to gain and which is not to be his home: the promised land, which for him is never to be the Possessed Land. God made it clear to him that he would not enter it. Moses might have used the poetic lines of one of our poets: "There's the life lying, and I see all of it, once I'm dying."[1]

It is a great picture, and small wonder that poets have made it the theme of their poems and artists have reproduced on canvas the picture of this lonely man viewing the longed for land and knowing that his feet would never cross the river. One would linger over that, wondering what was pouring through the brain behind that face. Was there angry resentment, the feeling that it was not fair that after forty years of traveling and leading, another should cross the Jordan ahead of the people into the land God gave to their fathers? Was he looking back and painfully regretting and repeating the pride and disobedience which had brought about the calamity and thinking the consequences out? Or, was he quietly and calmly accepting God's will, knowing that it was

---

1. This comes from a poem by Robert Browning entitled "Pisgah-Sights."

"MOUNT PISGAH—THE HILL OF VISION"—DEUTERONOMY 34.1–4

best, and content that another man was fitted for finalizing the work he had begun? We do not know and it is idle to speculate. What we can do and benefit from is to—

SEE IN THE PICTURE A PARABLE OF LIFE

Even if the reality is not always so dramatic or pathetic, life has many similar pictures. Here and there you find a man whose purposes are accomplished and who is complacent over his achievements. I do not want to be unfair, but often that means that such men sought lesser things to do and their cheap satisfaction is over no great decision completed. Most of us feel that our lives are of an unfinished character. We seldom attain all we strive for. Abraham left home to seek a country and found only a grave in it. David projected a temple he never built. Livingstone died with the source of the Nile undiscovered. "So much to do, so little done," sighed a great man.

In our own little ways, we are often unfinished and frustrated with our incompleteness. We set our hearts on things that evade us. Our dreams do not become deeds. Our futures are broken off. Sometimes the best is dangled before our eyes, within our grasp, and we reach for it and it changes to the second best or what seems the very worst. We see our promised land and it is shown before us, and then it is as if we are told "thou shalt see it with thine eyes, but thou shalt not enter it." That is all very pathetic, and very true, but it does not help much. What is there to say in view of these unrealized dreams, frustrated hopes, and incomplete lives?

First of all, that unfinished work and incomplete lives are neither fruitless nor wasted. They seem so to us, but not to God who is working this tapestry. He is weaving our lives into His great design. He cannot accomplish the whole through any one of us. He allocates one for this work and causes that work to be through other hands. You can almost hear Moses saying, "I have come myself and brought my people to the very border of Canaan and now the work of my life comes to naught." If you are reverent you will hear God say, "You have not failed, you have brought my people in sight of the land. That was your task and it is finished."

My friends, there is no failure if you have attested and accomplished the work God gave you to do. That life is not wasted which realized what God brought it into the world to do. Then "well done" is over the work that seems unfinished but that is what He asked. And remember this—the work you have done reaches onto the work others will do. Joshua was properly fitted for the work ahead, but he could never have done it but for what Moses had done before him. A little while ago, passing through Darlington, I saw one of the first of Stephenson's railway engines. It looked a truly little, insignificant thing. But it has made possible the mighty engines that can take us from London to Newcastle in a few hours. Your bit of work, faithfully done, though it seems incomplete, is preparing the way for others who will carry it forward and nearer God's ideal.

Now let us learn that divine judgment is of the heart. The world judges outward results, giving its flatteries and its favor to men who have succeeded. It thinks of "making good" use in terms of material conquests, it gives no credit for earnest effort that ends in apparent failure. But at God's judgment bar, the verdict is not given that way. "Man looketh on the outward appearance, but God looketh upon the heart."

That means this—you stand on your Pisgah looking at your unfinished work and know that you will never carry it to a successful conclusion. Maybe, like Moses, you think of something that has frustrated your progress and robbed you of success. But at that moment God is looking on your heart. That is where the greatest work is done. There is no true success for us apart from God's success and that is always in our hearts. Have you learned through success and influence, through disablement and frustration, through all of these forgiveness, to be patient, humble, tender, to accept God's will though it checks your will? Then have no fear. God has work in you and where he looks for success he sees it.

It means this too—God gives the victor's crown to the virtuous person. You have not accomplished all you meant to. Many things you projected have not been performed. You know that you will not enter the land of your vision. God judges you by your earnest venture. He knows the limitations that have beset you, the pressures under which you balanced, the blunders you have encountered. He knows what you have tried to be and measures you by what you have endeavored to do.

DO NOT OVERLOOK THAT PISGAH IS THE MOUNT OF VISION

Moses knew he would not enter the promised land, but he was granted a vision of it, and he knew his people would enter. Faith always has the Pisgah which commands a view of the glorious land ahead. It may be a disappointment that we shall never enter, but we know it is there. Our eyes see the glory of the coming glorious man, caught the glimpse of the dawn on the mountain summits. The golden age is in the future. God's day is dawning. We may not live to see the final triumph, but Jesus shall reign. Above all the ailments and doubts, we have seen a vision of a redeemed world and we shall not fail nor be discouraged. Our task is to do our part to hasten the coming of the glorious day. We must learn that—

INCOMPLETENESS IS THE PROPHECY OF CONTINUANCE AND COMPLETION

What does it mean that this world, for all its beauty, for all we achieve in it, so often disappoints and frustrates us? Surely this—there is a beyond for which this life is a preparation. We have longings that are not satisfied, hopes that are unrealized, work that is unfinished. I simply cannot believe that all this is intended to mock us in what will be written at the end of this life. There must be, my heart's faith is that there is a "land of pure delight where everlasting spring abides and never withering flowers."[2] We do not often hear this song now, but there is a Promise of Life that "Heaven shall make perfect our imperfect lives."

∾

---

2. This is a quote from an Isaac Watts hymn, "There Is a Land of Pure Delight."

"THE CALL TO THE CAPABLE"
—Judges 9.7

(Preached once at Katherine Road 2/9/36)

Judges 9.7 "And when they told it to Jotham, he went and stood in the top of Mount Gerizim, and lifted up his voice, and cried, and said unto them, 'Hearken unto me ye men of Shechem, that God may hearken unto you.'"

OUR IMMEDIATE CONCERN IS with what Jotham said rather than what was said about him. His speech was simply the telling of a fable, a fable to which some interest attaches because it is probably the first fable of which we have any record, as Lamech's is the first song. To understand the fable, you will have to remember that in Hebrew literature, talking trees take the place which in the literature of other lands is occupied by talking beasts and birds.

THE FABLE AND ITS SETTING

The fable is simple and straightforward and it is told in the way that is striking and impressive. Once upon a time, the trees came together to appoint a king. In turn they approached the olive tree, the fig tree, the vine, and saying, "Reign then over us." In turn each of these noble trees replied, "Shall I leave my fatness, my sweetness, my wine, to run up and down for other trees?" So each declined the honor and responsibility. Having failed with the kingly trees, the rest of the trees approached the bramble, representative of what was common and coarse, and asked him to be king. The honor refused by the great trees the bramble at once accepted, at the same time laying down the strongest conditions of his rule.

For the setting which gives point to the fable we have to go back through many centuries to the wild times in Israel's history when "every man did that which was right in his own eyes" and which was often wrong in God's sight. It was a time when there was no king in Israel and very little in the way of national unity and organization. Judges and chieftains rose up from time to time to lead and deliver the people. Perhaps the greatest and best known among these was Gideon, whose great exploit

"THE CALL TO THE CAPABLE"—JUDGES 9.7

with his gallant three hundred has always fascinated us. Not many of us have followed his career after his deliverance of the people from the hands of the Midianites. Unfortunately, it does not make very good reading. There is a blot in Gideon's escutcheon and the story of his later life hardly bears telling. Before he died the people besought him to become their king. This honor he declined for himself and his sons. But after his death, his illegitimate son, Abimelech, who had much of his father's endurance and strength, though without his sweetness and goodness, was approached and at once accepted the kingship. His first act was to murder all his brothers except Jotham, in order that his own seat on the throne might be the more secure.

It was while the feast of celebrating his elevation was in progress that Jotham appeared on a rocky eminence and told the fable of the Bramble King. You can see at once the point of the fable, and the biting sarcasm and touches of humor with which it is made. The bramble, the thorn, king over cedars and olives and vines! Jotham meant the people to see the folly and madness of electing a man like Abimelech to be their king. They were intended to mark the contrast between a man like Gideon and an unscrupulous place seeker like the man they had made their king.

THE MORAL OF THE FABLE

It is when we try to find the moral of the fable for ourselves that the difficulty begins. It does not pretend to have any religious significance. Yet there is a lesson standing out clear and convincing and as I see it, it sounds like the following. The highest places in the state, in the municipality, and in the church should be accepted by those most competent to fill them. In the terms of the fable the bramble should not be permitted to usurp the place of the olive tree, fig tree, and vine. Neither should the olive and the vine shrink from the responsibilities their gifts fit them for.

This is the sort of sermon one would like to preach at election times. Men who are graceless and gift-less ought not to be elected to positions of critical responsibility. If we are foolish enough to elect such men, whatever the length of their purse or their pedigree, however glib their tongues and their promises, it needs no prophet to predict, as Jotham did, that a fire will break out and consume much that we value. On the other hand, if men of noble gifts and character refuse to accept the responsibility of office and leadership you may be quite sure that less worthy and less able men will shift into the position. If the olive will not rule then the bramble will.

Preparing for this sermon I was reminded of a modern parallel—the French Revolution whose failures we mourn and at whose "excesses" we shudder. "What was the French Revolution?" asks Dr. Aked, "In one sentence it was the issue of fires from the bramble king, fires that blazed sky-high from hell to heaven and consumed the cedars of Lebanon. Every function that belonged to place and power, to responsibility and rule, had been abdicated by olive, fig, and vine, by noble, priest, and king . . . That was why the trees of the forest sought the bramble and the thorn, called to the Dantons, the Robespierres, and the Marrats to come and rule over them." So the modern application of the moral of the fable is—

THE CONDEMNATION OF THE UNWILLING

In the state and in the community. What a picture the fable gives of much that happens today. There are men and women who are gifted and eminently fitted for the service of the community. But they say, "I'm not interested. It's too much time. All parties are alike and a plague on all your parties. I'm too busy with my studies and the living of my own life. I do not covet any of these positions, let those who want them have them." It all sounds very humble. In reality it is often selfish slacking. The inevitable happens. Because worthy men and women will not undertake public service and sit in committees, the work gets into the hands of the incompetent and unscrupulous. That is not to say that all men in public life are either incompetent or unworthy. One gladly bears testimony to able and unselfish service of those who run up and down to serve the community. One honors such people and it is to help them and to multiply their numbers that this is said. But we all know that the old fable is true to life and that the bramble rules because the olive declines.

In the church. But my main concern is with the church. Listen to these words. "There is, perhaps, no danger more threatening to the efficiency and peace of the church in these realms than the grievous tendency of men of culture and refinement to decline from its communion and its service." That was written by Dr. Cox in 1872. It might have been written yesterday for it is true to the facts. Many of those who are best fitted to guide a congregation are either outside the church or, if within it, are content to pursue their own path rather than share its responsibilities and duties. They try, so they tell us, to be good in their own homes and that they are better and happier outside the organizations of the church. Anyway, it would be a waste of time.

Boiled down, it's the old excuse of the olive and the vine, "Should I leave my fatness and my good cheer to run up and down after others?" The temptation we can all understand. When men are wise and happy, cultured and refined, pursuing their own ways in peace and context, it is a peculiar temptation to leave the wild to go its own way. From the days of the disciples, men who have stood on the Mount of Vision and Contemplation have wanted to abide there and leave the demoniacs and sufferers to others. Some of the tasks can be so vulgar and some monstrous, some of the people helped are so ungrateful, fellow workers can be small and mean and jealous. It is always easy to persuade ourselves that we are doing better by keeping aloof. No useful end will be served by simply indulging in condemnation. So, let me translate the lesson into other terms.

THE CALL TO THE CAPABLE

You have special culture, refinement, goodness. You might not keep them to yourself. "If our virtues go not forth from us, tis all alike as if we had them not." *A call comes through the special lesson of this fable.* You are fitted for service, if you do not undertake it, other less fitted will have to do it. It will be idle for you to blame them or complain that the work is ill done. You say, "We need better men in the pulpit, in the leader's meetings, in the Sunday School." Exactly! What about you? It is because men and women of education and ability are shrinking that those of us who are less competent have to do the best we can.

The common life constitutes a call. We are a fellowship, a communion and no man is to live to himself. It would be a strange and quaint spectacle, says Dr. Cox, to see all the trees of a great forest stamping up and down in their roots to forward each other's welfare. But, he continues, there is a spectacle far stranger than that, and very common: it is that of a Christian church whose members do not go up and down, helping forward the common welfare, each according to his ability. If we have any special gifts of mind and heart we are debtors to our fellow members. To think only of our comfort and ease, ever only of saving our own souls, comes near to meaning, "Every man for himself and the devil take the hindmost."

Not to use our gifts is to lose them. Here the figure of the material fails us. The olive tree will not lose its fatness nor the fig tree its sweetness by not serving the other trees. But in the spiritual realm service is the law of increase and idleness means loss. All God's gifts thrive in work and increase in proportion as we are faithful stewards. From him that hath not is taken away that which he hath.

THE CALL TO THE LOWLY

There is one more word to be said. I can take nothing back that I have said, but I am anxious not to be misunderstood. And the last thing I desire is to discourage any lowly worker. There are some who are, and who know they are, not typified by stately and kingly cedars and oaks, but by the lowly bramble or hawthorns. Ask the hands of the people who go blackberrying. Let every tree bear its own fruit and do the best it can for the whole forest.

So, in the church, there are diversities of gifts and operations. Do the best you can with the best you have. If others who are better equipped than you shirk, try to make up for their indifference. Do not strive for mastery or place, do what you can, not in the spirit of lordliness, but in the spirit of lowliness. I can best drive home this closing lesson if I let that veteran warrior, Dr. Clifford, being dead, yet speak to us. Speaking of the great Earl of Shaftesbury, who sacrificed place and ease to serve chimney sweeps and ill-used toilers, Dr. Clifford said that the remedial acts got through were not so much acts of Parliament as acts of an apostle. And the doctor quoted these lines:

"Does it make you mad when you read about some poor, stained devil who flickered out because he never had a decent chance in the tangled meshes of circumstance? If it makes you burn like the fires of sin, brother, you're fit for the ranks—fall in!"

"Whoever has blood that will flood his face at the sight of a beast in the holy place. Whoever has rage for the tyrant's might, for the powers that prey in the day and night. Whoever has hate for the ravening brute that strips the tree of the goodly fruit. Whoever knows wrath at the sight of pain, of needless sorrow and heedless gain, brother, you're fit for the ranks—fall in!"[1]

---

1. This is a quote from a Masonic hymn, the author of which is unknown. It can sometimes be found in full under the heading "Our Social Problem" on Masonic websites.

"SAMSON—A CHARACTER STUDY"
—Judges 16.20

(Preached eleven times from Fentiman Road 3/12/22 to Mount Zion, Cornwall 5/16/43)

Judges 16.20 "And he awoke out of his sleep, and said, 'I will go out as at other times and shake myself.' But he wist not that the Lord was departed from him."

THE STORY OF SAMSON has so often been treated as a story for the entertainment of children that it is difficult to get for it the serious consideration it deserves. We will insist on thinking of Samson simply as an old-time Sandow, a slayer of lions, a fighter of Philistines, a man strong enough to pick up massive iron gates and walk away with them. We regard the story of his life as a giant story written to fascinate the infant imagination. Now all these things are in the picture, but they are as certainly not all the picture. I want to suggest to you that you have here a pregnant study in temptation and character that serious men and women cannot afford to neglect. You have a luminous illustration of how the decay of moral principle paralyzes power, and how the lust of the eye and the pride of life lead on to tragedy and failure.

If you have imagined that there is neither dignity nor profit in this story, let me remind you that one of the greatest of all Englishmen, himself blind and in danger, though with no moral fall behind him turned his thoughts to this story we have neglected. And if my setting of the story fails to move you, let me urge you to ponder Milton's *Samson Agonistes*. The story, as told in the book of Judges, is too long for detailed consideration in this hour of service, but we may get the heart of it under three propositions.

THE DECAY OF MORAL PRINCIPLE MEANS THE PARALYSIS OF POWER

Think of the Jewish Hercules as he stepped on to the stage of action. He was a giant in more senses than one. He was prayed into the world and born into an atmosphere of piety. The smile of God was on his birth and nature added her choicest gifts. In body, he was brawny and strong, and he was keen and smart in intelligence and wit, and his courage matched his strength and intelligence. The Philistines, the enemies of his country and his religion, were like witless clay in his hands.

Here we instinctively feel he was the destined leader and deliverer of his people. Everything promised that. Yet the life that opened so brilliantly went out in tragedy. The opportunities were tremendous, the attainments trifling. Samson had all the makings of a great man in him, but he never made a great man. There were just a few flashes of noble passion, true patriotism and heroic attainment—enough to show what might have been—and then the light was quenched. Failure is writ large over this man's life, and as you look in the tragic failure you are inclined to give a new turn to Whittier's words, "The saddest of all sad words are these, 'it might have been.'"[1]

The reason for the failure is not far to seek. Milton says, "But thee, whose strength, while virtue was her mate, might have subdued the earth." But virtue did not long remain the mate of strength, and so Samson subdued nothing. He did not "rule his own spirit," and he did not rule anything. His moral principle decayed, his purity went, and his power to bless himself and his fellows was paralyzed. The man who might have lifted his people up, let them down.

Was this nothing to say to you? Can you not match that? That searching analyst of character, Alexander Whyte, says, "Samsons in body are not born among us in our day, but Samsons in mind are sometimes given us in room of them. And it is not seldom seen that our greatly gifted youths work as little deliverance for themselves and for us as Samson did for Israel."[2] You can read that in life as well as in Dr. Whyte. We all knew the youths who at school and college stood head and shoulders above the rest of us. Easily and brilliantly they came out head of the examination lists and carried off all the prizes. With them, as with Samson, the slaying of lions was as the slaying of kids. Great things were prophesied and expected of them. And for all the brilliant promise there has been no performance. They have been easily outstripped by men with fewer gifts. Many of them have not only failed, they have looked too long and longingly on the wine red in the cup, have sought too often the excitements of the card table, and well, the other can be left unsaid.

God help us to lay the lesson to heart. It is great to have great powers, but there is something greater than intellectual greatness or flashes of genius. Recall Tennyson's knight "whose strength was as the strength of ten, because his heart was pure."[3] That is not a pretty poetic myth, it is life's great fact. Behind your brilliant intellect keep a pure heart. Let your moral principle be sound and strong. Then your power to serve your generation will be increased tenfold. Even if you are not an intellectual giant or

---

1. The actual quote of John Greenleaf Whittier, taken from the last two lines of the work, is: "For of all sad words of tongue or pen / The saddest are these: 'It might have been!'" This is a quote from a poem entitled "Maud Muller" (1856).

2. This is taken from Alexander Whyte's *Dictionary of Bible Characters* (1901), the entry on Samson.

3. From Tennyson's poem of 1842, "Sir Galahad."

a greatly gifted man you will be able to help your fellows if you are a good man and true. But without humility, purity, singleness of heart, your power will be paralyzed as surely as was Samson's.

THERE IS AN UNCONSCIOUS DEGENERATION AND LOSS OF POWER

He said, "I will go out as at other times. He wist not that the Lord was departed from him." Poor Samson! What a sorry awakening! The giant had become a weakling and without knowing it. You are not to suppose that his strength went from him in an hour because he told a woman his secret and let her shave his head. I take it that that is simply a dramatic and forcible way of telling how he degenerated and his strength left him. He had been gradually weakening, falling, departing from the spirit of his Nazarite vow. His power had been going without his knowing it and one day he awoke to find it gone.

Here again the story is true to life. This is the way strength usually goes in regards to physical strength, the invalid, after a few days illness, thinks he can rise and walk and work but finds his strength has gone. In regards to mental strength, politicians, preachers, singers, keep on after their power has gone. That is how moral strength goes too. Men smile superciliously when you suggest that trifling with wine cups, having a shilling in their fancy, sporting with Delilah may ruin them. "Is thy servant a dog that he should do this thing?" They know when to stop. But the question is stopping when you know you ought to. The evil you are flirting with is sapping your strength and will hand you over to slavery.

Religious strength goes this way too. We all know people who neglect the means of grace, allow the family altar to fall into ruins and the dust to gather on the Bible, and who are rather sarcastic towards earnest folk who keep these things up. They declare that they are growing broader and not weaker, and yet, we can read the story of Samson with a religious interpretation.

My friends, we cannot help the loss of physical and mental strength and there is no tragedy when they go. But we need not and ought not to lose our moral and religious energy. We can go from strength to strength. Is it not written that, though youths faint and be weary, they that wait upon God shall renew their strength?

STRENGTH MAY BE RECOVERED BY A RETURN TO FAITH

Turn now to the closing scenes of Samson's life. I have nothing to take back of the solemn and stern words I have tried to say, but I must proclaim the gospel Samson's closing days preach. Look at the man. "Ask for the deliverer now, and find him eyeless in Gaza, at the mill with slaves. Himself in bonds under Philistian yoke. With his heaven-gifted strength put to the labor of a beast." What a sorry spectacle! Sightless, a slave, ageing fast. But it is not the sorriest spectacle in that tragic life. In some respects, it is the most hopeful. Blinded by his enemies, Samson is recovering his inward sight. Never again will he look upon the dazzling sights of earth, but there is still opportunity to look upon the face of God. The lonely prison cell became a house of God, a place of prayer and penitence. In the night of his blindness Samson spoke with his God and held Him fast.

The day of his disgrace was his day of grace. The cutting of his hair was the outward sign of his inner dislocation and departure from God. In the prison, "the hair of his head began to grow again." He got back to purity, to faith, to the spirit of his vow. He prayed, "Remember me, O Lord, just this once." And you know the sequel. Call it a mean, petty, personal revenge if you will, I cannot join you. I have to judge this man in the light of his day, by the rude and rough laws of his time and not by Christian standards. I have to remember that the Philistines were the sworn foes of Israel's integrity as a nation and of their faith in the One God, and that slaying Philistines was thought to be serving God. And, anyway, I have to preach the gospel that the miracle of Samson's life may be worked in yours. His fall has not been yours, nor his temptations. But how many of us have failed to keep the vows, the purity, and the faith of other days.

Think of the vow you made at your mother's knee, when you gave yourself to Christ and joined the church. When God delivered you from some threatening trouble. Have you allowed the enemies of God and your soul to rob you of your strength, your faith, your purity, your zeal? I am here to call you back. Back! I pray you to the old pure vows. Back! To your loyalty to God. Back! To the old sense of separation to a holy life and Divine service.

For some of you, the day is far spent and the night is at hand. For others, the sun is still high in the sky. For all of you this gospel is that if you will return to your faith, your strength will return to you. If you will pray God will bless you with his reviving grace and make his strength perfect in your weakness. Pray Samson's prayer, "Remember me, O Lord." Cry, "Give me back my heart, my purity, my power." God always answers that prayer when it comes from a penitent heart, and in the abundance of the answer the failures of the past shall be swallowed up in the victories yet to be.

∼

"GOD AND BREAD"
—Ruth 1.6

(Preached twelve times including Spring Head Mission 9/20/36 and Prees Green 10/7/51; a Harvest Sermon)

———————————————————

Ruth 1.6 "The Lord had visited His people in giving them bread."

"The loveliest little idyll that tradition has transmitted to us." That is how Goethe described the book of Ruth, and the German poet was a judge of such matters. The book opens in tragedy and ends in sheer romance. It begins with a famine and ends in a harvest field. It contains a lovely love story leading to a romantic wedding. You are left with the picture of a sweet-faced granny crowing over a little boy. And you know that that boy was the destined grandfather of great David and an ancestor of great David's greater Son. The story is set in the background of a harvest field and it mimes to the swish of the scythes in the golden corn and the greetings of the song of the reapers as they bind the sheaves. That fact makes the book a happy hunting ground for preachers in search of a text for a Harvest Festival.

In it I found the simple and direct message which seems a word in season for us. As definitely as any passage I know the text relates the Harvest to a gracious Divine visitation. Standing in the midst of signs and tokens of an abundant harvest, seated at our well-spread tables, we can change our word, and read the text in the present instead of the past tense and say, "The Lord hath visited His people in giving them bread." Then the first fact to be emphasized is that of—

THE GRACE OF DIVINE VISITATIONS

That is not how we usually think of Divine visitation. In the presence of some inexplicable tragedy, some judgment of disaster and death, our juries return a verdict of "died by the visitation of God." We associate plagues and catastrophes with the same visitation, when we quote the words, "Prepare to meet thy God," we are positively afraid of the meeting. Doubtless God does sometimes come in swift condemnation of judgment of the sins of a people or an individual. But as Isaiah says, that is His "strange work."

God's ancient people were versed in this matter. They associated God's visits with mercy rather than with judgment, with compassion rather than condemnation. God visited His people when He saw their need and heard their sighs. He came down to deliver them. Their statement of redemption was, "God hath visited and redeemed His people." The day of Jerusalem's visitation was the season of God's loving pleading and patient waiting for them to turn to Him.

We ought to learn the lesson, to associate Divine visitations with redemption and blessing. Instead of dreading we ought to welcome and pray for the visits of God, to be thankful that He does not forget us or fail to come to us. We can decorate our church, sit at our tables, because God has seen our need and come down to meet it. Do not, I beg of you, associate God's visitation only with tragedies. Think of Him as you stand among the golden corn, as you listen to the song of the birds, as you enjoy the good things which are your daily possession. That leads us to the central thought of the text:

OUR DAILY BREAD IS GOD'S GIFT

Day by day we pray, "Give us this day our daily bread," but when the bread is given we do not always recognize whence it comes. One of the best services a Harvest Festival can render is to remind us of the connection between God and our daily bread. Living in towns and crowded streets we do not hear the song of the reapers or see the wagons laden "with four months' sunshine bound in sheaves." We see bread over at some modern bakery and almost think of the loaf as a manufactured article. Today we set the truth of the text to music and sing: "All good gifts around us are sent from Heaven above."[1] We see in the Harvest God's answer to our daily prayer.

---

1. This is not a reference to the famous song from Godspell, but rather an earlier hymn that actually provides the lyric for both the original hymn and the one from Godspell. Here are the particulars: "Harvest Hymn" by Matthias Claudius (1780).

> We plough the fields, and scatter the good seed on the land;
> But it is fed and watered by God's almighty hand:
> He sends the snow in winter, the warmth to swell the grain,
> The breezes and the sunshine, and soft refreshing rain.

> Chorus:
> All good gifts around us
> Are sent from heaven above,
> Then thank the Lord, O thank the Lord
> For all His love.

> He only is the maker of all things near and far;
> He paints the wayside flower, He lights the evening star:
> The winds and waves obey Him, by Him the birds are fed;
> Much more to us, His children, He gives our daily bread.

"GOD AND BREAD"—RUTH 1.6

That is not to deny man's part. In the natural as well as the spiritual, man plants and waters, sows and reaps, grinds and labors; but in both cases, it is true that without God there will be no increase. We talk glibly about the laws of nature and second causes, and those very laws imply a lawgiver and the second causes lead to a great First Cause. Don't stop your scientific investigation continue it. Trace back far enough and you are sure to come to God. Pay your tribute to the farmer, the miller, the baker, but do not forget that God hath visited us and given us bread, that "He opens His hand and satisfies the desire of every living thing."

Therefore, this day is the festival of the Divine beneficence and should be the occasion of the people's gratitude and praise. God has visited us in giving us bread. The heart should sing its thanksgiving and the people shew forth His praise. But instead of saying, "God be praised," we often murmur and complain because the bread is not buttered on both sides and jam and cream added. Bread stands for what satisfies the real needs of life. Most of our discontent springs from our desire for luxuries we do not need and that in some cases we are a good deal better without. What we need is bread, and not too much highly spiced confectionery. There is a book on my shelves called *The Durable Satisfactions of Life*.[2] The writer sees all those satisfactions in the things bread implies—health of a day, mental balance, power to appreciate beauty and truth, the rare delights of friendship, love and home, ties that bind us to the unseen world, and faith which fills even the dark hours of life with the light of immortal hope.

All these are ours, and God did not spare His only Son, but gave Him to be the Bread of Life. Eat your bread with singleness and thankfulness of heart. Try to count your blessings. The task is impossible but it is a good exercise. All you can do, and this you ought to do, is form a grateful heart to sing your Doxology praising God who has visited his people, giving them bread.

∼

---

2. A book by C. W. Eliot, published in 1910.

"DAVID HARPING BEFORE SAUL"
—1 Samuel 16.17, 23

(Preached six times from Lumberhead Green, undated, to Katherine Road 2/24/35)

---

1 Samuel 16.17, 23 "Saul said unto his servants, 'provide me now a man that can play well.' And it came to pass, when the evil spirit from God was upon Saul, that David took a harp, and played with his hand: so Saul was refreshed, and the evil spirit departed from him."

THESE WORDS CANNOT BE understood apart from the man to whom they refer. You will have to look at Saul before you look into the words. When you look upon the first king of Israel you are looking upon one whose story is told in the Old Testament. You are also looking upon one whose failure was as complete and tragic as any recorded in Scripture. When Saul is first introduced to us our hearts go out to him. He was a man every inch of him—tall, strong, comely. Modesty mingled with strength, humility with bulk, and a gracious magnanimity with conquering power. He had a keen eye, swift powers of judgment, and was ready and strong in action. Discovered by the man of God, acclaimed by the people, he looked the heaven-sent leader of his people.

But alas! The promise of those early days was blighted. The blossom never heightened into the fruit of great and worthy achievement. He struck a few brave blows for freedom. There were a few bright flashes, but after that the dark. The first king of Israel died by his own hand, a miserable failure, a striking revelation of how, notwithstanding great gifts and early promise, a man may miss his chance, fail in his task, and miss his high destiny. The Bible is a faithful book and there are no stories more powerfully told than those in its pages. You cannot forget the story of Saul and you cannot miss its lessons. For our immediate purpose, we hone it down to one or two lessons appropriate to the occasion. We begin with—

THE KING'S DEMAND FOR A MINSTREL

"Provide me now a man that can play well." The demand came out of a condition that needs examination. The king had fallen into a distemper, a fit of melancholy and

"DAVID HARPING BEFORE SAUL"—1 SAMUEL 16.17, 23

depression and the old way of describing his condition was to say that an evil spirit from the Lord was tormenting him. That was the popular notion of the time. We do not now think of such spirits as coming from the Giver of all good things. Putting the whole story together we can see what happened. In Saul's earlier days, the Spirit of God was welcomed, followed, obeyed. Later on, that Spirit was refused, rejected, disobeyed. Humility giving place to pride, Saul preferred his own way to God's. The Spirit of the LORD departed from him because, to borrow a word from the New Testament, Saul "grieved the Holy Spirit." "My Spirit shall not always strive with men." The gracious, willing, guest found no acceptance or welcome, and departed. The effect of that departure was that from that hour the gracious king became a prey to gloom and melancholy, a victim of the torturing jealousy which goaded him to undo and mar the fair promise of the early years.

In less dramatic fashion, what happened to Saul occurs in our own day. When men shut God out of their lives they leave room for all manner of evil spirits. We try to live without the God for whom we were made, and for whom our souls cry out, and we leave the door open for torturing evil. Jesus saw and taught that in the parable of the house without a tenant.

I am not unmindful of the physical causes that so often make for shattered nerves and disordered minds. But a large part of the trouble of our times is the forgetfulness or rejection of God. The root cause of much of our pessimism, our fears, our cynicism, and some of our nervous wrecks, is to be found in the forsaking of God. Nothing can save us but the return to God and the recovery of His Spirit.

For mark the expedients to which a man resorts when he rejects God. The man who used to send for a prophet and seek counsel with God cries for a minstrel and sends for a musician. Later on, he turned to the witch at Endor and sought counsel of the dead. What a come-down! That is not simply strange. It is what always happens, and what is happening now! Men and women trying to live without God are hungry and unsatisfied. Everywhere there are frantic cries for the minstrel, for the man who can amuse, entertain, make us laugh and forget. You know the modern minstrel—pictures, revues, dances, and entertainments. I am saying nothing against these things in themselves. I am saying that it is an awful indictment that we are afraid to live with ourselves, that we are calling for a fiddler when our souls cry out for the living God. And I am saying that that way folly and failure lie. "You can never satisfy the soul by the tickling of a sense." You may get an evening's forgetfulness and fun out of a fiddle and a song, out of a dance and a play, but you cannot get what will satisfy an immortal soul made in the Divine image and destined for eternal glory. Oh, it is pitiable to see men and women craving for the happiness and frivolities of life when what they really need is God. It is not the minstrel, or his modern equivalent, we need, it is God and the God revealed in Jesus. Now turn to the other side, a complimentary lesson.

LUMINESCENCE

CONSIDER THE MINSTREL GOD SENT

You might almost call it God's last appeal to Saul. In the good providence of God, it was David who went to play before the depressed, distressed, and diseased king—not a mechanical or professional buffoon, but a bright, clean, healthy, cheery youth, fresh from the sheepfolds and fellowship with God. A youth "with God's dew on his gracious gold hair."

One of the finest things in modern poetry for me is Browning's description of David harping before Saul. He pictures Saul seated in the gloom of his tent. David said not a word, but tuned his harp and played. First, he played the tune with which the shepherd calls home his sheep in the gloaming, then the song of the reapers, a funeral dirge, a marriage hymn, and a battle song. Then he sang of the beauty of God's world and the good gift of life. Then he tuned his harp to the story of Saul's life, his boyhood, his honesty, his beauty, and his brave deeds. The king was touched and troubled, and "there in the darkness Saul stirred." But the work was not yet done. Again, the minstrel bent over his harp and sang. The song was the blessed gospel, the assurance that by Divine mercy the past may be blotted out and a new man rise from the grave of the old. Then the look of care passed from Saul's face, and a great gentleness came over him, he drew the lad towards him, and for long sat stroking David's yellow hair.[1]

Thank God there are Davids as well as Sauls. If there are warped, weary, wizened men and women, there are fresh, eager, happy, pure souls too. And this incident suggests a ministry they can exercise. I would like to say to them—keep your soul young and clean, pure and glad, and your very presence will be an inspiration to sad and dispirited souls. Though you don't know a note of music, God will make your life a song "that comforteth the sad, that helpeth others to be strong, and makes the singer glad."

I know youth calls to youth and that you will want the company of those of your own age and outlook, but give some of your time and some of your youth and freshness to the old and depressed, to the sick and the suffering. Just by going into a home you may brighten it. One of my own loveliest memories is of going into a home in this district to visit an old lady. While I was there two of our own young people came in. It was their half-holiday and they were giving part of it to cheer a lonely old woman. Their incoming was like the coming in of spring, and I marked with joy how the old lady's face brightened. One of those young folk had a lovely reward. The old lady had nothing to give but her thanks and her blessing, and one other thing. She had one spray of lilies of the valley in her garden and she had saved it to give to the young lady who made music in her heart and home.

And do not let us forget, in His service, the ministry of music is our debt to those who find sense in it. Music may be something men seek to tickle a sense when the soul is hungry for God. It may be the tones in which the voice of God reaches

---

1. He is referring to the 1890 poem "Saul," a lengthy narrative poem by R. B. Browning.

"DAVID HARPING BEFORE SAUL"—1 SAMUEL 16.17, 23

wandering and weary souls. The service of song may be a performance intended only to attract and please, or it may be part of the attempt to cheer, gladden, and uplift. There is tremendous power in song. Music both has charms to sooth a savage heart, to soften rocks, or bend a knotted oak. Of some songs, it is written: "Such songs have power to sooth the restless pulse of care, and come like the benediction which follows after prayer. And the night is filled with music, and the cares that infest the day, just fold up their tents like Arabs, and as silently steal away." How many hearts have been moved to finer issues by the singing of "home, sweet home?"[2] Strength and courage are inspired by the singing of "John Brown's Body." Hearts and minds have been made tender and kind by "Lead, Kindly Light," and comforted by "The Lord's My Shepherd." "Abide with Me" catches the heart of any audience from that in a cathedral to that in a football field.

Let us consecrate the power of song to the service of God and weary and tempted men and women. Do not be content to sing for amusement or applause. Sing so that depressed and lonely souls will be lifted and cheered. Above all, let the ministry of music be enlisted in the service of evangelism. Use it to cast out evil spirits. Sing as David sang to Saul of the grace of God, of the new chances God gives, of the new life that is offered. Let evangelistic singing cooperate with evangelistic preaching. Let us answer the world's "Provide me now a man that can play well," with a gospel ministry of sacred song.

∼

---

2. This is a quote from H. W. Longfellow's famous poem "The Day Is Done."

"THE GREEN EYE OF THE YELLOW GOD"
—1 Samuel 18.9

(Preached twice from Fentiman Road 3/15/25 to Katherine Road 2/23/36)

---

1 Samuel 18.9 "And Saul eyed David from that day and forward."

IT WAS ON THIS wise—David the young and newly appointed commander of the hosts of Israel, had gone out on a campaign against the Philistines. As he returned after winning a great victory, the daughters of Israel met him with singing and dancing. In the experience of their joy they exalted the new commander over the king. "Saul," they sang, "hath slain his thousands, and David his ten thousands." With a lowering countenance, Saul stood in the background, and in that dark and terrible moment he gave jealousy place in his soul. He was wroth and said, "They have ascribed unto David ten-thousands, and to me they have ascribed but thousands, and what can he have more but the kingdom?" From that moment, David could do nothing right for the king. Saul could not bear the sight of his face or the sound of his name. The eyes that followed David wherever he went were blinded by jealousy to everything good. Everything the son of Jesse did angered the jealous king. And as jealousy struck its fangs deeper into his soul he saw in David only one who must at all costs be removed.

Follow the story. It is not long before you are reading how the king in his jealous rage flung his spear at the youth who was trying by music to charm the devil out of him. And but a little later, you are told how Saul sought to bait a death trap for his fancied rival with his own daughter's love and flesh. It is a terrible story, and I do not hesitate to dwell on it a moment or two longer in order to point out the kind of man who was mastered, embittered, and spoiled by the entering of the demon of jealousy into his life. Saul was a man of fine parts. In his moments of sanity and reasonableness he was a gallant and magnanimous man. But his whole life was cursed and the big man became petty and small, a would-be murderer of the vilest sort, because he gave place to the devil of jealousy. He made David's life unbearable, and he consigned himself to the hell of a tortured spirit. That is the story and—

"THE GREEN EYE OF THE YELLOW GOD"—1 SAMUEL 18.9

IT IS TRUE TO THE FACTS OF LIFE

It would be hard to mention a sin which can do mischief on a larger scale, as well as more subtly poison the springs of character, you can find illustrations in the Bible, in general literature, and in life. It was jealousy that made Cain slay his brother Abel. It was jealousy that made Joseph's brother meditate and attempt the murder of their brother and sent them home to their father with a lie on their lips and a blood-stained coat in their hand. From literature, take one great illustration instead of many small ones. Part of my reading in preparation for this sermon was Shakespeare's *Othello*. How Iago stirs up the spirit of jealousy in the Moor until in a blind passion, which has turned mole hills into mountains and seen in the most trifling incidents causes of suspicion, smothers Desdemona. Listen to the haunting words: "O, beware, my lord of jealousy: It is the green-eyed monster which doth mock the meat it feeds on."

Advancing civilization has not exercised this demon. You can see it at work in the life of today. Think of the racial jealousy which blinds nations to their need of each other and the horrors of war that turns the world into an armed camp. Think of the class war inflamed by the same demon of jealous suspicion. Read in your newspapers the tragedies of life and the wreaks of homes caused by the green-eyed monster. You can see politicians and profession men who can do no sort of justice to one another because their vision and judgment are jaundiced and warped by jealousy.

NO ONE IS EXEMPT FROM THE INSIDIOUS ATTACKS OF THIS SUBTLE DEMON

If you think there is no need for me to warn you against this evil, let one remind you of some things that ought to put us all on our guard. There were men who had been called by Jesus into fellowship with Him. For three years, they had lived with Him, listened to His gracious words, watched His great example, and been under His helpful influence: and yet, on the last night of His life, under the very shadow of the cross, they were all jealous of one another! Their Master had to wash the jealousy from their hearts as He performed the task they had all declined and washed the dust from their feet. Even in the glorious days of the early church, hurtful divisions arose because of little, spiteful jealousies. And how often we have known the peace and effectiveness of modern churches marred because lovers of Christ were jealous of one another!

Even into our homes this spirit enters. Brothers and sisters quarrel and one has seen the house of death turned into a place of shame, and an angry scene take place over a coffin, because of unworthy and jealous suspicions. And there are few of us who could not name the time when we have suffered ourselves or done injustice to others because of jealousy. There is need to say, "O, beware, my master, of the green-eyed monster of jealousy."

Any man who eyes another as Saul eyed David can do no justice to him. Such feline watchfulness and morbid suspicion will blind us to all the good in another. There may be as much courage and virtue about him as there was in David's life, but a jealous man or woman will not see it. The fairer face of another, gifts possessed, success achieved, victories won, will be seen through jaundiced eyes. The green eye of the yellow god never sees with appreciation. Jealousy makes men skilled in the easy art of subtle detraction. Let that demon in and if the man you are jealous of succeeds you will argue favor, if he fails you will argue justice: you will never be decent to a successful rival.

There is a couplet in Othello which sets forth a further evil wrote by jealousy. "Trifles, light as air, are to the jealous confirmations strong." A handkerchief, innocently dropped, was though enough to inflame Othello to the murder of Desdemona. Eyeing David as he did, Saul saw in David's most innocent words and actions something subtle and deep. And always the jealous man turns trifles into traitorous acts and sees in simple things something aimed at his own honor or place. So it often happens that jealousy leads to murder. Sometimes literally. Oftener to the casting of the javelin of slander and detraction at a good name. Many a man's chances have been killed by jealousy. Many a home has been wrecked. Many a friendship murdered. I understand that some years ago some splendid butterflies were introduced by the authorities into Battersea Park, but they were torn to pieces by the gutter sparrows. So the lives of some of the most gifted and delightful of the sons of men have been blasted by base jealousy and envy. "Love is strong as death: jealousy as cruel as the grave" (Song of Songs 8.6).

JEALOUSY REACTS POISONOUSLY ON THE JEALOUS

Saul intended to hurt David, but blasted his own life. The large, magnanimous man became a bitter, morose, and blighted man. Base emotions always recoil on themselves. They poison the atmosphere of the soul in which they live until nothing bright and glad can live in it. When jealousy infects the soul, it destroys the very possibility of joyfulness. The green eye is at once the cause and the sign of an ulcerated soul. The passion of jealousy is fatal to those who cherish it. Can there be any hell worse than that in which a jealous man spends his days? For your own sake as well as that of others we urge: Beware of jealousy!

HOW SHALL WE SAFEGUARD OURSELVES?

The first piece of advice is deliberately put bluntly. Stand up to the demon. Give no place to it. From the temptation to jealousy perhaps none of us are exempt. To see others succeeding where we failed, winning the place we coveted, doing the work we wanted, brings the devil to our doors. But brave and true-hearted men and women kick him out. Crush down all envious feelings and pray for grace to congratulate the man or woman who passes you in the race of life. If something happens that you cannot understand, do not harbor unworthy suspicions, either ask or wait for an explanation. Take yourself thoroughly in hand and never eye your fellows in the jealous and suspicious way Saul eyed David.

Yet show I unto you a more excellent way. Turn jealousy into right channels. "I am jealous over you with a godly jealousy," Paul wrote to the Corinthians (2 Cor 11.2). There is a godly jealousy. Do you not sing, "Arm me with jealous care"? Godly jealousy is a jealousy which God has. "The Lord our God is a jealous God." But the jealousy of God is a solicitude for truth, purity, justice. It is a sensitiveness to anything that hurts the good. He is not jealous *of* people, but *for* their welfare. Turn your jealousy into these channels. Be fearful lest anything sully your purity or stains your honor. Be careful that nothing offends or hurts those around you. This is the jealousy of love, and love thinks no evil, rejoices not in iniquity, but rejoices in the truth.

"STRENGTHENING A MAN'S HAND IN GOD"
—1 Samuel 23.16

(Preached twelve times from Fentiman Road to Roker, Sunderland. Dated for Spring Head Mission 9/24/36)

---

1 Samuel 23.16 "And Jonathan Saul's son arose, and went to David into the wood, and strengthened his hand in God."

DAVID'S BODY WAS HIDDEN in that wood, and his soul was sinking in a Slough of Despond. Enemies were closing in on him and discouragement and despair were shadowing his spirit. His heroic deeds for his own people seem to have been forgotten. Saul was seeking his life to take it. The men of Keilah, whom he had just delivered from a marauding band of Philistines, instead of being grateful, were preparing to hand him over to his enemies. So he fled for his life and hid himself in the wood. That wood may well stand for—

THE MOOD OF DEPRESSION

All noble souls, at times, find themselves in it. None of us are likely to find ourselves driven into a desert by an armed band or betrayed by graceless folk we have succored. But it is easy to think of many modern foes that discourage and drive to despair. There are some whose life is one long struggle with diverse circumstances and physical infirmities. The other day I called at a home and saw an old woman who cannot see to read, cannot speak, and cannot walk. There's a thick enough wood for you. Other sensitive souls are depressed by consciousness of moral failure, and constantly mourn their lack of success in their appointed service. Many find seeming providential discrepancies and the glaring injustices of life a constant source of doubt and fear and discouragement.

Mrs. Herman, whose insight into the moods of the soul is most penetrating, says, "There is no disease of the soul more common than discouragement, no source of sin more prolific, no cause of inefficiency more widespread." She continues, "If the eyes of our imagination were opened to see how hard that most human lives are, and

"STRENGTHENING A MAN'S HAND IN GOD"—1 SAMUEL 23.16

how heavily the chill chord of discouragement presses upon hearts that seem cold and sullen, we would surely seek to strengthen the weak hands and confirm the feeble knees where now we stand aloof as critics."[1] That introduces the very word of our text. If David in the wood represents a mood of the soul, Jonathan reveals—

THE MINISTRY THE MOOD NEEDS

"Jonathan went to David into the wood and strengthened his hand in God." In Isaiah's words, God bids us "strengthen the weak hands and confirm the feeble knees." The literal translation of these words, according to Moffatt is, "Put heart into the listless, and brace all weak-kneed souls, tell men with fluttering hearts, 'have courage, never fear.'" Here is the mark that distinguishes true human beings. They are encouragers, and they will never lack compliment. The supply of encouragement is limited because few give it and everybody needs it. "Ninety-nine out of every hundred people," says one writer, "want encouragement all the time, and the hundredth wants it for only twenty three hours and fifty nine minutes every day."

If that sounds like hyperbole, it is a fact that thousands are hiding away discouraged and depressed, needing someone to do for them what Jonathan did for David. And I would enlist you all in the noble army of encouragers. But before we can render effective service we must realize—

WHAT IT IS WE HAVE TO DO

The sacred writer uses a striking and suggestive phrase to describe what Jonathan did for David. He "strengthened his hand in God." He nerved him afresh for his task, turned him from despair and set him to work again. That is the art and the end of encouragement. Like all good things, it is imitated. There are substitutes which are not only worthless but harmful.

It is one of the easiest things in the world for sloppy sentimentalism to pass for sympathy. Even well-meaning people make mistakes. Instead of encouraging the diffident and depressed into confidence, we may simply flatter them into conceit. Instead of putting grit and grip into the man who has let go, we may only minister to his complacency. It is not our task to make people comfortable in the Slough of Despond, we must help them out. You haven't finished your task when you've said, "I am sorry for you, old man, you are having a bad time." The fact is there are few arts that need more mastering than the art of encouragement. "The Lord God," said the prophet, "hath given me the tongue of a disciple, that I should know how to speak a word in reason to him that is weary." Encouragement is a divine art and a secret of discipleship. We need training in the school to which the prophet went if we are not only to soothe

---

1. I could not track down who Mrs. Herman is.

and ease but revive and restore. And that is what we have to do—to put heart into the listless, help a man to gird himself afresh for his pilgrimage, and strengthen his hand for his work. Now let us try to realize—

HOW WE CAN TRULY ENCOURAGE

Jonathan did a great deal for David by just going to him in the wood. What distresses and depresses many is the thought that nobody cares or understands. Many a man would shake off his despondency and stand up to life if he knew someone was with him. Many a soul lets go and sinks through sheer loneliness. You can be the one man or woman who encourages with your presence and hand shake. It is so easily done and it means so much.

I spoke just now of the ailing old lady who cannot speak or walk. She lives under the shadow of our mission. The other day I heard it was her birthday and my wife and I just dropped in to wish her well. It didn't take five minutes but I wish you could have seen the old face light up and the tears of joy that fell. That isn't an isolated case. Some time ago, thinking of people who cannot get to the house of God, I started a little Home Service. No ministry of mine has brought me greater joy or more expressions of gratitude. It is just that lonely folk find the wood less lonely if someone visits them in it. It is so terrible to feel you are forgotten.

And if you can carry a word of honest praise so much the better. A bit of praise helps many a fainting heart and cheer the jaded spirit. There is no limit to the power of good cheer. Carry a bit of brightness and joy to a despairing man or woman and you will dispel foes and awaken brave resolves. Gladden a man's heart, and you will strengthen his hand. Don't be afraid to praise, most people get enough of the other thing to keep them humble.

In this noble sense, you can encourage by reminding people of what, for the moment, they are forgetting. Jonathan not only strengthened David's hand, he "strengthened his hand in God." He brought him the reminder of the truth David had often eloquently expressed, the truth that through rough and trying circumstances God works His sovereign will. "You will be king yet," said Jonathan, "and my father knows it well." Assure men and women that behind a frowning providence there is the smiling face of God, that God is working His purpose out, and you will do them real service. Open a man's eyes and you will strengthen his hand. Restore his faith and you will revive his courage.

And you greatly encourage men when you pray with them and for them. It is recorded of David and Jonathan, in this incident, that "they two made a covenant before God." What they covenanted we are not told, but my own picture is of those two men kneeling together before God there in the wood. No wonder David's hand was strengthened. "We kneel, how weak, we rise, how full of power." Get a man to pray.

"STRENGTHENING A MAN'S HAND IN GOD"—1 SAMUEL 23.16

Kneel by his side and pray with him. And that is the surest way you will strengthen his hand and his heart in God.

∽

"THE GRACE OF HUMILITY"
—2 Samuel 7.18

(Preached once at Spring Head Mission 7/2/39)

---

2 Samuel 7.18 "Who am I, O Lord God? And what is my house that Thou hast brought me hitherto?"

I WISH TO SPEAK on the Grace of Humility. It is by no means the most popular of the virtues, but it is not a minor virtue. Indeed, it may be claimed that it is chief among the virtues because without it none of the others come to full beauty and power. It would have been easy to take a conventional text in which the word occurs and where it is emphatically stated that God Himself resists the proud and gives grace to the humble. But to see a grace embodied, to set it forth in a shining example, always seems to be a better way than arguing for it in the abstract.

In the incident before us, indeed in the whole life of David, humility has a lovely setting and makes a great appeal. It was the quality which gave balance and beauty to the king's character. It was the grace which, despite his grievous falls, made him the man after God's own heart and the beloved prince of his people. It was this virtue too which gave religious significance to his reign and made it so powerful. He held his throne from God and knew that he so held it. And he sought the guidance and help of his overlord.

THE INCIDENT SET FORTH IN OUR TEXT

David was at the zenith of his power and his throne was established. The prophet had just told him that his name was to endure and his glory to continue in his house. The son coming after him was to build a house for God's glory. In a lesser man the promise of such glory would have erected pride and vanity. A meaner man would have said: "Look at me, at the success I've achieved, the glory I've won." But David went in and set humbly before the God who had taken him from the sheepfold and set him on a throne. His words were not "Look at me," but, "Who am I and what is my father's house?" I know no picture of truer humility than this great king sitting in humility and giving the praise and the glory to God. Now we can turn to the lessons the incident has for us.

SUCCESS AND EXALTATION NEED NOT SPOIL A MAN

They so often do that. Many people are afraid of them and fear for those who become prosperous and rich. But prosperity as well as adversity may be God's gift and can be used to His glory. There is nothing sinister in the bright things given us by God. Here was a man to whom the brightest luminaries had come, and because he maintained a humble spirit, he was not only unspoiled, his success ministered to his own good and was made a blessing to others. It would be a shame not to acknowledge that there are other men and women who have gained success and honor and who have remained humble and unspoiled. They have regarded themselves, not as self-made, but as God-made and their riches and honor have been used for God's glory and the good of their fellows. Cultivate a church in the grace of humility and you need not fear, but rather rejoice, in all the good things God gives you and your friends. But let us go further and learn a lesson that applies to more of us.

THE GRACES OF HUMILITY AND GRATITUDE ARE ALWAYS LINKED

It is humility that makes us gratefully accept the unmerited favors and undeserved mercy of God. It is pride that makes us take things as a matter of course and all the gifts of Providence and of grace as if we had a right to them and no right to be grateful. Too often we ache or a pain calls forth a lament but the joy and light of years call forth no hymn of praise. "What have I done," we ask, "that I should suffer and remain poor? Who is David, or the other man, that he should be prosperous?" Ah! It is our pride breaking out. Why should we not take our share of hardships? Who are we that we should be spared? And there is a precaution. Instead of lamenting the adversities, try counting your blessings. Who are we? What have we done that the blessing of health, the gift of love, and friendship should be ours? Who are we that the incredible mercy of God in Jesus Christ should be ours? If in infinite wisdom God casts our lot in circumstances not as bright as others enjoy, who are we to question His appointments. Let us cherish the virtue of humility and counting our blessings and we shall bring our song of praise for the streams of the mercy God sends.

HUMILITY THE TEMPER IN WHICH TO RECEIVE NECESSARY REPROOFS

For the last lesson, we leave this incident and turn to another which reveals the same temper. There was a time when the king had done wrong and stained his name with the deepest sins. The prophet Nathan was sent to rebuke him and fulfilled his ministry faithfully, bringing the king's guilt home to him. Again, you can understand how a proud man would have acted. He would have said, "Who are you to speak to the king so?" Instead, this humble man said, "Woe is me." Instead of bursting into passion and standing on his dignity, he melted into repentance and confession and poured out his soul in the 51st Psalm.

How some of us cannot bear being corrected and reproved even when we know we are wrong. How we resent those who speak words of rebuke even when we deserve them. And always it is our pride that puts us in a passion. Who are we to be thus spoken to? The way of humility, David's way, is the nobler way, the only way into peace and joy.

Let us strive to be among the humble souls who see their own emptiness and poverty, who accept correction and reproof in a humble temper, and who, to say the least, find themselves among God's own children. Let us say from humble hearts, "Who am I that this incredible mercy should have reached me?"

∼

"CONCERNING THE SAFETY OF YOUNG PEOPLE"
—2 Samuel 18.29

(A Decision Day sermon preached four times from Patricroft 5/29 to Katherine Road 10/16/29)

---

2 Samuel 18.29 "Is the young man Absalom safe?"

BEHIND THE TEXT IS one of the most dramatic and moving stories of the Old Testament. David, as you know, had been driven from home and throne by the rebellion led by his handsome and cruel son Absalom. When the messenger came from the field in which the decisive battle was fought, the king was lost in the father. David's first question was not, "How has the battle gone?" but, "Is my son safe?" When the news was broken that his soldiers had triumphed, but his son slain, all the glory of the victory was gone, all his son's base ingratitude was forgotten, and there came from David's broken heart the most poignant wail of sorrow that ever fell from mortal lips: "Absalom, my son, would God I had died for thee!"

It was necessary to say that much about the story and some day we must return to it. But for this special day I want to lift the text from its context and ask the king's question concerning our young people. Are they safe? Is it well with them? I deliberately put the query in Dr. Moffatt's colloquial translation—"Is young Absalom all right?"

We are familiar with the question as it relates to the physical, mental, and material well-being of our young people. We consult a doctor about their health. We sacrifice our comforts to educate their minds. We try to secure them a business appointment that will give them a safe job for life and a comfortable pension. And no sane man quarrels with that! Our quarrel is with those who are careless and slip-shod in these matters and who allow their children to go out into the world with ill-nurtured bodies, badly equipped minds, and into blind alleys.

But even when we are satisfied that our young people are fit in body and mind for the battle of life, there is a further question to be faced: is all right morally and spiritually with our young people? That is the supreme question and we have not given it the consideration it deserves. The days in which we live make it imperative that we should face it. Our young people are facing dangers that did not exist for us. The conditions of life and labor expose them to enormous risks. The liberty they demand and are taking is fraught with peril for them.

Reading some of the horrible cases brought by the papers to our notice we have wondered what parents were about that they did not know where or with whom their young folk were. One can only conclude they supposed it was all right. And I insist that when the safety of your young people is concerned, you ought not to be content with suppositions. Of course, I know that you cannot always be with them and that as they grow up they will choose their own way. But there are some things you can do to safeguard them and secure their well-being.

You can forearm by forewarning them. It is quite clear that in these days they cannot live the sheltered and shielded life of years ago. At school, in business, in books and pictures things are freely discussed that once would have been forbidden. Your young folk will learn many things you did not know at their age. It is for us, and especially those who are parents, to take trouble to find out what they are learning and where. Do you know what they are reading? Or what films they go see? Do you take trouble to perform the delicate and difficult task of informing them and safeguarding them against the temptations peculiar to youth in these days? Reverently and earnestly I say, don't for God's sake and their sake let them learn life's most intimate things from rotten yellow-backed novels or unworthy films. You needn't preach at them, you can wisely and lovingly forewarn and so forearm them.

Further, it is impossible to exaggerate the safeguarding influences of godly lives and pious examples. Many a young fellow is kept straight in the midst of temptation by the memory of what his father was. Many a girl simply cannot go wrong while memory keeps alive her mother's example. Make your religion the everyday business of your homes and your example such that your children can never excuse the reality. What you are and do profoundly affects the children of the home. You cannot be surprised that a lad wants a ticket in a sweepstake if he knows his father has a flutter in the Derby. It isn't easy to preach temperance to young folk who see drink on the home table. Bring up your young folk in the instruction and admonition of the Lord and you help to make them safe.

And be sure your example brings them under the prayerful influence of the sanctuary. Frankly, I am going to say that I'm nervous about young folk who treat church attendance lightly. But can we expect young people to treat seriously what we take lightly? "I have tried every way and can't get them to go to church," said a father to a minister. "There is one way you haven't tried," said the minister. "What is that?" "You haven't tried taking him." Let your young people see how tremendously these things count with you and as they are surrounded by the influences of the sanctuary they are more likely to be safe.

On this Decision Day I am going to say what I believe every day: It is not well with our young people until they have come to definite decision for Christ. Your fathers and mothers said to you, "Twill save them from ten thousand snares to mind religion young." It will save your children too. I simply dare not think of what my own life would have been but for an early decision to be a Christian. That is why this day means so much to some of us and ought to mean more to all. I cannot believe that all is right with our young people until they have given themselves to Christ and joined His church. I say it about them and to them. You will be surrounded by temptations and perils and your great safeguard lies in giving yourself to Christ and letting Him be your Savior from sin. It is in fellowship with Christ that strength is renewed that keeps us straight.

I spoke just now of David's agony and remorse, of his poignant cry, "Would God I had died for thee." When I preach on that text I shall have to point out that the deepest agony in that cry was the circumstances of his own sin and failure. We would die to save our young folk from sin and anguish. Would it not be better to live so as to save them? It is so easy for many of them to go astray, we ought to leave nothing undone that we can do. Sometime ago I read in a religious weekly (Methodist Recorder Oct 13/24) the story of a girl who had been tricked into sin. I marked this sentence in a letter she wrote to a minister. "All my life I, through my own sin, shall be a looker in at other girls' happiness." Poor girl! The Lord deal tenderly with her wherever she is. But the sin is not hers alone. I say nothing of the sin of the one who tricked her, but I wonder if she might have been saved if someone had taken the trouble to teach and warn her, and lead her to Christ? A looker in at the happiness that might have been hers!

Are young Ted and Harry, Florence and Kate all right? Are they safe? It is our Christian duty to see that they are as safe as loving counsels, earnest prayers, pious examples, and sincere efforts to lead them to Christ can make them.

"RELIGION AS LOYALTY"
—1 Kings 2.4

(Preached at Katherine Road 2/2/36 and Spring Head Mission 6/6/43)

---

1 Kings 2.4 "If thy children take heed to their way, to walk before me in truth with all their heart and with all their soul."

"Living loyally under His (God's) eye with all their mind and soul." —Moffatt

THE SUBJECT IS RELIGION as Loyalty and it was chosen before the text was decided upon. You will not find the word loyalty in either the Authorized or Revised Version of the Bible; though the thing itself is on almost every page. Dr. Moffatt rightly introduces the word in this passage. Walking before God in truth is living loyally under His eye.

Though the text was not chosen until after the subject, I am not ashamed of it. It sums up what I want to say. I am not at all surprised that the promise made to David was that, if his sons would be loyal to God with all their mind and soul, there should never be wanting a man to sit on Israel's throne. Men who live such lives are kingly men. But the subject is bigger than any text or incident in the Bible. The whole Bible is the text, and to be rightly conceived religion must be conceived as loyalty. Let us begin by asking an elementary question:

WHAT IS RELIGION?

Your dictionary will define it for you as "the outward act or form of which men indicate their recognition of a god or gods having power over their destiny." Or it will give you this as an alternative: "A system of faith and worship." Both definitions are true so far, and both are inadequate. If you have the soul of religion you will need a body in which it can express itself. For all our railing against creeds, I can't for the life of me see how you can do without one of some sort. Your creed is your thought form. Still, neither of these definitions is finally satisfying. At the heart of religion is the idea and the fact of a tie, a covenant. Religion is vision of God, fellowship with God, making for righteousness. It implies faithfulness in the Divine side and loyalty on the human side.

"RELIGION AS LOYALTY"—1 KINGS 2.4

My simple definition of the Christian religion is faith in Jesus Christ our Savior and loyalty to Him as Lord. That compels the facing of another question:

WHAT IS LOYALTY?

Once more I turn to the dictionary and learn that loyalty is faithfulness in allegiance, being true to word and duty, it is devotion, fidelity. You know what it is for a man to be loyal to his king and his country. The loyal man plays the game and is true when others are not looking and when no galley applauds. He keeps the flag flying when things are at their worst. "Thy coat is shabby," said a wife to her preacher husband in days when it cost to be loyal. "Yes," came the answer, "but it has never been turned." The loyalist is not necessarily the man who waves the biggest flag and gives the loudest cheer; he is the man who stays at his post, does his duty, never fails a friend but is faithful to the last. He is the man you can rely on. My point is that eventually religion is loyalty, an unswerving allegiance, a deathless devotion. It is something far more than correct views, right creeds, careful ritual; it is personal and passionate loyalty to the Lord, it means being bound to Christ by the soul's tenacious purpose.

NOT DAZZLING, BUT DEPENDENCE

That may seem to make religion a rather colorless thing. There are times when loyalty wins the Victoria Cross or some other distinction. But in the main, loyal people do not dazzle or attract. Generally, they are the people who just keep on keeping on. They pursue their given ways without pomp or blaze of trumpets. They are doing a great work and cannot come down to receive the rewards of men. Think of and thank God for the men and women who have never been disloyal to the troth they plighted at the marriage altar—and you never hear of them! The most loyal man I ever knew, a man who served God in China for thirty years, a man who never broke his word or failed a friend—Frederick Galpin lived and died in obscurity and few recognized the heroic soul he was.

A few years ago I heard of the daughter of Tom Hughes—hardly anyone knew the author of *Tom Brown's Schooldays* had a daughter and she had been living for thirty years in an East End tenement, seeking no publicity for the work she was doing. For thirty years, she had never had a holiday because the women she wanted to help couldn't afford one. In our hearts we know that if loyalty is not dazzling, it is something better, it is dependable. You can be sure of these loyal folk. You can lean on them and they will not let you down. We owe an unpayable debt to the loyalty of those who seek no publicity or reward, who shun everything obtrusive and vulgar, and whose glory it is that they are dependable.

LUMINESCENCE

LOYALTY IN LIFE

I am insisting that religion is loyalty. It is, as Moffatt's translation of the text says, "living loyally under God's eye with all their mind and soul." It means being loyal in the ordinary relationships of life. Tennyson said of Queen Victoria that she was "loyal to the royal within herself." That is where loyalty begins. "To thine own self be true, and it must follow as the night the day thou canst not then be false to any man" (Hamlet). It works out as in our great Bunyan, "True to ourselves, our fellow men and Thee." Christ does not ask less than the best of the best ethics and moralities. He asks more—"what do ye more than others?" So religion means loyalty to your word as your bond. It means loyalty to your friends and never letting them down. It means never betraying a trust or proving unworthy of confidence. It means being loyal to your wife, your parents, your home. It goes down to your thoughts as well as expresses itself in your words and actions.

LOYALTY TO JESUS

But supremely, of course, the Christian religion is personal and passionate loyalty to Jesus Christ. It does not mean just believing something about Him or singing hymns to His praise. There is something prior to loyalty and that is consecration. You make Him the captain of your salvation and then give Him a complete trust, a cheerful obedience, and an unswerving loyalty. It means following Him at all costs and ordering your life according to His mind and will. It means that, just that, but it does mean that Galsworthy has given us a play called "Loyalties" and made us see situations where there is a clash of loyalties. Most of us know such situations. But for a Christian the supreme loyalty is never in question. Our first loyalty is pledged to Jesus Christ and neither pleasure, nor care, nor enemies must reduce us from it. If He is the captain of our salvation it is His to call and command, ours to follow and obey.

LOYALTY TO CHURCH

The Christian religion means loyalty to the Christian church. For the church is the body of Christ, the agent through which His kingdom comes, the one instrument that exists alone to establish His reign on the earth. There are folk who entice the church and cheerfully argue that it is nearly dead. It is worthwhile remembering that the bitterest critics of the churches never enter one. These folk will draw their own conclusions. Don't you worry: The church can't die for the life of it. It lives because Christ is its Head. No other institution knows so well the mind of Christ or exists alone for the pastures of the kingdom. Boldly I say it, through the church alone can the world be cured of its poisonous hates, devastating materialism, and bitter despair.

"RELIGION AS LOYALTY"—1 KINGS 2.4

What the church needs is the loyalty of its members. If you ask me why you should make sacrifices for it, since it ever were the service comes before your own wishes, why you should care for its well-being and concerned that its congregations are small, there is only one reply—you are a member of it. Who asked you to join? Not me. I never asked one of you to join and never put a man's name on the roll without his consent. It is not for me to dictate, it is for you to ask what loyalty to your membership involves.

Be loyal to the church of your choice though it is far from perfect. My home may not be as elaborate in its appointments as some of the homes I stay in, but because it is mine, it commands my loyalty and service. Bring your best to it. Put your youth and vitality, your courage and your resources, your laughter and your high spirits, into it. Seek to make your church worthy of your Lord.

LOYALTY'S GOLDEN OPPORTUNITY

Days of defection and defect give loyalty its golden opportunity. Just because the days are difficult and things do not seem to be going well with the church is surely no reason for desertion and disloyalty. This is one great chance to show the sincerity of our loyalty. Let one illustration serve instead of argument. Whenever I want to renew a proper pride in a church of my fathers' and my choice, I take down Silvester Horne's history of the churches. In it, among many stirring stories of splendid loyalty I read the story of Vavasor Powell (182), the intrepid Welsh evangelist. He died in 1670 having spent eleven of his fifty-three years in prison for no greater crime than that of preaching the gospel. If you search in Bunhill Fields you will find his tombstone and on it these words—"In the defection of many he found grace to be faithful."

That is the grace we greatly need in these days. It is comparatively easy to be loyal when your cause is popular and your church is successful. But real loyalty is displayed when things are going wrong and the half-hearted scatter from what seems to be a sinking ship. "Then to side with truth is noble, when we share her wretched crust, ere her cause bring fame and profit, and tis prosperous to be just, then it is the brave man chooses while the coward stands aside, till the multitude make virtue of the faith they have denied."[1]

WHAT THIS VIEW OF RELIGION INVOLVES

Religion, I am insisting, is loyalty, loyalty to Christ, His church, and the wonderful life and service for which they stand. Such a view does not make religion easy, but it does make it simple and intelligible. It does not ask you to sign complex creeds or believe things that offend your intellect and tax your credibility. It asks you to consecrate your

---

1. This is a quote from James Russell Lowell and his famous poem "The Present Crisis."

life to a leader, a captain, and then to be loyal at all costs to Him. That is all I have a right to ask, but I have the right to ask that. It is not for me to say you shall not go here or there or do this or that. But if Christ says, "Don't go there or do that," will you obey?

That is religion—loyalty to the captain. Such loyalty transforms and transfigures. Perhaps the most moving writing of the war years was Donald Hawkins's "The Beloved Captain." He tells how literally loyalty to the beloved captain made a bunch of odds and ends into a company of perfect soldiers. Still more will loyalty to the captain of our salvation mean the transforming of ordinary folk into soldiers who, in the good fight, play the part of heroes.

"Live loyally under God's eye with all your mind and strength." Such loyalty will bring its own radiant reward. One of the outstandingly happy memories of my early days is the memory of Rallies of Christian Endeavors. I recall the crowds of clear-eyed, happy-hearted, full-throated, eager youths and maidens. They were keener and happier than the crowds I have seen at football matches or in entertainment halls. I recall their radiantly happy rendering of the hymn that was their Marseillaise, and I would to God we could sing it in the same spirit. "Peal out the watchword! Silence it never! Song of our spirits, rejoicing and free, peal out the watchword! Loyal forever! King of our lives, by Thy grace we will be."[2]

---

2. This is from the famous hymn writer Frances Havergal, "True Hearted, Whole Hearted, Faithful and Loyal" (1878).

"UNACCOMPLISHED AIMS"
—1 Kings 8.17–19

(Preached at Spring Head Mission 10/17/1943 and at Bishop Street 8/11/46)

---

1 Kings 8.17–19 "It was in the heart of David . . . to build a house for the name of the LORD . . . and the LORD said . . . whereas it was in thine heart to build a house unto my name . . . nevertheless, thou shalt not build the house, but thy son . . . he shall build the house to my name."

DAVID'S PURPOSE TO BUILD a house for the worship of God seems to have been altogether pure and generous. He could not bear the thought that, while he himself dwelt in a house of cedar, the ark of God rested under curtains. His proposition to build commended itself to the judgment of Nathan the prophet, who said, "Go, do all that is in thine heart." Yet for all that, David was forbidden to carry his scheme into effect: the purpose never became a performance. God made it clear to him that he was not to realize his heart's desire. The house would be built, but not by David's hands.

Though there are many fine things in David's life, I know nothing finer than the spirit in which he accepted the denial of his desire and the refusal of his proffered gift. There was nothing little or peevish about him when he learned that the desire he sought had been granted to another. I will come back to that presently, for the moment let us think of how this incident illuminates life's unaccomplished aims.

There are many whose generous purposes are broken off and whose grand designs never become deeds. The broken column in the churchyard is a symbol of unrealized dreams and broken hopes. But this thing is true to life as well as to death. There are reasons, physical, psychological, emotional, why many never fulfill all that it is in their hearts to do. They plan in marble, but have to build in brick. Their paths find extension in Anne Bronte's words: "I hoped, . . . with the brave and strong." We recognize that the lot of all is such.

Whatever it cost Solomon to build the temple, it cost David a great deal more to relinquish the grand design. However much some of us complain of the roles we are fulfilling, be sure there are those, denied our opportunities, who would give much to take our places and handle the spade and the trowel. The incident does more than set the problem, it supplies needed—

COMFORT TO THE DISAPPOINTED[1]

There are many things in this incident a preacher would be glad and thankful to pass on to the disillusioned and disappointed, but I must put several aside because of a special purpose I have in mind. *God knows, and accepts, the generous purpose.* "Thou didst well," He says, "that it was in thine heart." He, to whom the darkness shineth as the light, is not a glorified policeman looking for crimes. He sees and honors and accepts the secret purposes of the heart. As Browning says, "All I could never be, all men ignored in me, this, I was worth to God, whose wheel the pitcher shaped."[2] Do not be disheartened or cast down because you are not able to do all you have dreamed. The Lord looks on the heart and judgment is according to it.

But my special point this morning is that here we have a man who could not do all he would but who did what he could. It was made clear to David that his son would build the house of God. A lesser man would have been piqued and peevish and selfish. He would have said, "If he is going to have the honor, let him do the work and make the sacrifices." But David was cast in a nobler mold than them. He gathered material in abundance so that Solomon's work would be easier.

My dear friends, here is both a challenge and duty for us. So long as the work of God is done, what matter is it who does it? A good many of our regrets have self-will and pride in them. We want to do the work and are jealous of those who are chosen above us. Let us rather be grateful that Solomon executed what David proposed and that God always has those who will carry on the work. The duty is equally clear. We can make it easier for those who come after us to do the work. We can toil and sacrifice to give them the chance we never had, never mind who gets the honor when the temple is built!

A WORD TO THOSE WHO WILL BUILD THE TEMPLE

This is your dawning day and some thoughts for those who will build the temple we wanted to build and now know we never will. You must increase while we decrease. But there is no resentment in our hearts, only the prayer that you may succeed where we failed and build where we only planned. I want no dead hand to limit you in your task. But you will remember that you are taking on the task from the hands of those who planned and toiled—"died not having received the promise." That does not mean they have not gone to heaven, they have. And you have material lying in your hand

---

1. This subtitle, though legible, appears to have been marked through and excised from the oral sermon.

2. This is from Browning's poem "Rabbi ben Ezra."

"UNACCOMPLISHED AIMS"—1 KINGS 8.17-19

that was gathered by men and women who know they will never do all they dreamed. As David said to Solomon, "Thou mayest add thereto." You may alter the design and have to add to what they left you. The only word of advice I will give you is this—remember what it is you are to build, not simply a palace or a place of fellowship. You are to build a place of worship, where God's holy name is honored, where rich and poor—learned and illiterate, shall gather for fellowship and prayer. May God set your heart to the high holy purpose and give you strength and enduring grace. May God grant you the joy of seeing the accomplishment of your noblest dreams.

∼

"CAN RELIGION BE MADE EASY?"
—1 Kings 12.28

(Preached at Katherine Road 1/24/32 and Spring Head Mission 11/2/41)

---

1 Kings 12.28 "It is too much for you to go up to Jerusalem: behold thy gods, O Israel."

THESE WORDS WERE UTTERED by Jeroboam. And Jeroboam was a great fighter, a showy politician, and an unscrupulous man. He had split the kingdom of David and established a kingdom of his own in the north. The southern kingdom still held Jerusalem and was in possession of the national temple on Mount Zion. Jeroboam was shrewd enough to know how great was the pull of religion in the people and how strong was the appeal of the temple at Jerusalem. If the people he had made his continued to go up to Jerusalem to worship, he feared that their hearts would be taken from him, that they would return to their old allegiance and leave him without a kingdom.

So, within his own kingdom, he set up two sanctuaries. And he was wily enough to erect them at Dan and Bethel, two places having many sacred associations. In them, he placed two golden calves. They were not meant to be idols but to symbolize the Divine presence. Then it was that he said, "It is too much for you to go up to Jerusalem: worship here at home."

You can see at once what an attractive program this shrewd and wily king had worked out. You realize how subtle was the argument. It was the offer of an easier religion. It was too far to go to Jerusalem. The road was too long, too dangerous, it took too much time. He offered them a worship without effort, without expense, without sacrifice. And I believe it is not unfair or uncharitable to say that that is the kind of argument that still appeals to many people. They are not against religion, indeed they urge that it is a good thing and that they want to be religious. But they want it in easy and pleasant doses. Most of us are naturally indolent and hate effort of any kind. Promise to make religion easy, to run the church along the lines of a comfortable club, and there will always be those who will respond with *Amen*.

Can we respond to the demand for a religion made easy? Instead of answering that directly, let me remind you of one or two things. Have you found anything worthwhile in this world that is easy? Is business easy? Is education or music? I know preaching is not. Why, you are as skeptical about cheap, quick, and easy ways of accomplishment as my mother was of getting her washing done while she sat in a chair and read a novel. The only way to success, you know it, is the way of hard work and elbow grease. You must, as a clever writer in yesterday's paper (Helen Hope) said, "Put your back into it."

RELIGION NEVER PROFESSES TO BE EASY

Its first and central command is, "Thou shalt love the LORD your God with all thy heart, and with all thy soul, and with all thy mind, and with all thy strength." It demands all and everything. Jesus did not preach an easy religion. He pointed out that the gate was straight and the way narrow. He said, "If any man would come after me, let him deny himself and take up his cross daily and follow me." And, "whoever doth not bear his own cross and come after me cannot be my disciple." Paul made it a matter of taking one's share of hardness as a good soldier of Jesus Christ. John Bunyan found it hard. He had to pass through the Slough of Despond, up the Hill Difficulty, and down into the Valley of Humiliation. He had to fight with lions and giants. Someone has suggested that all that is altered and that there is now a bridge over this slough, and a Pullman running up the Hill Difficulty. Which is said ironically, for still the way is hard and narrow and long. Dropping figures, let us come to the large demands religion makes of us.

Religion makes demands on our purses. In this verse, you can't be really religious on the cheap. A religion that costs little is worth little. Of course, the minister is always begging, or rather asking, in the name of religion. You well know what is asked and expected, mind you the demands are not unreasonable. Let me give you a thing to do. Sit down and write down what your lodge costs you, your seat at the theater, the amount you spend on tobacco or chocolates, etc. Now on the other side of the page write down how much your religion has cost you. When religion makes demands on your purse it is God giving you the opportunity of helping Him to save the world.

Religion makes demands on us in worship. Worship is not an easy thing. To sit and criticize while the minister pours out his own soul, to look on at the choir as you would at an opera chorus, to pass judgment on the service as you would on a play, that is not worship! To come to church to see your friends and eager to gossip, that is not worship. When men worship, they not only fall on their knees, they fall on their faces before God. God takes hold of their soul and they take hold of His strength. In real worship the soul of man answers out of the depths the call of God from the heights. You cannot make worship just bright, brief, and breezy.

Religion's greatest demands are on personal loyalty. It calls for the high endeavor of holy living, the surrender of the self, the consecration of time. It calls for the giving of one's self to the service of the kingdom. No man knows when he answers the call,

"Follow me," where he will be led. He only knows he must, at all costs, be obedient to the heavenly vision.

How can religion be easy? Think of the price God has paid. It cost Him His only begotten Son. He spared not His only begotten Son, but delivered Him up for us all. We sing easily, "Jesus paid it all," but the price "none of the ransomed ever knew," or ever will know. It was paid by agony and tears of Gethsemane and the suffering and the blood of Calvary. For many it has meant many a sorrow, many a tear. How, then, can we expect it to be easy for us?

THE STRANGE PARADOX: RELIGION CAN BE MADE EASY

Have not men sung of its statutes becoming songs and marched to their battles with happy hearts and all the colors flying? And did not Jesus say, "My yoke is easy and my burden light?" The reasoning may be difficult, but the meaning is clear.

An illustration may make better sense than argument. The hardest work I know is mothering a child. I mean nursing it into manhood. It means travail, sleepless nights, restless days, the greasy tasks of the bathtub and vigils by a cot. There are no light hours for a mother. And ultimately a sword will pierce her heart. But ask her if it is hard. Or better still, watch her about her task. What lifts the load and makes the hard task easy? You know before I tell you . . . The service of love is perfect freedom. The only way to make religion easy is to meet and answer its stern and searching demands in love.

"MOUNT CARMEL —THE HILL OF DECISION" —1 Kings 18.20, 21

(Preached twice at Spring Head Mission 2/21/37 and Bishop Street 2/22/48)

---

1 Kings 18.20–21 "So Ahab sent unto all the children of Israel and gathered the prophets together unto Mount Carmel. And Elijah came unto all the people and said, how long halt thee between two opinions? If the LORD be God, follow Him: but if Baal, then follow him."

MOUNT CARMEL IS ONE of the best known of the hills of God. On its slopes was set one of the most memorable and striking scenes in Bible history. In earlier years, the text was heavily marked in the evangelist's Bible. From it many evangelistic sermons were preached. To this day, it holds the attention of many and is the theme of one of the greatest oratorios. It is a remarkable fact that at this very time London's largest hall is crowded with people to witness the dramatic reality of it. The dominating figure of the scene was not the king or his handsome consort, not any of the grandly dressed prophets or priests of Baal, but the rugged, roughly clad prophet who lived with God in the hills. Righteousness has a royalty above all earthly dignity. For all his rough garb, this man of clear eye, clean life, and consecrated devotion was the man of the mount and the moment as he stood lifting a standard for the living God against the fictitious deities of the pagan world.

There are many things in this scene hard to understand and most of them we must leave untouched. One thing, however, stands out clear as the sun in the Syrian sky—the prophet's challenge to his people, making them face alternatives and calling them to a definite and immediate decision. "How long," he called out, "halt ye between two opinions? If the LORD be God, follow Him; but if Baal, follow him." To that one point, we confine ourselves.

LUMINESCENCE

CLEAR-CUT ALTERNATIVES

The alternatives put before the people on Carmel were clear cut and well defined. They were God and Baal. Look at the situation and you will see just how untenable it had become and that a decision had to be made. King Ahab had brought home a foreign wife and that had involved political alliances with pagan nations. Under this strong foreign influence, particularly that of Jezebel, the worship of Jehovah had declined, altars had fallen into ruins, and the prophets of the LORD had been slain. At the same time, Baal worship was on the increase and Baal's prophets multiplying. He threatened to become Israel's national religion though the Israelites were still nominally the people of God. They were drifting to disaster. They felt that they ought to serve God, but they wanted to worship Baal. They didn't know what to do and were simply hesitating, conforming, and trying to combine something of each. Then this rugged man, impatient of hesitation and intolerant of fear, flung at the procrastinating multitude a clear-cut challenge, "How long halt ye between two opinions?" He called for an immediate decision, God or Baal.

Are the alternatives and the challenge facing us as clear and well defined? On the surface they do not seem so. The difference between the life that is religious and the life that is not is not so clear. The lines of demarcation are largely erased. One of the questions often asked in Commando Campaigns is "What's the difference between a good moral man and the man you call a Christian?" The bulk of people see things as neither black nor white but as grey. A writer in the *Nineteenth Century* magazine put it this way: "I can understand what is to become of the sheep and I can understand what is to become of the goats, but how are the alpacas to be dealt with?" The alpaca, with its long wool, is not unlike a sheep, but at the same time it possesses some of the characterizations of the goat. So many people seem to be "amongst the middlings" and they see no necessity for definite alternatives or decisions.

Under the surface, however, the alternatives are as clear as ever. We are still faced with two definite and distinct schemes of life. A greater man than Elijah said, "No man can serve two masters. You cannot serve God and mammon." It is God or mammon, Christ or the world. Someone or something must be supreme, and the supreme thing in your life is your god. You have to decide whether you will give God the supreme place in your life, whether Jesus should be your leader or not, whether or not you will seek first the kingdom of God. This may not seem much outward difference between the man who fears God and the man who does not, between servants of Christ and men of the world. But go down into the realm of the spirit, to motives and aims, and the differences are deep and profound. Jesus said, in words that no man can mistake, that there are two gates, and through one of them we must pass, two paths, and along one of them we must travel, two ends, one life and one death, and at one of them we shall arrive.

"MOUNT CARMEL—THE HILL OF DECISION"—1 KINGS 18.20, 21
NO REASON FOR DELAY

Between the alternatives many try to affect a compromise. In Elijah's day, the people wanted to accept Baal without renouncing Jehovah. In our day, there are those who camp out definitely on one side or the other. But many are delaying and declining decision. They would be mightily offended if you told them they were not religious or Christians, but they shrink from committal, they do not make up their minds to be definitely Christian. They give lip service to the Lord, but not heart loyalty. Religion, of course, is all right in its place, but they are hesitant to give it first place. Our main trouble is with those who halt between two opinions, half-hearted and undecided. The preacher's burden is to make people face the alternatives and to call them to a decision. How long halt ye between self-will and submission to the Lord's will, between conscience and passion, between Christ and the world? Let us get down to face facts and consider the causes of indecision.

Some wait for clearer light. There is something honest about that with many, and no man can be hustled into the kingdom. The cost has to be counted and the decision born in intelligence and thought. "If the LORD be God—or Baal." By all means think through the alternatives, and choose what is right. But have not most of us light enough to choose by? There are questions to be discussed, but the discussion need not delay the decision. You have enough to choose the high rather than the low, the right not the wrong, the way of Christ rather than the way of selfish ease. A brilliant Frenchman says, "The man who insists upon seeing with perfect clearness before he decides, never decides."[1]

Another cause is that selfish considerations delay the decision. It is never easy to decide definitely for the right. For one thing, the decision would be greeted with scorn and ridicule, some of it from friends. In a fine sermon on this text, L. W. Robertson includes excess of amiability and love of formality as reasons for failure to come to a decision. Most of us know that the choice of the right, the way of Christ, means meeting demands the world would never make. Thus, our selfish love of the easy, the pleasant, deters us.

Another cause for deterring decision is waiting for a more convenient season. What procrastinators we are! We are always "going to," but what we are going to do never gets done at all. "The road of by-and-by leads to the town of never in the kingdom of too late," says a Spanish proverb. The more convenient season does not come, the more powerful impulse does not stir us, and we are left in the old position of indecision and uncertainty. I will now turn from that to consider *the consequences of indecision*.

The position is unworthy of you. What have you a need for but to face the answer? What have you a will for but to decide? Your manhood, your womanhood, is

---

1. This is a quote from Henri-Frederic Amiel, who was a Swiss philosopher.

consulted when you are faced with the challenge, "how long halt ye?" Be men and women and make your choice.

The position is painful. The very word suggests the pain—"how long halt ye?" It is a word you use for the lame. Moffatt translates the text "how long will you hobble on this faith and that." The horns of a dilemma is an uncomfortable place to be in. Twixt two stools you fall to the ground. There is no satisfaction in the undecided life; you get neither Christ's best nor the world's.

Indecision means ineffectiveness. Whatever is to be said about the "alpacas," it cannot be said that they are effective in the battle of life. Following God means falling in and following one who is marching against the foe. You will never do that while you are holding on and hesitating, delaying and dallying. You will never do that until you have made your decision. "Passionately fierce the voice of God is pleading, pleading with men to arm them for the fight. See how those hands, majestically bleeding, call us to rout the armies of the night."[2]

Now let us consider the perils of indecision. I know how the old preachers would have dealt with this point, and it is not the fashion nowadays to say much about the perils. But delay is dangerous and he who hesitates may be lost. To use the danger of the day, you may "miss the bus." It was not an orthodox preacher, but a poet, that wrote, "Once to every man and nation comes the moment to decide," and who added, "and the choice goes by forever." A far, far greater man that Russell Lowell said in memorable words, "O that thou hadst known, at least in this thy day, the things that belong to peace, but now they are hid from thine eyes." So I bring you to the hill of God called Mount Carmel and say to you "how long halt ye between two opinions?" Why not have done with your indecision and hesitation and decide once and for all to be on the Lord's side?

∽

---

2. This is a quote from "The Suffering God," one of G. Studdert-Kennedy's famous poems. It is interesting that both Kingsley and Fred regularly draw on poetry, particularly the poetry of Studdert-Kennedy.

"THE BROKEN ALTAR"
—1 Kings 18.30

(Preached ten times including Patricroft 5/7/50 and Somerby 5/25/50)

---

1 Kings 18.30 "And he repaired the altar of the Lord that was broken down."

To the prophet, and the prophet's God, that altar of unhewn stones on the slopes of Mount Carmel, was the most significant thing in the land. God's eye is always on the altar, using that great word to describe the place of worship and of prayer. There is always a vital connection between the altar and the state. The destiny of the state is determined by the state of the altar. It is never well with the state when its altar is in ruins. By the place the altar is given, individuals and communities are judged.

GOD'S CONCERN FOR THE ALTAR IN ENGLAND TODAY

When God looks down on England, His concern is with the altar, the place where men worship and offer the sacrifices of broken and contrite hearts, the place to which they bring the sacrifice of praise. His main interest is not in the Stock Exchange, or Downing Street, or Whitehall, but is what Westminster Abbey and Wesley's Chapel represent, and the churches and chapels throughout the land. When the Lord comes to His temples, His first concern is not with our magnificent buildings, our splendid traditions, our elaborate ritual, but with the offerings of prayer and praise from devoted lives. So it is when He comes to our homes. We pride ourselves on our modern equipment, luxuries, furnishings, and artistic ornaments. There is no word to be said against these things, but God passes them and looks for the altar of the hearth. In the individual life, the determining factor is not our wealth and social status, but the flame of sacred love burning on the altar of the heart.

HOW STANDS IT WITH THE ALTAR?

Is that neglected and dilapidated altar in Carmel suggestive of anything in our own land and life? The last thing I want to do is to dim the lights and deepen the shadows.

But the question is too important to trifle with and facts must be faced. *How does the nation regard what the altar stands for—reverence, prayer, and sacrifice?* A visitor from another country might be pardoned if he concluded that for the bulk of the people, the main places of worship were music halls and cinemas, and our deities comedians and film stars. He would have to notice indifference to the places God counts all important.

Is the altar, the worship point, central in the churches? Our visitor might find abounding activity, the latest thing in organization and machinery, social activities and amenities, but would he find the supreme interest in prayer, the devotional life, and consecrated service? *Does religion maintain its sanctities in the home?* Is there in our homes a high regard for religion, the recognition of Christ's Headship, the example and atmosphere which make it easy for our children to be Christians? There are difficulties in these busy days, but surely prayer and Bible reading are not impossible.

How about the altar of the heart? Does that still stand? Are we not in danger of losing our reverence, our holy aspirations, and our responsive love to the love of God? One need be neither a pessimist nor a savage critic to say that there are many broken altars in our own land and time. Instead of simply criticizing and condemning let us get down to—

THE CAUSES OF THE BROKEN ALTARS

Once they stood in good repair and with the fire of devout inspiration and affection burning brightly in them. What has made the difference? Reading in the Revised Version we gather that the altar on Carmel had been "thrown down." Gladly we admit that that has not happened often to our modern altars. We certainly have no joy in the sight of these broken relics of bygone years, often they awaken feelings of shame and regret. Where then shall we find the causes?

There is one, and though it is not mentioned in the dramatic scene on Carmel, it is presupposed all the way through. You know it before I name it—neglect. No sacrilegious or iconoclastic hand has ever turned over the altars, but neither has any loving hand tended them. No worshippers have used them, their fate has been to be ignored. That is the story of our broken altars. We lose what we fail to use. They come to mean nothing to us. Laying no offering on the altar, it falls into disrepair. The church suffers more from the indifference of its friends than the attacks of its foes.

The context supplies another cause. Another god had been set up, another worship introduced. Baal, the new god, was a false god, and a popular god. The people went after him, laid their gifts on his altar. But you cannot have two gods and two altars. You cannot serve God and Baal, God and mammon, or God and anyone else. We think we are free from this charge. We say we have set up no new god and declare that we do not worship idols.

To such a claim the reply is that idols are not only the work of men's hands, they may be the imaginations of the heart. Anything the soul puts in the place of God is an idol. The heathen in his blindness bows down to wood or stone. But there are men in England who worship the check book, or pleasure, or fame. We have set up golden idols, goddesses of pleasure, idols of fame, and we are so long worshipping at their shrines that we have neither time nor desire for the worship of God. The altar of God always suffers in the dervish dance of the worship of the gods of this age. However, it has happened and most of us admit that the altars, the sacred places are down and sadly in need of repair.

A PLEA FOR THE RESTORATION OF THE BROKEN ALTARS

Elijah was a mere man, but began the work of reformation by the reframing of the altar. Every beneficent and lasting reformation begins there. Nothing is stable while God's altar is neglected. It was the old altar he repaired and not a new one he bought. In all work of religious revival and reformation we must connect ourselves with the past and not obliterate it. Every wise thinker, politician, and reformer knows that wisdom did not begin with him and that some principles of the past must be the foundation of his extension. I am in favor of new schemes and methods, but there are things in the past that must not be forgotten. There is only one foundation. It is the old altar, with its reverence, faith, and prayer. This we must rebuild.

We must rebuild the altar in the nation. Time was when in our national affairs God was recognized and consulted. In times of crisis men sought to know God's will. One of the saddest effects of the First World War was that sacred things went which have never been restored. Lots of people scrapped the fourth commandment and, as I believe, with disastrous consequences. If you scrap the fourth commandment, why should not other men scrap the sixth, seventh, and eighth? Instead of slacking in zeal, let us keep our chapels open and our service going. It is only in the House of God and at the altars of God the nations will be indissolubly joined.

We must rebuild the altar in the church. There is room in the church for many things our fathers did not know and would not appreciate. But we must restore our sense of proportion. We must not carefully keep the billiard table in order to neglect the Communion Table, nor give socials and concerts a larger place than prayer meetings and fellowship. The church must be a church and not simply a social center.

There are those who sneer at the simplicity of our church's building and services, and say we have no altar. But we have, on hand, the most sacred of all altars, only we called it a penitent-form, and at it men and women knelt confessing their sins and giving themselves in full and glad surrender to Christ. Let us be quite sure that in our modern buildings we keep in good repair the place where men and women kneel in faith, in love, in surrender.

We must rebuild the altar in the home. Religion is necessary to home. A place where we lodge and eat together is not necessarily home. Let us restore the family altar where father is the priest and mother the theologian, and where children are brought into the admonition of the Lord. Associate the first thoughts of the children with prayer and worship. There is no place like home—if Christ is the Head.

We must rebuild the altar in the heart. Here at least we are responsible. Unless we repair the altar here we shall fail everywhere. What a story of neglect the life of many of us is. Neglected opportunities, growing carelessness, lack of reverence, weakened love of the House of God, failure in the prayer life. Let us restore the altar. When the altar was repaired, and the offering laid on it, "the fire of the Lord fell." And God will demonstrate His power and send His blessing when we have repaired the altar.

"LISTENING IN AND LISTENING OUT"
—1 Kings 19.11

(Preached once at Katherine Road 1/17/34)

---

1 Kings 19.11 "Go forth, and stand . . . before the LORD."

THE SUBJECT WILL HAVE suggested that this is to be a topical talk rather than a direct exposition of a passage of Holy Scripture. It will be sufficient to remind you that Elijah was fleeing from the threat of the vindictive and vengeful Jezebel. The hero of Carmel was lurking within the safety of a cave. He was in, nurturing his wounds, when he ought to have been out, completing his victory. He was in, brooding over his trials, when he ought to have been out, doing his duty. He was listening in when he should have been listening out. There was condemnation and there was challenge in God's command, "Go forth, and stand before the LORD." At that moment, the challenge of God was for a man who was outside, standing with loins girt and ready for service.

Without going further into the interesting story of Elijah, we may here begin our application by remarking on the pleasure and peril of wireless in the home. One of the incidental ministries of the wireless is that it has made home more interesting. There is little need to have it in order to find entertainment. Every kind of knowledge and every form of entertainment come to us from the BBC. From a comfortable seat in the old armchair by our own fireside we can listen to the finest lectures and the choicest singers. The leading lecturers offer to us the treasures of their minds without one troubling to go hear them in a lecture room. Plays and pantomimes, and even the "thrillers," that necessitate "the sending of the children to bed and the locking of grandma in the bathroom" can now be brought across. If the day is cold and wet, or you cannot get a ticket, you can listen in to every important game of football described by an expert. And if it looks like rain or you don't feel quite up to the mark on Sunday, you can hear a long-way better sermon than you would hear at church, over the wireless. In a sense the poet never dreamed of, we can now sing, "Be it ever so humble there's no place like home." And one rejoices at all the treasure that is brought into the homes of those who listen in.

LUMINESCENCE

[Anything that makes home more the center of interest is doing us service. If listening in has deepened our love for the fireside it has ministered not only to comfort, but to strength. We have caught up with the demand for houses.][1]

And yet, what ministers to our pleasure may be a peril to us. For if home is the center of a man's life it ought not to be the circumference of his thought. The SOS message you listen in to you cannot respond to. And the peril is that you may be so busy listening in that you do not listen out for the SOS messages you could respond to. To listen in with comfort when you ought to listen out with compassion is to betray your trust and your fellows. Perhaps a personal illustration: When my church provided me with a portable wireless set it dreamed up for me sources of a hundred pleasures. So much so that the peril is that I want to stay in and listen to an interesting program when I ought to be out before God and my fellows in the attitude of service. I am not afraid of any attacks in the church from without—I think a little persecution would be a fine tonic. What I do seriously fear is that the friends of the church may let it down through their desire for the coziness and comfort of their homes.

You have not sung enough when you have to sing, "Ours is a happy little home." One of the liveliest things I know in these days is to watch a young couple building their home and finding their joy in it. But its coziness and comfort may spell peril. To let your interests be bounded by your little house, and its pretty decorations, its little garden, is proof that you are growing a little soul. Think of the wealth that is poured into your home. Where did the coffee or tea for their morning breakfast come from? How did the soap sponge for your bath reach you? Where were your tobacco or the ingredients for your chocolate grown? The thought, the music, the art that make up your wireless programs, these come from many countries and centuries. Do you who receive so largely owe nothing to those outside your homes? If your charity begins there must it stop there? The peril of listening in is that everything is a matter of receiving. You do not have to give even when you listen in to a sermon or a service. You cannot contribute to the good of your fellow worshippers and you cannot even give a threepenny to the collection. It was Jesus who said, "It is more blessed to give than to receive." Listen in by all means and gather all that your receiving set makes possible. Have your joy in your house and fireside. But do not forget to listen out so that you may share your best with those who most need it.

Let us go a step further and consider the wireless as a parable throwing light on the meaning of prayer. I am a novice in things wireless, but I know enough to know that there are definite conditions to be fulfilled before you receive what is being broadcast. Divine revelations are conditional too. And human preparation includes at least a susceptible soul, a trustful heart, and an obedient mind. Much of our knowledge of God we owe to men who listened in and out. No conditions. "I suppose he had a special lifeline," sneered a critic when a preacher urges that one of

---

1. This paragraph has been marked through in the handwritten copy, and appears to have not been included in the oral sermon.

the old prophets has received a special revelation. No. God has no favorites that way. He was broadcasting a message and this man obeyed the conditions and listened in. Indeed, God is always broadcasting messages for us and we do not hear because we are not listening in or not meeting the conditions. Oftentimes the din and noise of the world have to be blocked out. We have to be still and know. We have to get away and be alone. A prayerful attitude sets the soul in the listening atmosphere. There are some messages we can only hear as we enter our private room, shut the door, and wait for them.

But in this parable, there is a need for listening out too. Not all Divine revelations come in the quiet of a study or the seclusion of a convent. Sometimes God is discovered on the adventures of compassion and in the doing of duties. The message to Elijah in this case was, "Come out, and stand before God." The disciples wanted to build tabernacles and listen in on the Mount of Transfiguration when Jesus called them to come down to the place and listen out for the cry of human need. Often the revelation of God is for men to look to the poor. To selfishly shut them out is to foolishly shut God out. God has something to say to me for you as I sit in my study to pray. But He has something to pass on to me as I share the sacred service of your homes. Much we can all learn of God as we pore over His word and pray to the Father in secret. But there is truth in sayings like this one, "He that doeth the will of God shall know the doctrine." "He that followeth me shall . . . have the light of life." And in one of our own poets: "Heaven's gate is shut to him who comes alone: Save thou a soul, and that shall save thine own."[2]

If you have tried shutting yourself off from duty until your doubts were solved and your fears scattered, try the other way. Come out and stand before God as a servant ready for duty. Follow Jesus Christ in the work of seeking and saving the lost. What did not come to you through listening in may come through listening out to the voice of the poor and needy, the sick and the suffering.

There are few more known names in religion today than that of Albert Schweitzer. He is one of the foremost critical scholars of the day, a doctor of theology, of philosophy, of medicine. He is probably the world's greatest authority on the music of Bach and his work on Bach's music has been published in German, French, and English. He has played in the great orchestras of Berlin, Paris, and London. A few years ago, with the compassion of Christ and the need of his fellows in his soul, he left all to go out to Africa and to a desolate region in the Ogowe River. And there he is today serving in the healing art of a Christian physician. He has just been telling the world that following Christ and serving the least and lowliest of those Christ died to save, there has been born within him a new deep sense of religious reality.

By all means, let us listen in. And let us not forget to listen out for the SOS message there may be for us in the cry of the needy. Stand forth, girt for service. Be ready

---

2. This is from the "Two Rabbins" poem by John Greenleaf Whittier.

to serve the lowest. By serving the lowest you will hear the voice of the Highest saying, "In as much as you did it to one of the least of these ye did it unto me."

"A RELIGION THAT COSTS"
—1 Chronicles 21.23, 24

(Preached twenty-eight times from Batley 7/18/37 to Bishop St.10/31/48)

---

1 Chronicles 21.23, 24 "I will not take that which is thine for the Lord, nor offer a burnt offering without cost."

THE BACKGROUND OF THIS text is what, without exaggeration, may be called a perfectly lovely story. David had been commanded to build an altar and offer a sacrifice on a certain plot of land. No other plot would do, for on that particular spot God had wrought a great deliverance. The land belonged to a man called Ornan and David approached him and asked the price of the land. Here was the man's opportunity to drive a good bargain. Then, as now, prices were regulated by the law of demand and supply. Besides, the land was wanted by the government. But this man was no mere money grabber, he was moved by higher motives. The land was needed for religious purposes, and he said, "Take it, I give it to you. And take also the oxen that are ploughing it for a burnt offering, and the wheat growing on it for a meal offering. And take the wood of the plough with which to build the altar. I give it all." There's generosity for you!

But Ornan had to deal with a great and generous soul who was not prepared to be religious or cheap at another's expense. David's heart was overflowing with gratitude and he would not give God an offering that cost nothing. He rejected the gift so generously offered and insisted on paying the price.

So you have the pleasing picture of two men competing with one another in generosity. They were not Christians, one of them was not a Jew—Ornan was a Jebusite—and yet they set us a lovely example of elevated regard for religion. As we think of them, especially of David, we can hardly miss—

THE REBUKE TO OUR OWN NIGGARDLINESS

David had to build an altar and bring an offering. He was in such a mood of thankful love that to worship without cost seemed a mean and shabby thing. He simply had to bring something that cost. It would serve no useful purpose to fling about wild charges and one cannot be unmindful of the costly offerings that are brought to the church and given to God. One is often humbled and amazed in the presence of sacrificial gifts brought by the lowly and poor. But it is a fact that many of us give to God only the fag ends of our possessions. We give Him what is left over when we have gratified our own whims and fancies. It is a superfluity and not a sacrifice that we bring and lay on the altar.

I am not thinking only of the money we give, though there is need of faithfulness in our responsibility on that matter. We often speak of religion as costly and one needs to speak carefully. God is not unreasonable and we ministers of His should not be impertinent. But does what we give really impoverish us? Have we any right to talk about sacrifice when we have not forgone a single luxury? We talk about our outgoings, what about our incomings? The measure of what we give is in what we have left, and in what we spend on ourselves. You have to consider your passbook as well as your checkbook. But we are least niggardly in our gifts of money. We give gold where we withhold the greater gifts.

What about our gift of time? There are those who think they patronize the Almighty by giving an hour and a quarter a week to Him. We grudge the time we give to His house and service and we are not more generous with our thought. For our business, self-advancement, and our pleasure we exercise our brain to the full. For God's work we are too tired, indifferent, and indolent. If some men put no more thought into their business than they put into the church they would be on the rocks in twelve months. The same thing is true of our whole religious life. We are content to repeat orthodox creeds, sing popular hymns, and be respectable and conventional Christians. We fail when it is a case of living the life which means taking up a cross, denying self, and following Christ fully. It is when you carry your creed into your business, let it govern your thoughts, guide your speech, control your temper, make you charitable, forgiving, kind, it is then that religion begins to cost, and it is there that so many fail.

"I will not offer a burnt offering without cost," said David. And his fine conduct ought to shame us out of the cheap and the superficial and into something deep and sacrificial. Let me put what is in my mind frankly and bluntly to you—

CAN WE EXPECT GOD TO ACCEPT CHEAP OFFERINGS?

Would an earthly governor? I borrow the question from the prophet you call Malachi. He was reproving his people for bringing miserable offerings to God's house and altar, and he said to them, "Offer it now to thy governor, will he be pleased with thee? Or will he accept thy person?" It was a shrewd and searching question. They were offering to God what an earthly governor would not look at and which they would not have the cheek to offer him.

That is a searching test still. Apply it. It is not for me to blame or chide you if you are giving your best. But are you? Would you offer to an earthly foreman or manager what you offer in the way of thought, time, and service to God? Would you bring to someone you love on earth what you bring to the God you profess to love? I go further to ask—

HAS GOD TIME FOR THE UNREAL?

That is speaking after the manner of men, but it is the only way we can speak. Reverently I say that God is too busy with people desperately in earnest to bother with folk who are playing at religion. While men are praying in agony, "God be merciful to me a sinner," can you expect Him to trouble about Pharisees whose prayer is simply a piece of self-congratulation? Out in the Yunnan Hills are men and women who will tramp miles to attend Divine worship and spend nights in the mountains. I wonder if God will listen to some of us who will only cruise the road to church if it isn't too wet, or on the other hand, it isn't too fine.

I have been reading of an old woman in Ayrshire who, when surprised into revealing that her meal was only a crust of bread and cold water said, "It's only water, but He makes it taste like wine." God has people like that to listen to, can you honestly expect Him to listen to people whose only complaint is that there is too much salt in the soup? God will accept the smallest offering from the lowliest worshipper, even a cup of cold water does not fail of its reward, but you cannot expect Him to leave the widow casting in her all, two mites, to attend to people who are changing sixpence for a three pence because they think no one is looking. God cannot be pleased with our unworthy offerings.

WORSHIP ON THE CHEAP IS AS UNSATISFYING TO THE WORSHIPPER AS IT IS UNIMPRESSIVE TO OTHERS

When a man gives little to religion and gives it grudgingly it is precious little satisfaction he gets out of it. If you are trying to be religious on the cheap, you will never touch the heart of its joy. That's the trouble with many of us. We give only what is an insult to God and what can never satisfy us. There is a real place for counting the cost, but if a man is always counting the cost he misses the great satisfactions. Put yourself, your money, your time and thought into religion, and whatever the cost the return will be greater. Put more in and you will get more out. But while you live in a cold, calculating, miserly spirit there will be no glow of soul, no satisfaction of spirit, no joy of heart.

And such a religion will never impress outsiders. Can you expect them to believe that you are finding the pearl of great price if you are only willing to pay so little for it? By our own interest, devotion, sacrifice, others will judge what we recommend. And I say frankly that we shall never impress others with the supreme importance of religion if we are unwilling, reluctant, and niggardly with regard to it.

When David had paid the price, and laid the offering on the altar and called upon God, then fire from heaven fell. There was a visible sign of God's acceptance. Sometimes still we sing, "My all is on the altar, I'm waiting for the fire." Do we always sing the truth there? You won't have to do much waiting when your all is on the altar. The fire will fall, your own soul will be quickened, and revival will begin.

LOVE SO AMAZING, SO DIVINE, DEMANDS—

One has to listen to and to make many appeals to people to give their money and to give their time and strength to Christian service. If I wanted it, here is a text that would give one ample scope for using the spur and the lash on niggardly givers. I am deliberately declining it. For one thing it isn't much use, it is like flogging a dead horse and that is an unprofitable exercise. There is a more excellent way. You will never get at purse strings except through heart strings. You will never get people to give more, to do more, until love is kindled in their hearts. It is here the text helps.

David's heart swelled with grateful love because of what God had done for him, and he would not give what cost him nothing to God who had delivered him. God has done greater things for you and me. We survey the wondrous cross where God's love is most clearly revealed and where God wrought out the soul's deliverance. As we survey that cross, let us say, "Love so amazing, so divine, demands my soul, my life, my all." Before that demand, I cannot stand balancing a two shilling piece and half a cross, I cannot stand calculating how little I can give of service and of love. At the cross I can sing F. R. Havergal's consecration hymn, "Take myself and I will be ever, only, all for thee." I can change a word in Watt's great hymn and sing, "Love so amazing, so divine, shall have my soul, my life, my all."

∼

"GOD'S GOODNESS AND MAN'S RESPONSE"
—1 Chronicles 22.14–16

(Preached five times from Fentiman Road 9/21/24 to L. E. 10/14/34)

---

1 Chronicles 22.14–16 "Now, behold, in my trouble (in my poverty) I have prepared for the house of the LORD a hundred thousand talents of gold, and a thousand talents of silver . . . and thou mayest add thereto . . . Arise, therefore, and be doing, and the LORD be with thee."

Here is David with his heart set on the building of a temple for the worship of God. He begins with an apology that he has not been able to make more adequate preparations, to bring greater gifts. "In my trouble, my poverty, my low estate," he says, "I have not been able to do more." What he means is that the affairs of the kingdom have distracted him, wars have drained his exchequer, domestic duties have occupied his time, and well—he is sorry—this is the best he can do. We have heard men talk that way. Often, such talk has been preliminary to a miserable and unworthy gift. Men have made their trouble an excuse for a small subscription. But listen how David's speech reads. In the narrowness of my circumstances I cannot do all I would. I wish it were more and am sorry it is not. It is *only* a hundred thousand talents of gold, and a thousand talents of silver, and wood, stone, iron, and brass in abundance. Why, this is a magnificent, colossal, unheard of generosity. And yet, the man is apologizing for it! Mind you, the man is perfectly sincere. There is not a touch of complacency about him, none of the pride that apes humility. He means and feels what he says. He really thinks that he has not touched the occasion, that his gift is unworthy of the object of it.

THE MEASURE OF GIFTS

The fact is this man had learned how to measure gifts. He saw gifts in their true light. It is when men look only at their gifts of money, time, service, strength that they begin to think they have done enough, grudge to give more, and tell the man who pleads with them that he is always begging. But David compared his gift with what God is. He saw God as "the only wise God" who "delighteth in mercy," and was "from everlasting to everlasting." He was God glorious in holiness and doing wonders. It is in the vision of God's holiness, power, and grace that men rightly measure themselves and their gifts. When you remember that working for God, giving to the God and Father of our Lord Jesus Christ, you will lose all your pride and complacency, cease all your murmurings and complaints, and recognize that our greatest offering is an offering of poverty.

David measured his gift by what God had given. God had taken him from the sheepcote and put him on the throne. He had subdued his enemies and made his reign glorious. God had preserved him from his foes and given him friends. When his feet were well-nigh gone, God had upheld him. And when he had sunk into base and degrading sin, God had lifted him out of the miry clay and set his feet upon a rock, restored to him the joy of salvation and put a new song in his mouth. By the side of God's great gifts even a hundred thousand talents of gold and a thousand talents of silver seemed small and unworthy.

That is the way to measure gifts. What a magnificent giver God is! How manifold are His works and how great are His gifts! See them in the splendor and the resources of creation. Think of all this common life can give of rest and joy amid its strife. He has not made us kings but He has given us a kingdom where love is and laughter sings. And He has redeemed us, not with corruptible things such as silver and gold but with the precious blood of His own Son. Our sins which were many he has pardoned, our evil which was as crimson He has made white as snow. Before us he has set the open door of heaven. Why, we can never pay the debt, the best we can do is to acknowledge it. Always when men have realized the greatness of Divine gifts they have sung, "Were the whole realm of nature mine, that were a present far too small."

DAVID'S GIFTS WERE INSPIRED BY ZEAL

"The whole was prompted by a burning zeal for the glory of Jehovah," says a commentator. It was true of him and of his Greater Son that, "the zeal of Thine House hath eaten me up." To such zeal even great gifts and service seemed small. David wanted to do more, to give more. It is always so and we know it. When our faith burns dire, and love runs low, and zeal dies down, then we get sulky and talk of the strain of our resignations. Pray for a "calmly fervent zeal," and nourish and feed it. Then you will see the glory of giving and count your best gifts as only a slight contribution to the worthiest object. Look at this incident another way, and see how, instead of making his poverty an excuse for idleness and niggardliness—

DAVID TURNED HIS POVERTY INTO AN INSPIRATION TO GENEROSITY

He had a great purpose in his heart and a great plan in his mind, but when he set about turning them into a performance he found he was crippled by poverty and affliction.

"GOD'S GOODNESS AND MAN'S RESPONSE"—1 CHRONICLES 22.14-16

A small man would have relinquished his dream and made his low estate an excuse for doing nothing. David's greatness is revealed in his brave attempt to do his best. If he could not give all, he would give all he could.

Every man whose mind is set on great deeds in God's name soon feels his poverty, his limitations, and his lack of resources. It may be actual poverty, or want of education, or ill health, or trouble, or enfeebled strength, but it is there and it is very real. Well, what are you going to do about it? Little men and women will make it an excuse for inaction. They will talk about what they would do if they had more money, leisure, or gifts. They will probably look very wise and very pathetic as they say, "one can't do more than one can, can one?" But that isn't really very clever. It isn't true because one never knows what one can do till one tries. You can give more than you have because the real wealth of life has a way of multiplying as it is given. Great souls will make their poverty, their limitations, an incentive to greater service and more earnest attempts.

May I remind you that the greatest work of the world has been done out of poverty? Columbus discovered America in an old windjammer no one would put to sea today. Milton gave us *Paradise Lost* out of his blindness. Bunyan wrote the immortal allegory in prison. Turner painted his masterpieces out of broken tea cups. One of the greatest seers of the last century saw his glowing visions of ladders from Charing Cross to heaven as he sold matches and held horse's heads in London's streets, and he wrote them down on the backs of old envelopes and dirty scraps of paper.

When you come to the church, it has been built out of poverty. Of our Lord himself it is written, "He was rich yet for our sakes became poor." But out of His poverty He built the sanctuary where the heavy laden find rest, the sinful find pardon and cleansing, and the troubled find peace. Paul wrote of himself as poor, yet making many rich. In the early days of the church not many wise, not many noble were called, for the most part they were slaves and outcasts.

Think of the great Methodist Church to which it is an honor for any man to belong. We have had our scholars and our saints, but we have had no Parliamentary grants, no patronage of royalty or aristocracy, and few millionaires. No, why should we be ashamed to confess it? Methodism has been built up by plowmen, artisans, servant girls, shop keepers, who, out of their poverty, gave their penny a week and a shilling a quarter, and many another gift beside. And how are our churches maintained? We thank God for a few men and women who are consecrating their wealth to God's work, but in the main we pay our way by those who, out of their poverty voluntarily tax their limited incomes to support their church. We are successors of men and women who, "in their poverty"—

DID GREAT THINGS

David did what he could and said to his son Solomon, "thou mayest add thereto." That is our privilege and our duty. To carry on, to add to what others have given and have done. We are better equipped, we have had a better education, and we have more money and more leisure. We must not let them shame us and we must not let their work suffer. We must carry on and complete their work. We shall have to do it as they did with stiffened backs and gritted teeth. We shall be faced, as they were, with poverty, limitations, obstacles, difficulties. But we must not let our afflictions be excuses for indolence. Rather, let them be incentives to greater zeal and activity.

Out of your straightened circumstances, in spite of ill health, notwithstanding your crowded life and unceasing years, you can do great things for God, if you have the mind, heart, and zeal. And we all have more than we think we have in the way of ability, strength, and possibility. I can tell every one of you where you can dig and find treasure. I can tell you because a distinguished preacher, some of whose thoughts are in this sermon, told me. If you want to find treasure, dig in your ribs. It is there all right! It is in your heart. You talk about tight fists, but they open when the heart is touched. Men run in the way of God's commandments when the heart is enlarged. It was in David's heart to build a magnificent Temple and it was a delight to do what he could.

What is in your heart to do? Think of what God is. Remember His matchless, mighty, redeeming love. Then out of your poverty you will give and do your best. It will never satisfy you and will always seem small. But you will never bring less than your best: inadequate and unworthy as it seems to you, God will see in it the love, the consecration, the purpose of your heart. It will look poor to you, but it will look great and glorious to Him.

"A CHARGE TO KEEP"
—Ezra 8.29

(Preached Katherine Road 1/19/36 and Spring Head Mission 2/4/40)

Ezra 8.29 "Watch ye, and keep them, until ye weigh them . . . in the chamber of the House of the Lord."

LET US BEGIN AT what will seem some distance from the text—with this—what we call the life of faith includes two great committals. On the one hand, there is what we commit to God. The Christian life begins, continues, and ends in faith, in the trusting of our souls, our temporal and eternal well-being to God's love and His unwearied strength. "We know the love of God and we confide in it." On the other hand, we are guardians of something God commits to our care. We confide in Him and He counts on us guarding what He puts in our care.

The clearest and best setting of this twofold committal is in Paul's letter to Timothy—when the great apostle writes, "I know whom I have believed, and am persuaded that He is able to keep that which I have committed unto Him" (2 Tim 1.12) and then, "That good thing which was committed unto thee keep by the Holy Ghost" (2 Tim 1.14). The first committal usually gets emphasis, and rightly so. The measure of peace and strength is the measure of our trust. But it is with the second committal that our main concern is just now.

The question I want us to face is this, *we are sure of God—can he be sure of us?* What we have committed to God is safe. He never fails and they who trust in them are never confounded. Our souls and all our interests are safe in His hands. That is never in doubt with Paul, knowing Him whom we have believed, we are persuaded that He will keep what we have committed unto Him. With God as security there is no room for anxiety. But can God trust us? Is what He has committed to us safe? If He so sacredly guards our deposit we ought not to fail Him. It was God's complaint against His ancient people that they were "children in whom is no faith." They counted on God's faithfulness but were themselves unreliable. We realize the trouble of that. And we owe it to Him who guards us that we keep what He has committed to us. It is against failure here and faithlessness that I would warn you. It is to prayerful vigilance that I call you. You are kept by God and you ought to be keepers for God.

It is to illustrate and enforce this duty that we turn to the story of the pilgrim priests. The two passages from Timothy would have served, but the subject gains in colors, interest, and purpose when set in the little-known story from which the text is taken. A company of Jews was returning from Babylon to Jerusalem. A brief halt was made on the edge of the desert to get things in order for the perilous journey. To twelve priests as guardians was committed the treasures of gold and silver vessels to be used in the service of God's house.

Think of that company setting out, of the long journey, the perils of the way, the risks of attacks and robbers. The treasure had to be guarded until it was weighed and placed in the temple. The men who were responsible were both trusting and trusted. They committed themselves to God, and with fine courage refused an escort of Persian soldiers. They accepted as a sacred charge the treasure of the temple. You can see what an apt illustration this is of our Christian life and responsibility. We are pilgrims journeying along unknown and often unfriendly ways. We do commit ourselves to the sleepless love and unfailing care of God. And there is that we have to guard against all foes and keep at all costs; something God will require at our hands when we come to the end of the journey and stand before Him.

There is no time to do more than hint at the treasures we have to guard. First, there is the rich and real treasure of ourselves. I am not forgetting what is indeed fundamental in my faith, that "the Lord is my keeper." But: "Our sacred selves! Have we no charge to keep o'er this divinity that lives within ourselves." The difference is perfectly clear and there is no contradiction to my own mind. I am trusting God to save and keep me, and yet I know that if I fail to watch and pray there are forces that will get under my guard and over my defenses and pollute my soul. God sends me forth as His child and I must take heed lest in trying to win the world I lose my own soul. I have to remember that nothing I have or can have is as important as what I am. Your task and mine is so to live, so to watch and pray, that we come through with humor unsullied and with soul unstained.

Second, it may be that God has committed another soul to our charge. Children are a heritage from the Lord and a responsibility to be guarded for Him. It is time we had done making vulgar jokes about the coming of children to our homes and realize that with the advent of the "little stranger" God is saying to those of us who are parents, "Take this child and nurse him for me." Our responsibility is only discharged when we can say, "Here am I and the children whom thou hast given me." And in this matter our charge is wider still. It is far too late in the day to ask, "Am I my brother's keeper?" You are; God has appointed you this task. There is the brother or sister in the home, the weak brother, the friend who trusts you and will follow your lead. These are part of the sacred trust God has committed to you; fulfill it so faithfully that you will be able to say, "Of those Thou hast given me I have lost none."

Third, then there is faith. Dr. Moffatt's translation of the second passage in Timothy is, "Keep the great securities of the faith intact." There is a stand we are to make for the faith of our fathers and for the faith that is in Christ Jesus. There is no plan for the forms of faith over which many struggle and fight, but for the central things of the Christian faith. We must guard these when others speak lightly or slightingly of them to seek to set them aside for their own devices. But it is another tune I wish to give to the thought. Through the grace of God, we have ourselves come to believe in Christ. We have won our way to faith. Having so far won, we realize the truth of Wordsworth's words: "Tis the most difficult of tasks to keep, heights which the soul is competent to gain."[1]

"Let no man take thy crown," wrote Paul to Timothy. The enemies of the faith, the robbers who try to take it from us, are known to every believer. We have all been tempted to deny our Lord and sometimes to forsake Him. Men try to laugh us out of our faith, offer us their bribes to leave it, by their threatenings try to drive us from it. Drowsiness, weariness, worldliness settle in us at times and our faith is in danger. We are so to guard the faith that nothing drives us from it.

Fourth, God commends his cause to us. He puts the purpose of His name and the interests of His kingdom into our keeping. He counts on us and His cause suffers if we are faithless. His kingdom tarries when we are slack and is advanced by our devotion. We are only true to our task when we let our light so shine before men that they see our good works and glorify our Father.

Mark the solemn admonition. We can understand how solemnly Ezra charged those guardians of the temple treasure—"watch these and keep them. Guard them until you deliver them safely in the House of God." Our task is more delicate and difficult than theirs, it demands more earnest heed to the solemn admonition. We must watch as if everything depended on our wakefulness, watchfulness, and wariness. The price of liberty and every virtue is eternal vigilance with a vigilance surpassing that with which men guard the crown jewels, or our coasts, their homes, their interests. Let us guard what God has committed to us: "Watch as if in that alone, hung the issues of the day." If we are to keep what is committed to us, we must "pray that help may be sent down."

We must watch and pray. "That good thing which is committed unto thee keep . . . by the Holy Spirit." We do need to pray in private, but we need too the help which comes through fellowship and prayer in the sanctuary. "My feet were almost gone," said the psalmist, "until I went into the sanctuary." Many a man would have let go his faith and been disloyal to his trust but for the help coming from there. And many a man has gripped and guarded his treasure with a firm hand because of the fellowship and help of the sanctuary.

Any lack of vigilance or failure to pray may spell disaster. Readers of Sir Walter Scott's *The Talisman* will remember how one brief hour of failure in Sir Kenneth's

---

1. This is from a very long poem entitled "Excursions," bk. 4, *Despondency Corrected*, l. 139.

past meant the banner of England being dragged in the dust. The strongest among us cannot afford to be careless or prayerless; the weakest may safely guard the treasure through watchfulness and prayer. So let us give the more earnest heed to the familiar words: "Help me to watch and pray, and in Thyself rely, assured if I my trust betray, I shall forever die."[2] Only, if we watch and pray we shall neither betray nor die, we shall stand before God, with the journeyings, dangers, and foes all behind us and be able to say with Paul, "I have kept the faith."

∼

---

2. This is a line from Charles Wesley's hymn "A Charge to Keep I Have."

"RIDICULE AND REBUILDING"
—Nehemiah 4.2–3

(Preached seven times from Fentiman Road, undated, to Spring Head Mission 10/6/40)

Nehemiah 4.2–3 "What do these feeble Jews? Will they fortify themselves? Even that which they build, if a fox go up, he shall even break down their stone wall."

"Reith's Task: To Build the New Britain." So ran a headline in my paper the other day (October 4, 1940). The reference was to Sir John Reith's appointment to the new Ministry of Works and Public Buildings. It might have referred to Nehemiah about the middle of the fifth century BC. At the request of his people, and still more at the call of God, the great Jewish patriot undertook the task of rebuilding Jerusalem after the devastation caused by the Babylonian conquest. The task was difficult enough and the new minister decreed the cooperation of all the people. But there were those who opposed and used every weapon at hand to hinder and frustrate the work.

Perhaps the most deadly of all their weapons was *the weapon of ridicule*. That is the weapon used in the text, "What do these feeble Jews? Do they think to restore and rebuild the city? Why, if a jackal ran up against what they build he will push it over!" You can see the sarcastic smile on Sanballat's face as he speaks. You may be quite sure that to carry on in the teeth of sneers and ridicule was a harder task than clearing away rubbish and lifting the heavy stones for the walls. Ridicule is a most deadly weapon. So Dr. Samuel Johnson, who could speak from experience, wrote: "Of all the griefs that harass the distrest, sure the most bitter is a scornful jest. Fate never wounds more deep the generous heart than when a blockhead's insult points the dart."[1] Many a man has given up in despair, not because his work was hard, but because it was ridiculed.

Today the odes of Keats are reckoned among the loveliest in our language. Yet, when the poems first appeared, the receiving magazine rained scorn and ridicule upon them. According to those who are in the know, these scornful rejections hastened the tuberculosis that killed him. After a week of sleeplessness, he arose one morning to find a red spot in his handkerchief: "That drop is my death warrant. I shall die," he

---

1. *London*, line 165. *Imitation of Juvenal*, Satire, III. V. 152.

said.[2] And so, when he was twenty-six, his friends lifted a marble stone above him in a graveyard in Rome upon which was written, "Here lies one whose name was writ in water."

RELIGIOUS BUILDING AND REBUILDING

Some of you have determined to build your life according to the Divine Architect's plan. You have realized that it is more important to build a worthy character than a wealthy business. You are striving to build your life on a sure foundation and of worthy materials. You want your life to be not a Palace of Art or a Theatre of Pleasure, but a Temple of the Living God. Some of you, maybe, are attempting the harder task of rebuilding your life after it has been wrecked by some sin or has crumbled and decayed through carelessness and neglect. It is middle life with you and only you and God know how hard your task is.

Or, one may make our reference to the work of building the City of God, the Kingdom of Christ, where are now only the rubbish heaps of sin. We have seen a vision. God has shown us His plan for the world and we are trying to make things according to His pattern. Much of the material seems poor and some of it has to be recovered from scrap heaps. We are builders of that city, and it has to be built in waste places.

NEHEMIAH AND SANBALLAT

Every builder of character knows that every Nehemiah has his Sanballat. They stand round and sneer. They make fun of the man who is trying to build on a right foundation. They ridicule the very idea of the reconstruction of a wasted life. And they smile in a superior way at effort to build the City of God. They see only something to laugh at in endeavor to reclaim and restore those who are broken down. There is not one of you trying to build up a Christian character to reclaim a broken life, to build up the walls of a Holy City, but has to endure the scoffs and the sneers, the jibes and the jeers of men. They mark your attempts, sneer at your wishes, ridicule your work, and say "What do these feeble Christians?"

Such ridicule can still be a very deadly weapon. Many a man who faces without flinching deliberate opposition and bitter persecution breaks down before mocking laughter. Peter drew his sword and faced a crowd in defense of his Lord, but thrice denied him before the sneering question of a servant girl. Not many of us care to cast

---

2. The exact quote is found in a comment by his close friend Charles Brown. Brown later wrote, "He mildly and instantly yielded to my request that he should go to bed . . . On entering the cold sheets, he slightly coughed, and I heard him say, 'That is blood from my mouth . . . I know the colour of that blood;—it is arterial blood . . . that drop of blood is my death-warrant;—I must die.'" See http://hcl.harvard.edu/libraries/houghton/exhibits/keats/year_1820.cfm.

stones at him. We live in glass houses. I would not be unsympathetic for I know the courage it takes to carry on in the face of ridicule. No man likes to be thought a fool. It is desperately difficult to stand up for goodness where it is held in contempt. For a young man to stand up against his team and refuse to play football on a Sunday. So many good things are smiled at as simple and old fashioned. The very idea of a few Christian men and women doing anything for the good of the world is ridiculed. What does the church do? Why don't these people turn their attention to politics or social reform and do something practical? Well, it is hard to go in the face of such sneering questions.

There are few things I'd rather do than say some heartening word to ridiculed builders in the realm of character. *There is no need to be cranks.* I will speak as frankly as I can, and say nothing I do not believe with my whole heart and am trying to live out in my life. There is no need to be a crank, an oddity, for the sake of it. Someone has said that the Lord has His dear ones, and His queer men. He has. The cause of God has suffered because of the angularities and peculiarities of some professing Christians. It is not for me to condemn folk who are better and braver than I am, but I do not think Christ calls us to be anything simply silly. There is no need to exalt fads to the position of prominent tradition.

What I do want to urge is that you shall not be so weak as to give up what you believe to be right because you are laughed at. You will get nowhere and do nothing unless you are prepared to stand up against the weapon of ridicule. A fool's cap can be worn as bravely and proudly as a crown. To be a fool for Christ's sake is an honor. For His sake, men have endured the loss of all things, surely you can endure the mocking laughter of critics and cynics.

OUR DEBT TO RIDICULED MEN

They have done far more for the world than the men who have laughed. Any fool can sneer. A place in the seat of the scornful makes no demands on the occupant. Many a man who has been laughed at has built what has been a love to his fellows while his sneering critics are only remembered for their failure to recognize genius. Columbus they sneered at as a visionary. Galileo they thought mad. Luther they said was troubled. People laughed when shrewd men utilize the refuse of certain industries, yet fortunes have been made out of what was once thrown away!

So men have sneered at efforts to build "wastes" into worthy social structures. They ridiculed the work of Jesus, but He found men like Zacchaeus and women like Mary Magdalen and built their lives into the kingdom of God. Primitive Christianity was riddled with sarcasm and ever since revival has provoked the sneers. Students sneered when Wesley and the members of the Holy Club at Oxford went to work in the prisons, but sinners were turned into saints whose boots the critics were not worthy to black. Sanballats, some of them were in the churches, made merry when

William Booth began work in what was literally the Mile End Waste, but some souls came from the waste. The world does nothing to its sneering Sanballats.

Never mind the scoffs and the jeers of the world. You will accomplish nothing unless you can stand up to ridicule and *do what Nehemiah did*. Keep your spirits up by turning in prayer to God. Leave Him to humble your critics and you get on with your job. You will not get through life without being counted a fool, better be regarded as one now than find out at the end of the day that you have played a fool's part and built your life on shifting sand. Whatever men say and do, play your part in the building of your character and the City of God. "Stand by your conscience, your honor, your faith; stand like a hero and battle till death." And when you are very sorely tempted to give up, remember your Lord and what He endured: "Bearing shame and scoffing rude, in my place condemned He stood."[3] Now you stand and bear it for His sake.

∽

---

3. This is a line from Philip Bliss's hymn "Hallelujah! What a Savior" (1875).

"THE HERITAGE OF YOUTH"
—Psalm 16.6

(Preached twenty-three times including Katherine Road 10/25/31 and Spring Head Mission 10/17/37)

Psalm 16.6 "I have a goodly heritage."

WHEN WE THINK OF a heritage or our inheritance we usually speak in terms of the material. What is "left us" we generally measure with values in cash or real estate. Or thinking on a higher level we speak of the good name, fine example, gracious influence handed on to us by those who have gone before us. But the heritage I want us to think of now is in none of these things. It is the heritage that belongs to youth as youth and not to a favored few. There is no youth or maiden here but can say, "I have a goodly heritage." It would be possible to say, and with truth, that "youth is in itself a goodly heritage." When Wordsworth caught the enthusiasm of the stirring of new life in the French Revolution, he cried out, "Bliss was it in that dawn to be alive, but to be young was very heaven."[1] That comes near to the psalmist's utterance which is literally, "A blissful heritage is mine."

There was a time when it was a positive handicap to be young, when youth was told that it must be seen and not heard. Paul had to warn others and encourage Timothy with this, "Let no man despise your youth." And in our own history, William Pitt, who became prime minister at a very early age, had to defend himself against "the atrocious crime of being a young man."

Well, all that is past. This is the age of youth. Many prefer the energy and enthusiasm of youth to the wisdom and experience of age. Many a man finds, to his surprise, that he is regarded as too old at forty. Mind you, I am not accepting that dictum nor is anything I say in my enthusiasm for youth to be interpreted as meaning that a man's chance is past when he is forty, or that I fail to note the achievements of age. There is a scene in our own political history, and we have not to go very far back for it, which I glory in. At a time when most men are laying down burdens, the Grand Old Man was girding himself for a great fight. Those who had the privilege of seeing Gladstone in

---

1. This is from Wordsworth's long poem "The Prelude."

the House of Commons in those days, tell us that it was a wonderful sight to see this old man meeting and beating the attacks of young men though they were led by "the agility of a Chamberlain and the subtlety of a Balfour." And too often have I seen old men gallantly carrying burdens young men declined because they were blind to the possibilities of age. But even the grand old men will agree with me that the heritage of youth, to be young, is as Lowell says, "a heritage it seems to me, a king might wish to hold in fee."[2]

Let us work that out and see if, whether you have inherited money and a fair name or not, you have not a goodly heritage. What enters into the heritage of youth? First of all—

THERE IS ENERGY

That does not mean that every young man is energetic. Sometimes the opposite is the case. One has known young folk listless, dilettante, blasé, not exerting energy enough to keep themselves warm. There are even "good" young men who are wanting. It is not sufficient surely for a man to be an ignorant Christian or a lazy teetotaler. Sometimes the energy is wrongly directed. Some young folk are energetic with wrong direction. They can tell you all about cricket averages and derby winners, but are "sticks" at their business. They will put any amount of energy into a football match and none into the greater game of fine living.

But energy is part of the heritage of youth, wrongly directed as it may be, but it is there in normal youth. You can make efforts, carry burdens, undertake work, without being weary and that is a great gift. Some of us who do not call ourselves old can already feel the lessening of energy with the advancing of years. The things we were once able to do with ease we now do, if at all, with an effort. It was a sad day for me when I had to return from the football playing pitch to the stand—not simply because it meant no more football, but because it meant the knowledge that energy and strength were lessening.

Nor does this apply only to physical energy. Mental energy is part of the heritage of youth. Youth is the time to tackle new subjects and master great problems. One has noted the difference a few years make in the power of students to grasp lessons. And there is peculiar spiritual energy which belongs to youth—L. W. Bonner's testimony and one's own experience attest to that. Youth is the time to do great things because you have the strength and energy to carry them through.

---

2. This is from James Russell Lowell's poem "The Heritage."

"THE HERITAGE OF YOUTH"—PSALM 16.6

THERE IS FREEDOM

I use that great word with a special significance. What I mean is freedom from ties and bonds, freedom to do the thing you dream. Start with something very practical. "My six reasons for taking no risks," said a man in the American Civil War, "are a wife and five children." When a man has given hostages to fortune in that way, he is bound. Freedom from family ties makes endeavor possible.

Then custom and habits become a tie. Hy Drummond used to say that a man does not often change the shape of his collar after he is forty. I know that it is true that some of my friends have tried to persuade me to wear a clerical collar, and my one fancy is for a wing collar, but I know now that I shall wear a polo to the end of my days. We become the creatures of habit, our ruts become too deep to get out of. Grooves are in danger of becoming graves.

And too often, in older men, sin becomes a chain that binds them. Light as a gossamer thread once it has hardened into adamant links until a man has literally become the slave of sin. He is never at an age when the great Deliverer cannot set him free, for the Lion of Judah can break every chain, but it is not easy for him to make a new choice and turn in a fresh direction.

Youth is the time of freedom, when a man can afford to take risks, can as a soldier of the cross take a place in the forefront of the battle. Youth is the time when you are free to say, "I will take this way, the way of Jesus, the way of unselfish service."

THERE IS AUDACITY

There is just one other thing I want to mention in the heritage of youth. That is audacity. I might have called it courage, but it is a special kind of courage I am thinking of. It is courage with a plus, courage carried to a point of risk, courage mercifully blind to dangers. And youth is the time for such courage. How often you are told that you are audacious young things! Youth is the time for that kind of thing: "When all the world is young, lad, and all the trees are green, and every goose a swan, lad, and every lass a queen."[3]

As Robert Louis Stevenson says: "If we wish to scale a mountain, or visit a thieves' kitchen in the East End, to go down in a diving dress or up in a balloon, we must be about it while we are still young. It will not do to delay until we are dogged by prudence." He goes on to say, "Youth is the time to see the sunrise in town or country: to be converted at a revival. It is the time of venture."[4]

I stood for a long time this summer and watched the speedboats at Scarborough do a roaring trade. It was a master thrill and you paid a pound for the privilege of

---

3. This is a quote from Charles Kingsley, a nineteenth-century Anglican clergyman Fred greatly admired, and named his son for. This is taken from a poem called "Water Babies."

4. These quotes come from Stevenson's work entitled "Virginibus Puerisque."

getting drenched. I enjoyed watching but had not the slightest inclination to go. I noticed that all who came up soaked and smiling were young folk. Youth is the time of daring, devil-may-care audacity.

And it is that in other things. How many of us look back on the things we did in the name of Christ and His church in our youth. We went into lodging houses, stood in the streets, we entered pubs for the purpose of bringing others out. It all seemed so natural and saw nothing especially courageous in it. You don't mind being a fool, even God's fool, before you are forty. That is part of your heritage, the faith and courage that laugh at impossibilities and cry that it can and shall be done.

That is your heritage and I think I have the right to ask, *what are you going to do with it?* Society and the nation have a right to expect that you shall not squander it, but use it. There is no part of our national life where we do not need the energy and courage of youth. We need them in business, and in politics. We need not cranks, but young men and women of vision and with strength and courage to turn their dreams into deeds.

But I am pleading especially for Christ and His church. He needs you and we need you. If only we had your energy, your freedom, and your audacity, we could attempt greater things. The kingdom of heaven suffereth violence and the violent take it by force, and you are the fellows to do it. I am, I declare, not unmindful of the veterans. It is as true for the church as it is for the nation that: "Thank God, when the young lads fell, sir, we still have the brave old boys." But the call is to youth because youth is strong and free and dare to do. You are leaving too much to the "brave old boys," and I shall call on you tonight with the courage and daring of youth to come out boldly and range yourselves on the side of the great white captain, Christ. Consecrate your splendid power to the doing of His will, the building up of His church, and the winning of the world for Him.

ADDENDUM: WHAT YOU CAN DO WITH YOUR HERITAGE[5]

You can fling it away. You can squander your energy and waste your freedom as I have known men fling away the money and fair name they inherited.

You can fritter it away, use it on things of no importance as you will if you have no definite end or reason with words borrowed from the words of this service.

You can dedicate it. Devoting your energy and courage to some great cause, to the good of yourself, your country, or another great cause. The inscription on General Gordon's monument. You do that and do not forget the last thing—"his heart to the Lord."

∼

---

5. The following notes were included on a loose piece of paper, written in a different ink, and placed in the pages of "The Heritage of Youth."

"THE FEAST IN THE PRESENCE OF FOES"
—Psalm 23.5

(Preached six times from E. N. R., undated, to Spring Head Mission 9/15/40)

Psalm 23.5 "Thou preparest a table before me in the presence of mine enemies."

AT VERSE 5 IN this well-known psalm, there is a sudden transition from the figure of a flock to that of a feast. Such transitions are characteristic of Hebrew poetry. Having spoken of life as a journey, the psalmist speaks of it as a conflict. The Good Shepherd becomes Host. Instead of "green pastures and still waters," you have a well-spread table and an overflowing cup. In the text is the picture of a hunted, hard-pressed fugitive who claims and finds the shelter and protection of a friendly shepherd's tent. His enemies are so near that he can see their frowning faces and hear their cries of baffled rage, but he rests and acts at leisure, and his enemies are powerless to interrupt the feast.

I had little trouble in finding an almost literal fulfillment in the physical place we inhabit in these days. We eat our meals while enemy planes try to level our courage and lurking submarines hurl torpedoes at supply ships. The bountiful provision for our needs, the abundant harvest, calls for special thanksgiving and praise. Our gratitude ought to go out to God the Giver, and to men who have run the gauntlet of warplane and submarine attacks to bring supplies to our table.

But important as our food supplies are for the body, I am thinking mainly of the greater harvest, the table God spread for our souls in the presence of our enemies. The soul of man is invited to be the guest of God. The fellowship of the table speaks of spiritual entertainment, good cheer, and friendship. The Divine host provides security for His guests in the midst of danger, peace in the heart of strife. Here is more than a figure of speech, there is an actual and stern fact. Life for all of us is a conflict, and there are many adversaries of the soul. As we go to meet them, in the midst of the struggle, we may be the guests of God and share the refreshment of good cheer and of fellowship with Him. As we go to meet our foe we can sing, "My table thou hast furnished in the presence of my foes."

Take this truth in relation to life's daily conflict. We speak of the battle of life, and that is what it is for all of us, only not so much a pitched battle as a long-drawn-out conflict. Though we triumphed yesterday, the enemy awaits today. You can see their frowning faces and hear their devilish rage as you contemplate your day's work. But you need not go into the conflict unprepared. God not only spreads the table at which you eat your breakfast, for the battle of life you may be strengthened and satisfied. The spiritual table is spread, do not go into battle without having set down to it.

Let us go into some details of the conflict. Think of the temptations that lie in wait. Even our Lord had to face these foes and there is no exemption for any of us. Even as I speak some of you are naming the temptation that berates your path and dogs your steps. There is no expecting the conflict. Even if the grosser forms of temptation make little appeal to us, the devil lies in wait for us as he did for Jesus, tempts us to doubt our sonship, presume on God's law, and compromise with evil. But the God whose angels ministered to Jesus does not forget us. When Bunyan's Christian was almost beaten by Apollyon, he was fed and refreshed by the bread of God in preparation for the next conflict. God draws near to us and it is blessedly true that: "Temptations lose their power when Thou art nigh."

Or, think of the perils of persecution. Our foes may be flesh and blood enemies. They are not now emperors who threaten to confiscate our property or take our lives, but people who ridicule us, who scoff, men and women who try to browbeat us out of this way of life. There are critics of the faith we hold and antagonistic to the church we love. Often the foes seem overwhelming and the fight against them hopeless. But while they surround and attack us, God spreads the table, calls us to communion, and in the fellowship we are calm and strong. He grants us His peace and gives us a sense of security. There is a picture which shows a Christian girl the night before martyrdom. Her persecutors, in a final attempt to stamp out her faith, have put her in a cell separated only by iron bars from the lions to which she is to be cast on the morrow. Through the bars can be seen the hungry eyes of the lions as they glare upon their prey. The girl is seen sleeping on the rough ground as placidly as an infant on its mother's breast. God not only provided a table but gave rest, and he will not fail us.

Looking on we know that darkness and sorrow may afflict us. The sorrows of life encompass us. We suffer from events unto which we can put no meaning. There are problems that perplex and tragedies that almost drive us mad. The best we think we can sing is, "light after darkness." That is blessedly true, but it is not all the truth. "Unto the upright there ariseth light in darkness." There is not only "a calm beyond life's fitful fever," there is calm in the midst of it. God spreads a table and the promise of his presence makes it a sanctuary. In the house of mourning He lights the lamp of hope. In the dreary wilderness, we ask with the Jews of old, "Can God furnish a table in the wilderness?" He did and he can. In the wilderness, His table is spread and in the

"THE FEAST IN THE PRESENCE OF FOES"—PSALM 23.5

desert waters break forth. "Peace, perfect peace, with sorrows surging round, on Jesus' bosom nought but calm is found."[1]

Let me give, as I draw to a close, an application. This will mean little to the young folk, they may well spare a few minutes for the old. The fear of old age. That is a very real foe to many. They dread old age as an enemy. I heard an old lady say some time ago, "Enjoy life while you are young, no one wants you, and there is nothing for you when you are old." To her as to others, old age seemed dreary, the foe of life and pleasure. That is why the old pagan saying says, "Whom the gods love die young."[2] It took a Christian optimist to say, "Grow old along with me, the best is yet to be."[3]

God spreads a table and the foe we dread cannot touch our joy and peace. In fellowship with Him his own find happiness and rest. It is written of them that they shall bring forth fruit in old age. Life becomes deeper as it lengthens and at every time there is light. Asked at the close of a long life if religion still meant much to her, Julia Ward Howe replied, "All the sugar is at the bottom of the cup."

What a wonderful God ours is: spreading our tables bountifully even in the presence of our foes, giving us at all times rest and peace and the joy of fellowship. And even that is not the last word. The earthly table is the prophecy and foretaste of the Marriage Supper of the Lamb. The earthly fellowship is the prelude to the heavenly. "And if our fellowship below in Jesus be so sweet; what heights of rapture shall we know when round His throne we meet." In the last word is the best word, "I will dwell in the House of the LORD forever."

---

1. This is a line from a hymn of the same name by Edward H. Bickersteth written in 1875.
2. This is a quote from Menander speaking about the mythological figure Trophonius. See Robert Graves, "Cleobis and Biton," in *The Greek Myths* (New York: Penguin, 1990), 1:450.
3. This is another quote from Robert Barrett Browning.

"WORSHIP IN THE BEAUTY OF HOLINESS"
—Psalm 29.2

(Preached at Katherine Road 1/24/32)

Psalm 29.2 "Worship the LORD in the beauty of holiness."

THE OTHER SUNDAY MORNING, I listened, as I usually try to listen, with attention and sympathy, to hear what the word of the Lord was for me in the anthem the choir sang. There was a word for me and it was the word of our text. I have been thinking about it ever since and I am certain that there is only one greater word on the worship in the sanctuary, and that is the Lord's saying, "God is Spirit and they that worship Him must worship in spirit and in truth."

This is one of the texts that will stand alone, and without troubling you with references to the context, I may treat it as a call to make one worship carefully and becomingly. Let me just point out that in the translation of the Revised Version you have the alternative rendering "in holy array," while Dr. Moffatt translates "in festal attire." Putting these translations together we get the figure of a happy-hearted throng of worshippers, arrayed in their best, going up to the House of the Lord to worship their God.

WORSHIP ASSOCIATED WITH BEAUTY

This applies to what we call the place of worship. It has been a fine instinct which through the centuries has made devout hearts ill at ease until they saw the House of God made beautiful. Recall the anthem of the prayer when the Jew's first temple was built. And the greatly tuned hearts of the Jews who saw the temple restored and rebuilt—under Nehemiah's leadership. Yes, and recall what you have seen and felt, when, in modern days, some little company of worshippers has been able to beautify their sanctuary. The place set apart for the worship of God should be made and kept as beautiful as loving hands can make and keep it. That is why it cuts some of us like a knife to see irreverent handling and flippant use of the sanctuary and its furniture.

"WORSHIP IN THE BEAUTY OF HOLINESS"—PSALM 29.2

This applies, too, to the service within the sanctuary. The praise should be as beautiful as can be, with nothing slovenly and tawdry about the singing and nothing careless about the reading of God's word. The prayer, you will agree, should be as soulful and deliberate as talking with God ought to be and the sermon as fittingly phrased and delivered as is becoming of the eternal gospel. And this is not only for preachers and members of the choir, but for all. The idea is of worship in company, communal worship if you will. And you have not worshipped if you have simply been present at a service, you must participate in it. If you have a voice like a crow it is evident that the Lord did not mean you to be in the choir, and it is no use getting cross with the choir master because he won't have you. You are not thereby refused admission into the chorus of praise. I hope the day will never come when paid singers or skilled musicians do all the praying for us. "Let the people praise Thee! Let all the people praise Thee!"

But the main reference is to the worshippers. They are to come "in holy array." It matters what you are arrayed in. It was a true instinct which made our fathers and mothers talk about putting in their "Sunday best" for worship, and that caused church festivals to be the occasion for wearing new clothes. But what matters supremely is not the clothes put on your body, it is the raiment of your soul. The beauty is to be the beauty of holiness. Acceptable worshippers are clothed with humility. They have on the robe of reverence, the silk of sanctity, the broadcloth of benevolence, and over all they "put on love." Even the most acceptable sacrifice is that of a contrite heart and a prayerful spirit.

This is the real beauty of acceptable worship. Not simply that we have handsome buildings or services that are pleasing displays of entertainment in speech and song, or a well-dressed congregation. There have been times when eternal beauty got in the way of spiritual worship and when men deliberately went back to the simplicities. We have all known churches when the building lacked material beauty and the order of service was anything but ornate, and yet where the worship was in the beauty of holiness. One of the most pathetic things I know is to hear people excuse themselves from the service of God's House because they have not the clothes to come in. He would be a bold man who said that the worship of a meeting in an unadorned building, attended by people in robes grey, was unacceptable to God. My own home chapel is among the least of our United Methodist Zions or Bethels, it had a very amateur choir—I was in it—and its preachers were often crude and uneducated men, but in it I have known that God came down to greet our souls and glory to crown the mercy seat.

By all means, let us rejoice in our beautiful buildings, let us bring the best of music and elocution to our service. But remember that "God looketh on the heart," and it is in the beauty of holiness that we are to worship. There is little time left for the other two associations of worship, but they must be mentioned.

WORSHIP ASSOCIATED WITH GLADNESS

That is the reference from Dr. Moffatt's translation—"in festal array"—clothed as for a feast. "I was glad," said the psalmist, "when they said, 'let us go up to the House of God.'" We gain from this association that we should not be so reluctant and weary on a Sunday morning. Too often we come simply from a sense of duty and stay away at the slightest pretext. We must have missed the meaning of worship. Yet God has been at pains to make it clear that worship is to be joyous. The gospel is the best of good news. "Come, sinners to the Gospel feast, let every soul be Jesus' guest" catches the right note. If you want it set to better poetry and music, you have it in this: "This is the hour of banquet and of song, this is the heavenly table spread for me, here let me feast, and feasting, still prolong the brief bright hour of fellowship with Thee."

Put on your festal array and come to church as to a banquet. You don't want to be fetched or carried to a feast and you don't go as if you were going to your execution. Put on with your "Sunday best" the garment of praise, and join in the happy song, "Glad was my heart to hear my old companion say, 'Come, let us seek our God today.'" That is how you are to worship, in the beauty of holiness and gladness and singleness of heart.

WORSHIP ASSOCIATED WITH WARFARE

"In holy array" means not only what we are arrayed in, it means the way men are marshalled for some great contest. Often, we read of the army being set in array. In a matter of fact "Array" was the word of command given of old to English archers. Perhaps you have already realized the similarity between "Array" and "Hurray." All our services, and most notably the most sacred of all, our Commemorations, Communions, and Convocations. Our hymns are our rallying songs. The church is the Armory. Sermons are the reminders of the work Christ has done and that He is doing in the world. And we come as Christian soldiers who are marching as to war. This may seem like a mixing of metaphors, but the truth is single and straightforward. We do worship in the beauty of holiness and with gladness of heart, and in the very act of worship we are arrayed for that war in which there is no discharge, the endless warfare to keep ourselves unspotted from the world and to win for our Lord the kingdom over which it is His right to reign.

"KNOWN IN ADVERSITIES"
—Psalm 31.7

(Preached at Fentman Road, undated, Spring Head Mission 7/4/40, and Bishop St. 7/14/49)

Psalm 31.7 "Thou hast known my soul in adversities."

THIS IS ONE OF those pithy and pregnant sentences with which the book of Psalms abounds, which it pays to ponder. You might easily pass it by and think little of it, but once you have paused with it you find it full of meaning and comfort. It fell from the life of a man who had been through the furnace of the affliction and who came out with something he could take consolation in. God had seen his affliction and taken note of his distress. Ponder that and it will yield for you good fruit.

DIVINE REMEMBRANCE

To begin with, it brings an assurance of Divine remembrance in contrast to the forgetfulness of many. It is one of the commonplaces of our morals that the world encourages prosperity and shuns adversity. Perhaps we have ourselves suffered at the hands of those who flattered and fawned over us when all was well with us, and who passed us by when trouble and misfortune dogged our steps.

One of my dearest friends "came down" in the world. In his days of affluence, he displayed hospitality with a generous hand. Speaking of those whom he had often helped, he said with pain in his voice, "They don't want me now." Let us give that a larger setting. Gotthold, the German philosopher whose work brought comfort to countless people, tells of one who, by the calamities of war, sickness, and other afflictions, had been reduced from affluence to pennies. This man came to Gotthold in great distress. He complained that he had met a former acquaintance who had not condescended to bow, much less speak to him. He said he felt as if a dagger had pierced his heart. "Don't think it strange at all," said the teacher, "it is the way of the world to look high, and to pass unnoticed that which is humble and lowly. I know of one, however, of whom the royal prophet testifies, 'Thou hast known my soul in adversities.'"[1]

God remembers when the world forgets. He welcomes us when others are ashamed of us. Instead of driving Him from us our distress draw us to Him. His home is with us, with the humble and He dwells with the lowly. Here is the great comfort of the text. When other helpers fail, and sometimes they do, when comforts flee, and sometimes they have wings, He is the help of the helpless and he is already with us. He knows our soul in adversities. But there is a deeper note to sound. The Lord had not only remembered and helped the man when others passed him by, you have to put the emphasis on the "soul," which means the real self.

GOD KNEW HIS SOUL

The comfort of the psalmist was that God knew his soul in adversities. God was aware, not only of the circumstances that encompassed him, but also of the spirit in which he was meeting them. There is real comfort here, for so many men misjudge the state of our souls. Many are so made that they cannot reveal their souls to others, they must hide their hearts. They meet us, chat with us, and smile at us, when often their hearts are heavy and sad. Many a mother, worried ill, struggles on bravely and hides her infirmity from her family. The father deep in his own difficulties and worries, puts on a brave face and lets no one know. Everywhere is the camouflage of the courageous—cheerful looks, brave words, and proficient work—when the soul is heavy and cast down. In my own little way, in the discharge of my ministerial duties, I have had to go from the chamber of death to a marriage feast, and seem as happy as if there was not a sorrow in the world! The heart knoweth its own bitterness, and often the world is ignorant of it. Often the world is not only ignorant, it misjudges it. It mistakes courage for carelessness and heroism for hardness. It condemns where, if only it knew, it would comfort.

Or, like Job's comforters, men charge in with folly and in their ignorance give advice that only mocks us. They are well meaning, but because they do not know our souls, they are insistent and not helpful. With the best of intention their ceaseless chatter is like rubbing salt into a wound and we wish they would go. There is a poignant example in *Uncle Tom's Cabin*. A poor mother's child has been taken from her and sold. The trader who sold the child clumsily tries to console her. He says he knows that she is a smart, reasonable woman who will see it was all for the best. To which she replies, "O master, if you only will not talk to me now." Even the callous trader felt that there was such quick and living anguish in the words that he pressed no further. But not everyone has the sense of the trader. They talk and talk, and pass out platitudes which hurt far more than they heal. They do not know our souls.

1. He is in fact referring to Gotthold Lessing, the famous German philosopher of the eighteenth century.

And further, there is a point at which human knowledge at its best fails and beyond which human sympathy cannot go. Jesus came to a place where, even to the man who loved Him best, He had to say, "Tarry ye here while I go and pray yonder." Into the deepest recesses of our own Gethsemane, our most understanding and sympathetic friends and lovers cannot go. "Oft through the world we smoothly go, hiding some secret curse, our nearest, dearest, may not know, which God alone can share."

That is the statement of the case and holds the promise of comfort. God knows our soul in adversities. He knows its real state, its deep needs, and can sooth and hush and calm it. He never mistakes or misjudges. Known to Him are our secret cares and open to Him are the innermost recesses of the soul. That was the psalmist's comfort and it should be ours.

GOD'S KNOWLEDGE IS NOT IDLE CONTEMPLATION

Active intention is implied in it. To say that God takes note of the soul in its distresses is the same as to say He cares for it. He loves as well as knows. He looks on no grief he cannot comfort, nor on any wounds He is not ready to bind up. When God says, "I have surely seen the affliction of my people," He immediately adds, "And I am come down to deliver them." The psalmist was sure God had seen his adversity because he had experienced God's delivering power. It was when his soul had been lifted from its adversities and limitations into a large place that he wrote with gratitude and joy, "Thou hast known my soul in adversities." He was remembering not the distresses but the deliverance. He knows God had known and bowed and helped. We have his experience to build on, and the experience of many another since his day, who have found God's knowledge and love all sufficient. To our plaintive cry: "Be with me when no other friend, the mystery of my heart can share; and be Thou known when fears transcend, by the best name of Comforter." Then comes the answer: "Well I have thy troubles, O my servant true! Thou are very weary; I was weary too. But the toil shall make thee someday all mine own, and the end of sorrow shall be near my throne." Yes, God knows our soul in adversities for the Son has passed through them all.

"THE AUSTERITIES OF THE HILLS"
—Psalm 84.5

(Preached at Spring Head 2/21/37, and at Bishop Street under the title THE CHALLENGE OF THE HEIGHTS 2/15/48)

Psalm 84.5 "Blessed is the man whose strength is in thee; in whose heart are the ways of them."

As it stands in the Authorized Version, that does not sound like a suitable text for a sermon on the austerity of the hills. Indeed, this verse has often puzzled devout readers. A man is hard pressed to find any clear meaning in it at all. It is a text that needs clarifying. Moffatt helps in his translation:

"Happy are they who, nerved by thee, set out on pilgrimage!"

But the real meaning of the text is brought out in the Vulgate Version of the Bible:

"Blessed is the man who, nerved by thee, hath set his heart in ascents."

That makes the meaning of the text perfectly clear and gives us a very suitable and helpful starting point for our meditation on one of the most dramatic beatitudes of the Old Testament.

THE CALL

Let us begin at once with the challenge of the heights, and read in it the call to something instinctive in man. There is a call from the heights to the depths of man. That in him are the common levels of ambition. Men have been challenged by literal mountains and have given their lives in attempts to scale them. You may call it folly but it is much more than that. There is something in humankind that will not let him rest until he has stood upon the roof of the world.

In social life, the heights challenge us. We have our ups and downs, but we are inveterate climbers. We say that if only we could reach a certain level we would be content. But we are not. Every goal reached becomes the starting point of fresh endeavors. Every success becomes a threshold to a new effort. Each victory sets us trying to win some other victory.

"THE AUSTERITIES OF THE HILLS"—PSALM 84.5

The history of man may be written as "the ascent of man." Tennyson writes of man as "moving upward working out the beast, and letting the ape and tiger die."[1] After two very nasty conflicts in one generation we are not so confident. But in spite of falls and setbacks something within a human being keeps his heart set on the heights. He was made to have dominion and gradually he is getting things under his feet.

But it is of the realm of the Christian life that we are thinking specially. Often, we are low enough, God knows and we know. But when we were born again we were born for the heights. When we became "partakers of the divine nature" something was given us which will forever be seeking the hills of God. The heart of every man nerved of God will be set in the ascents. Often enough we are down in the valley, but we lift our eyes and our hearts to the hills. We are challenged by the heights, and in our best moments we want to ascend unto the hill of the Lord and we can never be content in the valley.

THE CALL OF THE IDEAL

Interpret the challenge of the heights as the call of the ideal. The vision of the ideal calls men to attempt its realization. In the midst of things as they are they see a vision of what might be and should be and then they seek to translate deeds into dreams and visions into realities. Again, we are thinking mainly of the ideal of the awakened nature. Whatever we have been and are, we have seen a vision of what might be in Christ. We needs must have the highest when we see it. Of course, we may dim our light and darken our vision until we are like Bunyan's man with the muckrake grasping for straws and missing the crown that is held out. But we have not come to that yet.

On the Damascus Road, Paul saw a vision and was not disobedient unto it. Years after, he conferred that he had not comprehended all that the vision held but he was still following, striving, ascending. That is how it is with us also. Years ago, we saw a vision of the man and woman God meant us to be. The vision still shines before us. We have not yet ascended and we are not yet satisfied. But still the vision haunts us and climbs before us. There can be no complete satisfaction until the ideal becomes the actual. It is God who nerved us for the ascents. He is always saying "come up further," calling us to the heights of holiness, to be emptied of evil and filled with good, to be more like the ideal revealed in Jesus. It is not without significance that we seek the higher life. Seek for a heart in every thought renewed and full of love divine. Lift your heart toward the high way, toward the ascents that lead to the hills of God, and strive toward the goal of the ideal life.

---

1. This is from one of Tennyson's most famous poems, "In Memoriam."

LUMINESCENCE

THE CHALLENGE OF THE DIFFICULT

It follows, inevitably, that the call of the hills is the challenge of the difficult. Mountain climbing is not for the soft, lovers of ease. It is for those who are not afraid of difficulties and danger and are willing to face a stern contest with unrelenting forces. It taxes the limbs and nerves and heart. Of those who ascend mountains of eminence and influence, Longfellow says, "They, while their companions slept, were toiling upward in the night."[2]

It is not for me to say that spiritual mountaineering, the ascent to the ideal, is easy. There are competing interests and levels of contentment with incomplete attainments and the unfulfilled ideal. There is the lure of the easy valley. The youth who "through an alpine village passed," and who bore a banner with the strange device that told of his intent to scale the heights may well be a parable of a spiritual ascent. He had to face the dark and lowering tempest; the roaring torrent that was deep and wide. The old man said, "Try not the pass," the maid urged, "Oh stay and rest thy weary head." Does that sound a bit romantic and highfalutin? Well, you try tomorrow to live the ideal life and you will find it is not fancy but fact. Unless you are prepared to face difficulties, brave dangers, and endure hardships, you will never become what God means you to be. You will never ascend the hills of God. It is harder to climb the hills of God than to climb Mount Everest, and you will make the ascent the same way, by careful planning, feeling every inch of the way, and referring to the leader.

THE GOSPEL FOR THE CLIMBERS

There is no mistaking the austerities of the hills, nor must we forget the gospel for the climbers. It is God who set the instinct for the heights and the love of the eternal in our hearts. He nerves us for the ascents, helps our quest, and advances our purpose. We persevere in the ascents of grit and we do not forget the ascents of grace. "He will make my feet like hind's feet." The deer is swift and sure footed. "There is a way for man to rise," sang Thomas Binney, and he went on to sing of something more than a way—a Holy Spirit's energies.

Maybe you will tell me that my own parable tells against me. You will quote another verse from Longfellow's poem: "A traveler, by the faithful hound, half buried in the snow found, still grasping in his hand of ice, that banner with the strange device—Excelsior!" I have not forgotten that verse, but remember that that is neither the end nor the climax. "And from the sky serene and far, a voice fell like a falling star—Excelsior!"[3] His body lay stiff and cold on the alpine slopes but his soul had ascended the heights of the sky. And if we hold undeterred in our way we shall come where we

---

2. This is from stanza 10 of the poem "The Ladder of St. Augustine."
3. This is from a different poem by the same poet, a poem entitled "Excelsior."

"THE AUSTERITIES OF THE HILLS"—PSALM 84.5

want to be. For "he will lead us safely in the paths that He has trod, up to where they gather in the rest of God."

In a little church yard in Switzerland on the stone that marks the resting place of one who perished in an alpine accident, it reads "he died climbing." He had heard the call of the heights and lost his life in response. Let us love climbing, ever seeking the things which are above. We shall not lose our lives, but gain them and find our way into the glorious liberty of the children of God.

∼

"THE SOUL'S STRONGHOLD"
—Psalm 91.1

(Preached at Spring Head Mission 7/5/42)

Psalm 91.1 "He that dwelleth in the secret place of the Most High shall abide under the shadow of the Almighty."

OF ALL SONGS OF happy and perfect trust in Divine protection, this is perhaps the sunniest and best. It follows the solemn sadness of the nineteenth psalm "like a summer morning after a night of pain." It was the favorite psalm of General Gordon and has been the favorite of many folk. Through a long life, it was the stay and strength of one of my old friends (Chris Baver of Centenary Rd.) and in death it was her comfort and hope. It was as I read it to her when she was nearing the river that this sermon was born.

THE PSALMIST'S PROBLEM AND OURS

The psalmist was facing a problem as old as the hills and as new as today's sunrise, the problem of preserving the soul uncontaminated and inviolate in the teeth of the antagonisms and assaults of the world. We are all subject to influences that make for deterioration and destruction. The forces which war against the soul abound at every turn. It is our task to keep ourselves pure and at peace, to come through undefiled and undisturbed. The problem is where we can find a sure refuge and a safe stronghold from the assaults of evil and the looming cares and racking anxieties of life. Where may the soul dwell in security, purity, and peace?

THE STRONGHOLD OF THE SOUL

The psalmist found such a dwelling place, tested and proved it, and then laid bare the secret. He that dwells in the secret place of the Most High dwells in safety and abides in peace. The "secret place" probably suggests the Most Holy Place in the temple. That temple had an outer courtyard, a porch facing east, a central hall, and an inner sanctuary. In the Temple not made with hands there is a similar arrangement. Many never get beyond the outer court. It is the choice souls who get through to the inner sanctuary who dwell in peace and security and are kept unspoiled from the world.

The secret places are not geographical points but spiritual experiences. To dwell in them is to pan through all the externals of religion to a union with God and fellowship with Him. It is to find the spot where spirits blend and Jesus sheds the oil of gladness on our heads. Note, too, that the suggestion is not that of paying occasional visits but abiding, dwelling there. That means unceasing prayer and unbroken fellowship. We have to live in the world, face its responsibilities, and carry our burdens. We live in the world, but we must dwell in the secret place if we would find the soul's refuge.

Before I go in to speak of the value of all this for our lives, let me point out that the psalm passes from a general statement to an expression of personal faith. It is worthwhile spending a few minutes in examining the structure of the psalm. The first verse has the general statement. In the second verse you have the psalmist's solemn act of self-dedication—"I will say of the Lord, He is my refuge and my fortress." Perhaps it was the solo in the anthem. Then follows the statement of the blessings that follow such personal dedication. Perhaps that was where the choir took up the chorus. At verse 14 another voice is introduced. It is the voice of God and gives His loving response to personal trust. What I want to emphasize just now is this—the general statement is true, "he that dwells in the secret place of the Most High shall abide under the shadow of the Almighty." But faith is far more than intellectual acceptance of great truths. It is one thing to say, "He that dwelleth, etc.," and another thing altogether, "I will say of the Lord He is my refuge." The psalmists were never afraid of the use of the possessive pronoun. "The LORD is my shepherd," "the LORD is my light and my salvation," "the LORD is the strength of my life." It is not until you put in your claim and make God yours by personal acceptance that the blessings named become yours.

VALUE FOR PRACTICAL LIFE

It is clearly stated and is attested by experience:

(1) We begin on the negative side. The "secret place," the soul's stronghold, is neither a coward's castle nor a funk hole. It is not a place to which people run to hide from the responsibilities and burdens of life. Here is no promise of immunity from adversity, trouble, temptation, and pain. It is not exemption from these things but security in the midst of them that is promised. They may all come, but the soul that dwells in the secret place is entrenched in an impregnable stronghold.

(2) Consider the promises on the positive side. "He shall deliver thee from the snare of the fowler, etc." The snares and assaults of evil will be in vain. Neither subtle secret temptations nor open bullying evils shall overcome the soul that dwells in God. God's truth is the soul's shield and buckler and no harm comes to it.

(3) The soul is invincible as well as invulnerable. "Thou shalt tread upon the lion and the adder, etc." We can not only resist the evil, we can triumph over it and make conquered foes the stepping stones to nobler heights.

(4) As we have seen at verse 14, the psalmist speaks for God and no words of mine can equal the eight "I wills" of God. Listen to them: "Because he has set his love on me: I will deliver him. I will set him on high. I will answer him. I will be with him in trouble. I will deliver him. I will know him. With long life, I will satisfy him. I will show him my salvation." Why not say here and now, "I will say of the LORD, He is my refuge and fortress, my God, in Him will I trust?" Then, instead of living under the shadow of a great fear, you will abide under the shadow of God's throne and find peace and purity.

"SETTING THE LAW TO MUSIC"
—Psalm 119.54

(Preached at Spring Head Mission 9/12/43 and Bishop Street 8/4/46)

Psalm 119.54 "Thy statutes have been my songs in the house of my pilgrimage."

"When the eastern traveler takes shelter from the scorching heat of the sun, or halts for the night in some inn or caravanserai, which for the time is the house of his pilgrimage, he takes the sackbut or the lyre and sooths his rest with song—maybe of war, romance, or love. But the poet of Israel finds his theme in the statutes of Jehovah." With these words, Horace Bushnell begins his great sermon on this text.[1]

Later scholars have seen deeper meaning within the text, and we shall come to it. But that is no reason for overlooking Bushnell's interpretation and his comment. It is not too much to say that men are judged by their songs. If a man's delight is in songs that are vulgar and smutty you do not need telling what kind of a man he is. If he listens often to songs that are comic and youthful or chatters through classical music, he stands condemned as having a trivial and trifling spirit. When a man finds his joy in singing or listening to the songs of Zion we know that in his heart is love of the heavenly and eternal.

Most of us know that we are on pilgrimage. We talk about the journey of life and passing its milestones. There is nothing wrong, but a great deal of good in finding resting places where we can cheer our hearts by singing the Lord's songs. Nor is it surprising that some of our sweetest songs speak about peace and singing in someplace of eternal rest. In this way, God's statutes, the Divine Will, God's ways and works, are the theme of the songs we sing as we rest along the way.

We sound a deeper note, however, when we say that the list sets us to learn the music of obedience. It teaches us, not only to sing of God's statutes when the day's marching is done, but to set the life of obedience to those statutes to a marching and musical strain. That is not always the spirit in which we keep our Lord's commands. We talk of duty as the "stern lawgiver" and tread the hall of obedience with reluctant

---

1. This sermon by Bushnell is entitled "Obligation a Privilege," and it can be found at http://biblehub.com/sermons/psalms/119-54.htm.

hearts and leaden feet. If we set the statutes to music, it is in the minor key. If we sing, "Thy will be done," we sing it as one who only accepts it because it cannot be avoided. "But," says a great thinker who had to learn her own lesson on the hard road, "obedience is not the prudence of invalids. It does not crawl along life's backways, it marches to music along life's highway in the vanguard of a victorious army."[2]

We all know how the striking up of a band gives a lift to the head and a lift to the spirits of soldiers who follow it. I think we should think of ourselves as Christian soldiers marching to a real war, with the cross of Jesus going on before, and keeping in step with the saints and martyrs who marched to their battle to the music of great songs. What a difference it would make to us! What an impression it would make on the world, if instead of stumbling along like weary walkers we stroll along the hall of obedience saying bravely and ever gaily, "Have thine own way."

But there is the rub, you say. The commandments of God are stern and forbidding, they interfere with our liberty and satisfied life with statements of "thou shalt not." How can we sing as we go? It is here that we sound the deepest note of our text and consider how the statute becomes a song.

Nothing seems less singable than a statute. It seems unthinkable to set laws to music. Yet here is one who has learned the secret and declares, "Thy statutes have become my songs." For this man, the Law had ceased to be burdensome and become pleasant, duty had become delight, and statutes had turned into joy. He had learned the music of obedience. That is the music we are set to learn, not only to march to music, but to turn the statutes into songs, to find the delight and life in the duties of life.

Our music master is one greater than the psalmist. He is our Lord and Savior who in the face of difficulties, danger, and death said "I delight to do thy will, O my God." We have to follow and learn from Him whose desire forever it was to do the Father's will with gladness. Whose life was not that of a sullen, reluctant, constrained obedience, but one of free, glad, and willing service. In Jesus, the statutes were songs sung to do the will of God.

How then, for us, can statutes be converted into songs? Through clearer knowledge. It is when we are ignorant and ill-informed of the Divine requirements that we find the laws restrictive and repellent. What is it that the Lord requires of thee? Once that is your question you have learned our first lesson in the music of obedience. Pray with the psalmist, "Open thou mine eyes that I may behold wondrous things out of thy Law," and the answering vision will reveal the delight of duty. The statutes of the Lord are right, rejoicing the heart, says the man who had learned His lines. When you hear the line of Wordsworth, do not forget to finish the sentence: "Stern Lawgiver! Yet thou dost wear, the Godhead's most benignant grace; nor know we anything so fair, as the smile upon your face."[3]

---

2. I cannot find the source of this quotation.
3. This is from Wordsworth's poem "Ode to Duty."

"SETTING THE LAW TO MUSIC"—PSALM 119.54

Through clearer knowledge the binder becomes life and the statute becomes a song. An honest and earnest attempt at obedience is one thing. It is when we hesitate or repudiate the laws of God that they appear unpleasant or irksome. The man who sets himself to keep them discovers that they become easy and pleasant. The law of the Lord has given both facility and felicity of execution. What I mean by this is illustrated by learning to play the piano. How tiresome are those finger exercises! But with patient endurance the lines of music are mastered and what a delight the sound becomes!

Like many of you I was brought up by the good and wholesome lines: "Honor thy father and thy mother," "children obey your parents." That was not always easy, especially when their will contradicted my wishes. But now life holds far greater songs than that of doing anything that gives my mother joy. Reform to the demands of God and you will find they are all congenial. Practice your scales, however distasteful it is, you will find joy in it. It is by constant practice that the statute becomes a song.

Love transforms the statute into a song. When God's love kindles love in our hearts and we love Him with all our hearts, the rest is easy. Love transcends legality. I never ask a bride to promise to obey, when she and her husband love one another there is no need. When there is real love, duty received becomes delight. Love makes its own laws. Professor Seeley says, "Love, wheresoever it appears, is in its measure a lawmaking power. Love is dutiful in thought and deed."[4] If we love our Lord we shall not want for commands, but we shall not always follow His will and articulate His command. Jesus knew that and the only guarantee He asked or took was love. The more the law of God is obeyed in our hearts the more completely is obligation forgotten in privilege. The ideal is reached when the only constraint is the love of Christ. That was the secret of Paul's expectant enthusiasm, and it will be the source of a glad service and patient endurance. "All's Law," say some. Yes, say the poets, and they add, "All's law, yet all's love." We set ourselves to keep the laws of God and find the task distasteful, but with clearer knowledge, persistent practice, and growth in love we find that keeping the commandments we are dwelling in God's love. What we discover is that "God's commandments are not the external mandates of an impersonal law-giver, they are love in the imperative mood."[5]

As so often, Bunyan has the master illustration. One whose name was Secret gave to Christian a letter from her husband's king, which "smelt after the manner of the best perfume, also it was written in letters of gold." Said Secret, "I advise that thou put this letter in thy bosom. That thou read therein to thyself and to thy children until you have got it by heart. For it is one of the songs thou must sing while thou art in the house of thy pilgrimage." "If you love me," says Jesus, "ye shall keep my commandments." Keeping them for love's sake will turn the statutes into songs.

---

4. This quote can be found in Richard Tudor, *The Philosophy of Church Life*, vol. 2, 620. Tudor is dealing with a quote from William Wordsworth.

5. I cannot find the source of this quote.

"DISTANT AND NEAR"
—Proverbs 17.24

(Preached fifteen times from Katherine Road 7/12/36 to Thornhill, Sunderland 10/28/51)

Proverbs 17.24 "Wisdom is before him that hath understanding; but the eyes of the fool are in the ends of the earth."

THERE IS A DISEASE of the eyes known to oculists as hypermetropia. Those afflicted with it are able to see distant objects with comparative clearness, but are almost blind to what is close at hand. There is a similar disease of what the Bible calls "the eyes of the heart," and this proverb has reference to it. With the bluntness characteristic of this book the man is called a fool who is forever stargazing into blue distances and neglecting what lies close to hand.

We have a good-natured proverb of our own which suggests that we have not outgrown the ancient folly—"far fowls have fine feathers." It is still one of our habits to magnify the distant and despise what is at our own door. The house with the golden windows is always at the other side of the valley. That is not to say that all farsighted men are fools. It is reasonable and wise for every man now and then to lift his eyes from the immediate to the distant. To lift one's eyes to the hills at times is to find strength for the trudging of life's rough roads. Beholding "the land that is very far off" strengthens faith and confirms the hope of the Golden City that is to be. There is no rebuke here or anywhere in Proverbs for men and women who, in moments of exalted vision, see past what is to what is to be, and who glimpse far more than they grasp.

The rebuke is for those whose eyes are always in the ends of the earth and who fail to find any interest, romance, beauty, and service in their immediate surroundings and the present time. All such deserve the rebuke, for obviously such stargazing leads to neglect, blindness and probably disaster. In Switzerland, there is a monument to an artist who was killed while painting, on the precipitous shores of Lake Lucerne, the mountain peaks on the other side. The distant vision filled his eyes and his canvas with beauty but he did not ponder the path of his feet. More than a few have stumbled to moral disaster and death through spiritual hypermetropia. Let us mark some of the ways in which the folly reveals itself in modern life.

"DISTANT AND NEAR"—PROVERBS 17.24

IN FAILURE TO RECOGNIZE BEAUTY AND HEROISM IN OUR IMMEDIATE SPHERE

It is a commonplace that many are unconscious of the material beauty that surrounds them. Swiss tourists, we are told, marvel that tourists travel hundreds of miles to see their mountains, and we know that Londoners only visit their historic spots when entertaining country cousins. Still greater is the folly of those who scoff at their lot and think that happiness lies only in another sphere. The "trivial round, the common task" furnish interest and beauty for those who have eyes to see. Writers like George Eliot and Charles Dickens have shewn, and with fine sympathy, how rich in interest and romance are the ordinary lives of common people. It has been pointed out that Robert Burns lived in sight of grand mountains, but found his chief interest and the subjects of his poems in common tipped daises, field mice, and a little group gathered about a family hearth and altar. In noble strains he sang, "To keep a happy fireside clime for weans and wife, that's the true pathos and sublime of human life."[1]

Where are our eyes? We go into raptures over the painted beauty or the latest film star, and miss the infinitely greater beauty of some little woman who, without murmur or boast, lives a life of self-sacrifice for the sake of her man. We shout ourselves hoarse over the hero of a fight or a race or a game and miss the greater courage of the man who fights an unending battle against poverty, temptations, and discouragement that he may give his children a chance and leave them the inheritance of an untarnished name. We suffer ourselves to be discontented and are happy because our sphere is narrow and straight when we might find interest and love and a great opportunity in it.

FOLLY APPEARS IN FAILURE TO FIND THE WORK OF LIFE CLOSE AT HAND

"Do the duty that lies nearest thee," says Carlyle.[2] But the farsighted fool sees no near duty. His eyes are in the ends of the earth, he sees only beams of the duty at a distance. We talk glibly about the service of humanity. What needs to be done and ought to be done for humankind. In his interests, legislation needs to be speeded up and social reforms introduced! They do, heaven knows they do. But legislation is slow and time is fleeting. Your duty and mine is to humans. It is easy to talk about humanity and its needs. I can do it with my feet encased in comfortable slippers and as I sit with a healthy appetite before a good meal. But my duty lies with a poverty-stricken or ailing family on the next road—that means kicking off my slippers, leaving my comfortable study, going out into a germ-laden atmosphere to speak a word of comfort and lend a

---

1. This is a form of a couple of lines from a humorous poem by Burns, entitled "Epistle to Dr. Blacklock."
2. This is from Thomas Carlyle's *Sartor Resartus* (1833–1834), bk. 2, ch. 9.

hand. The missionary call is the grandest that can come to anybody, and I pray it may come to some of you, meanwhile your duty is in your own borough, at your own door.

We feel quite good as we sing "From Greenland's Icy Mountains" in a warm and comfortable room, we can see the colors and we don't feel the cold. We can see a lovely picture as we sing of "Africa's sunny fountains," and we don't have to swelter under a broiling tropical sun, endure the malignant flies, or suffer with black water fever.[3] What's the good of saying what we would do for the Chinaman we have not seen if we neglect our own neighbor?

Come nearer still. We are all fond of saying we would die for those who love us if a crisis arose. We would die for them, but they don't want us to. The demand is far simpler and the duty much nearer. You'd die for your old dad! Will you go for a walk with him some time and give him your confidence? You'd die for your old mother! Will you man a dance and stay in a night or two to wash up pots and darn socks? The test of our love is not in talk but in actions. It is not my eloquent speech at the mass meeting that counts so much as the way I treat the tired bus conductor who brings me home. Call in your eyes from the ends of the world, stop talking about what you would do, just "do the work that's nearest, though it's dull at whiles, helping where we meet them lame dogs over stiles."[4]

When I hear people talking loudly and shirking badly, I want to quote Kingsley again and use the full blooded language of Saunders MacKaye to the tailor poet—"What the devil! Is there no harlotry and idolatry here in England that ye maun gang speering after it in the South Sea Islands . . . If God had meant you to write about the Pacifics, He'd a'put you there . . . because He means you to write about London he's put you there."[5] God has put you and your work together. Find it and do it, your reward for going it will be the only reward honest men seek—more work and a wider sphere.

SEE FOLLY IN FAILURE TO SEE ROMANCE AND OPPORTUNITIES IN WHAT WE ARE PLEASED TO CALL DULL AND PROSAIC DAYS

There are people who are forever talking about the specious days of old. "When every day brought out a noble chance, and every chance brought out a noble knight."[6] If only they had lived in the days of Cromwell, they would have shewn his sternness and his strength. They would have died at the stake if they had lived in the martyrs days of old. If they had lived in the first century they would have eclipsed the fervor and faith of Whitefield and Wesley. But for them, there is no romance, there are no golden opportunities in these days. They are buried in the past and dead to the present. Their

---

3. He is quoting a hymn by Reginald Heber (1819), the first line of which is "From Greenland's Icy Mountains."
4. This is another quote from Charles Kingsley, from "The Invitation."
5. This is taken from a work by Kingsley entitled "Tailor and Poet."
6. This is from Tennyson's poem "Morte d'Arthur."

eyes are in the faraway past and so they are blind to the splendor and grandeur of the churches of their own time. What shall it profit a man if he lives in the past and is a slacker in the present.

Others there are whose eyes are always in some distant golden future. They postpone all their reformations and resolutions. They are always waiting for a convenient reason only they call it the psychological moment. When shall he learn that this is our golden time and that our days are rich in opportunity? With green branches Russell Lowell warns and lashes us—"We're curus critters, now ain't jes the minute that ever fits us while we're in it. Long ez twas the future, 'twould be perfect bliss. Soon ez it's the past, that times with ten o' this. And yet there ain't a man that need be told that now's the only bird lays eggs of gold."[7]

If you want it more seriously than that, let another American poet, Longfellow, tell you the same truth. "Trust no future, how'er pleasant! Let the dead past bury the dead! Act—act in the living present! Heart within and God o'erhead!"[8] And if you want it from the Word of God, here it is, "Now is the accepted time and now is the day of salvation."

Look at now. Keep your eyes open. Every day will bring you your chances of getting and doing good. This year of our Lord is as rich in opportunities as every year if you have a willing mind and a ready hand. And let me add the word without which this would not be complete as a gospel sermon. Too often our eyes are in the ends of the world when we think about salvation. We seek for Abanas and Pharpars far away. If we were bid to do some great thing we would do it. But salvation is so near and so simple that we miss it. The Savior is here, seeking you now. His hand is on the latch of your heart's door. He is waiting to come in and bring you pardon, peace, and power. Today, here and now, "If ye will hear His voice, harden not your hearts." Bid Him enter and He will save you now.

∼

---

7. This comes from *The Complete Poetical Works of James Russell Lowell*, part 11.
8. This is from Longfellow's poem "A Psalm of Life."

"THE HEARTH OF GOD"
—Isaiah 31.9

(Preached seventeen times from Fentiman Road to Swannington, dated only for Spring Head Mission 2/7/37)

Isaiah 31.9 "The Lord, whose fire is in Zion and His furnace in Jerusalem."

THAT SOUNDS LIKE A terrible and terrifying text. Fire is so often the symbol of consuming and destroying energy. In the Bible, it typifies the wrath of God. A little later on, in the thirty-third chapter, the prophet speaks of the devouring fire and the everlasting burnings. When men have tried to describe hell, they have talked of a place where the consuming flames are never quenched. No wonder, then, that this is a text we have skipped.

But if only we had given time and attention to it, we should have realized that most great forces work in two directions. The same force that on one side consumes and destroys, has a side that comforts and heals. Water may come in floods and destroy and devastate, but it may come to cleanse and quench. Fire can consume and devour, but it warms our homes and boils the water for our cup of tea. Electricity may kill, but it's very handy to switch on in a dark night.

We can carry the truth over to Divine forces and to God Himself. Here, too, there are the two sides. The chapter from which our text is taken provides a striking illustration. In verse 4 there is a magnificent picture of a young lion roaring in the majesty of his strength—the sort of animal we would wish to avoid. But it is used as a metaphor for God defending His people. The tremendous strength and energy are used for protection and peace. God is represented as the strong one standing over Israel and daring their strongest foes to come on.

Later on, the figure changes and God who was represented by a strong lion is pictured under the figure of a mother bird, fluttering over her nest and spreading her wings to protect her young. You get the same idea of God in Jesus. To those who believe He is a tried and precious stone, but to unbelievers He is a rock of offence. "Whosoever shall fall on this stone shall be broken: but on whomsoever it shall fall it shall grind him to powder." This ought to prepare us for the truth that—

"THE HEARTH OF GOD"—ISAIAH 31.9

THE FIGURE USED IN OUR TEXT HAS A DOUBLE ASPECT

Doubtless there is a sense in which the fire of God is consuming and His furnace for destruction. But the emblem is as rich in joy and blessing as in warning and terror. Dr. Moffatt's translation brings out the gracious and tender aspect at once: "Whose hearth is in Zion, and whose home-fires are within Jerusalem." And if I may take another minute for exposition, Dr. George Adam Smith has a suggestion worthy of note. He sends us back to chapter 29 where Jerusalem is called Ariel, which means "the hearth of God."

Now the idea should be clear. God as fire is a terror to evildoers and a consuming and devouring energy towards evil works. But His presence in His city is as a fire for the comfort and defense of His happy people. And my special point here is that, if God dwelt in this way in Jerusalem, it is true also to say that He dwells in the city of great David's greater Son, that is the Hearth of God where the home-fires burn. Now we ought to have a figure pregnant with lessons for the whole church. Let us begin with the literal picture of—

THE CHURCH AS THE HEARTH OF GOD WITH THE HOME-FIRES BURNING BRIGHTLY

This, to an Englishman, suggests almost the last word of comfort and contentment. In cold weather the ideal is to gather round the blazing fire in what we call a circle—like Bob Cratchett we mean half of one—with loved ones and genial companions in happy fellowship and helpful talk. Travelers and colonists tell us that, notwithstanding all the advantages of central heating, they miss the cheery fire round which friends can gather. In the dark days of the war nothing gripped the hearts of exiled sons and lonely fathers and mothers like, "Keep the home-fires burning."

I say that the church is intended to be the hearth of God. We often speak of this "cold world." The church is the opposite. It is the place where the home fires brightly burn. "The Church's task," says James Reid, "is to give to the social outcast the feel of home and the sense of a family life." The church is indeed a fellowship of warmed hearts. Around the glowing fire men and women gather for glad fellowship. That idea is central in the Methodist Church.

The Methodist Class Meeting was started as a place where redeemed men and women could gather to warm themselves at the fire and talk of their redemption and Redeemer. Whether we go back to the old forms of fellowship or not, I crave few things more for the church, our own church and all the churches, than that it should be the hearth of God to which those who have found the world cold and hard may turn and find themselves within a circle of light and warm fellowship. When the church is what it was intended to be, there is no need for men to warm themselves at the world's fires. So do you who are members of the church keep the home fires burning and find a place and give a welcome to all who come in? Let us follow the same line a little further.

THE PRESENCE OF GOD AS FIRE IN THE CHURCH MEANS THE PRESENCE OF A FLAME OF SACRED LOVE

In every land and language fire is the symbol of emotion, ardent love, fervent feelings, and blazing enthusiasms. And to say that God is in the church is to say that He dwells there in pure and passionate love. "How comes it," asks Dr. Maclaren, "that so many churches are the ice-houses instead of furnaces?"[1] That is a pertinent and searching question. Many of our churches are cold and hard. Methodist churches used to be described as furnaces. You would not so describe many of them now. Someone said of a certain church that it was "the cream of nonconformity." "Yes," someone else said, "but it's the ice cream." A cold church is a contradiction in terms. Such a church will attract no outsiders, and those inside will be stunted in their growth. The strangest malady I know is for church which is the hearth of God to be lukewarm, callous, and indifferent. If you want to know what Christ thought of such a church read the letter to the Church at Laodicea.

How can a church which is the hearth of God be an ice house and not a hot house? I only know one reason—we do not get near enough to the fire. We attend the services, sometimes. But we do not go to get near to God. We go to hear a preacher, to meet our friends, to find recreation and social fellowship. All good things in their way, but they are only the porch, and porches are cold, draughty places. The hearth fire is the altar fire, you only get near it when you get near the place of communion sacrifice. If we realized God's presence in the church is a flame of sacred love the spiritual temperature would go up immediately. More than that, our own hearts would catch fire and we should radiate the light and warmth of Divine love.

I am often told that there is the danger of an "emotional religion." I am also told that we are cutting out emotion, that love is giving place to the science of eugenics and that kissing is not hygienic, that really enlightened people don't do these things. Well, I don't believe it, and I can make you skeptical in ten minutes. Take a walk down your local Lover's Lane and see the number of strong arms encircling slender waists and the tired heads resting on manly shoulders. I have no use for an emotionalism which has no foundation in intelligence and principle, which is not regulated by wisdom, and which does not work or its living. But I simply cannot understand a religion without emotion, and I cannot imagine a religion which is fellowship with Eternal Love being too devout to sing and too phlegmatic to be stirred to enthusiasm. Instead I want to sing, "Oh that all might catch the flame!" Let us draw near to the hearth, commune round the fire, then we shall catch the flame and be mightily moved by love to holy

---

1. This is from a sermon on Isa 31.9 by the famous preacher Alexander MacLaren.

heroism, great endeavors, and whole-hearted consecration. The flame of sacred love will be kindled in the altar of our hearts and will burn with me inextinguishable blaze. There is another thought and it is complementary to what has been said.

THE FIRE WHICH WARMS CLEANSES ALSO

We are becoming familiar with the idea of cleansing by fire. Up-to-date towns have their disinfecting ovens. Fire is a better cleanser than water. Water cleanses the surface and is infected in the process. Fire cleanses within and without and is not tainted thereby. High temperature kills disease and germs and infected articles come out pure.

The cleansing of the soul is as by fire. John baptized with water, but Jesus with the Holy Ghost fire. God purifies the soul, not by some external application, but by getting up the heat. In the sacred temperature, the poison germs of sin die. That is not only a figure, it is a fact. In the warmth of God's love our love of sin perishes. The passionate enthusiasms He kindles bar unworthy passions. That is a great line in one of the hymns, "Perish self in Thy pure fire." We might well make the whole verse a prayer. "Holy Spirit, Love Divine! Glow within this heart of mine, kindle every high desire, perish self in Thy pure fire."

Let us release this great truth for our church. Our God is a consuming fire and nothing contrary to His nature will stand before Him. But in His church, He is the flame of sacred love, and we may draw near and find ourselves warmed and comforted, inspired and quickened, cleansed and transformed.

"THE UNDISCOURAGED SERVANT"
—Isaiah 42.4

(Preached at Katherine Road 1/6/35 and at Spring Head Mission 7/6/41)

Isaiah 42.4 "He shall not fail nor be discouraged till he have set judgment in the earth."

THEN HE, WHOEVER HE may be, has a secret that is worth our while to discuss. For the trouble with us is that we are so often discouraged. It is comparatively easy to start out with confidence and high hope, and just as easy for faith to burn low and hope to die away. Our high enterprises burn in enthusiasm and often burn with tears. Here is one who, as we shall see, faces the great task and carries it through without being discouraged.

OF WHOM SPEAKETH THE PROPHET?

The text is set in one of the "Servant" passages of Isaiah's work. The "Divine Servant" is undoubtedly set forth as the ideal for Israel. The nation was intended to be God's servant commissioned to carry out the Divine purpose in the world. The nation never fully realized the ideal. What was an unrealized ideal in the Old Testament becomes a realized fact in the New Testament. Matthew claims this very prophecy for Jesus Christ. He fills in all the details, reveals all the spirit, and does all the work of the ideal Divine Servant. In turn Jesus becomes the ideal for all who believe in Him. As He was commissioned and equipped so He commissions and equips His followers for Divine service. As the Father sent Him so He sends others, and as He is in the world so are they. The text, then, sends us to Jesus and to Jesus as our ideal and pattern in service. If we are to learn how not to fail or be discouraged we must get at the secret of His unfailing optimism and undying faith.

THE GREATNESS OF THE DIVINE SERVANT'S TASK

It is stated in the terms, "to set judgment in the earth." What is the judgment? Whose is the judgment? It is not judgment in the judicial sense of a sentence. In that sense,

"THE UNDISCOURAGED SERVANT"—ISAIAH 42.4

Jesus did not come nor are we sent to judge the world. He came and we are sent to establish God's judgment, His mind and will, to put men right with God—personally, socially, civically, right with God. And of the ideal Servant it is recorded that he shall not fail nor be discouraged until that Divine judgment is established and accepted in the whole world.

That is a task to tax the brain, heart, and strength of giants. It is in the greatness of the way that we are wearied and discouraged. The difficulty begins with ourselves. We make our New Year's resolutions, or in some great moment we determine that God's judgment shall in all things be our standard. But how difficult it is to keep those resolutions and translate our good desires into actual facts. We forget and fail so often that we begin to lose faith and hope in ourselves and the possibility of goodness.

In our endeavor to set up the standard of God's judgment outside we are constantly "up against it." We are distressed by delays, disappointed in our fellow workers, almost disgusted by the indifference and cynicism of those we set out to help. The task seems utterly hopeless and if we do not altogether relinquish it we are discouraged and lose our zeal.

NEITHER FAILED NOR BECAME DISCOURAGED

We mark not only the greatness of the task but the fact that the Ideal Servant did not fail and was not discouraged. That is to say, the Servant who is our Master met the demands of the great task without pessimism and discouragement. He, too, had to meet indifference, delays, and desertions. He was rejected by those He had come to help and must have constantly suffered from the misunderstandings and failures of His friends. He moved among those who were as broken reeds and smoking flaxes but His faith did not break nor did His hope burn dimly. Men cast Him out, spat on Him, crucified Him, but He went to His cross praying for his murderers and declaring that He would draw all men unto Him. He turned the cross on which men nailed Him into a new standard of God's judgment in a fuller measure of His love. His was the love that did not fail, but thought and hoped the best to the end. He did not fail, He was not discouraged.

THE SERVANT'S SECRET

The final and supreme question for us to face is what is the secret of the Servant's courage and strength? It lies in the sense of a Divine call. The service is a vocation. The Divine Servant is a servant of the Divine. He is called and chosen. Jesus at the first said, "I must be about my Father's business," and later, "My Father hath sent me." Realize that you are sent of God and you have tapped the first secret of strength. Make your service for man a service for God and you will find new strength for it. Remember that behind your commission is God's purpose and you will not be discouraged. Make "whose I am and whom I serve" the working rule of your life, and neither this year nor any year will you fail or be discouraged.

Note the assurance of Divine equipment. "Behold my servant . . . I have put my Spirit upon Him." When God sent forth His Servant-Son it was in the power of the Spirit. In that power, Jesus as Servant triumphed over temptation, did His work, kept his faith and courage. When Christ sent forth His servants He promised them His Spirit, and in the Spirit, were all the resources and equipment they needed. The Spirit inspires and sustains, directs and controls, instructs and inspires. God calls and equips by the indwelling Spirit. All power was given unto the Son by the Father and all sufficient power is ours through the Son. It is spirit filled men and women who neither fail nor grow discouraged until judgment is set in the earth.

Our knowledge of the heart's deep longings. Men and women everywhere need what we are commanded to preach. And in their better moments they know it. They need the truth as it is in Jesus, the grace and strength He brings. There are foes of the gospel within my own heart, but there is something within me which cries out for the living God and which longs to see His throne set up within me. Men and women range themselves alongside the foes of God, but in some revealing moment they cry out, "the Lord helps me." "Far and wide through all unknowing, pants for Him each mortal breast." Let us not be unbelieving nor discouraged. The world needs the God revealed in Jesus for He alone can save it. It is our solemn and blessed duty to bring the two together. To that work we are called, for it we may be equipped, let us not fail nor be discouraged until the twain meet.

∼

"BLIND TO HIS BEAUTY"
—Isaiah 53.2

(Preached at Fentiman Road, Advent 1922 and Paradise Road, Passion Week, undated)

Isaiah 53.2 "He hath no form nor comeliness; and when we shall see Him, there is no beauty that we should desire Him."

FOR OUR IMMEDIATE PURPOSE, it is not necessary to stay to ask in a critical way, "Of whom speaketh the prophet this?" We can begin, as Philip did, at this Scripture and preach Jesus. In Christian thought, He has been the "sapling springing out of a dry ground" in whom men have failed to see form or comeliness or beauty that they should desire Him. It is as the text has appealed to Christians since the days of Christ that we interpret it now. Only remembering that, to see the final fulfillment of this prophecy in Jesus, it is not necessary to refuse to see the Suffering Servant in Israel also. It is not an exceptional thing for good merit to be misunderstood and ignored. Indeed, it is hardly too much to say that part of the penalty of greatness has been that the great man had to die before he was appreciated. "Seven cities quarreled over Homer dead, through which the living Homer begged his bread."[1] Inventors, scientists, poets, reformers whose fame will last as long as the world lasts, were misunderstood and rejected by their own generation.

But the great Misunderstood is Jesus Christ. The Son of God came in the likeness of man and men cast Him out and crucified Him. The light shone in darkness and the darkness comprehended it not. The world saw no beauty in its Savior and would have none of Him.

We think we are wiser and that we know better how to appreciate and treat genius and goodness. Perhaps we do, but there really is a doubt about it. An able critic, who is somewhat of a cynic, said: "If Demosthenes were to come back, if he were to speak in Westminster, and his speeches were to be reported in the morning paper, I tell you, you would begin to skip them. If Shakespeare were amongst us today, you would

---

1. The lines have been attributed to several writers, including Thomas Heywood (d. 1649), who wrote: "Seven cities warred for Homer being dead; / Who living had no roofe to shrowd his head." Thomas Seward (1708–1790) is accredited with the lines: "Seven wealthy towns contend for Homer dead / Through which the living Homer begged his bread."

mistake his magic mirror for a bit of common looking glass. If Milton were here your critics would declare that his golden trumpet was brass. If St. Paul or St. Chrysostom had been elected by this church as its pastor, it would not be long before somebody had been getting together quietly in a corner and saying that a change was desirable."[2]

How we should treat Jesus if He came to us as He went to the Jews can best be seen by the way we treat Him as He stands in our midst a historic figure and a living spiritual presence. What are the facts? Crowds ignore Him. They claim to admire His person and His ethic, but they are indifferent to His practical claims. There is little of bitter antipathy but there is colossal indifference. It is easy to picture Him standing in our crowded cities and crying, "Is it nothing to you, all ye that pass by?" Keeping to the figure of our text let us ask how it is that men fail to see the glory of Jesus Christ and are blind to His incomparable greatness and merit.

DEBASED TASTE BLINDS TO HIS BEAUTY

A sapling springing out of a dry ground looks starved and colorless by the side of the grand growths of a well-watered garden. And it is the splash of color and the flaunting beauties that so often catch the eye and dazzle the senses. Cockatoos are said to charm savages for whom the iridescent neck of a dove has no charm. Have we altogether emerged from the savage stage in this respect? Flaunting vulgarities and self-assertive claims to beauty captivate vulgar eyes to which the serene beauties of goodness seem insipid.

Think of what passes for beauty in decorations, ornaments, and pictures—in the feminine world. It is one of the ironies, if not one of the tragedies of life, that real beauty is overlooked for the artificial and superficial, that gaudy tinsel is chosen in preference to gold. Think of the way crowds can be attracted (S. A. Tipple). The crowds that attend brutal boxing matches. "Odd world, is it not," says somebody, "that sends its Bunyans to gaol and gives its jockeys ten-thousand a year."

Thus explains the blindness of many to the beauty of Christ. The unattractiveness is not absolute nor real, it is only "that we should desire Him." The desire is for something more dashing and poignant than the meek and lowly man of Nazareth. Or, the portrait is all right, but its setting is homely, the place of its hanging lowly, and the frame plain. Can any good thing come out of Nazareth? Art Thou, poorly clad, homely looking creature, a King? Men come to Christ in a merely carnal, secular, intellectual spirit and see in Him no beauty that they should desire Him. A debased taste blinds Him to His beauty and worth as a Savior, a leader, a Captain, and they say, "Not this man, but Barabbas."

---

2. As far as I can tell, this a quotation from the sermon "The Great Misunderstood," by the Rev. W. L. Watkinson in 1903. See https://paperspast.natlib.govt.nz/newspapers/NZH19030822.2.60.46.

"BLIND TO HIS BEAUTY"—Isaiah 53.2

FAMILIARITY BLINDS TO HIS BEAUTY

Familiarity, we say, breeds contempt. Oftener it breeds blindness and insensibility. The dwellers of the Swiss mountains and lakes are often blind to the beauties visitors travel thousands of miles to see. The children of the home are often insensible to the love and devotion of the noblest parents. "Do you know, Hughie," asks Ronald MacDonald of the minister's son, "do you know what sort of a woman you have for a mother?" Alas, Hughie did not. And there are thousands as blind to the beauty that is at their side every day.

Familiarity with genius blinds people to it. The Cumberland peasants had not a great opinion of Wordsworth and the Lincolnshire residents did not think much of Tennyson. Percy Ainsworth preached the sermons that sell by thousands to mere handfuls of people and the stewards put him in a house that gave him the fever that took him before he was forty. Familiarity can blind us to the beauty, holiness, grandeur of the most sacred places, occasions, and services. And here is a season for our blindness to Christ's beauty. We have read the story so often, the teaching has sounded in our ears since we were children, the glory of the gospel has been always before our eyes, until familiarity has bred indifference and the romance, the thrill, the rapture has gone.

While we who are so familiar see nothing to charm and thrill us, those who see and hear for the first time are enraptured. The gypsy boy and heathen ask the missionaries "Why did you not come before?" The rapture of new converts. The joy of the returned prodigal often surpasses that of the Elder Brother, and yet, "Son, thou art ever with me and all that I have is thine." Familiarity, instead of blinding us ought to open our eyes to new beauties and our hearts to new thrills.

PREOCCUPATION BLINDS TO HIS BEAUTY

As we noted earlier, we have not now to contend with antipathy and opposition to Christ so much as with apathy and indifference. There are many who admit his beauty and even praise it, but they are so busy with other things that they do not allow it to have its full effect upon them, "We needs must have the highest when we see it." Yes, but we must see it clearly and steadily before we can have it. At first glance, some pictures seem only blotches of color, it is only to the clear, steady gaze that they reveal their beauty. Of some people, we say that they grow on us. The Bible draws a fine distinction between the look that is a mere glance and the look that is an attentive gaze. "They looked unto Him and were lightened." "They shall look upon Him whom they pierced."

If we would but give ourselves to such looking we could not be blind to His beauty. But we are busy about so many things. There are so many things that demand and hold our attention, and some of them are such sorry, vulgar pictures by the side of His beauty. And while we hurry past or postpone our looking unto Him, for us the vision fades, we lessen our power to appreciate it.

With an old Russian legend that illustrates this point I draw to a close. When the wise men were searching for the Christ-child, says the legend, they called at the house of a peasant woman and invited her to join them in their search. Said the woman, "When I have made the fire and prepared the meal and swept the room, then I will follow and find Him." But when her work was done the wise men had passed on their way across the desert, and the star shone no longer in the darkened heavens. She was so busy that she missed Him.

Have you ever paused to ask why you are blind to the beauty of Him who is and has been to thousands the fairest of ten thousand and is altogether lovely? Why is He nothing to you and all-in-all to others? Face that question now. Is your blindness due to the debased taste or the low level of maturation? Is He a "sapling out of a dry ground" and not "the Rose of Sharon and the Lily of the Valley" because you have never passed to look, to examine, to investigate? Have you passed by with the crowd instead of passing to look and listen? Stop! Stop now, and if your eyes are blind, remember that it is His mission to open blind eyes. Pray! Pray as you have never prayed for anything before: "Oh send Thy Spirit, Lord, now unto me, that He may touch mine eyes, and make me see, shew me the truth concealed within Thy Word, thus in the Book revealed, I see the Lord. Bless Thou the truth, O Lord to me, to me, as Thou didst bless the bread by Galilee, then shall all bondage cease, all fetters fall, and I shall find my peace, my all in all."

"THE FOOL AND HIS PENKNIFE"
—Jeremiah 36.23

(Preached at Fentiman Road 1/13/1924)

Jeremiah 36.23 "And it came to pass when Jehudi had read three or four leaves, that the king cut it with the penknife and cast it into the fire that was in the brazier."

IT IS DANGEROUS TO put a penknife into the hands of a child or a fool, for each of them is likely to use it to their own hurt or to the danger of something of value around them. This particular penknife had got into the hands of an exceptionally foolish king and he used it according to his folly. *The story is worth telling.*

Jehoiakim, the king in question, was the one of the last two kings who reigned in Jerusalem. He was about the worst specimen to occupy the throne. He had all the vices of an eastern monarch and none of the virtues. His stock in trade consisted of a vast amount of obstinacy and bravado. He had a tremendous opinion of himself and just about as much foolishness as a man can well carry. Of real courage, manliness, and wisdom there does not seem to have been even a spark. He was steeped in vice and dragged the nation down with him to godlessness and immorality. In politics, he was a miserable blunderer and did nothing but lead his people to destruction.

The redeeming feature of the times was the fact that Jeremiah, the clear-eyed statesman, God's prophet, was exercising his ministry. Though the people so resented his honest judgments and his stern condemnations of their sins that he was excluded from the temple and public places and went in danger of his life. Because he would neither flatter nor hide disagreeable truths his tongue was silenced. However, the wrath of men was made to praise God. This temporary and partial silencing of Jeremiah led to a new departure which made the influence of his teaching more extensive and permanent. He was commanded to commit his prophecies to writing. So the restriction of his ministry bore much good—like the imprisonment of Paul, the exile of Athanasius, the incarceration of Bunyan.

Jeremiah dictated the prophecies to Baruch, the scribe, who wrote them down on a scroll. Afterwards Baruch read these words to the people assembled in the house of God. The king was not present but his princes carried the roll to the palace and read it there. It was not a pleasant reading. There was no flattering in it and there was a good deal of straight talk. Jehoiakim did not like it, and it was then that he took the knife and cut the offending columns out of the roll and cast them into the fire, thinking that that would end the matter. It was the end of that particular roll, but not of the awkward truths it contained. *Truths cannot be abolished by burning the parchments on which they are written.* Now it is time to leave the story and come to the text and the applications thereof. Though I do not grudge the time taken if it has helped us to the right point of view.

THE KING'S PENKNIFE HAS SURVIVED HIS AGE

It has always been a favorite weapon in the hands of those who disliked parts of the word of God. The easiest way out has seemed to be in the destruction of what was unflattering and unwelcome. It is so simple to put down what we do not want to believe as an accretion, a variant, a Babylonian myth, or to say "out with it." In the same way men have often cut out the passages that were not altogether favorable to their own ecclesiastical position. But it is not only critics and ecclesiastics who are in danger of emulating Jehoiakim's conduct, and I am far more concerned about the ways in which ordinary folk reflect this folly.

We should not dream of desecrating the material Bible by using a penknife on it, though we often do what is far worse. We cut away, whittle down, its sacred truths if they interfere with our pleasure or comfort. There are commandments which cut clear across our desires—the fourth commandment for example—so we call it a piece of antiquated legislation and out it goes! There are exhortations in the New Testament, calls to repentance and whole-hearted consecration, exacting demands of the kingdom, that we call local and temporary in their application. Think what a difference it would make if we took the sayings about forgiveness, ceasing from worry, doing as we would be done by, and practiced them instead of whittling them away.

To come closely to our text. The roll contained mainly warnings, prophecies of evil, promises of judgment. Jehoiakim treated them with contempt and used his penknife on them. Perhaps there is nothing in Revelation that today is treated more lightly than the doctrine of punishment. This may be a reaction against an unchristian way of presenting Christian truth, but even admitting that, it does remain true that again and again the Bible rings out the warning that "the wages of sin is death," that "the soul that sinneth, it shall die." Jesus taught that as well as Jeremiah. It is still the duty of preachers to sound warnings about truth of retribution. "Knowing the terror of the Lord," said Paul, "we persuade men." One gladly confesses that this is not the highest form of appeal. It is higher than to say, "Do right because it is right, and love God because he is God." But exhortations against sin on the ground of its consequences is part of the Divine message. The preacher who would declare the whole counsel of God must sound the trumpet of warning. Why not?

"THE FOOL AND HIS PENKNIFE"—JEREMIAH 36.23

THE WARNING COMES FROM LOVE

God does not cease to be love when he warns of evil consequences. What sort of a world would this be if men might live as they like, and do all the evil they like, and then go free? Caprice and anger have no place in the Divine Being, but His throne is set and men must be judged according to what they have done, whether good or evil. We are part of a settled order and have to face an inviolable law, and it is part of the mercy of God that the consequences of wrong doing are made clear. There was love behind the roll the king burned. "It may be that the house of Judah ... may return every man from his evil way: that I may forgive their iniquity and their sin." God wills not the death of any, even of a man like Jehoiakim. He sends a warning in the hope that he will repent.

Any preacher who is worthy of the name has entered to some extent into the passion of God and must warn men of the penalty that follows sin. The warnings are all the more necessary because of the sophistries that are around us, the deceitful allure of sin, and the siren voices that whisper to our hearts "you shall not surely die."

FOLLY LIES IN REJECTING THE WARNINGS

What a conceited ass Jehoiakim was! *Facts are not altered by neglecting them. Judgment is not averted by refusing to believe in it. You cannot break consequence by burning the paper that states it.* The preacher proclaims, "The wages of sin is death," "God is not mocked," "We must all stand before the Judgment seat of Christ." Well, there is no wisdom in saying with derision and contempt that these words mean nothing and are only stories to frighten children with. That is but the same story of the foolish king cutting the roll and burning the words.

The penalties of sin are slow in coming, but the day of reckoning comes. God is patient and long suffering, therefore sentences against evil are not executed speedily, but the inevitable hour creeps on. If you break the laws of health, you cannot dodge the consequences. If you break the law of your country, you pay the price. You may tear your life in pieces, but the debt stands. The lookout man sings out, "Breakers ahead," you do not abolish the reef by ridiculing his warning, you will go on to destruction. It is foolish to despise the warnings that are given in love. Wisdom is in giving heed, turning from the ways that are leading to ruin.

INCREASED PENALTY FOR DESPISING WARNING

There is an increased penalty for the man who despises his warning. Jehoiakim burnt the roll, but another was written, "There were many like words added." The fact that we are warned increases our responsibility. "It shall be more tolerable for Tyre and Sidon," said Jesus, than for the cities that had had the privilege of his own ministry.

Added privilege brings added penalty. With all my heart I believe, and with all the earnestness I can command, I preach that: The love of God is broader than the measure of man's mind, and the heart of the Eternal is most wonderfully kind. It is broad enough to take us all in and kind enough to warn us where we are going wrong. It is His love that shakes us when we are in danger and gives us time to repent.

It is not often I preach on judgment and tell you that unless you repent you will perish. I do it tonight in love. If you reject the warning, the responsibility is yours. It is not simply an arbitrary penalty I declare, and there is nothing unjust in it. Rejection will make you more obstinate, and your continued sin will be against you. Let me beseech you not to play the part of the foolish and contemptuous king. I will show you a more excellent way. A few years before this happened, Shaphan had read a similar roll to Jehoiakim's father, and it is written "Josiah, the king, rent his clothes." That was an outward act signifying an inward repentance, and reform and blessing followed. May the warning lead you to repentance and to Jesus, so that you may not hear, and never experience, the judgments of which you are warned.

"THE LIKENESS OF MAN ON THE THRONE OF GOD"
—Ezekiel 1.26

(Preached at Katherine Road 12/10/33)

Ezekiel 1.26 "And above the firmament that was over their heads was the likeness of a throne . . . and upon the likeness of the throne was the likeness as the appearance of a man above upon it."

EZEKIEL WAS ONE OF the most exalted thinkers among the Old Testament prophets. The book bearing his name records the most majestic visions that ever met mortal eye. The great seer of Patmos was more indebted to Ezekiel than we think. Yet probably no book of the OT is read less than Ezekiel. Our reason for this is undoubtedly the difficulty of understanding these visions in which the glories of heaven and earth are thrown together in such rich profusion. In our age of rush and hurry we cannot find time for the understanding of any thinker whose truth is hidden in visions and imagery. We want everything put so that he who sees may read. We want our thinking and reading made easy. And our indolence is our impoverishment. I want you to think seriously about this introductory vision.

LET US SURVEY THE PROPHET'S SURROUNDINGS

That may give us the key to his vision. Ezekiel was prophet in the days of Israel's captivity in Babylon. Like Isaiah, he became aware of his vocation through a vision of God. Seated on the banks of the river Chebar, his attention was attracted to a storm cloud forming in the North and advancing towards him across the plains. The cloud may have been an actual phenomenon, the natural basis of the theophany which follows. Falling into a state of ecstasy, the prophet sees the cloud grow luminous with unearthly splendor. There was the hearth of glowing coals, the four-headed, four-winged figures, running and returning like a flash of lightning, the mysterious wheels with eyes in, and above all the flushing movement and splendor the Throne of God.

The meaning of the vision. Just what these weird figures and moving wheels mean it is difficult to say. He would be a bold man who claimed to have threaded all the mazes of this mysterious vision. They may simply represent the servants of God corresponding to seraphim of Isaiah's vision, the actual form in which they are set being borrowed from Babylonian art and ritual. More likely they are representations of the gods worshipped at the time. The eagle was the particular symbol of the national god of Assyria. The ox or bull was the well-known symbol of the Babylonian god, Marduk or Merodack. The Chaldeans were great believers in guardian spirits who preserved their goings out and comings in and presided over their destiny.

The supreme and unmistakable thing in the vision is that over all these living forms and turning wheels there is set the Throne of God. The law they must all obey comes from it. That was the message Ezekiel and his people needed. It made the prophet and it saved the people. For the Jews were losing their faith in Jehovah. They were not only setting down to the ways of Babylon, they were beginning to worship Babylonian gods. We must not be too hard on them. Their temptation was great. Evidences of Babylonian splendor and power were all about them. Babylonian armies were victorious. Must not their gods be supreme?

It was Ezekiel's vision and message which saved them from becoming idolaters. He made it clear that the Throne of God was set in the heavens and that His kingdom ruleth over all. The eagle of Assyria and the ox of Babylon were the servants of the Living God. Above all human agencies and fancied and real spiritual activities was God's throne. "The great gods of Babylon were only as draught horses to draw the chariot of the Lord."

THE MESSAGE FOR TODAY

That was the message for the Jews and it is needed today. The lion and the eagle and the ox have been very much to the fore. We put a lot of faith in social, political, and ecclesiastical machinery, we have wheels within wheels far surpassing anything Ezekiel dreamed of. Our danger, too, is that of forgetting the central and supreme power. We are so taken up with "thrones, dominations, princedoms, powers," as Milton called them, that we forget the eternal throne and the everlasting kingdom. We do not, of course, believe in genies who give fortune and victory, but we are not averse to mascots and lucky tokens. And we put a lot of faith in what was typified by the four figures. The ox, labor. The lion, power. The eagle, foresight. The man, reason. And, I repeat, our danger is that of forgetting or neglecting God in whose hand our breath is, and who is the creator and sustainer and governor of all the earth. That is the first lesson for us from the vision. The Lord, He is God. His throne is set in the heavens and He ruleth over all.

But the prophet carries us further and gives us a *truth appropriate to the season*. He saw the throne, and on the throne "the likeness of a man." "Likeness" means the

"THE LIKENESS OF MAN ON THE THRONE OF GOD"—EZEKIEL 1.26

external, visible form or representation of a thing. The Throne of God and on it the form of a man! That was a great thing to see six centuries before Christ came. It was so strange that the prophet hardly dared proclaim it. But it was true, and in the light of the incarnation we can see it more clearly and expand the thought. Here is a gleam, a hint, a prophecy of the truth fully revealed in the coming of Jesus.

THE HUMANITY OF GOD

God is enthroned in the heavens, above all the might and powers of earth, our destinies are in His hands. And He who is the world's governor and the Lord of life has all the noblest thoughts and failings of humanity. He is good in the sense that every honest man understands that word. We must not be afraid to say it—man is like God, made in his image. And God is like man. Whittier tells of the minister's daughter who said of God: "Oh, I fear Him! And I try to love Him, too, but I wish He was good and gentle, kind and loving as you."[1] If we were always as honest and outspoken we should sometimes express the same wish. Well, God is as good and gentle, as kind and as loving, and infinitely more so, than the best you have known. Will you believe that? That the Throne of God is supreme, and that the occupant thinks and feels for us and with us. Believe as Whittier's minister came to believe when: "Lo! From the bloom and greenness, from the tender skies above, and the face of his little daughter, he read a lesson of love. No more as the cloudy terror of Sinai's mount of Law, but as Christ in the Syrian lilies the vision of God he saw. And, as when, in the clefts of Horeb, of old was His presence known the dread Ineffable Glory was Infinite Goodness alone." Believe it, for it is true. Above all the noise and tumult of earth is the Throne of God. And "through the thunder comes a human voice saying, 'O heart I made, a heart beats here! Face my hands fashioned, see it in myself.'"[2]

THE NATURALNESS OF THE INCARNATION

If you accept that truth you will see that the Incarnation was the manifestation in the plain of time of what God eternally is. The coming of Jesus did not change God, it revealed Him. Ezekiel saw the likeness of a man on the Throne of God. Men saw God as man walking the fields of earth. And on the throne still is One who, not only has human thoughts and feelings, but who has worn our flesh and borne our mortal griefs. "Thou knowest—not alone as God all-knowing—as man our mortal weakness Thou hast proved." What Ezekiel glimpsed in part, we may firmly grasp. On the throne set in the heavens is One akin to us. That is why Faber could sing so sweetly and so

---

1. This is from Whittier's poem "The Minister's Daughter."
2. This is from Robert Browning's "The Strange Medical Experience of Karshish."

truly: "There is no place where earth's sorrows are more felt than up in heaven. There is no place where earth's failings have such kingly judgment given."[3]

THE DIVINITY OF HUMANITY

"The likeness of the appearance of a man" upon the throne. That teaches us what God is like. It teaches us, too, what man is destined for. Humanity is to be crowned and sceptered with God. That is made clearer for us in the Incarnation. Jesus revealed God and reveals human possibilities. His disciples are to be like Him, to be with Him, to share His throne. That is philosophic as well as prophetic. A human being becomes like what he worships. Association means assimilation. Fellowship with Christ means transformation into His likeness. Partnership in His sufferings means sharing His glory. In the face of Jesus, we see the glory of God, with Him we come to the Throne of God. Man on the Throne of God! We do not see that yet. Often, we see him degraded and deformed. "We see not yet all things put under his feet, but we see Jesus . . . crowned." Where He is, we are destined for. Let us trust Him and follow Him and we shall arrive. "Follow you the star that lights the desert pathway, yours or mine, till you see the highest human nature is Divine."

∼

---

3. F. W. Faber is hymn writer, and the hymn has two arrangements, one entitled "There's a Wideness in God's Mercy" and one entitled "Souls of Men Why Will Ye Scatter."

"PUT YOURSELF IN HIS PLACE"
—Ezekiel 3.15

(Preached twenty-four times from Fentiman Road to Sunderland, dated only at Patricroft 5/2/37)

Ezekiel 3.15 "I sat where they sat . . ."

THAT IS WHAT EVERYONE must do if he is to judge right, speak wisely, and act well. You can form no true estimate of your fellow human being, come to no real understanding of his needs, or make no adequate contribution to his well-being, unless you "put" yourself in his place.

Ezekiel did that literally. He was charged with a stern and searching message to his people, his heart was hot within him and he was prepared to deliver the message in terms of fierce condemnation. Fortunately, "the hand of the Lord was strong" upon him, and a higher spirit took possession of him. Before he spoke, he went and sat quietly with his countrymen by the river Chebar. He sat where they sat, entered into their distress of body and mind. The experience struck him dumb and for seven days he could not speak. When utterance came back, he cut out of his speech the fierce philippic and the fiery denunciations and talked with "good sense of fine sympathy." You may be sure that his message was more sweetly reasonable and far more effective because he had made himself one with his people and argued from firsthand knowledge of their condition.

It is not always possible for us literally to put ourselves in another's place, but we can really, if imaginatively, sit where he sits, see what he sees, and feel what he feels. We can enter his life, into his thoughts, and into his trials, difficulties, and temptations. And not until we do are we in a position to estimate and minister to his needs. It is no exaggeration to say that half our misjudgments and mistakes spring from—

THE BLUNDER OF ALOOFNESS

We jump to conclusions, and often jump wrong. We do not take trouble to see things from another's point of view, and so we err in our judgment and find our words and our schemes rejected. A ready-made illustration comes to mind. Some years ago, a very popular and very able London minister made certain, very severe criticisms of British working men. The immediate result was a newspaper storm, and the men concerned called the preacher, well, anything but an angel. Fortunately, the immediate result was not the only result. The preacher was invited to a meeting of Trades Union representatives. He accepted the invitation and afterwards said, "I realize that, although all I had said was perfectly true, I had not taken account of the working man's point of view." The strictures were resented, not so much because they were unjust, as because they were made by a man who did not share the privations and disabilities of those with whom he found fault. The preacher set himself to see things from the point of view of those he had criticized with the result that he became a welcome speaker on their platforms and an eloquent advocate of their cause.

For the moment, I am not discussing his attitude and action. I am only using his experience to illustrate my claim that the point of view makes a world of difference. That carries us a long way and there is only need to indicate briefly some of the ways in which it will be all to the good that we "put ourselves in the other man's place."

CONCERNING LEARNING AND TEACHING

We are only beginning to learn that in order to understand a great teacher's message we must take pains to get his point of view. You cannot possibly understand Browning apart from his point of view. "In Memoriam" only yields its full message to those who know Tennyson's grief at the loss of his friend Arthur Hallam. *Pilgrim's Progress* becomes a new book when, in thought, you sit by Bunyan's side in Bedford jail. I am not particularly concerned with that as a principle in general educational methods, but as it applies to our understanding of religious truths.

How much more vital and valuable the Bible becomes if we put ourselves in the places of those who first uttered its truths. It saves us from fantastic interpretations. Stand by some grief-stricken father who has come from his days of toil to find his home in ruins, his children slain, and his wife carried off, and you will understand why in the collection these are "vindictive psalms." Sit with the captive Jews on the banks of the river Chebar and the Lamentations of Jeremiah and the rebukes of Ezekiel will take on a new meaning. Gather with a few humble Eastern saints in an upper room at Corinth or Philippi and you will understand Paul's epistles as never before. Still more does the truth apply to our endeavor to teach Christianity. Educational experts are declaring with increasing emphasis that the teacher must study the pupil's point of view. He must sit by the scholar's side.

For Christian teachers, this is a primary necessity. The preacher who would be effective must project himself into the experience of his people. The Sunday School teacher must learn this lesson. The only way to success is for the teacher to become a child. We must sit where they sit. That is where so many fail, we sit on them and not

"PUT YOURSELF IN HIS PLACE"—EZEKIEL 3.15

with them. If we are to teach wandering and wayward people the way of life we must never stand above them in a lordly or patronizing way. We must sympathize with them, come down to them in a generous sense.

That is what overseas missionaries are teaching us. They begin with the heathen where they are and lead them in, just as Philip sat with the Ethiopian statesman in his chariot and took the book he was reading, and "beginning at the same scripture preached unto him Jesus." Think, too, how this would effect—

OUR ESTIMATE OF OTHER PEOPLE

When he sat with his fellows the prophet was astonished. We have a saying that our half of the world doesn't know how the other half lives and if they did, there would be some surprises. But we don't know and we don't try to understand. So, we scream at one another across the intervening spaces. From a distance, we see a great deal to be criticized and condemned. It makes all the difference when we get at close quarters with the situations we have judged or envied.

It would do some men good to have a week at home doing the work they think so easy in comparison with their work in shop or office. There is a humorous song called, "When Father Was Mother for a Day." That day yielded weird results and father didn't want any more such days. And it might possibly make some women a bit less extravagant and a bit more sympathetic if they had a few days at the office.

Any man can criticize the preacher and lots of people think they could do his job better—until they try. If some folk would only try the pulpit they would understand the meaning of some words painted over a Californian pulpit in the wild and wooly days: "Don't shoot the preacher, he's doing his best." And I know some preachers, and one in particular, who would do a good deal better if they sat in the pew for a while.

Every critic of the church might be less noisy if they would sit for a time with the much-criticized men and women who are striving to keep a conscience void of offence toward God and humankind and striving in their way to cleanse and save the city. The clash of class against class would not be so bitter if Capital could sit with Labour and Labour with Capital.

None of us would be so hasty and bitter if we did what the prophet did. When we try to understand the position of some who have done wrong we realize that not always do we know all the facts and forces. Some have resisted more than we ever knew existed. In all directions saner, kindlier judgments would result from sympathy. It must now be obvious that seeing things from another's point of view and seeking to enter his experience would—

LUMINESCENCE

DEEPEN OUR SYMPATHY AND ENRICH OUR CHRISTIAN SERVICE

Indeed, what is sympathy but fellow feeling, and how can we share a fellow's feeling unless we sit where he sits. Too often what passes for sympathy is only a superficial kind of pity which is not always free from contempt. If you would really comfort and help the suffering and the sad, put yourself in their place. Don't be so eager to talk and tell them what to do or you may be only "Job's comforters." Often you won't have much to say, but sit with them, let them know you are trying to understand, and your presence will be a comfort and your sympathy will help.

This is the only effective way in the work of saving the lost. You must pray for grace to stoop to the fallen and walk with the wounded. Too often our words are empty, our service cold, and our whole attitude Pharisaical. We shall never resume the perishing and lift up the fallen in any contemptuous or ever patronizing spirit. We must be willing to make ourselves of no reputation and sit with the erring, make them feel that we are trying to enter into their experience, and then we shall really help.

"Readers of Oliver Twist will remember and well remember," says one, "how the sweet, pure girlhood of Rose Marylee came into touch with the soiled soul of poor Nancy, and for one awful moment projected itself into the sins and sorrows of Nancy, and in the presence of that marvel, Nancy burst into tears. 'Oh, lady,' she cried, clasping her hands passionately before her face, 'if there were more like you there would be fewer like me—there would, there would.'"[1] It is easy to pass from that to my last word.

HE SAT WHERE WE SIT

Ezekiel was following the Divine Ideal. When God visited and redeemed His people He sat where they sat. That is the meaning of the Incarnation. The name of our Savior is Emmanuel—God with us. God with human beings and suffering with them, pleading with them, and dying for them. For us and for our salvation, God came in the likeness of flesh. He made Himself of no reputation and He tabernacled with us. Let us remember that where we are lonely, sad, and despairing, we have a High Priest who has learned sympathy by suffering. There is no place where earth's sorrows are more felt than up in heaven for He who sits enthroned came down to be a man and die.

Let us remember it, too, that we may follow in his steps. There is nothing Diviner and nothing more effective in the saving of men. Stoop to conquer and stoop to save. Stoop that you may sympathize. Follow Jesus in ways of lovely and loving service. Sit where He sits with the sad and sinful and lonely and there you will sit with Him in the Heavenly Places.

---

1. An episode from Charles Dickens's *Oliver Twist*.

"SHOWERS OF BLESSING"
—Ezekiel 34.26

(Preached at Fentiman Road, undated, and Spring Head Mission 7/14/40)

Ezekiel 34.26 "And I will make them and the places round about my hill a blessing; and I will cause the showers to come down in his season; there shall be showers of blessing."

WE ARE THINKING AT this Flower Service in terms of holistic lives, and trying to see sermons in gardens. We are following the Lord's example and considering the flowers. Let us think of a garden when, after a period of drought, the blessed rain falls in refreshing showers. Can you imagine anything more fresh, fair, and fragrant? It is like looking upon a new earth. The flowers lift their heads as if in gratitude and as though they were giving thanks. But there is no need to multiply words. You have walked in such a garden and felt the spell.

The point I want to make is that He who waters the earth refreshes the soul and renews the church. Is it not written, "Thy soul shall be like a watered garden"? That is what this text says. It is God's promise to send showers of blessing upon His people, not only renewing and gladdening them, but making them a means of blessing to all around.

Let us begin with the simple but necessary thought that showers of rain are not more essential to the fertility of gardens than are showers of blessing to the growth and beauty of the soul. That sounds commonplace, but it is a truth that needs to be remembered.

In prayer, there is no petition we offer so often as that the blessing of God may rest upon us and ours. That is our tacit admission that we can no more live without it than flowers can without rain. When at meal times we pause and say, "Give a blessing, O Lord, with this food," we are acknowledging that, in addition to the natural ingestion of food to sustain bodily strength, there is needed a certain superintendence and favor of heaven. Divine wisdom and strength are needed to maintain even physical health and to make the best use of it when we have it. When we ask God to bless the labors of our hands, we acknowledge that, beyond all our planning and working, there is need of something which comes from God. In our temporal affairs, we need the blessing of Almighty God.

But it is in the spiritual domain that we require most the need and value of the blessing of God. Without "showers of blessing" there will be no growth and sharing of the fruits of the Spirit in our souls, no harvest of good in the world around us. Paul and Apollos may and must do all within their power, but without the help of heaven their labor will be in vain. That is why in times of spiritual drought and unfruitfulness we pray: "There shall be showers of blessing, send them upon us, O Lord! Grant to us now a refreshing, come, and now honor Thy word."

In the spiritual realm, the falling of the showers of blessing is conditional. In the natural world, God makes the sun to shine and the rain to fall on good and bad alike. The refreshing rain falls on the garden of evil as well as in the fields of the righteous. In the spiritual world, we can take it for granted that drought is a part of God's plan or purpose. He is more ready to send than we are to receive. When the love of God has free course, there are abundant showers of blessing. The obstacles are in us. Again and again in the Bible we read that, for His people's sin, "He shutteth up the heaven that there be no rain." On the other hand, we read that in their repentance, "He giveth rain."

Take one or two examples. "It shall come to pass, if ye shall hearken diligently unto my commandments . . . I will give you rain for your land in due season." "Take heed to yourselves, that your heart be not deceived, and ye turn aside, and serve other gods, and worship them; then shall the Lord's wrath be kindled against you, and He shall shut up the heavens that there be no rain."

Whatever that means in the natural world, its application to the spiritual world is clear. Disobedience means drought! The showers of blessing do not fall when and where God's people are worldly and sinful. It is not irreverent to say that they cannot. How can the Divine blessing rest on what is contrary to God's will? How can God enrich us while we impoverish ourselves by sin? While we harden our hearts in unbelief and selfishness, even if the showers fell they would do no good. The first thing, if we really want these showers, is to trust and obey. God will then add grace to welcomed grace.

"But for the showers we plead." The showers are conditioned by circumstance of need, and they fall in answer to believing prayer. "Ask ye of the Lord rain . . . and the Lord shall make bright clouds and give them showers of rain." That is God's promise to Zechariah. Do we really want the showers of blessing? Are we anxious that our lives shall be rich and abundant flowers and forests of holiness and love? Do we want our church to be renewed and refreshed in its life? Is the great longing of our heart to see revival in our land? If we do, let us pray for the blessing and it will not be denied. It is as sure as God's promises that on individuals and the church the showers will fall when we want them earnestly enough to plead with God to send them. Do not hesitate to pray the full prayer: "Mercy drops round us are falling, but for the showers

"SHOWERS OF BLESSING"—EZEKIEL 34.26

we plead." "Showers of blessing," that is the promise of love. Ask for them, plead for them, take no rest and give God no rest until they fall in revival on all around. This "plenteous grace" will be given.

Do not miss the last thought of the text: the diffusiveness of God's blessing. It is God's nature not only to bless us, but "I will make them and the places about my hill a blessing." He sends precious, reviving showers upon the people and His church so that they may be a blessing. There are Christians in whom this purpose is realized. Refreshed by His grace they exhale fragrances wherever they move. There are Christian homes that radiate happiness. There are Christian churches out of which blessings flow to the neighborhood, their city, their country. We ought to be such Christians, have such homes, and be such a church. Such indeed we shall be if we are willing and obedient, trustful, and prayerful. Let us make the simple hymn our earnest prayer: "There shall be showers of blessing! Oh, that today they might fall! Now as to God we're confessing, while now on Jesus we call."[1]

---

1. This is from the hymn "There Will Be Showers of Blessing," by Daniel Whittle (1883).

"THE CHURCH AS BENEFACTOR"
—Micah 5.7

(Preached fifteen times from Fentiman Road, undated, to Bishop Street 10/14/44)

Micah 5.7 "And the remnant of Jacob shall be in the midst of many people as a dew from the LORD, as the showers upon the grass that tarrieth not for man, nor waiteth for the sons of men."

THOUGH IT COMES FROM the Old rather than the New Testament, here is a singularly apt description of the church and its beneficent ministry. It is part of a separate oracle, has no direct connection with its context, and can be considered apart from its setting. The whole sermon is on the text, but we can come at once to the truth it enshrines.

REMNANT AND CHURCH

First of all, the close kinship between the "remnant of the Old Testament" and the "ecclesia" of the New. "Remnant" is a favorite word with Old Testament writers. It means the residue, what is left over. Its first reference is to those who expected captivity and death. The suggestion is always that of a remainder of a few. When the word is carried over into the spiritual realm it is used to describe people who, in days of apostasy and nominal religion, were loyal to God and actually religious. In a broad sense, the prophets could speak of the whole nation of Israel as the people of God, in the same way as we speak of England as a Christian nation. But there was a people within the people, a nation within the nation, and such people were in deed and in truth, and not merely in name, the People of God. They were the "Remnant." They had escaped the common formalism and indifference. The hope of the nation was in the "Remnant." It was God's witness, God's servant, God's agent. It was always made up of a few, it was small compared to the bulk of the nation. It was a "Remnant," but through it religion kept alive, irreligion was repaired, and revival came.

In the New Testament, the word hardly occurs at all. The word "church" takes its place. The true church is the "*ecclesia*." That is, it is made up of those who have heard the call of God and responded to it. As I have said, we speak broadly about the

"THE CHURCH AS BENEFACTOR"—MICAH 5.7

whole country as Christian, but the real Christian country is but a remnant of the whole. It consists of those who have heard God's voice and are truly seeking to obey it. Not all who are outwardly members of the church belong to the *ecclesia*. There is a church within the church: its members are distinguished from formal members by their vitality and their obedience. Like the "Remnant," the true church is made up of those who are witnesses to good in days of evil, loyal to God in days of apostasy, lovers of Christ more than anything on earth, more anxious to see God's will done than to secure any gain or comfort for themselves. Such people are always a few in the midst of a multitude. They are literally a "remnant."

APPARENT INSIGNIFICANCE OF THE CHURCH

That brings me to the thought of the apparent insignificance of the church. Earnest, religious, whole-hearted, fully devoted men and women have never been in a majority. They were few in the days of Isaiah and Jeremiah. Elijah said he was the only one left. The writer of our text said there was not one near to be trusted. Even when you have allowed for the discouragement and depression of these men, it remains true that real lovers of God were few. Our Lord himself left but few followers and the first church roll had but 120 names.

What concerns us most just now is the fact that after two thousand years, the church is but a remnant of the people. It is often ignored and skeptics scoff at its insignificance. As we look at our sparse morning congregations and think of the crowds that pass our doors, we feel that we are few and feeble. The same feeling must often come over those who are witnessing for God and find themselves holding lonely outposts in the social life of today.

We are so apt to judge matters by bulk, to trust in majorities, and anticipate victory for huge combines and big battalions, though it ought to be clear that in every realm quality counts for more than quantity in the long run. A light well-tempered rapier is a more effective weapon than a great, clumsy, ill-made sword. A handful of trained and disciplined and brave men can hold the pass against undisciplined hordes. The one man with a message, a keen eye for the opportunity, and effective powers of speech can win the debate and the country is his forever. No one can measure or weigh the power of prayerfulness and piety, or calculate the effect in the world of the influence and example of godly men and women.

BENEFICENT MINISTRY OF THE REMNANT

It is because of this that the prophet speaks of the beneficent ministry of the Remnant. "The remnant shall be . . . as a dew from the LORD, as showers upon the grass." The people who made up the Remnant were the benefactors of their nation and the world. Their ministry was silent but saving, modest but mighty. Think of what the dew and showers meant in that semi-tropical land. From the beginning of April to the end of October, the dry seasons, from the "latter" to the "former" rains, the herbage depended for moisture and life in the dew. After long periods of drought, it was the shower that quenched parched sods, raised drooping plants, and made harvest possible. The "Remnant of Jacob" was to fulfill a similar ministry. It was to be as a dew from the LORD and a shower upon the earth. But for it, goodness would die. As Paul says, "Unless the Lord had left unto us a very small remnant we should have been like unto Sodom and Gomorrah."[1]

HOPE OF REVIVAL

So too, in the apparently insignificant church is the world's hope of revival. The world ignores, despises, and ridicules the church, but it owes more to it than it knows. Often, we despise ourselves as we are so few and feeble. But we are set in the world to be its benefaction. Our influence is greater that we know. No man can measure the power of piety and prayer. But for your witness, the protest of your godly life, evil would go unrebuked and unchecked. Be faithful to your duties as a Christian and a church member, and your example will win others. Live your life for God at your lonely outpost and someone will note it and be helped by it. Let the church continue to pray and to order its life according to Christ's will, for in these things is the only hope of revival. Apart from the spiritual life of the Remnant, the springs of goodness will dry up and the world become barren of spirituality and vital goodness.

MINISTRY OF DEW AND RAIN

Let us state our ministry in terms that no one can misunderstand: the ministry of the dew and the rain. The "Remnant of Jacob," the church of Jesus Christ, are to us the dew and the rain. What does that mean? Our own prayer to the Spirit of God is: Come as the dew, and sweetly bless, this consecrated hour: May barrenness rejoice to own thy fertilizing power. In response to that prayer the guiding influences of the Spirit fall silently upon our lives and victories are brought to birth. What God's Spirit does for you, you in your lives and according to your capacity are to do for others. Your life is to be spiritual and true and there it will be as the dew, weak in itself, but cooling and refreshing, preserving the life it touches, giving itself in blessing.

Again, at times we sing: "There shall be showers of blessing, precious, reviving again." We do well to sing that and pray that "today they may fall." It is as God grants them that our spiritual life is refreshed and strengthened. And again, in a measure, the influences of our own life should fall as showers of blessing on the world. It was our Lord who said, "If any man thirst, let him come to me and out of him shall flow rivers

---

1. This is actually Isa 1.9, not Paul.

of living water." We are blest that we may be a blessing, saved that we may serve, filled with God's fullness that our hearts may over flow in kindly thought and glowing word. God grants us grace, not that we may simply contemplate our own salvation and enjoy our privileges, but so that our lives may be as showers of blessing in their quickening, reviving, life giving power.

Again, I urge—do not imagine you are doing nothing that the church does not count. God has done some of the greatest work through despised and ridiculed agencies. Go on living your life after the pattern of Christ, maintain your piety and continue in your prayers, and He who uses the dew and rain to enrich the earth will use His Remnant; the church, and a few and feeble folk, to bring in the revival which will change the moral desert into a paradise of holiness and peace.

But if God is to use us in this way, if we are to fulfill our beneficent ministry, the text has two other things to say to us. First, the dew and the showers only bless the earth as they come into contact with it. The remnant of Jacob is to be "in the midst of many people." The figures Jesus used to describe His followers imply that they will helpfully affect the world by contact. Leaven leavens the lump by being in the midst of it. Salt saves from corruption by being rubbed in. Lights are needed in the darkness. We need not and must not bid for cloistered cell our neighbor and our friend farewell. We must not withdraw ourselves nor hold aloof. Do not murmur or complain that your lot is cast in a dry desert place. Do not cold shoulder those who differ from you. Rather, give thanks for the opportunity afforded and try to make your life as dew and showers to barren and faithless souls.

Second, if the church and Christian people are to be in contact with the world, there is a real sense in which they must be independent of it. Of the dew and showers to which he likens the remnant, the prophet says, "They tarry not for man, nor wait for the sons of men." The plain meaning of that I take to be this—we have not to want for the world's permission or its smile, until what we are constrained to do is powerless. If we have some God-given indication of our work, there must be no hesitation, but swift obedience. The world is constantly trying to tell the church what to do and how to do it. But we take our orders from the Head of the church and when we have His command we "confer not with flesh and blood." Let the church and its members tackle their task "in the name of the Lord," and then and then only will it fulfill its mission and be as dew and showers which quicken spiritual life and usher in the revival which is the world's greatest need.

"TO THE WORK! TO THE WORK!"
—Haggai 2.4

(Preached twenty times including at Katherine Road 11/8/31 and at Horsehay 8/5/42)

Haggai 2.4 "Be strong . . . saith the Lord, and work: for I am with you, saith the Lord of Hosts."

HAGGAI WAS PERHAPS THE least of the men we call the Minor Prophets. It has to be admitted that his style was simple, homely, unadorned, and lacking in imagination. In his theme, too, he was limited. He reveals little knowledge of world problems and no indication of solutions. He is concerned almost entirely with the rebuilding of the Jewish temple.

There are critics who sneer at what they are pleased to call his "crabbed and jejune style," and at his interpretation of the Word of God as only a call to hew wood and lay stone on stone. They see in his book a collapse of the prophetic spirit. But most of us are not critics. The homely and direct style of the man brings him nearer to us. What we see is a man who felt what the moment needed, and who made clear the stern hand way of the nearest duty. That, for us, is the mark of the true prophet.

Nor do we quarrel with him because his insistent call was to the rebuilding of the material temple. That temple was sacramental, a symbol of the nation's relationship with God. It was essential to the continuity of Israel's religion. It was the House of Prayer, the place where men were reminded of God's presence, recognized His power, and remembered the covenant betwixt Him and themselves. Any man who calls the people of his time to the task of building a place for prayer and praise and preaching is doing a service to the strength of the nation's life.

OUR OWN TASK

We have to build and maintain the material fabric of a church. That is important, but we have a greater task. We have to build up a spiritual church, to bring what the Apostle Peter calls "living stones" into contact with the "Living Stone" that there may be a strong and effective church of the living God. The question is—what has this homely prophet to say to us as we attempt our work? The answer to that question demands some knowledge of—

THE PROPHET AND HIS TIMES

Briefly summarized, here are the facts. The captivity in Babylon was practically at an end. Most of the Jews had returned to Jerusalem. The altar there was erected and the foundations of the temple laid. But the builders had allowed the difficulties of the task and the opposition of the Samaritans to depress and deter them. The glowing enthusiasm of the return had died down and the work of rebuilding was held up. The people were pessimistic about the accomplishment of the task and turned to the securing of their material comfort.

To such a people at such a time came Haggai. It was due to his ministry, along with that of Zechariah, that the people were stirred up, the builders heartened, and the abandoned task taken up with an enthusiasm and determination that carried it to completion. The heart of the prophet's message is in our text. To a people nervous and afraid, delaying and dallying, shrinking and shirking, he rapped out his message—blunter even than the Authorized Version suggests. "Courage, all the people of the land and get to work." It was a clear and ringing call, reminding the people of what they could do for themselves and bidding them do it. Let us spend a few more minutes in exposition before we apply that clear ringing call.

A SHREWD ANALYSIS OF THE SITUATION

In that analysis, the weakness of the people is revealed. I am anxious we should examine it for it is so strikingly true of the present situation. Haggai said three things about the religious people of his day that might have been as appropriately said yesterday.

He pointed out that the people were saying, "The time is not come, the time that the Lord's House should be built" (Hag 1.2). That is precisely what people are saying today, only they do not say it so simply. They say, "We are waiting for the psychological moment." That sounds wise and inspiring, but how much indifference is hidden behind the imposing phrase. There are "tides of the Spirit" and a place for waiting in the religious life. But in the face of clamorous need and abounding opportunities, it is foolish and sinful to play the part of a Micawber "waiting for something to turn up." Haggai knew, and the people knew, that it was idle to say, "The set time does not come." For us, too, the set time has come. Our duty is not to wait and see, it is to come and build, tackle our task, and get on with the work lying to our hand.

By the side of what they were saying, the prophet set what the people were doing. In Haggai 1.4, he asks, "Is it a time for you, o ye, to dwell in your ceilinged homes, and this house be waste?" You can see the suggestion. It was not the time to build God's House but they were getting on very well with their own. They were building large, comfortable, and ever magnificent residences for themselves. The house of prayer was unfinished, but they had completed their own mansions and seen to the last thing in luxury as those ornamented ceilings testified.

I want to speak carefully and not to fling about wild charges. Everyone is justified in seeking to have his life and furnish his home in comfort. I will go further and say that thousands of men and women lack the comfort to which they are entitled and live in homes that are neither fit for heroes or any of God's children. But, I am convinced we are touching here one of the chief sources of weakness in the church of Christ. We have got things in the wrong order. We are giving God superfluities and not sacrifices. Our spiritual devotion has not kept pace with our material prosperity. The luxuries of our fathers have become necessities with us. We are positively afraid to be poor. We must have our own comfort, our ceilinged houses, whether the House of God is built or not. God help us to see and to set things in their right order.

Just another thing in this analysis. *The people were contrasting their own days with the good old days.* In Haggai 2.3, the prophet says, "Who is left among you that saw this House in its first glory? And how do you see it now? Is it not in your eyes in comparison of it as nothing?" They were saying that things could never be the same again. If things were only as they used to be! That is what we are always doing and saying. We talk about the good old days, the old preacher, the old prayer meetings, in a tone that is not without contempt for the present. There is nothing wrong in going over the past to find inspiration for the present. I am the very last man to sneer at the fathers and their great deeds and mighty victories. But I get a bit tired of talk that suggests that God worked himself out in their day, and that nothing great can happen in these days. God did nothing in those old days that He cannot surpass in these. God who made them mighty can make us mightier yet. Talk about the good old days and give God thanks for them, and then look and work and pray for the best that is yet to be. That is the situation as Haggai saw it and as it is today. So, we may apply to ourselves—

THE RINGING CALL, "COURAGE . . . AND GET TO WORK"

The need is great and the opportunities abound. The set time is come. The House of the Lord lies waste and the people are in want. We have delayed and dallied too long. Be strong and work. Don't wait for something to turn up or to be done by magic or miracle. Get to work. Stop criticizing and theorizing and do something. Forget your comfort and find your task. Give up for a while talking about the glorious past and make the present and the future glorious. "Hats off to the past, coats off to the present." There the glory of the past shall pale before the greater glory of the present. As you go to your task, take with you—

"TO THE WORK! TO THE WORK!"—HAGGAI 2.4

THREE GREAT PROMISES FROM THE PROPHECY

All of the promises were made and meant for courageous people who get to work. "I am with you saith the Lord of Hosts" (2.4). You can face anything with a promise like that. Think who it is who is with you, "The Lord of Hosts." Lord of the hosts of heaven, of earth, of hell. Dare you take on unsurmountable difficulties with a promise like that? What foe need you fear if the Lord of Hosts is with you?

"I will fill this House with my glory" (2.7). You do your part, arise and build, be strong and work. God will light up your sanctuary with glory. What is the glory? I cannot define it. It is the brightest and holiest you can think of—the glory of God's presence, His redeeming love, his saving and sanctifying power. Let it stand as it is, "I will fill this House with my glory."

"In this place will I give peace" (2.9). Peace to the builders, the worshippers. Peace to distressed minds and troubled hearts. But more than that, here come the supreme values of God's House. It is when the Temple of God is built that peace comes to the nations. Haggai is at one with the great prophets. Both Micah and Isaiah saw and said that when God's House was exalted that nations would learn war no more. It has been said, "If we all dwell in our own houses, and provide no place where all men can be equally at home because it is their Father's house, then we shall be sowing the seeds of which the harvest will be decay, anarchy, and misery." Be strong and work. Build the house of God where men and nations can meet on a common basis of brotherhood because of the Fatherhood of God.

That is Haggai's message for his own day and ours. And I gather it all up in the words of a hymn we seldom sing but can ill spare. "To the work! To the work! We are servants of God. Let us follow the path that our Master has trod. With the balm of his counsel our strength to renew, let us do with our might what our hands find to do."[1]

---

1. This is from Fanny Crosby's hymn "To the Work! To the Work! We Are Servants of God" (1869).

"A WHITSUNTIDE ASSURANCE"
—Haggai 2.5

(Preached seven times from Spring Head Mission 5/16/37 to Bishop Street 6/5/49; a Pentecost sermon)

Haggai 2.5 "My spirit remaineth among you, fear ye not."

"Whatsoever things were written aforetime were written for our learning, that we through patience and comfort of the Scriptures might have hope." So wrote Paul in his Epistle to the Romans. And it is still true that, though we live in the New Dispensation, the record of God's dealings with men in the earlier Dispensation may bring to us patience and comfort and inspire hope. In particular, living as we do on this side of Pentecost, and knowing more about the work of the Holy Spirit than did the men of God of old, we may yet turn to the movements of the Spirit in the old days for many a lesson for the life of today. That is why on this Whit Sunday we turn for our text to the Old Testament.[1] There are few narrations more inspiring for Christian workers than that which is the setting of our text. If you can see the situation which Haggai addressed there will be no difficulty in making the applications of the text, they will make themselves.

Haggai exercised his ministry after the return of Judah from the Babylonian captivity. Behind him lay the seventy years when "Zion was ploughed as a field, and Jerusalem became heaps." But the message of forgiveness had been proclaimed and God had constrained Cyrus to let the captives return. On returning to Jerusalem they set about the task of rebuilding the temple and restoring worship. But the work was so hard, the difficulties so many, the opposition so great, that the builders lost heart and gave up in despair. The work ceased because the workers became lukewarm and indifferent. For fifteen years, the work of rebuilding the temple was neglected and the people gave themselves to the work of building and beautifying their private homes. Even the few nobler souls could only sigh as they remembered the glory that had been and compared it with what was. So the situation was difficult, discouraging, and enough to drive the people to despair.

---

1. Whit Sunday is another name for Pentecost Sunday.

"A WHITSUNTIDE ASSURANCE"—HAGGAI 2.5

However, addressing the situation, Haggai's message was cheery and hopeful. He reminded his people that God's arm was not shortened and that the Lord was in command of the situation. Their God, who had been with them all through their captivity, was with them as they faced the present difficult and discouraging situation. Let them be strong and get to work. They need not bewail what had been, for they would see greater things. The desirable things of all nations would come to them and the glory of the Lord would be revealed. The prophet gathered all this up in the reminder that God had pledged his word to them and that His covenant could not be broken. "I am with you, saith the Lord of Hosts according to the word which I covenanted with you when ye came out of Egypt, so my Spirit remaineth among you, fear ye not." They were fearing and faltering and failing because they were forgetting God's covenant that through all changes His Spirit remained with them. "Realize the presence of your divine ally," said the prophet, have done with your fears and get on with your work.

We, too, forget what they failed to remember. And we too are often downcast and despondent because we forget. Our work as individuals and as a church is so heavy and tiring, there is so much indifference and opposition, that we lose heart and give up hope. We, too, talk of the good old days and even while we talk of the glorious past we lose the vision and settle down to a dreary acceptance of things as they are. We say that times have changed and that it is useless to expect anything better or to try to restore worship to its old place.

To us there comes the message of comfort and hope. And it comes to us reinforced by the experience of the church at Pentecost. The promise is to us and ours. The Spirit outpoured has never been withdrawn. We are neither helpless nor friendless. Our Lord has pledged to be with us and His eternal covenant He will never break. We can say even more surely than Haggai could that God's Spirit remains among us, and that assurance should scatter our fears and inspire confidence and courage. But instead of leaving the text to apply to our difficulties and discouragements generally, let us apply the truth to some special needs in the modern situation.

Like these Jews, we think and speak of a glorious past and contrast it with things as they are in the present. We say, "Ah, there were giants in those days," and we talk of great and mighty victories. There is no need to belittle the past. Let us think of it that our hearts may glow. But let us remember that the giants of those days said, "It is not by might or power of our own, but by God's Spirit that great things are accomplished." Then let us quote our text to ourselves—"My Spirit remaineth among you." Then the present and the future may be yet more glorious because the Spirit who made our fathers mighty is still with us.

Or we think of defections and deaths. From one cause or another our workers leave us. Death works in our midst and our trusted leaders are taken. We are left with depleted ranks. The work is great and the laborers are few. But, let us never forget, "My Spirit remaineth among you." God is with us and we need not fear. Again, we think of our own defects and sins. We know how unworthy we are and how often we have grieved the Spirit. As with David, our fear is that God should take His Holy Spirit from us. But for all our fears, God's promise still stands and His Spirit remains among us.

What, then, is our duty? Certainly, not to sit down and expect everything to be done by God's Spirit apart from us. Look again at the setting of the text: "My Spirit remaineth among you, fear not, be strong and work." The Spirit is our ally not our substitute. He works, not apart from us, but through us. Let us tackle our tasks in a fearless and courageous spirit, and we shall find God working in us and through us and leading us to success and triumph.

∼

"WOUNDED IN THE HOUSE OF FRIENDS"
—Zechariah 13.6

(Preached at Spring Head Mission 11/7/38)

Zechariah 13.6 "And one shall say unto him, 'What are these wounds in thine hands?' Then he shall answer, 'Those with which I was wounded in the house of my friends.'"

THESE WORDS ARE SIMPLE enough, but the task of discerning their precise meaning is difficult. The words may refer to false prophets who had cut themselves with knives after the manner of heathen priests, or to the hurt those prophets had received in the foolish and sinful service to which they had given themselves, or to what faithful prophets had suffered in their endeavors to save foolish folk from backsliding from the worship and service of God. Scholars differ widely and it would be wrong for ordinary persons to be dogmatic.

Christian thought has long been on the side of that interpretation which applies the words to faithful and suffering servants of Jehovah. It has gone further and seen in the text a prophecy of the suffering Savior who was wounded by those He came to save, and from whose side flowed the mystic stream which cleanses from sin and uncleanness. Having admitted that there are these possible interpretations, I am going to follow the example of the older preachers.

Whatever the correct exegesis of the text, it is true that our Lord's wounds were afflicted in the house of His friends, and it is of Him that I am thinking and of him I want to speak. And let us lead up to our main thought along the avenue of human experience. Wounded in the house of friends! Smitten by hands pressed in love! Such are surely of all wounds the most painful and hard to bear.

ILLUSTRATIONS IN LITERATURE

Literature has been described as "the reflection in words of the great pageant of life." Great literature does not shrink from life's darkest experiences and among the darkest it does not hesitate to place the ingratitude and treachery of friends. The old Greek poets tell of Agamemnon coming scarless through battle and tempest only to find shame and death awaiting him through the treachery of his wife. Our own Shakespeare tells of Julius Caesar stabbed by friends, of King Lear driven frantic by the cruelty of his daughters to whom he had given his kingdom, and gives us the better known figure of Wolsey wailing at the end of his life—"O Cromwell, Cromwell! Had I but served my God with half the zeal I served my king, He would not in mine age have left me naked to mine enemies!"

When we turn to the greatest of all literature, the Bible, we find David drinking of the bitter cups of ingratitude and treachery. His own son, Absalom, and his trusted friend, Ahithophel, played him false. Listen to the pathos and the pain of this psalm—Psalm 55. "For it was not an enemy that reproached me. Then I could have borne it: neither was it he that hated me that did magnify himself against me . . . But it was thou . . . my guide, and my acquaintance. We took sweet counsel together, and walked unto the house of God in company." Now let us pass from literature to—

PARALLELS IN LIFE

It is a common experience for a man to be "wounded in the house of his friends." Those to whom we give one love have the greatest power to hurt us. We do not often read nowadays of poison cups and deadly daggers, but ingratitude and treachery are not unknown. A not uncommon headline in our papers is, "Robbed by the man who befriended him." One of my friends who had, as we say, "Come down in the world," said somewhat bitterly of friends who had shared his hospitality, "They don't want me now that I'm poor." Parents lavish the wealth of their affection on children who sometimes prove ungrateful and unworthy. A man marries a woman he credits with qualities she does not possess and finds out afterwards that she is shallow, frivolous, heartless. Or a woman gives a whole, pure, loving heart to a man who turns out to be a brute. A girl I know married a colonial soldier who took her to a foreign land and forsook her. I shall never forget her father saying to me, "She gave him her all, and he left her to die alone."

Often our kindness is taken for softness and imposed upon, our service taken lightly and soon forgotten. Many a politician and public benefactor murmurs in silence that the public have short memories. We can steel ourselves to "grin and bear" the wounds of our enemies, but wounds afflicted by those we trusted and loved, we have no heart or courage to endure. The hostility and persecution of opponents we expect, but to be wounded by friends is the unkindest cut of all. Now we come where you expected I should arrive to—

THE SUPREME ILLUSTRATION OF OUR TEXT

The supreme illustration of our text is the experience of Jesus. Of all the sons of men He stands out as the despised and rejected. Wounded! Bruised! Chastised! All in the

"WOUNDED IN THE HOUSE OF FRIENDS"—ZECHARIAH 13.6

house of friends. His was the fullest cup of suffering ever drunk, and the bitterest drops were added by those He loved. The pain in his soul was harder than that which pierced His hands and side. He came unto His own and they received Him not. His unselfish devotion was marked and spurned. Upon the face that beamed a benediction, they spat. The hands that had healed the sick they nailed to a tree. His loyal and loving heart was abandoned and betrayed. Truly he was the man of sorrows, acquainted with grief, and "wounded in the house of His friends."

So far, I have only reminded you of facts you know. Part of my purpose is in the reminder. But I want to go further by putting these facts together and point out one or two lessons. First of all—

A WORD TO THE WOUNDED

Some of you know the truth of what I have been saying by bitter and painful experience. You have been wounded and your foes have been of your own household. Your love has been repaid with hate and those you trusted have let you down. I want you to see that in Jesus you have a fellow and a sympathizer. He has been through what you are suffering and you can turn to Him in full assurance that He understands your case by personal experience.

And what is more, He teaches us how to think and act towards those who wound us. I know what your instincts are and share them. But we are not to be at the mercy of instincts. If we are Christians we have to ask what Jesus did. And you know what He did before I tell you. When He was reviled, He reviled not again. He suffered in silence, and it was not the cold, hard silence of a Stoic. He was patient with the follies and sins of those He loved. His love did not change though His friends forsook Him in the hour of his agony. He prayed for those who pained Him and carried not wrath or bitterness in His heart for those who nailed Him to the cross. As He forgave them, He put the best possible construction in their action—"they know not what they do."

That is what you must do even when you are wounded by those you trust and love. You must never let injustice make you unjust or unmerited suffering make you bitter. You must continue to love though your love is spurned. Even when you have broken your costly box of spikenard over the feet of one who turns coldly away, you must be ready to break another over the same feet. You must have love like the thirteenth chapter of First Corinthians.

How hard a saying this is I know full well, but it is Christianity. It is what Jesus did and what he hands down as the law of His kingdom—"Bless them that curse you, pray for them that despitefully use you and persecute you." Remember He did it, and when you find it hard, find comfort and help in His presence. Now—

LUMINESCENCE

A WARNING AGAINST WOUNDING

None of us would set out deliberately to stab a friend in the back or let down one who trusts us. But by our experience of those who trust us it ought to be clear how often the evil is wrought and how deep is the wound. When we are greatly loved, it is so easy to give pain. Sons and daughters do it by neglect. Husbands and wives do it by thoughtlessness. Friends do it by forgetfulness and disloyalty. As you turn with loathing from treachery take warning lest you become those who wound trustful and loving hearts.

It is easy now to pass to the thought of Jesus and the sacred head once wounded. Our anger often rises against those who nailed Him to a cross and plunged a spear into His side. But in the New Testament (Heb 6.6) there is a reference to "crucifying the Son of God afresh." It is a terrible possibility and may be our reality. If Jesus lives and is gladdened by goodness, He can be hurt and wounded more by faithless friends than by cruel foes. We should no more set out to wound Christ than we would to hurt our friends. But we may cause him pain as we do them. We can all see how He is "crucified afresh" by the glaring sins of those who profess His Name. What we do not see is that our incongruities and inconsistencies hurt love, and make the thorns prick again and the nails tear afresh. We wound Him when we cause needless pain to others, for "inasmuch as ye do it unto the least of these, ye do it unto me." What must he feel when through pride or cowardly fear we disown Him? Perhaps we wound Him most by our neglect and the easy way in which we break solemn pledges of loyalty.

Take for its own sake, and as an illustration, what is in our minds tonight. He did say, "With desire have I desired to eat this Passover with you," and, "As oft as ye eat this bread and drink this cup ye do show forth the Lord's death till He come." Where we who are members joined the church, we promised to obey this word of His. No one made us make the promise, we made it ourselves. And yet we often fail and with excuses that are worse than our absences.

By the love He bears you, by all He once suffered, by all your deepest and finest feelings, I not only warn you against wounding Him, but urge you, in your real love and loyal life, to let Him see the travail of His soul and rejoice: "Ah, then let me strive, for the love Thou hast borne, to give Thee no longer occasion to mourn."

"THINKING UPON GOD'S NAME"
—Malachi 3.16

(Preached twice on 10/9/38 at Spring Head Mission and 10/16/38 at King's Hill)

Malachi 3.16 "A book of remembrance was written before Him for them that feared the Lord, and that thought upon His Name."

THE REFERENCE IS TO the faithful in dark days. The days were dark, very dark. Wickedness was rampant and appeared to be triumphant. It seemed of no avail to serve God. Then it was that the men and women who feared God gathered and talked together. There was "a confederation of godly souls for godly ends." It is true that they aired doubt and uttered complaints. God harkened and what is remembered is that "they feared the Lord and thought upon His name."

THEY THOUGHT UPON HIS NAME

It is upon these words that I am mainly concerned. That was vital. Of the wicked it is said that God is not in their thoughts. That can sometimes be said of those who cannot be described as wicked. It is sometimes true of the righteous. They are preoccupied, obsessed with fears and thinking only of the dangers around them. In ordinary as well as critical days, there are peace and strength in the thought of God. "Thou wilt keep him in perfect peace whose mind is stayed on Thee."

SOMETHING MORE THAN A CASUAL THOUGHT OF GOD

Be patient with Bible study that is necessary to get to what these people really did. Consider those passages in the Old Testament that help to give the true meaning of the word thought. Isaiah 13.17 "They (the Medes) shall not regard silver." The only thing we need from the passage is the fact that "regard" is the same as "thought." Isaiah 33.8 says, "He regardeth no man." Again, the only thing needed is the fact that you have the same word as thought in our text. In a terrible day man was not thought of, no value was set on him. Isaiah 53.3 says, "We esteemed Him not." Again, here we have esteemed which is the same word as thought.

These passages have no direct connection with our text, but they throw rereading light on it. What these people did not do about silver, about man, about the Suffering Servant, the people of our text did about God. They valued Him, considered Him, and esteemed Him. All that is included in the statement that they thought upon His name.

A STEP FURTHER

There is something more supplied in the word *thought* than has yet been stated. Let us turn to the New Testament. Philippians 4.8, "Whatsoever things are just, pure, honest, etc., think on these things." The word used there means "reckon," "keep in mind," "carefully estimate the value of," and in a free translation, "take an inventory." The Philippians were to reckon their wealth, not in gold and jewels, but in things honest, honorable, lovely, and of good report. The Septuagint, a translation into Greek of the Old Testament, uses this word for "thought" in our text. They thought upon God's name and reckoned up their wealth in it. Now we are getting closer to home. These people had—

A WONDERFUL HERITAGE IN THE NAME OF THE LORD

He had revealed Himself by names continually. To them He was the great and only "I Am." With his names, they associated some of their greatest deliverances. Take an outstanding illustration. When God met their father Abraham's great need and provided the sacrifice, he called the name of the place, Jehovah Jireh. The name lived on and whenever Jews thought of it they remembered that the Lord would provide. These people thought on the name of the Lord, regarded it, esteemed it, and counted their resources in it. Living in the Christian era, on this side of the Advent of Jesus we have—

A RICHER HERITAGE

Our thought of God is enriched by all the Jesus taught and revealed. What's in a name? What about when it is the name of God? Think of the names by which we know God. We sing of Him as "our maker, defender, redeemer and friend." We begin our daily prayer with "Our Father." We are baptized and blessed in the name of the Father, Son, and Holy Ghost. Think upon His name. Reckon all you have in it and rely on its resources. Remember that you have in God a father, redeemer, friend. The name of the Lord will then be your strong tower and your defense.

"THINKING UPON GOD'S NAME"—MALACHI 3.16

THE FELLOWSHIP OF THE THOUGHTFUL

A word of conclusion about what may be called the fellowship of the thoughtful. There was something more than a few scattered men and women thinking upon God's name. They met and spoke unto one another. You say we are tired of endless talk. But what did these people talk about? Surely, they talked of what they thought, of God's name and their mutual possession in it, of their joy in the name, of their sorrow that so many ignored it. You can see the value of that. There is always strength in fellowship. Here is the reason for your class meeting, your group meeting. In such gatherings, you can speak about the deepest things. Apart from organized meetings, those who think upon God's name might well get together and talk of their mutual heritage and treasure. In all such fellowship, there is strength for those who fear God, and it is always out of such fellowship that revival comes.

SERMONS FROM THE NEW TESTAMENT

"THE UNWANTED CHRIST"
—Matthew 8.34

(Preached at Spring Head Mission 7/13/42)

Matthew 8.34 "And, behold, the whole city came out to meet Jesus: and when they saw Him, they besought Him that he would depart out of their coasts."

THE NEXT VERSE READS, "He entered into a ship and passed over." They begged Him to depart and He departed. He was not wanted, and He did not and does not stay where He is not wanted. That gives us our subject, the unwanted Christ.

UNWANTED, BUT NEEDED

What we want and what we need we are, maybe, two very different things, though we do not always realize the difference. One of the sad things of our time is that so many seek only what they want. That way is the way of disaster. We do not leave our children to decide whether they want education. We insist on their going to school because they need it. To decide about religion by our wants with no reference to our needs is tragic. A minister tells how he found in a bookstall a book about salvation priced two pence. He inquired the reason for the cheapness, and was told that no one wants salvation nowadays. "No one may want it," he replied, "but everyone needs it." That is the point. People may not want to go to church, to pray, to find God's love. It simply does not appeal to them. But that does not disprove the fact that they need God. Everybody needs Jesus Christ, though to many He is the unwanted.

Let us look at this truth in the case set before us. The Gergesenes, of whom our text speaks, were largely Gentiles and it was a sheer act of grace on our Lord's part to visit them. Immediately after He landed He worked a miracle and cast demons out of two possessed men. We do not understand all that is meant by demon possession, but it is clear that the two men were the terrors of the neighborhood and that nothing could be done with them until Jesus healed them. He changed them into good men and law-abiding citizens.

You would have thought that would establish him in their good graces, make them glad and grateful, and desirous of keeping Him in their midst. Instead they besought Him to depart. They were perfectly polite about it, but they made it quite clear that they did not want Him. I want to be quite fair to them. They were taken with a great fear. They wondered what this wonder worker could do next. But a fair reading of the narrative shows that it was the owners of the swine who preferred the request, and that they associated the healing of the demoniacs with the destruction of their property. They were more concerned about their pigs than about persons, about their own loss rather than the community's gain and the welfare and happiness of the two men.

MODERN SETTING

Whether that is a true interpretation of the incident or not, the fact is it describes the attitude of many today. There are multitudes of people so occupied with selfish and unnecessary concerns that they have no time for Jesus Christ, no desire for His presence, no enjoyment in His freedom. They think more of worldly loss than of spiritual gain. They care more for possessions and pleasures than for purity and piety. To use our modern terms Jesus commits the unpardonable crime of offending against vested interests. He challenges the ways in which men make money and insists that human interests come before interest in capital.

Some of us He offends by interfering with the pleasure we want and the ease we love. Many of those who are rejecting Christ are not doing it because of intellectual difficulties, though they are clever at inventing them. They want to do what they like and Christ insists that they shall do what is right. They resent any preaching that interferes with the things they want to do. Some of them make a profession of religion and claim to be better than those who go to church, but because Jesus calls them to a spiritual attitude they are unwilling to adopt, and challenges their ways of living, they will have none of Him. With His steady eyes upon them they cannot continue in sin, so they bid Him depart. Of course, they bid Him depart nicely. There is little of what the prophet called despising and rejecting. They are far too polite for that. They just show Him out. They do not always put the dismissal into words. A visitor can be made aware that he is not wanted without telling him so. Indifference and taking part in things He does not approve of often makes it plain that there is neither room nor time for Jesus.

HE DEPARTED

They bade Him depart—and He departed. That is the nemesis of rejection. If we bid Him depart no thunderbolt will fall from heaven. He will take us at our word and go. We have seen Watt's picture of the rich young ruler with his back turned to Jesus going sorrowfully away. There is a sadder picture than that, it is the picture of Jesus turning sadly away from people who do not want Him. I do not want to paint that picture too black. You know the hymn "Jesus of Nazareth Passeth By," which tells that He is passing but will always stop at the cry of need and faith. I can sing all the hymn except the last verse: "But if you still his call refuse, and all His wondrous love abuse, soon will He sadly from you turn, your bitter prayer for pardon spurn."[1] To be honest, I have to be silent when that is sung. I do not believe that he will ever spurn a prayer for pardon. What I am concerned about is the state of those who dismiss him.

I am very anxious to speak the truth in love. Let me give you it in some of the tender words of Jesus which I have been trying for forty years to read with the right emphasis. He was weeping as He uttered them, "O Jerusalem, Jerusalem, which killest the prophets and stonest them that are sent unto thee: how often would I have gathered thy children together as a hen doth gather her brood under her wings, and you would not. Behold your house is left unto you desolate." The word "desolate" is not in the best manuscripts. Probably some copyist introduced it because he felt it was needed to describe a house without Christ. But there was no need to add the word, for there can be no more ultimate desolation than this, that Jesus of Nazareth passeth by and men are left to take the way they have chosen. Years ago, Coulson Kernahan wrote a book, *The World without a Child*. What a picture of desolation! But think of a world without Christ. In your hearts, you must know that the world today is overrun with demoniacs because it has asked Christ to depart.

Think of your town without Christ. Will you brighten it by introducing Him? Sometimes we sing, "O happy home where Thou art not forgotten."[2] What of home without Him? What of the heart without Him? Without the peace, pardon, and comfort He brings with Him?

HE WANTS TO BE DESIRED

If you bid Him depart He will go, but His desire is to be desired. He wants to be the Savior of the nation, the city, the home, the heart. In uttermost love, He comes and stands at the door seeking entrance. He is willing to forgive the ingratitude and sins of the past. All He wants is for you to want Him. Let me briefly put another story by this story of rejection. Jesus walked with two men on the Emmaus Road. When they reached their destination, He made as though He would have gone further, but they constrained Him and He went in to stay with them. Constrain Him by your faith and prayer and He will abide with you.

And I am taking back no word I have said when I declare that though you bid Him depart you do not destroy His desire to come to you. I can best put it this way. I remember years ago T. C. William preaching a sermon on a pathetic text in the book

---

1. This is from a hymn from 1863, written by Emma Campbell, "Jesus of Nazareth Passeth By."
2. This was originally a German hymn written by Karl Spitta in 1833, but it was later translated into English by Sarah B. Findlater in 1858 under the title "The Happy Home."

of Hosea 5.15. "I will go and return to my place, till they acknowledge their offense, and seek my face: in their affliction they will seek me earnestly." No one will forget that great preacher's words, "God goes away but He leaves His address." You know where to find Him when you want Him. And I will venture to add that He keeps coming back to see if you have changed your mind. "Would you believe, and Jesus receive, if He was standing here? Will you believe, and Jesus receive, for He is standing here?"[3]

∽

---

3. This is from a hymn by Caroline Sawyer entitled "Would You Believe?" (1899).

"THE SERVANT'S TEMPER AND METHOD"
—Matthew 12.19, 20

(Preached at Katherine Road 1/13/35 and Spring Head Mission 8/10/41)

Matthew 12.19, 20 "He shall not strive, nor cry: neither shall any man hear His voice in the streets. A bruised reed shall He not break, and the smoking flax shall He not quench."

IN THE LAST SERMON, we noted that the Ideal Servant of the Old Testament only appeared in fact in the New Testament.[1] The ideal was only realized in Jesus and He in turn becomes the pattern for all who would be Servants of the Most High. We may well turn then to the Servant passage in the New Testament, and as applied by St. Matthew to our Lord. Last week we tried to find inspiration in the Master's confidence and courage. Let us now consider Him as our example in the Servant's temper and method.

Against all contending forces the Divine Servant is undismayed and undiscouraged. He is to set the Divine Judgment as a standard to the whole world. He will neither fail nor be discouraged until He "carries religion to victory." It is a great task the Servant sets out to accomplish and at first sight *the servant does not seem adequate for the task*. The mission seems to demand a man of purpose and power, who comes with the sound of a trumpet blast and armed with the forces that break down opposition and crush foes. What we see is a quiet, patient, sympathetic figure who seems far more concerned about the weak and the suffering than about smashing thrones and setting up a new empire.

If we are disappointed it is not surprising. John said that the Messiah would come with an axe and a fire, to bring swift judgment upon the ungodly. When Jesus came, He brought neither axe nor fire, and John was so disappointed that he sent his servants to ask, "Art Thou He that should come?"

But the meek and lowly Jesus is the world's conqueror and the pierced hand has proved mightier than the nailing fist. And still the servants of the Most High do not always look the part. The meek inherit the earth, and the kingdom of God comes

---

1. See above the sermon entitled "The Undiscouraged Servant."

through the patient efforts of unlikely men and women. We shall not overcome the world by copying the methods of its warlords, but by being servants of God after the pattern of Jesus Christ.

OMISSIONS IN CHARACTER OF THE SERVANT

It is only carrying the same thought a little further to mark the omissions in the character of the Divine Servant. What is given us is a striking list of negatives. He "shall not strive, nor cry . . . He will not break the bruised reed, nor will He quench the dimly burning wick." The assumption is that men of the world would strive, cry, and break down those who stood in the way.

It is easy to sneer at negatives and absences, but the Servant of God must be content to differ. It must be true of him that he have no sin, no selfishness, no pride. We are too prone to think that the only way to save the world is to adopt its methods. The fact is that the only way to save the world is to be separate and distinct from it. The trouble God has with many of us, and the reason for our ineffective service, lies in our conformity to the world. Many things we must let go before we can say, "Truly I am Thy servant." We have to renounce the world, the flesh, and the devil.

TEMPER OF THE SERVANT

Note the temper of the Servant as it is revealed in Jesus and ought to be in us. He shall not strive or wrangle. That does not mean he shall never contend—he "contends earnestly for the faith"—it means he is not contentious. The wrangler wastes time, strength, and temper by contending for "a point." There is a time for argument and discussion, but with the Servant of God the end is never personal triumph or the scoring of points: it is always the triumph of truth. The scribes and Pharisees continually tried to lead Jesus off into striving and wrangling about knotty points and little matters of the Law. In our own day men would have us spend our time and get up excitement about "points," points of order, points of ritual, points of constitution. But men who are concerned by a great mission do not wrangle. Servants of God, like their Master, are too busy with the work of saving the world to fritter away time over trivialities.

"He shall not . . . cry, nor shall any man hear His voice in the streets." That is not an argument against opening our meetings; it is a warning against self-advertisement. The man of the world cries to call attention to himself and one of our own dangers is that of boosting and boasting. I'm sure Christ would revise some of our advertisements, some of our columns in the religious press. His most withering scorn was poured on paraded piety and street corner prayers and almsgiving. He commanded men to pray in secret and if a man needs to carry a big Bible to let you know he is religious, there is something wrong with his religion. The Divine Servant is no screamer. His strength is in his quietness and confidence. We shout to keep our courage up and

"THE SERVANT'S TEMPER AND METHOD"—MATTHEW 12.19, 20

when we are not sure. Jesus was quietly confident, a strong and silent servant. As we follow Him we too reveal the temper that is free from wrangling and money, showing parade.

METHOD OF THE SERVANT

Note the method of the Divine Servant. It was marked in Jesus by gentleness and patience and is expressed in two beautiful figures. He did not break bruised reeds or quench dimly burning wicks. What others would have cast aside as useless, He, with infinite gentleness and patience restored. A bruised reed needs gentle handling or it will be broken beyond repair. A smoking wick is an offense to the eyes and the nostrils and may easily be put out altogether. But Jesus healed the bruises, put strength into the weak, and turned smoking wicks into shining lights. Have we the Master's gentleness and patience? Do we not lose our patience with the dull and slow and sometimes crush what is already bruised?

It needs courage and strength to take the way of Jesus and we shall fail unless we have His equipment. Of the Divine Servant God said, "I will put my Spirit upon Him." It is our privilege to have the mind of Christ and the Spirit of Jesus. The fruit of the Spirit is . . . meekness and gentleness.

"LOVE'S LABOR NOT LOST"
—Matthew 26.8

(Preached sixteen times from Fentiman Road to Somersby, dated only at Pleck 5/18/41)

Matthew 26.8 "To what purpose is this waste."

HERE IS AN INCIDENT preachers love. It bristles with suggestive points. But for any immediate purpose I must have it myself to a particular application rather than a general exposition. A woman lavished her costly love offering on Jesus. To many standing round, it seemed sheer waste. They criticized her gift and declared that it might have been put to more practical uses. But for the fact that our Lord threw around her the mantle of His protecting commendation, the woman might have gone on her way thinking she had done a foolish and wasteful thing.

In our own day, it is still possible to bring a love offering, expressed in sacrificial service, and lay it at the Master's feet. And there are still utilitarian, not to say Philistine people who ask, "To what purpose is this waste?" They suggest that the time and strength spent in Christian service might and ought to be given to what they are pleased to regard as more practical work. What is more, sometimes those who are bringing the gift ask the same question. There is no service so costly as Christian service. It costs in time a money, and still more in patience, heartache, and love. And often the price seems paid in vain, it looks like "love's labor lost."

And there are those to whom we appeal for service who count the cost and who shrink from paying the price. They think they can spend their strength to better effect. I am not particularly anxious to answer the question as it is asked by those who stand idly by and ask it with a sneer. Probably no answer given would satisfy them. They do not understand our scale of values and will probably go on thinking as fools who squander what might have been sold. But it is another matter altogether when the question is asked by those who are giving and doing their best, and those who are hesitating before giving themselves to sacrificial service.

There are those who are saying we have labored in vain. We have given our best to win our children, our neighbors, our friends for Christ, to build up our church and school in strength and goodness and it has all gone for nothing. After years of sacrifice and toil we have nothing to show but a diminished membership and a weakened cause. What's the good, they ask, of pouring forth our best when it is unappreciated and ineffective? We might just as well have put our strength into something that would have increased our comfort and our wealth.

Such a question, asked in so serious a spirit, is deserving of our most considered answer. And never more than at a Sunday School anniversary. What can be said to those who are giving their strength and service, and who are asking "Is it worthwhile?"

LOVE'S LABOR NOT LOST

Well, I will say this first. We must judge fairly and honestly. We must not let cares of failure, or apparent failure, blind us to success. A great deal of the service rendered issues in positive gain. It is not love's labor lost. There is visible success and we ought to recognize it. I am not going to argue so much as bear testimony. I could tell you of a poor widow who slaved and saved to give her son an education. The story ought to end by saying that her labor and sacrifice were in vain and that he turned out ungrateful and unworthy. But as a matter of fact, he proved entirely worthy of her sacrifices and to her joy and the good of others became a good minister of Jesus Christ.

Sometime ago at a Sunday School Anniversary a gentleman who occupies a very prominent place in London's commercial and religious life took the chain. With frankness and sincerity and humility he told the children and teachers that years ago, he was a dirty, uncared-for youngster, wearing old clothes. "I was taken in hand," he added, "by Sunday School teachers and I owe all I am and have to their teaching and care."

For twenty-five years, I have gone to an Anniversary in Lancashire where there is a band of men who count it a great honor to serve their church. It is all due to the work of a gardener who had a Young Man's Class where he taught his scholars to love Christ and serve His church.

Let me add my own experience for what it is worth. If I am able to attempt any work as a minister of the gospel, it is due almost entirely to the devoted interest and work of Sunday School teachers in one of the least of our little Bethels. Let us be fair, and realize that all our labor is not in vain. The prayers of godly parents, the toil of Sunday School teachers, the influence of good people, often avail and bear fruit in associated lives.

THE FAR-REACHING ISSUES OF SUCCESS

And I want to remind you that nowhere does success mean so much as it does in Christian service. Again, illustration must serve. In a little Congregational church in Cheshire the deacons and the minister were in despair because in twelve months only one name had been added to their church roll, and that was the name of an under gardener. But when Robert Moffat's name was added to the church roll, Africa was added to the kingdom of Christ.

In a Methodist Church, some local preachers held a mission and one night there was great concern because the only convert was a lad of sixteen. But the lad became, "the greatest soul winner since Wesley." He was Thurman Cook. I am not talking high-falutin nonsense when I say that there may be a Robert Moffat or a Thomas Cook in your home or your class. It doesn't seem likely! No, but neither did it in that Congregational church or that Methodist church.

APPARENT FAILURE MAY BE DEFERRED SUCCESS

It is because we see no immediate fruit for our labor that we are inclined to think it is in vain. Remember what the promise is and give it a wider application than you usually do. "Train up a child in the way he should go, and when he is old he will not depart from it." The one who is breaking your heart may be more deeply impressed than you think and the labor you think wasted may bring fruit beyond your hopes. Longfellow sets the truth in "The Arrow and the Song."

This truth is verified in experience. Years ago, when I was a Sunday School teacher, there was a lad in my class who was a terror. His name was Fred, and that may account for much! When I left him he was still well and wayward. When I returned to conduct a mission in my old church, Fred was the first to respond to the appeal. In one of my churches was a similar lad—the stormy petrel of the Band of Hope, and came near to breaking the leader's heart and wrecking the meeting. The Great War came and he was one of those who went and did not come back. Among his belongings when they came home was a scrap of paper on which he had made his will just before going over the top, and he had left the few pounds, all he had, to the Debt Extinction Fund at his old church. You will reap if you faint not. You will come again with rejoicing bearing precious sheaves. Don't rob yourself of the good of the harvest by impatience and despair.

LOVE'S LABOR NEVER LOST

Finally let this be no mistake, even where visible success is never seen, honest toil is near lost, and sacrifice and service are never wasted. The Africans have a saying, "Though the meat is boiled to shreds, it is still in the pot." The answer to the question, to what purpose is this waste? Is, "Your labor is not in vain in the Lord." The sweetness of your sacrifice is not wasted in the driest air, it is a sweet-smelling savor unto God. It is in the world sweetening and saving it.

Jesus died on the cross and that seemed the supreme waste. But we know He did not die in vain. Nor did the martyrs for their blood become the seed of the church. You live a life of sacrifice and service and what seems waste will further God's purposes in the world. The world's sordid critics are as far from the truth as was Judas

"LOVE'S LABOR NOT LOST"—MATTHEW 26.8

when he criticized Mary's generous act. Let yours be the faith that can labor and want, and the love that can labor without seen and tangible reward. Give yourself to wonderful service. Keep on with it in spite of sneer and criticisms, and in spite of your own discouragements. It is life worthwhile and it is the only life worth living.

∼

"DARKNESS AND DAWN"
—Matthew 28.1

(Preached at Spring Head Mission, Easter 1937, preached five other times from Fentiman Road to Bishop Street, undated)

Matthew 28.1 "As it began to dawn."

LITERALLY, THE WORDS SIMPLY mark a point of time, they tell us that Christ rose from the dead very early in the morning. But the sacred writers, apparently by accident rather than design, use a word that expresses the poetry of a great occasion. "Dawn" is just the word that fits and suits. "Night" would be incongruous. But "dawn" flows easily from the tongue, and the "Resurrection morning" is as appropriate as "Resurrection night" would be jarring. So, we will take the poetical and mystical wording rather than the literal.

So we take the words of the text as gathering up and expressing in a poetic symbol what Easter meant to the disciples and means to us. Just as the rising of the sun changes the whole aspect of the landscape, making what was cold and dark shivering to glow with light and warmth and beauty, so the resurrection of Jesus poured light and warmth and joy upon shadowed hearts. It was the perfect fulfillment of the old prophecy, "The sun of righteousness shall rise with healing in his wings." It meant the scattering of the shadows of doubt and sorrow and the rebirth of faith, hope, and love. One of our own poets has the word: "While Christ lay dead, the widowed world wore willow green from hope undone, till, when bright Easter dews impearled the chilly burial earth, all north and south, all east and west, flushed rosy in the arising sun; hope laughed, and Faith resumed her rest, and Love remembered mirth."[1]

DAWN OF JOY

Let us put it this way—Easter represents the passing of the night of sorrow and the dawn of the morning of joy. What an awful night the disciples had passed through!

---

1. This is from a poem by Christian Rosetti entitled "Our Church Palms Are Budding Willow Twigs."

"DARKNESS AND DAWN"—Matthew 28.1

They had seen their loved one and Lord betrayed and crucified. The triumph of his enemies seemed complete. Their hearts were in their sandals. They had trusted that Jesus would redeem Israel, and he had died in the gallows. What remained but to bring spices to anoint his dead body? For these the sun had gone and the night of sorrow gathered round their souls.

But "it began to dawn." In vain they sought their Lord in the tomb. Early as they were at the sepulcher He was risen before they reached it. He was not amongst the dead but the living. In a while they would come to this reality like a dream. It all seemed too good to live. But the dawn grew into the perfect day. Then were their hearts filled with laughter and from their lips flowed songs of purest joy. True, shortly after he was taken from the sight of their eyes, but He lived forever in their hearts. They knew He was alive forevermore and with them all the days. Their master of the Galilean fields was the Christ who came and bade them be of good cheer. They had passed through the darkest night but their sorrow had been turned into joy. People marveled at their gladness. Forever after, Easter was to the disciples the day of rejoicing and thanksgiving, they donned their whole sacrament and greeted one another with "He is risen."

For us, too, Easter is the dawn that follows darkness. That is why our Easter hymns end with a triumphant Alleluia and why we place lilies on the Communion Table. Through the centuries, Easter has been the great day of the Christian year and no festival of the church is happier. It is not only that the light of gladness beams on hearts that have been sad at the thought of their Lord's passion and their own passions. It comes and reminds us that our afflictions are for a moment and that the glory is eternal. "Sorrow may endure for a season, but joy cometh in the morning." Sorrow is a lodger tarrying for a night, joy is the abiding guest. Isaac Watts sang: "In darkest shades, if Thou appear, my dawning is begun."[2] At Easter, we are sure of the presence of our Lord. It begins at dawn, and the dawn grows into the perfect day.

GOOD OVER EVIL

The joy is intensified and increased as we remember that Easter stands for the triumph of good over evil. Calvary seemed to be the triumph of evil and the powers of darkness. The prince of darkness seemed to have his way when the Holy One and the Just was crucified. What sort of a world was it in which Barabbas was released, Judas rewarded, Pilate commended, and Jesus crucified? That was what made darkness for honest hearts. It seemed pointless to be good, or to believe in goodness, if goodness came to such an end. But the seeming triumph of evil was short lived. It lasted three days, and then . . . "it began to dawn." When Jesus rose the powers of darkness were scattered, and it was proclaimed that the throne of God is set in the heavens and His kingdom ruled over all. God reigns in a world where evil is doomed to destruction

---

2. This hymn by Isaac Watts is entitled "My God the Spring of All My Joys."

and defect: "He threw their empire down, his foes compelled to own, o'er all the great Messiah reigns."[3]

Here is the secret of joy for us. So often it seems useless to fight and hope for the victory of the good. Evil is so strongly entrenched and has command of such vast resources. We have witnessed the blighting of so many hopes that passivism threatens to settle upon us. But despair can never be the final attitude of those who know what Easter means. Nothing worse can happen than what happened the first Good Friday, and after that day, "it began to dawn." The Resurrection is the living proof that Right the day must win. The cause of Truth may have a temporary setback. But the day of Truth's triumph has dawned and we can step out joyfully and fight hopefully knowing that the dawn will grow into the perfect day. We see not yet the final triumph of right, but we see Jesus crowned. That is enough.

LIFE OVER DEATH

And lastly, Easter prophesies the victory of life over death. Often it is not sin but doubt and fear that make our night. A little ridge in a graveyard that would scarce stop a child in its race, constitutes a bigger problem and causes more doubt and pain than the world's problems of evil. We watch our friends pass into the shadowland and our hearts are dark and desolate. Or, we feel in ourselves the sentence of death and all seems black as night.

Once more the Dawn Gospel brings comfort and hope. The resurrection of Jesus makes a new day dawn. It speaks to us not only of an empty tomb, but of empty tombs. We lift our eyes from graves to blue skies. We think reverently of God's acre where the mortal remains of our loved one's rest, but we must not think too much even of consecrated graves. It is only the "body of humiliation," the one that served for here, that was left in the ground. Standing in the dawn the angel asked, "Why seek ye the living among the dead?" That is a message for all who stand at a grave side. "They are not here, they are risen." The old, old question, "If a man die shall he live again?" has to answer—"Now is Christ risen from the dead and become the first fruits of them that slept." When "up from the grave He arose," it began to dawn. We speak of death as "going west." Easter bids us look toward the east and tells us that the grave opens toward the sunrise. "Heaven's morning breaks, and earth's vain shadows flee."

With the first Easter, "It began to dawn." Already we can see sorrow being turned into joy, seeming defect into glorious victory, and life even triumphing over death. We are moving, the world is moving, not towards the night, but towards Monday splendor. Out of the darkness of night, the world rolls into light, it is daybreak everywhere.

∼

3. This is a line from a poem by Benjamin Rhodes entitled "Messiah" and written in 1787, which was later transformed into a hymn entitled "My Heart and Voice I Raise."

"EMPHASIZE YOUR FAITH"
—Mark 4.24

(Preached at Katherine Road 1/10/32 and Spring Head Mission 7/24/41)

Mark 4.24 "Lord, I believe, help Thou mine unbelief."

THE MAN WHO SAID that commands our attention at once. He says two things in the same breath and one seems to contradict the other. He says he believes and that he doesn't believe. We have no difficulty in understanding his seeming contradiction. We often find ourselves in the same predicament. We are conscious of the same conflict of faith and doubt in our own minds. Many are drawn through various influences to the Christian religion. Some things about Jesus and the Christian religion they do believe. Yet, they hesitate to commit themselves because there are some aspects of religion that they cannot accept. And not a few who have accepted Christ as master find their faith challenged and doubts and fears creeping in.

JESUS' REACTION

Let us note at the outset how Christ treated this man in whom faith and doubt mingled. That is important because it settles what must be our attitude to men and women who have doubts. We make much, and never too much, of single, whole-hearted faith. Such faith saves, strengthens, and secures peace and joy. But with the example of Jesus before us we can never turn down or treat harshly those who have not yet found their way to undivided faith. For Jesus did not reject or rebuke this man. He came to Jesus as he was, believing and doubting, and he was welcomed with what little faith he had, and told, "All things are possible to him that believeth." Nor is this an isolated case of the welcome Jesus gave to those whose faith was not unmixed. Most of those who came to Him had doubts mingling with their faith.

There was a woman who came for healing. She did believe but her faith was mixed with superstition and she thought to secure a cure furtively by touching the hem of Christ's garment. And Jesus granted what she sought and said, "Go in peace, thy faith made thee whole." It is not for me or for any preacher to condemn you because you can sing without qualification, "I do believe, I will believe." If you have doubts and fears, reserves and qualifications, it is for you to come just as you are and to confess your whole mind to Christ. Be sure he will not reject your faith because it is mixed with doubt. Jesus never asks any man to be untrue to his convictions or even to his doubts and scruples. He wants all men to be honest.

THE QUESTION FOR US

The question I want to face is this, what shall we ourselves do when we find in our minds the conflict between faith and doubt? Well, for one thing, let us make sure that our doubts are honest. I am far from suggesting that all doubts are born of sin and stubbornness. But are they real? Have we examined the evidences? Are we really seeking the truth and are we prepared to accept it? In the words of Browning who has written so strongly of the faith: "What think ye of Christ, friend, when all's done and said? Like you then Christianity or not? It may be false, but would you have it true? Has it your vote to be so if it can?"[1] I am answering that there is something you believe and that you are honest in your search for the Truth and intent to do it.

EMPHASIZE YOUR FAITH

From the case of the man before us I can say this: emphasize your faith. This man put his faith first, "Lord, I believe." Too often we take the opposite course and put the emphasis on what we do not believe. The question of emphasis is more important than we think. Remember I am not asking you to guise or minimize your doubts. I am asking you to emphasize your faith, put it first, and let it determine your action. Perhaps what I mean will come more clearly by way of illustration. Here is the Bible, the great Book which has challenged the minds of men for centuries. It claims to be the Word of God and to make plain the way of salvation. But in these critical days it is challenged and men have difficulties in yielding to the claim. There are some things in it which they cannot accept or believe to be true. There are those who refuse to see divineness in the Bible because of the story of Jonah and the whale, or because of the cruelties which seem to be commanded or commended in the Old Testament by God Himself. You tell me you simply cannot believe these things not the accounts of some of the miracles recorded. Very well, then, let them wait. I believe that a longer and deeper study will bring you acceptable explanation.

But are there not some things in the Bible you do believe? Do you believe in the majestic revelation of a growing redemptive purpose, the loveliness of the gospel of grace, the wise and sleepless love of a Heavenly Father? Because you cannot believe that Balaam's ass spoke to him, that is no reason why you should not believe that God

---

1. This is from Browning's poem "Bishop Blougram's Apology" (1855).

spoke to men through the lips of Jesus Christ. You cannot believe in the virgin birth, in the glorious stories of the Nativity, you cannot accept the theories and dogma men have woven about the person of Christ. Well, what think you of Him as the master of life and the Lord of all good living, as a perfect example, and as one who has men and women to better things?

In the realm of life, you say you do not know what to believe, that you cannot accept some of the accepted Christian positions. Well, what do you believe? You believe in the good, the true, and the beautiful. Emphasize that. When Horace Bushnell was a college student he completely lost his faith in the God of the Christian revelation. All that he could find surviving in himself of his former conviction was a mistaken belief in "the abstract principle of right." But he held fast to that. He had no other god and he confesses that he actually said his prayers to an abstract principle. He says it was a dreary prayer. But it was a true prayer and it was the best he could do. Years afterward, in a voice broken by emotion, he told his students how God came to him in his act of faith and commitment. L. W. Robertson had almost a similar experience, and he became the wisest and most sympathetic helper of doubters in his day.

Too often we allow our faith to bask in the dark background of ambiguity while we emphasize our doubts. What you do not believe may be far greater in magnitude than what you believe, but the potency is in the faith. It is what a man believes that moves mountains. What he doesn't believe accomplishes nothing. So, emphasize your faith.

PROCEED POSITIVELY

The next thought follows inevitably: proceed in the positives. Act on your belief. There are many things about Christ the man of our text could not understand, but he believed Christ could save his child. That was enough for the moment and he came and won his case. There are some things in the Bible you cannot understand or accept. But you believe in the teaching of the Sermon of the Mount. Follow that teaching then and embody it in your character and conduct. You cannot accept all the mystical and theological writings about Christ, but you believe He was the ideal man and the Lord of all good living. Well, make him your pattern, live so that all your actions would be commended by Him. You cannot believe all that is taught about God. But you believe in goodness, in purity, in truth. Well, mind you proceed in what you do believe. Be a good, pure, true man. That is the way of enlightenment. I am bold to say: Let a man walk in what light he has, let him follow the truth he does believe in, he will find his faith growing and expanding. If you want to know the whole truth live out what truth you know. Increased capacity comes through increasing obedience. Faith always enlarges and strengthens itself as it is followed.

LUMINESCENCE

FAITH OVER DOUBT

Let me put another thought and urge you to, in your intercourse with others, talk of your faith rather than your doubts. I am sure that will be a good thing for you. It is not a good thing for us to be continually talking about our physical ailments, the psychological effect is bad. It is not a helpful thing for us to be always airing our doubts. Give your faith the blessings of fresh air, sunshine, and exercise. Talk if you will to someone older and wiser who may help you to overcome your doubts. But be sure to talk generally about the things you believe.

And Jesus said it is good for others for you to talk of your faith. Even the great German poet Goethe said, "Tell me of your beliefs, I have doubts enough for any man."[2] If Elle Wheeler Wilcox is a minor poet she wrote sound sense when she wrote: "Talk faith. The world is better off without your uttered ignorance and morbid doubt. If you have faith in God, or man, or self say so. If not, push back upon the shelf of silence all your thoughts, till faith shall come. No one will grieve because your lips are dumb."[3]

Especially let us show then mercy to the young. Do not lay the burden of your mind upon them or anticipate the days when they will feel the burden for themselves. It is faith that saves and lifts and makes men of us, not doubt or unbelief. It is the affirmations of faith that we need. There may be a hundred and one things you doubt, but if you can say, "One thing I know," say that. In your speech cultivate the habit of emphasizing your faith. I cannot leave you without adding *bring your doubts to the master*. That is what the man of our text did. Bring your doubt and your unbelief where he did and pray his prayer, "Lord I believe, help Thou mine unbelief."

∽

---

2. The full quote is: "If you must tell me your opinions, tell me what you believe in. I have plenty of doubts of my own." This can be found in *The Maxims and Reflections of Goethe*, translated by Thomas Bailey Saunders (Macmillan, 1906).

3. This comes from a speech poem entitled either "Speech" or "Talk."

"CHRIST AND GOOD YOUNG PEOPLE"
—Mark 5.21, 22

(Preached seven timed from Old Hill 6/9/42 to South Moor, Stanley undated; a sermon for Decision Day)

Mark 5.21, 22 "And Jesus looking upon him loved him and said unto him, 'One thing thou lackest, go, sell whatever thou hast and give to the poor, and thou shalt have treasure in heaven, and follow me. But his countenance fell at that saying, and he went away grieved.'"

OF ALL THE MEN who came to Jesus in the days of His flesh, the Rich Young Ruler represents the type of sinners the average minister faces when he conducts the ordinary ministry. Occasionally men and women come into our services who have wandered far from God and who's stained and maimed lives witness to the laws of life they have broken. But their presence is exceptional. The type represented by the Young Ruler is continually with us and it is worth our best endeavors to win them.

THE YOUNG RULER

Let me begin by looking at the portrait of this young man. He was wealthy, cultured, and occupied an important position. But the really important thing about him is that when Christ challenged him with, "keep the commandments" he could say, "all these have I kept." That was not the answer of a Pharisee, but the truth. Jesus accepted the assurance at its face and full value. He did not claim to be more than he was. He admitted there was something lacking in his life. Reverently, humbly, urgently, he came to Jesus confessing his lack and kneeling before Him asked the way to perfection.

He is the type of thousands in the churches. They have been trained in good things and well brought up. Influenced for good by home, Sunday School, and church, strengthened by friendships, they have been kept back from course and vulgar sins. They are clean in word and deed and their mothers bear witness that they are good lads or girls. They are not without interest in religion and are willing to help the church and attend its services. Yet they shrink from avowing themselves Christians, and indeed know they are not actually Christians. Those who know them best are anxious about them. They are just the sort who, if they would take the next step, would bear effective witness and do great work.

There is no more important question to be faced than this: how shall we treat this type? With the example of Jesus before us the answer is not difficult. Jesus looking on this young man "loved him"—loved him for what he was, a clean, healthy, promising specimen of young manhood. He was not in the kingdom but he was not far from it. He was not perfect, but there was much that was excellent in him. We have not always been as sure in our view and our judgment. We have been tempted to regard all outside the kingdom as whited sepulchers and their righteousness as filthy rags. We have charged them with sins they have not committed and expected a form of repentance that was only due from old and hardened sinners.

Let us have the mind and the view of Jesus. Do not charge them foolishly. Let us thank God for what they have kept firm and rejoice that they have kept the commandments. Love them as Jesus did and see in them the finest recruits for the Christian Army and glorious possible members of the church. For myself, I am trying in this service to take Jesus' view of the young folk.

TENDERNESS AND SEVERITY

Loyalty to that view demands that I shall go further and say that, if there was tenderness in Christ's view, there was severity too. He did not seek to take the promising young man on easy terms. He did not tone down His demand and say more than was true. The young man was not far from the kingdom, but he was not in it. There was something lacking and Jesus did not hesitate to say so. A man may be near to the best, and yet: "The little more and how much it is, the little less and what worlds away." And recognizing the good in you, and trying to have the mind of Christ, we cannot flatter and say that because you are like the Rich Young Ruler nothing more is expected. It would be no love for you just to say you're jolly good fellows and that because you come to church and play a decent game of snooker no more is required. Your very good may be the enemy of your best, and indeed one of our greatest dangers arises from the fact that so many are content if they can say, "All these have I kept from my youth up."

THE DEMAND OF CHRIST

Let us get right down to the demand of Christ. To the young ruler, it was a demand to part with his possessions and give to the poor. That was meant literally in this case as it has been sometimes since. That was the demand on Frances and Associates and others. But obviously, that cannot be the demand on all. Jesus put His hand on the one thing that keeps a person out of the kingdom. With this person, it was his great riches.

That is not the obstacle for most of us. But for most of us there is one thing that is our special temptation and stumbling block. I do not know what it is for you nor you for me. But we know the way, hear the call, and feel the pull, "one thing" stands in the way of our response. Pride—selfishness—envy—drink—or with some, as Studdert Kennedy says, "I cannot get at Jesus for the glory of your hair."[1] There are many who imperil their souls for a woman's smile or a man's attractions. You know the "one thing" in your life. And Jesus is here enough, loves you enough to say it, "it must go." There may be only one thing wrong, but it may ruin your life and wreck all your prospects.

THE POSITIVE CALL

Jesus goes further and gives the positive call. "Follow me." The center, the main interest of this man's life was money, and in the long sense, as the psychologists say, "character crystallizes round the supreme interest in life." This man's life centered around his goods and chattel, his wealth. His life was self-centered. Jesus said, "Make me the center, the main interest, and follow me." He says that still and I dare not tone down the demand. He claims the right to be Lord of your life and it is your wisdom and the only way to the perfect life to accept Him. You will never be all you might be until you "crown Him Lord of all."

I am recognizing the good in you and will not charge you foolishly. You are keeping the commandments. Thank God for that. It is good but not good enough. Have you, will you, make Jesus Christ the center of your life and the interests of His kingdom supreme? He demands that and only as you bring your life with all its promise and power under His Kingship will you find satisfaction and peace.

THE DIFFERENCE MADE

The difference it will make if you respond to Christ's call. Illustration will make sense better than argument. The Rich Young Ruler turned away, but there was a very similar young man who did respond. It was Saul of Tarsus. He, too, had kept the law. He had set at the feet of the greatest teacher of his day. But there was something lacking in his life. There came a day when the call came and he was not disobedient. He acknowledged the Lordship of Jesus and his one question was, "Lord, what will Thou have me do?" At once, his life was flooded with peace, filled with joy, devoted to the highest ends. Self-centered, his life lacked direction, power, inspiration. Christ-centered and Christ-controlled, it became enriched and enriching. I do not know what it will mean in the details of your life if you yield to Christ, but I am persuaded that it will make your life happier, more purposeful, and more serviceable.

---

1. This is from the short poem "Temptation," in the volume *The Unutterable Beauty* (1927); although the original line reads, "And I cannot get to Jesus for the glory of her hair."

LUMINESCENCE

The Rich Young Ruler broke down before the test. His countenance fell and he went away—sorrowful, but he went away. G. F. Watts has painted a picture of him and all that you see is his back.[2] He looked into the face of Jesus and then turned his back on Him. It was his golden chance, his great opportunity and he missed it. What happened afterwards? Did he change his mind, take up his cross and follow? We do not know, we are left with the picture of a downcast face and a back turned towards Jesus.

What will you do? In the mercy of God, you have your chance. Christ is challenging you, calling you. He is challenging the good with the best, calling you who have lived a good life to put away everything that hinders and follow Him. Gracious influences surround you, earnest friends constrain you, your own heart prompts you, Christ waits and longs. It is your golden chance—what will you do with it? Do not turn your back on Christ, do not go away. Follow Him. Go home not sorrowful, but joyful, and all the years to come will witness that in choosing Christ, you chose well.

∼

---

2. George Fredric Watts (named for Handel, on whose birthday he was born) was a Victorian painter (1817–1904). He was part of the Symbolist movement, painters who painted ideas, rather than scenes, usually. The reference here is likely to his painting, "For he had great possessions." See http://www.tate.org.uk/art/artworks/watts-for-he-had-great-possessions-n01632.

"THE DAYSPRING FROM ON HIGH"
—Luke 1.78, 79

(Preached at Katherine Road 12/21/30, an Advent Sermon)

Luke 1.78–79 "Through the tender compassion of our God, through which the daybreak from on high will come to us, dawning on those who now dwell in the darkness and shadow of death, to direct our feet into the path of peace." (Dr. Weymouth's translation)

"THE TENDER MERCY OF our God." Let us begin with that, not only because it is the first phrase of our text, but because it is the source of all that Christmas means. But for it, there would have not been the "unspeakable gift" of the Christ-child, and there would not have been all the joy that springs therefrom. "The tender mercy of God," Dr. Weymouth translates "the tender compassion." That helps if you remember how Jesus was "moved with compassion." He saw the hungry, wounded, leaderless folk, and was moved to help them by the stirrings of pity and mercy and compassionate love. God saw the world in its darkness and bondage and, moved with compassion, gave His Son to be a light bringer and deliverer.

But that is not sufficient. The original of this phrase is, "the mercy of the heart of our God." To the Hebrew, the heart was the seat and center of life. So mercy, compassion, is at the center of God's life. It is of His essence, His life. Christmas reveals the very heart of God. Nor is this all. With his keen eye and his masterly power of expression, Spurgeon saw and said, "The mercy of God's heart means His hearty mercy, His cordial delight is mercy...God made heaven and earth with His fingers, but He gave His Son with His heart that He might save sinners."

We are thinking most at this time of the coming of the Son, do let us remember that the coming of the Son originated in the heart of God. It was God's earnest, hearty, and cordial endeavor to redeem and deliver man. All the joy of Christmas comes from "the tender mercy of our God." For through that, "the dayspring from on high hath visited us." Now, having put the glory where it rightly belongs, let us consider the beautiful and fitting metaphor under which the coming of Christ is presented.

LUMINESCENCE

"The dayspring from on high hath visited us." The figure, of course, is that of the rising of the sun and the dispelling of the darkness. Charles Wesley caught the idea and gave it as in one of our best know Christmas hymns: "Hail the Heaven born Prince of Peace, hail the Son of Righteousness! Light and life to all He brings, risen with healing in His wings." The figure is familiar as it is beautiful. You have it in Isaiah, "For behold darkness shall cover the earth, but the Lord will arise." And in Malachi, "Unto you that fear my Name shall the Sun of Righteousness arise." Peter looking back wrote of taking heed to prophecy as "unto a light that shineth in a dark place until the day dawn." And one of our favorite titles for Jesus is "the Light of the world."

DAWN IN THE DARKNESS

Literally the coming of Jesus was the sunrise, the day dawning on a world that was in darkness. There is no need to talk in theological terms about total depravity or the unregenerate heart of man. But before Christ came, the world was what Peter called "a dark place." Human beings were "in the darkness and the shadow of death." With all its boasted wisdom, the world knew not God. It was in the dark concerning the most important things. Ignorant of God, it could not truly worship, or rightly value man, or understand the meaning of life and death. Perhaps our picture of the world into which Jesus came has been faulty, but let anyone read books which describe the environment of early Christianity, with its story of sin and slavery, or neglected children and degraded womanhood, let him read of the declining of the old religions and the inadequacy of the substitutes, and he will know that the world's great need was the need of light!

LIGHT BEFORE DAWN

That is not to say it was wholly without light. God has never left Himself without witness in any land or in any time. There have always been brave, fearless seekers after the Truth of God. The Hebrew prophets carried a lighted lamp. And outside the elect nation there were glimmerings. There was light from Zoroaster, and from Socrates, and in the Greek religions. But it was only the light of a lantern. It left people groping. It could not clear the darkness or banish uncertainty. It was only enough to make men long for the sunrise, for the Light of Life. You have still to picture the world as a dark place, with here and there some lantern bearer lighting the way for himself and a few disciples. And when the end of life came there was nothing for them but a "leap in the dark." Upon the bulk of the people the night of ignorance of sin and sorrow hath settled.

"THE DAYSPRING FROM ON HIGH"—LUKE 1.78, 79

THE RISING SON

Then the Sun rose. "Through the tender mercy of God" the Sun rose in the darkened world. The people that walked in darkness saw a great light, and in that light they have been walking and shall walk till traveling days are done. With Jesus came a revelation of the Father that at once and forever dispelled some of the world's darkness. It was the dawning of a new day, the illumination of life. He brought a new knowledge of God, gave a new meaning and value to life, and lighted the lamp of hope that has never been put out. Contrast the difference between BC and AD and you will know the difference Christ's coming has made. It was not for naught that Christmas was fixed at the date when men kept the festival that marked the conquest of light over darkness and the lengthening of the days. When Jesus came, the darkness was past and the true Light shone.

"The dayspring from on high" is not to be confined to the approach of the Son of God in the flesh. There is a birth of Christ in the heart. Philips Brooks wrote: "Though Christ a thousand times in Bethlehem be born if He's not born in thee thy soul is still forlorn."[1] Wherever Christ is known, to some extent, men must walk in the light. But the clouds of unbelief and sin and sorrow often shadow life. There are darkened minds and souls that are closed to and against the light. Holman Hunt's pictures represent the Light of the world as seeking entrance into a human heart.[2]

I am thinking specially of those who have crowded Christ out of their lives and who are afraid of His coming in it. Why are you afraid? His coming to you would mean what it meant to the world, the dawn of a new day, the rising of the sun. He would enlighten your mind, warm your heart, and guide your steps into the path of peace. Welcome Christ and you welcome light. Shut Him out and you condemn yourself to darkness. Let the light shine in your hearts this Christmas time. Keep Christmas by opening your souls to Him whose birthday it is. Then a new day of peace and gladness will begin. And if the clouds of sorrow have been about you, may "the dayspring from on high" visit you and bring the light of comfort and hope.

∼

---

1. Actually, this is a line from a seventeenth-century hymn by Johann Angelus Silesius, later translated into English.
2. He is referring to the famous painting by Hunt entitled "The Light of the World" found in many churches today.

"THE SIGN TO THE SHEPHERDS"
—Luke 2.12

(Preached at Spring Head Mission, Christmas 1936)

Luke 2.12 "And this is the sign unto you, ye shall find a babe wrapped in swaddling clothes and lying in a manger."

To the watching and wondering shepherds there had just been made the greatest proclamation in the world's history. The nations were looking, longing, wanting for a Savior and an angel had announced His advent. The long-expected Jesus had come! Surely there ought to be some sign of so momentous an event, some token of His presence. There was, but it was not such a sign as men looked for or as we should have expected. "This shall be the sign unto you," said the angel. Not "a" sign, but "the" sign, definite and distinctive. And what was the sign? "Ye shall find a babe lying in a manger."

That is where the disappointment comes in. We expected something more dramatic and distinctive and glorious as the sign of the Savior's coming. A baby, and obviously one born in poor circumstances. A child for whom there was no room in the houses or inns of the country. Yet it was the sign. And we need to ask what was the significance for the shepherds and for us.

First of all, it is the sign that Divine comings are not necessary or generally with accompaniments of outward pomp and show. We have become accustomed to the enthronement and proclamation of kings, and we think of stately pomp and pageantry. Perhaps it is all necessary. But when God fulfilled His promised word and the Word became flesh, there was no outward trappings of purple and ermine. The sign of His presence was a baby in a manger. Men were looking for a king and for the golden crown and accompaniments. He came in a quiet and lonely way, forsaking "his starry pathway, love's highway of humility to take."[1] Men saw no significance in the sign and

---

1. This is a paraphrasing of a verse of Evelyn Underhill's poem "Immanence." The lines in question are actually: "I come in the little things, Saith the Lord; My starry wings I do forsake, Love's pathway of humility to take: Meekly I fit my stature to your need."

"THE SIGN TO THE SHEPHERDS"—LUKE 2.12

he was crowded out. Later on, He came, "meek and lowly and riding upon an ass" and men who were lacking in spiritual perception "knew not the day of their visitation."

It may be the tragedy of our lives that we do not read the sign and so miss the visit. Many of our Christmas legends put the truth in a tale. They tell of the King's coming in rags, in a working man's raiment, and men failed to recognize Him, they were too busy, or too proud, to welcome Him. We ought to be aware of His comings for we have the sign. Let us look for Him in homely guise and coming in at lowly doors.

Further, a babe is the sign and promise of what is to be. A baby is a beginning, a promise. We have to want to see into what he grows and what he will accomplish. The babe as a sign was a sign that men had to wait. There were the hidden years, the period of working in a carpenter's shop, the experience of misunderstanding and rejection. But the babe was the sign of the Savior's presence and the rest was guaranteed. Trace we the Babe, who hath retrieved our loss, from the poor manger to His bitter cross.

Part of our trouble is that we get impatient with men and with God. Continually we offer the prayer, "Thy Kingdom come," and we want it to come in a hurry and with a rush. The best things never come that way. They come slowly. When we receive Christ into our hearts, not all at once do we see all He is going to do in us. He gives us the right and the power "to become." "It doth not yet appear what we shall be." We have the sign of His presence and it assures us that we shall be like Him.

So, into the world He has come. Not yet do people fully know Him or are all things put under His feet. He grows in the world in the gradual unfolding of His purpose. He winds His way and His kingdom spreads and grows. Simeon did not see as much as we see, but when he had seen the child he said, "Mine eyes have seen Thy salvation." The babe is the sign that God has begun and that He will perfect.

We strike the deepest note when we say that the babe is the sign that the world's redeemer assumed true humanity. He entered through lowly doors, came as a babe, and no child has been poorer than He whose cradle was a manger and whose first cry was heard in the courtyard of an eastern inn. Once more, we can "trace the babe" through all the struggle of human existence and the bearing of human burdens. The Divine became incarnate and incarnation means sharing all that falls to the human lot. So, Jesus shares in our gladness and cares for our sadness. He learned sympathy by suffering, and now "there is no place where earth's sorrows are more felt than up in heaven," because there is one who has lived our life and shared our sorrows.[2] All the carols tell of His humility, His lowliness, and His poverty. One of the best services Christmas renders is to give us the sign. When we have that we need not fear because God has shared our life, is with us in all our struggles, is afflicted in all our afflictions, and will bring us through "more than conquerors."

∽

---

2. A line from the hymn "There's a Wideness in God's Mercy," by F. W. Faber, is cited here.

"THE PILGRIMAGE TO BETHLEHEM"
—Luke 2.15

(Preached at Spring Head Mission; Christmas 1936)

Luke 2.15 "Let us go even unto Bethlehem and see this thing which is come to pass."

THE SHEPHERDS WERE THE first of a long line of those who have made the pilgrimage to Bethlehem. Millions have followed them and sought to locate the sight of the inn and the stable. Bethlehem has become the world's most sacred shrine. Round it gather sacred memories and holy associations. For most of us the literal pilgrimage is out of the question, but we can send our minds on the pilgrimage and "ponder . . .God's love in saving lost mankind." One of the values of a quiet Christmas morning service is that it gives us a chance, in the midst of the hustle, to send our thoughts out to Bethlehem to ponder the meaning of the happenings there.

WHAT'S FOUND IN BETHLEHEM

What do we find at Bethlehem? The assurance of God's love. From the manger cradle there is preached a great sermon and the text is, "God so loved the world that He gave His only begotten Son." The Christ child is the "impeccable gift," the crowning gift. The Gift reveals the Giver and no good thing will He withhold. Out of His pure love arose the thought of our redemption and to translate the thought into fact God gives His Son to be a Savior. Read the problems of pain and suffering in the light that shines over the manger. You will not find an answer to all your questions, but you will realize that God loves and in the assurance of His love you can want in faith and patience.

Let us go on the pilgrimage that we may find *inspiration to love and goodwill*. If Bethlehem is the place where love is revealed it is also the place where love is inspired. In its atmosphere jealousy and hatred die and goodwill and generosity lives. Where we learn love greatly we have been loved and where we have been generously forgiven, we can forgive and forget. We can shake hands over the cradle of Christ with our enemies, forgive those who have wronged us, and live at peace with one another. For the sake of Bethlehem's Babe cast out of your heart all bitterness and anger, forgive as God for Christ's sake has forgiven you.

BETHLEHEM'S GREAT IDEAL

Let us go to Bethlehem that we may dedicate ourselves to Bethlehem's great ideal. The Christ child is the Prince of Peace and He came to "guide our feet into the way of peace." God's ideal for the world, set to the music of heaven, is "Peace on earth and goodwill towards men." God was in Christ reconciling people to Himself and to one another. Hymns of hate are out of place at Bethlehem, you must sing carols of peace and love. Humans at war with humans, nations suspicious and envious of other nations, hear not the love song the angels sang. It would be a great thing if a world conference could be held at Bethlehem. Meanwhile, let us go to Bethlehem, see the Holy Child, listen again to the song of the angels, and then dedicate ourselves to the ideal of peace.

"THE DOCTRINE OF THE DEPARTING ANGEL"
—Luke 2.15; Acts 7.10

(Preached at Katherine Road 12/28/30)

Luke 2.15 "And it came to pass, as the angels were gone away from them."

Acts 7.10 "Forthwith the angel departed from him."

THE COMING OF THE angels we understand and appreciate and give thanks for. In their departure, we see only something to regret. We magnify the grace that sends the angelic ministries and think the great moment is passed when they go. But there is a really helpful doctrine of the departing angel, and it is that I want to preach. My point is that great and intense spiritual experiences must be tested and translated in the ordinary hours of life. The time of test for the watching, waiting shepherds was when the angels had finished their song and returned to heaven. Peter's test came when the angel left him beyond the gate. Our own testing time is not in the moment of some extraordinary spiritual experience but in the hours when we have to treat the trivial ground and put our hands to the common task.

The first lesson of the departing angel is in this. The angelic ministry for us is when God grants us some season of special vision, a "season of clear shining," of extraordinary exaltation, a deeper sense of His presence, and richer experience of His grace and help. From time to time we are, as we say, on the mountaintop. But, let us keep close to the facts of life. For most of us the pilgrim way lies along level stretches in the valley. *God does not reveal Himself in a continuous ministry of miracle.* In the main life is made up of commonplace days and ways. Now, far be it from me to belittle the exalted and extraordinary experiences. But I must not allow myself and you to dispose what life is mainly made up of. Let us thank God for all the angelic ministries He sends. But let us remember, too, that we cannot live on "thrills," and that the ordinary days are part of God's appointment. Let us go further and learn to translate the vision and glow of the mount into practical life and service in the valley. You are missing the

"THE DOCTRINE OF THE DEPARTING ANGEL"—LUKE 2.15; ACTS 7.10

meaning of your extraordinary experience if you are letting it make you impatient, unsettled, and contemptuous of the ordinary.

Put it this way, we have been permitted to keep Christmas with its hallowed association, its happy fellowship, it abounding gladness, its great thoughts and feelings. It is not too much to say that the angel of Christmas has been in our midst. What are you going to do now the angel has departed? Are you going back to your working life irritated and impatient and like children wishing Christmas came every week? That is no way to do. You must give thanks for all its joy and inspiration and carry its brightness and gladness into all the other days.

Always you prove the reality and value of your extra special experiences in the common things of life. Because an angel has visited you, you must not look down on men and women. Because you have had a special season of grace you must not shun the ministrations of grace through ordinary channels. You must bring a finer spirit to lowly folk, experiences, and duties.

Perhaps an illustration will be the best emphasis. During the heaviest stress of the Civil War, when many matters of great stress were occupying his thoughts, Abraham Lincoln, walking one day through the woods came across a fledgling which had fallen from its nest, and whose life was consequently in danger. He picked up the little bird, examined the branches of the overhanging tree until the nest was discovered, and then tenderly placed it there. And the one who witnessed the act rightly regarded and recorded it as one of the greatest he has seen Lincoln accomplish. There you have it. A man of great power and of great opportunities fulfilling a lowly task in a great spirit.

WHAT ANGELS DO

There is another lesson of the departing angel. The angels come to do for people what they cannot do for themselves. Peter in the inner prison was helpless until the angel struck off his chains and threw open the door. Then the angel went and Peter was left to use his own powers. The angels gave the shepherds full instructions and left them to go to Bethlehem. In extraordinary difficulties men may reasonably look for extraordinary help. Our extremity is God's opportunity to dispatch His unusual powers to our aid. But, to put it bluntly, we must not whine when the angel has gone, we must look about us, call up our own resources, and do our part. "Why comest thou unto me? Speak to the children of Israel that they go forward." God expects no more than we can do but He does expect that. He works the miracle of the new birth, but we must "work out our own salvation." He divides the Red Sea, but His people must set their hands to the task of conquering the land. Do let us be reasonable, and let us remember that when the angelic ministry is withdrawn there are powers at our disposal that always remain. The departure of the angel is the signal for Christians to better themselves, gird up their loins, and do their best.

LUMINESCENCE

ANGEL'S DIRECTION

The third lesson comes to us especially from the angels that sang the Savior's birth and then departed. The angels directed the shepherds. The shepherds went to Bethlehem and verified the angel's message and then they returned glorifying and praising God and making known what had been made known to them. The angels never come without leaving a message. They have come again at Christmas with a message of peace and goodwill. Now come the ordinary days with their opportunities of passing on the good news. Christmas is gone, but its effect on us ought to last all the year. In every vision, in every exalted spiritual experience there is a call. The angels depart, the vision fades, but the duty remains. We must be obedient to the heavenly vision. We must spread the joyful tidings.

My friends, have the angels of God sung to you, uplifted you, or delivered you? Has God set you on some mount where you saw wondrous things? Have you seen Christ transfigured? Has there come some experience of extra joy and peace? Do not now turn from the commonplace as though it were unworthy of you. Turn to it, give your best to it, and share your vision, your message, and your joy with others. And as you trample the dusty highways doing your duty and helping your fellows, you will find the romance of the commonplace and it shall be true of you as it was written of one of old "Jacob went on his way and the angels of God met him."

"LAUNCH OUT"
—Luke 5.4, 5

(Preached at Katherine Road 1/12/36 and Spring Head Mission 1/7/40)

Luke 5.4,5 "Launch out into the deep, and let down your nets for a draught . . .Master we have toiled all the night, and have taken nothing. Nevertheless, at thy word I will let down the net."

HERE IS A STORY that has always been dear to the church. It tells of Jesus meeting with weary and disappointed men and so dealing with them that they went back to their work with new heart. They had failed, but at his word, they took up the task again and in such a way that the place of their failure became the scene of great success. And for fishers of men the miracle has always been a parable of their own work and need. The Sea of Galilee has broadened out into the sea of life in which they were commanded to catch men. Those empty boats have often seemed the symbol of the success that did not follow. The gracious presence and word of the master have represented their great need. Again and again, the church has been heartened by this incident; Christian workers have been cheered, and failure has been transformed. I want to use the incident in the old way.

TOIL THAT FAILS

"Toiled all night and taken nothing." The grey morning found these men after their night's toil with empty boats, aching arms, and heavy hearts. For all their labor, they had nothing but what Americans call a "water haul." They had brought their job skill and experience as well as willing hands and hearts. It was not the failure of the incompetent and lazy, it was the non-success of the skillful and industrious. At once we strike the problem of our own service. Toiling for nothing, laboring in vain! The failure of the foolish and idle is not a problem, it is a foregone conclusion in any sphere. It is the failure of those who bring instructed and consecrated hands and hearts to Christian service that baffle us. Many have heard the call to be fishers of men and obeyed it, yet for all their subsequent praying and toiling they have little to show. With nothing and almost breaking hearts they too say, "We have toiled all night and taken nothing."

I have no final answer to the problem nor can I explain the want of success. One thing I am sure might be said very definitively—the failure is not always or necessarily the faith of the workers. You must not push your fellow toilers or yourself as we so often do. If you have honestly brought your best to your task, God Himself can do no more and he asks no more of you. You cannot command success, you can only deserve it. Can you say you have "toiled all night?" That is your responsibility and you must not carry a burden that God does not intend. I will come back to that.

HE DID NOT SCRAP THEM

Just now let us continue the parable and see how the master treats the toilers who had failed. He did not scrap them! I put it that blunt way deliberately. It is to men who had failed that He says, "Launch out and let down your nets." You will not see the force of that unless you remember the scant mercy the world shows to the men who fail. "Stand aside and let a better man try." That is the world's word to a failure. It says you have had your chance and failed and you must be superseded. It is all very plausible and it may be very cruel. Sometimes we dismiss ourselves. In our sadness and despondency, we charge ourselves foolishly and cruelly, and send in our resignations. We fancy we have proved unworthy of our high calling and are no good.

Thanks be to God, Christ is kinder than us. To those who have nothing to show but empty nets, and who are despised and self-despising, He says, "Try again." Instead of scrapping us, He gives us another chance and bids us launch the boat again.

It may seem a bit forceful, but I am sure that it is right to emphasize the fact that *He sends us back to the old sphere in the old boat.* He sent them back to the old waters, to the very place where they had failed, and with the old tackle. I want to stress that because so often when we are disappointed with our lack of success we get disgusted with the old sphere. If only we could fish in fresh waters, with a new boat and tackle, and other companions, we think we should do better. There are times when our location must be changed and I am no apologist for old methods, but it is not so much a new sphere we need as a finer spirit, not the last word in boats and tackle, but more courage and hope. There are fish in the old waters. Often there is more courage in going back than in moving out. It takes courage of a high order to launch out to the place of failure, and after a faultless night it takes earnest resolution to embark in a new adventure.

It was in that spirit that Miss Adams wrote the hymn "I Feel the Winds of God Today."[1] She was disappointed and discouraged in her work as leader of a women's

---

1. This hymn was published in 1906 and set to music by one of the great composers of the twentieth century—Ralph Vaughan Williams.

meeting, but she wrote: "If hope but light the water's crest, and Christ my bark will use, I'll seek the seas at His behest, and brave another cruise."

FURTHER OUT

Yes, back again and further out. Our failure tends to make us cautious even to the point of cowardice. In our fear of further failure, we cling to shore and are bound in the shallows. We are afraid of making fools of ourselves by further adventures. In failure, we will play for safety. Or we fear the storms of criticism and opposition. And against all this comes the clear singing call of Jesus, "Launch out into the deep." What if our timidity has contributed to our failure? Anyway, the master is calling us to make bolder ventures, tackle bigger tasks, attempt greater things. He is calling the church to take its life in its hands, and in these days when men sneer at its failures, to lift its sail and launch out into the deep where there is work to be done and men to be caught.

THE CORRECT RESPONSE

The men responded. They were weary, disappointed, oppressed with the sense of failure, but at the master's word they pulled for the deep and let down the nets again. That brings us back to the question I promised I would return to—the question of failure and success. Our tendency is to judge by what is in the boat, and judged by that test many are failures. That is not the only test or even the real one. The real test, says one, is not what is in the boat, but what is in the heart. You have toiled all night and taken nothing. Can you say, "I have toiled all night and caught nothing?" The boat is empty. Well, what is in your heart? Have you the faith, the courage, the strength, to try again at Christ's command? If you have, I say it deliberately, you are not a failure, and you are a glorious success. All honor to men and women who in spite of discouragement and seeming failure will "seek the seas at His behest and brave another course."

Shall we respond? The master is calling us back to our old task. Shall we go? And with fresh inspiration and new courage? Shall we answer His challenge with a courage not lessened by failure or the passing of the years? "At Thy word," that, as C. H. S. says, is the watchword of the saints.[2] The word at which Abraham "went" out not knowing whither he went. The word at which Moses "refused to be called the son of Pharaoh's daughter." The word at which "men subdued kingdoms and wrought righteousness." At that same word, let us "launch out into the deep," take up the task He appoints, go forth in new adventures. We may or may not "enclose a great multitude of fishes," see marvelous success or what people call failure. That is not our concern, our business is to listen for the word of the master and at his word attempt the very thing He commands. "The livelong day I toiled in vain, my net no fishes fill, how can I dare to try

---

2. This is surely a reference to Charles Haddon Spurgeon, perhaps the greatest of the British Baptist preachers of the nineteenth century.

again? Yet at Thy word I will. How often shall my brother sin? Must I forgive him still? Hard hearts can never pardon win; Lord, at Thy word, I will. How can I strive or ought to strive so scanty is my skill? Be perfect'—the command is Thine, hearing Thy word, I will. Harder than any work, methinks, to suffer and be still; though at the thought the spirit shrinks, Lord, by Thy grace, I will."[3]

∼

3. This is surely from a revival hymn, but my search could not produce a source.

"RELIGION ON THE DOORSTEP"
—Luke 5.9

(Preached at Katherine Road, undated, and at Spring Head Mission 8/25/40)

Luke 5.9 "Tell them, 'the Kingdom of God is at your door.'"

THAT IS NOT HOW you will read the text in your copy of the Authorized Version of the Bible. There you will read, "The Kingdom of God is come nigh to you." It is Dr. Waymack who gives us the picturesque rendering I have just read—"The Kingdom of God is at your door." This text can stand by itself, but it gains when considered in the light of the background. Jesus has sent forth seventy of His disciples, two by two, on a missionary tour. They were to speak the words and do the work of the kingdom. They were to carry the message into the cities and villages, to the homes of the people. It was their duty, and their privilege, to bring the kingdom, the news of it, the power and grace of it, to the very doors of the people of their time.

Though the commission still holds, I greatly fear that we are not anxious to avail ourselves of the privilege or very eager to fulfill the duty of carrying religion to the doors of the people. I have often had to make appeals for doorstep ministries and have never been overwhelmed with responses. I have not myself fulfilled such a ministry as I ought to have done. It would be foolish to suggest that the only way of commending religion is that of house to house visitation. It has to be admitted that that kind of work has been done in a way that sired resentment. But that must not blind us to the possibilities of the work or the urgent call for it.

MINISTRY OF THE DOORSTEP

The need and the call for it are grounded in certain well-attested facts. The church of Christ can never allow the indifference of the world to be the last word. If outsiders will not come inside, the insiders must go outside and fetch them. The Lord of mercy came to seek and save the lost. It was Jesus who said, "Go out . . . and compel them to come in." We are commissioned to carry on his mission. It is not enough to be willing to respond when the interested appeal to us, we must carry religion to the doors of the indifferent. We must not be content to say, "Come and welcome," to those who apply; if we are true to our Lord and our mission, we must go out and say, "Neighbors, will you travel with us?"

The work must be done through the people. The evangelist is not always welcome on the doorstep. That is putting it mildly. I have done enough to know the sort of reception that is often given. (The Bishop of London's story of visitation.)[1] Though when sympathetically done, the work becomes less resisted than we fear. (F. A. Atkins and his experience of visitation.)

WORK FOR ALL

Some people have a natural genius for this kind of work, but all can cultivate their ability. Men like C. M. Alexander and Dan Crawford had special gifts. (Story of C. M. Alexander—durable satisfaction.) We have not all these special gifts. Some are shy and retiring. But as it has been said, in a striking sentence, "Deep calleth unto deep, and those whose hearts God has touched can find their way easily to the hearts of others." Learn to say with sympathy and sincerity, "O let me commend my Savior to you."

The power of such a ministry is illustrated in the rise of the Labour Party. I am old enough to remember the time when a Labour man was regarded as a crank and his contesting a constituency a farce. Yet I have seen a Labour party in power in England! The rise to power was certainly not due to wealth or the influence of the press. It was due to the work of volunteer propagandists who at street corners, in train cars, and on doorsteps would talk and talk about what they regarded as the truth. Without depreciating them or their work, I declare that we have better news and a nobler cause.

You can lead a horse to the water, but you can't make him drink. But you can lead him to the water. You cannot make people religious or force them to open the door to God, but you can carry the good news to their doorstep. You cannot save a soul but you can tell of the Savior, and there are not many places where they will turn you away. You may have your greatest success where you expect your biggest rebuff. (Story of Chadwick's life, if that doesn't work take the story from H. P. Hughes's life.) Ask for grace to conquer your fear and give you courage, then go to the doorstep with your good news.[2]

THE THRESHOLD OF THE HEART

If the kingdom of God is not brought to the doors of our homes, God sees that it comes to the threshold of our hearts. His love will not let us go. His loving and seeking

---

1. This note is included in the text, but the story itself is not. There are several notes of this type in this sermon text, each included in parenthesis.

2. This obviously is more like sermon notes than a complete sermon manuscript, as none of these stories are included here, nor the persons mentioned identified.

"RELIGION ON THE DOORSTEP"—LUKE 5.9

Spirit uses many ministries to bring the kingdom close to us. He uses the example and influence of godly parents, the solicitude of Sunday School teachers, the memory of old days in the old churches, and they all bring the kingdom near you. Even when you are careless and indifferent, when you are immersed in frivolity and pleasure, something is constantly making you think and bringing the kingdom to your door. Just as Browning says, "Just when we fancy we're safest, there's a sunset touch, etc."[3]

Our services and ministries, crusades and campaigns, are not simply pieces of human organization. They are God's ways of bringing the kingdom and saving us out of apathy and indifference. God will not fail or leave us alone. He will send many a minister, not always in a black coat and white tie, with the message, "Repent, for the Kingdom of heaven is at hand."

Even when the kingdom is at your door, all is in vain unless you open the door. It is our glory that an Englishman's home is his castle. Not even the king can enter without consent. You can keep all visitors on the doorstep. God has put the key of the castle of each person's soul in each person's hands and submits to wait for the door to open. The kingdom is at your door now. The King stands knocking and will enter if and only when you open the door. "Have you any room for Jesus?"

∽

---

3. This is from Browning's poem "A Sunset Touch."

"THE GOSPEL OF A TOUCH"
—Luke 5.13; 8.46

(Preached at Spring Head Mission 5/31/42)

Luke 5.13 "And He put forth His hand and touched him, saying, 'I will: be thou clean.'"

Luke 8.46 "And Jesus said, 'Somebody hath touched me: for I perceive that virtue is gone out of me.'"

THE LINK WHICH BINDS together the two texts, and the passages from which they are taken, is the fact that each is the story of a touch. In one there is the touch of the Master's pity. In the other there is the touch of a woman's faith. In both there is the virtue that heals. Put together the incidents provide a parable and a gospel.

THE TOUCH OF CHRIST'S PITY

Consider the first incident and the pathetic figure at the center of it. Remember it is a medical missionary, Luke the physician, who tells the story. That gives added interest to the statement that the man was "full of leprosy." It reveals a medical man's interest in a serious case. The seriousness of the case interprets also the man's earnestness. "He fell on his face and besought Jesus, saying, 'Lord, if Thou wilt, Thou canst make me clean.'" He was full of a disease which not only meant the sentence of death, it gave the patient a sense of uncleanness. People gave him a wide berth. He was cast off from relatives and friends, and his piteous cry of "unclean, unclean" made him a lonely wanderer on the face of the earth.

It is interesting to note that the man had no doubt about Christ's power to heal. "If Thou wilt, Thou canst." He needed assurance only of Christ's willingness. That and more he got when Christ laid His pitying and powerful hand on his emaciated and disfigured body. Like the outcasts of India, he was one of "the untouchables." People shrank from contact for fear of contamination. That hand laid lovingly on him was the sign of Christ's understanding and the assurance of His sympathy. It was the sign of His willingness and the channel of His power. With the hand the health and power in Jesus went forth to meet and master the disease. "Immediately," says the doctor evangelist, "his leprosy departed from him."

THE TOUCH OF A WOMAN'S FAITH

Now turn to the equally pathetic incident from which the second text is taken. The central human figure in it is a woman who had hemorrhaged for twelve years. She had not only lost her health she had spent her means. "She had spent all her living on physicians, neither could be healed of any." So, hope in her was nearly starved to death.

Then Jesus came her way. She must have heard of His grace and power and felt He could do something for her. She was nervous and timid, but desperate necessity sometimes flowers into courage, and taking despair by the throat she came behind Jesus and touched one of the tassels of His robe. "And immediately," again it is the medical missionary speaking, "her flow of blood stanched." For her, too, then was healing in a touch. "Who touched me?" asked Jesus. And with "the general obtuseness of the good" His disciples replied: "The multitude throng Thee, press Thee, why sayest Thou, 'who touched me?'" But Jesus insisted: "Somebody hath touched me." It was not the crowd, nor casual hangers on, it was "Somebody," somebody with faith and earnest longing. He knew it, for health had gone out of Him to cure the disease of another. That brought the woman to the front with her grateful confession, and brought her the further and humble blessing, "Be of good comfort, thy faith hath saved thee, go in peace."

Put this picture by the side of the other. Do they not make a parable and preach a gospel? The gospel of a touch. I want to preach that gospel. The first thought I deliberately put as simply as I can is that: because Jesus is who He is—

HE CAN TOUCH AND BE TOUCHED BY US TODAY

There is a sense of immediacy which he creates. To think of Him is often to feel Him near. To pray humbly and sincerely is to find Him at our side. Ask him to help you and you will find that He carries you through. That is the proof of His Deity for me. Whatever scientists say or biologists discover, Jesus holds and will hold the hearts of men because they feel Him near them and find in Him a reservoir of inexhaustible moral and spiritual health and energy on which they can draw. He understands and sympathizes and there is healing in His truth.

A simple story told by Dr. S. D. Gordon has always appealed to me and is verified in more than one experience of my own. A woman began the day by thinking of the duties awaiting her. As she thought, they assumed tremendous magnitude and she began to worry. When her husband kissed her on leaving for business he said, "You are feverish, better take the day off." A day off! Just like a man! She had got into the way of having a few minutes of quiet after breakfast and that morning her daily Bible reading included the words, "He touched her hand and the fever left her." She knelt and breathed a prayer for the touch of the Master's hand upon her own fevered hand. It came as she remained there for a few minutes. She had to entertain some ladies from the church for lunch. The meal was not so elaborate as she had planned, but it was happy. A strong impulse came over her to tell her friends what had happened. She shrank from it, but at last told them quietly and simply. As they listened, the touch of the Master's presence seemed to fall on them all. When the husband returned, he said, "You did what I suggested, the fever has gone."

Yes, He still has the power to heal and is both able and willing to use it. He makes fevered minds calm, unclean men clean, and men whose sins were as crimson He makes white as snow. The outcast's hope is in the touch of the divine Healer. We may not understand what the theologians say about Him, but: "The healing of His seamless dress is by our beds of pain. We touch Him in life's throng and press and we are whole again."[1]

THE SPECIAL APPEAL TODAY

The terms in which this gospel is stated make a special appeal today. It is the gospel of a touch, and in our ordinary life we are continually talking about getting into touch with people. One of our commonest words is "contact," and we are continually trying to "contact" people. With your wireless set by turning a knob or pressing a button, you can get into touch with London, Paris, or New York. In the higher spiritual realm, everything depends on the touch, or making contact. The incident from which our second text is taken provides the illustration. There was a jostling crowd pressing all round Jesus, but He said, "Somebody hath touched me." Still the crowd is round Him and the many press but few touch. You say you come to church, read your Bible, say your prayers, and nothing happens. The trouble is you have not made contact, you have not touched Him nor asked Him to touch you.

I wish more people read their Bibles, but even then, there is reading and reading. There is a reading that skims the literary surface and a reading that penetrates to the spiritual surface. It is possible to say prayers without praying. You are in this service in the crowd that is around Jesus—are you reaching forth with the prayer of desire and faith in the effort to touch Him? Are you a "somebody?" If you are, I know what will happen. Have you ever, in the dark, thought that the child at your side was afraid, and put forth your hand to feel for him and then found that his hand was feeling for yours? You seek to touch Jesus and you will find Him reaching out His hand to touch you. The tragedy in the lives of many is that they do not keep in touch. Once they touched and were touched, but the contact was broken. Now our fevers and fears are back upon us. Let us take once again the way of the leper and the woman and then make

---

1. These are lyrics from the hymn "Immortal Love, Forever Full," but they come from Whittier's poem "The Master" ultimately.

it our prayer that we may evermore be kept in touch. In that unbroken contact is the secret of spiritual healing, moral victory, and peace of heart.

OUR CONSECRATED HANDS

Let me add another thought, this time on the side of our responsibility. Christ wants to touch some people through our consecrated hands. As someone says, we are to "carry the touch of Jesus to others." He takes our consecrated hands and makes them move at the impulse of His love. There is an idea of mechanically transmitted grace which we reject, but there is a true doctrine which teaches that ordinary people learn to trust God when they make contact with someone who trusts and whom they trust. Some folk cannot believe in Divine forgiveness because they have never been granted human forgiveness. They cannot believe in the gospel of a touch because the only hands that touch them are stiff and cold with condemnation and contempt. The human touch may be the medium of the Divine. In the simple words do not miss the sublime truth: "Touched by a loving hand, wakened by kindness, chords that were broken will vibrate once more."[2]

You may introduce a man to God with a handshake. In his book of literary sketches taken from him medical experiences, Sir Frederick Treves tells of a man afflicted with a dreadful disease which made him a kind of human monster. He was known as the "Elephant Man" and was being shown for a few cappers to crowds in East London—the very picture of despair. Later on, when he was cast on the streets, a place was found for him in the London Hospital. At first it was difficult to make him feel that anyone cared. Then came a lady who at the surgeon's request came into his room, wished him good morning, and shook him by his hand. He burst into tears. It was the first time a woman had smiled at him. From that time his transformation began, and it was completed when one day Queen Alexandra paid him a special visit. She entered his room smiling, shook him by the hand, and talked with him as a person she was glad to see. After that everything was changed. He used to remark, "I am happy every hour of the day." It was the touch of sympathy and kindness that brought his soul out of the Castle of Despair into the way that leads to the Celestial City.

I come back and finish with the central thought. Christ is both able and willing to touch with cleanness and wholeness, health and peace. If you will reach out in faith and prayer you will make contact. Your faith may be feeble and your prayer imperfect. He will understand and respond in words far better than I can command. Let us state the faith and offer the prayer: "Thy touch hath still its ancient power, no word from Thee can fruitless fall, hear in this solemn evening hour, and in Thy mercy heal us all."[3]

∽

2. This is from Fanny Crosby's hymn "Rescue the Perishing" (1869).
3. This is from the nineteenth-century hymn by Henry Twells "At Evening When the Sun Was Set."

"WHERE IT IS GOOD TO BE"
—Luke 9.33

(Preached once at Spring Head Mission 10/6/40)

Luke 9.33 "Peter said unto Jesus Master, it is good for us to be here: and let us make three tabernacles; one for thee, and one for Moses, and one for Elijah."

THE COMMENTATORS SEEM AGREED that Peter was not at his best when he uttered these words. They regard the saying as born of bewilderment or childish impatience. The best they can say for Peter is that he was half asleep when he said this thing. Dr. Horton, in his book *The Cartoons of St. Mark*, imagines the conundrum when the disciples discussed which of them should be greatest in the kingdom. He represents Peter as saying, "Well, I was the first to confess Him," and another disciple as replying, "Yes, and you were the man who uttered that inexplicably foolish thing upon the mountain about the three tents."

Yet, the commentaries notwithstanding, it must have been good to be there. And something is to be said for Peter that he realized that fact. It is not without significance that his words have passed unto our common religious speech. When we want to describe a particularly inspiring meeting we declare, "It was good to be there." And Dean Stanley does us a real service when he sets us singing the hymn: "Lord, it is good for us to be high on the mountain here with Thee."[1] It is a good thing. By this I mean it is happy and helpful to share such an experience as that Peter was engaging.

CONSIDER WHAT THE EXPERIENCE INCLUDES

Literally these men had got away from the crowd and climbed a mountain. They were free from the distractions of the multitude there. And, let it be remembered, they had gone there to pray. The key to the transfiguration is, "He took Peter and John and James, and went into a mountain to pray." The mountain is not always literally possible, but solitude, elevation, and prayers are, and they make a communion glad and good. It is not a vain emotion which prompts the words: "O, the pure delight of a

---

1. A. P. Stanley wrote this nineteenth-century hymn entitled "Lord, It Is Good to Be."

single hour that before Thy throne I spread: When I kneel in prayer and with Thee my Lord, I commune as friend with friend."[2]

And there was excellent company and good talk. It must have been good to be in the company of men like Moses and Elijah and to listen to their conversation. And it is always good to be in the company of the good and those who fear the Lord and speak often one with another what He has done for their souls. One regrets and wonders that the Methodist Class Meeting, with its opportunities for fellowship with the saints concerning the things of God, has lost its attraction for many. Even when attendance at class is not possible there is always the possibility of a meeting. Where two or three are met together, Another draws near and hearts are warmed and spirits glow. I'm all for the "get together" movement and for quiet talk about God and the soul.

That leads us to what surely was best in the experience. They were "with Him." It is our strong Protestant belief that, without the presence of priest or church, we can be "with Him" and walk with Him and talk with Him. Yet how slow we are to avail ourselves of our privilege, and how much we miss! It is His presence that puts us on the path to where He is in heaven. Like Enoch, we may walk "with Him" and travel through Emmanuel's ground. That can mean nothing but good. So, I suspect that it is both happy and helpful. It is good to be there.

CONSIDER WHERE PETER WENT WRONG

Something is to be said for the commentators. Even the Evangelist who tells the story suggests that Peter spoke impulsively, "not knowing what he said." He was wrong in suggesting the three tabernacles and a prolonged stay. It was good to be there, but the experience was intended to be good for something. It was intended as a preparation for the journey to the cross and the service awaiting in the plain. Peter's suggestion was not adopted. The tents were not set up. They had to go down the mountainside and there they found a demon possessed lad and a heartbroken father awaiting the ministry of healing. The need could only be met by those who had been prepared and encompassed by prayer.

That is where we go wrong. Where we find it good to be, we want to stay. Our Lord's posture is that we should enjoy the fellowship and in it be prepared for service. With his usual insight, John Bunyan makes one of the most dangerous parts in the pilgrimage the Halfway House, "a pleasant arbor, made by the Lord of the hill for the refreshment of weary travelers." There Christian, pleasing himself, fell asleep, lost his roll and nearly lost his soul. By all means, let us go where it is good to be, but let us ever be ready to follow our Lord in the way of the cross and in the field of service.

∽

2. From Fanny Crosby's "I Am Thine O Lord" (1875).

"WHAT SETS ANGELS SINGING"
—Luke 15.10

(Preached thirty times from Katherine Road 2/16/36 to Waltham 4/28/50)

Luke 15.10 "Likewise I say unto you, there is joy in the presence of the angels of God over one sinner that repenteth."

I DO SOLEMNLY DECLARE that that is almost, if not quite, the sublimest utterance in human speech. Indeed, it is hardly the language of earth at all, it is the golden speech of heaven. We have it on the authority of one alone. We should not have known it but for the word of Jesus. We must be content to take it on His word. Only, let us remember that He described Himself, not only as, "the Son of Man which came down out of heaven," but as, "the Son of Man which is in heaven." He knew, as no other ever did, what was in humans and what was in God. The language of heaven was his mother tongue. When He speaks of heaven He speaks what He knows. And He says, "There is joy in the presence of the angels of God over one sinner that repenteth." We shall only rightly understand this passage if we—

SET HEAVEN'S GENEROUS JOY AGAINST EARTH'S PEEVISH PIQUE

The key to the fifteenth chapter of Luke hangs at the door. You will never rightly read the three parables if you skip the first two verses. The publicans and sinners, the scamps and the scapegoats, were coming to Jesus, and instead of resenting their presence, He welcomed them, talked with them, ate with them. Let me put it in homely words—He made a fuss of them. And the Pharisees and scribes stood up with curling lips and sneering looks, "This man receiveth sinners," they said. They meant, "You can tell a man by the company he keeps." They were peeved because He was making more fuss of sinners than of them. They thought He ought to have companied with them rather than with this scum of the earth.

Jesus told the parables to vindicate His own action and to declare the attitude of heaven. Accept, for the moment, their own valuation. They, the Pharisees, were good.

They stood in no need of the soul's physician. And if these publicans and sinners were as bad as the scribes claimed, they were the very people who needed the attention of a Savior. He was only bringing to earth the spirit of heaven, where He declared there is more joy over one sinner that repents than over ninety-nine just persons which need no repentance. Now we can begin the application of the truth, and with this—

THE TEXT CASTS AN INTERPRETING LIGHT ON THE LIFE OF HEAVEN

At best, "our knowledge of that life is small," but we have not even troubled to try to get the best knowledge available. Our commonest jokes are about Peter and the gate and we make merry at the idea of cherub boys with dreary eyes floating round in fleecy clouds. We think vaguely of golden streets trodden by white clad figures who do nothing but play harps. Heaven is a happy land far, far away where saints in glory stand doing nothing for ever and ever.

You cannot think or speak like that in the light of this text. The next world! What is next means "nearest." What if the "happy land" is not far away at all, but mingles with the life of our own world? Here the truth is that heaven is interested in what happens on earth. The angels, whether you think of them as members of a higher hierarchy or as the spirits of past men made perfect, are not floating round in fleecy clouds or simply playing harps, they share God's sense of loss over wandering sinners and they share the Shepherd's joy over the found sheep and the Father's glad welcome to His homecoming son. The joy of the Lord is never dropped into the laps of angels or men like a gift from the blue, it comes to those who have shared God's sorrow and God's search. We have to be partners of His sufferings before we can be sharers in His joy.

That makes heaven more like home, doesn't it? And though I must not stay with the thought, it ought to rob us of our fear of dying and passing to the other life. For the moment, let it be sufficient to stress the thought that heaven is so interested in earth, mourns over the wandering sinner, and shares God's joy when the wanderers come home. But let us go further into details and consider just—

WHAT IT IS THAT SETS ANGELS SINGING

That which stimulates the interest and inspires the joy of the higher world must surely be of surpassing interest. Even to other countries or hemispheres we do not cable or wire unimportant or even casual happenings. What is it then that sets angels singing and heaven's joy bells ringing? Why, the news that one sinner is repenting.

Now don't just say, "Of course, we know that." Consider its significance and suggestiveness. Do you believe it? That heaven rejoices, not only over mass movements and the action of a crowd, but over one, one, and that one a sinner. One person can set heaven rejoicing. That one a sinner, a sinner repenting of his sins and turning from the error of his ways. One person in a far country turning his face to God and home saying, "Father, I have sinned." That is what Jesus declared, that one repenting sinner sets angels singing.

T. R. Glover has noted the parallelism of the text with Job 38.7. Even as the morning stars sang together at the Creation and the sons of God shouted for joy, so at the recovery of the lost there is joy among the angels of heaven. "We can believe in such joy when God made the world, but can we believe that there was the same joy in the presence of God yesterday when a coolie (or some woman of the streets) gave his heart to God. Jesus does. That is the central thing in His teaching about God. If we can assimilate, 'appropriate' this central thought, the rest of the Gospel is easy."[1]

If you think the cause is not big enough for the effect, think again. Think how great a thing repentance is. It is the issue of conviction and it is marked by intense sincerity. It is confession, changing, turning. If you think it is easy, try it. Try fessing up that you have been wrong and turning away from the wrong. The hardest thing in the world is for some of us to confess and turn again. And when humbled, sorrowful, sincere, a man says, "I have been all wrong, and now please God, I'll go right." That sets angels singing.

Repentance is only the beginning, but it is the beginning of great things. When a sinner repents, he has much to learn and far to travel. But the will is surrendered, the Rubicon is crossed, and all good things and great achievements are possible. When the prodigal turned his face and his feet towards his father's house the great thing was accomplished. And though the repentant sinner is not yet a saint, repentance puts him in the way to that greatest of attainments.

The angels sing because they know all the joy that awaits the repentant sinner. They know that the loneliness, the restlessness, the bondage, are over and that a welcome awaits, that peace will come, and singing abound. Dwelling in the Father's presence they know what fellowship means and their rejoicing is over all that awaits the returning sinner. But even more they sing in sympathy with the Father's joy. Never forget that all through this chapter the sense of loss emphasized is in the heart of God, and the joy in finding is God's. The angels know that God's joy is in fellowship with His children, that the Good Shepherd rejoices when he finds the sheep that was lost. "And all through the mountains, thunder-riven, and up from the rocky steep there rose a cry to the gate of heaven—Rejoice, I have found my sheep and the angels echoed around the throne—Rejoice, for the Lord brings back His own."[2]

You say that God is able and willing to save. It is a great truth, but it is only a fraction of the whole truth. God longs to save, loves to save, and gave His Son to save. By the grace of God Jesus tasted death for every person, and where one person, any

---

1. This is from Glover's book *The Jesus of History*, part 4.
2. These are lines from the nineteenth-century hymn entitled "There Were Ninety and Nine," written by Elizabeth C. D. Clephane.

person, accepts that salvation, God's heart is glad and the angels sing in unison. For the father's joy is shared by His children and His friends. That paves the way for the final thought—

THE TEXT CASTS REVEALING LIGHT ON THE IDEAL LIFE OF THE CHURCH

The church is a colony of heaven and it ought to share heavenly experiences. Its members ought to be akin to the angels. They ought to share God's sorrows over His wandering and erring children, to join Good Shepherd's search for the lost sheep, and to join the angels and Jesus in singing to welcome the returning prodigals. We know, now, what sets angels singing—what sets a church singing? You can test a church by that. Is your greatest rejoicing over increased collections and growing congregations? Do you keep your sweetest and gladdest songs for returning prodigals? Is there joy in the presence of the church of Christ when one sinner repents, when one little child says, "I want to be like Jesus?"

When I want to say a good thing I nearly always find that someone has been before me and said it better. What I want to finish with has been beautifully said by Ian Maclaren. When Flora Campbell, who had run away from Drumtochty to London, returned and was well enough to go to the kirk, that saintly soul, Margaret, said to Flora's father as they sat in the backseat and caught the faces of the people, "Everybody's pleased. This is the first time I've seen the fifteenth of Luke in Drumtochty. It's a bonnie sight, and I'm thinking it is still bonnier in the presence of the angels."[3]

That's what I wanted to say. The bonniest sight in the church of Christ is when the fifteenth of Luke is in it. For the rest, let me finish the story of Flora's homecoming. "Then the minister asked Burnbrae to pray and the Spirit descended in that good man, of simple heart. 'Almighty Father, we are all Thy poor and sinful bairns, who wearied of home and went away into the far country. Forgive us for we did not know what we were leaving or the sore heart we gave our Father. It was weary work to live with our sins, but we would never have come back if it had not been for our Elder Brother. He came a long road to find us, in a sore travail He had before He set us free. He's been a good Brother to us, and we've been a heavy charge to Him. May He keep a firm hand on us, and guide us on the right road, and tell us all we need to know till the gloaming come. Gather us in then, we pray Thee, and all we love, not a bairn missing, may we sit down forever in our own Father's House. Amen.'"

---

3. Ian Maclaren was the pen name for Rev. John Watson, a Scottish theologian and minister of the second half of the nineteenth century. He wrote many books, both fiction and nonfiction. This quotation is from p. 120 of *Beside the Bonnie Brier Bush* (Dodd, Mead and Company, 1894).

"THE GRACE OF GRATITUDE"
—Luke 17.17

(Preached five times from Spring Head Mission 1/15/39 to Bishop St. undated)

Luke 17.17 "Were there not ten cleansed? But where are the nine?"

THE OTHER DAY I came upon an extract from the autobiography of Mr. G. K. Chesterton. It read, "If I had my time over again, there is one doctrine I should always have liked to teach, that is the idea of taking things with gratitude and not taking them for granted." Immediately there came to mind the story of nine men who took a great blessing for granted and of one who took it with gratitude. It seemed the ideal story from which to preach on the grace of gratitude. It will be worthwhile spending a little time to set.[1]

THE GRACE IN THE LIGHT OF THE STORY

Jesus was on His way to Jerusalem and was met by ten men who were lepers. There is no more pathetic picture in the Old Testament than that which the Levitical Law gives of the leper—see Leviticus 13.45. "The leper in whom the plague is, his clothes shall be rent, and his head bare, and he shall put a covering upon his upper lip, and shall cry unclean, unclean." The cry was for warning that healthy folk might keep at a distance.

In those days as in these, news traveled and it must have been noised abroad that Jesus of Nazareth not only had sympathy with lepers but power to heal them. Anyway, as the ten approached him their voices were lifted up in a new cry which was a prayer, "Jesus, Master, have mercy on us." And He whose mercy was overflowing responded, and said, "Go shew yourselves to the priests." Then "as they went, they were cleansed." No longer would the dreadful cry, "Unclean, unclean," come from their lips, they were cleansed!

---

1. This autobiography is simply titled *G. K. Chesterton* and is still available from Ignatius Press (2006).

"THE GRACE OF GRATITUDE"—LUKE 17.17

THE NINE AND THE ONE

Our chief concern is what happened after the cleansing. One of them, we are definitely told, when he saw he was healed, returned, glorifying God and kneeling at the feet of Jesus and gave Him thanks. It was a graceful manifestation of the courtesy of gratitude and our Lord was obviously touched by it. There is no reference to what the nine did. Presumably they went their way to the priests. The question of Jesus implies that He felt their absence. "Where are the nine?" He knew they were cleansed and His question was intended to awaken the heart and conscience of the onlooker to the importance of the grace of gratitude. Ten cleansed and only one returning to glorify God. A thoughtful writer says that we may see the world of men in that band of lepers.

THE UNGRATEFUL NINE

It would be easy to make excuses for the nine. They did not intend to be neglectful or cruel. They were full of their newly given blessing. There were friends that they were anxious to see. There was much to be done. As it was with them so it is with many of us. It is often said that there is no gratitude in politics, and there are others besides politicians who mourn the short memories and the lack of gratitude. Dr. John Watson says rather a pointed thing, "In times past men hated their enemies and loved their friends, but now we forgive our enemies and forget our friends."

We do not mean to be cruel, but in these days of hurry and hustle, with so many things in our hands, there is little time for the courtesy of gratitude. Besides, we flatter ourselves that we are but little indebted to others. We have blazed our own trail and our own strong right-hand has carved our career. So, we forget and fail. And parents who have made sacrifices for us, friends who have helped us, and companions of other days are pained and discouraged.

Nor do we always remember the Best of Friends. Was that why, when He broke the bread, He said, "This do in remembrance of Me?" He died that we might be forgiven and made good, He stooped to save these poor hearts of ours, but how seldom there flashes from our eyes the glow of our thanksgiving. We are oftener found murmuring for some little thing denied than giving thanks for the great things He has done.

If you think the proposition is wrong and that there cannot be nine ungrateful men to one who returns to give thanks, think again. Take any street in this town on any Sunday morning and for one who comes up to the House of God with hymns of grateful praise, you will find more than nine who stay at home to pursue their own pleasure. Think of the numbers who, when a crisis was upon us and was threatened, came up to the Intercession Service and compare them with the number who have continued to give thanks. The question still is, where are the nine?

THE ONE WHO RETURNED TO GIVE THANKS

Thank God there was one who took the gift of healing with gratitude, and that he still has comrades and followers. Our Lord spoke of him as a "stranger," he was a Samaritan and might have been pardoned if he had failed. And often still we find gratitude where we least expected it. How refreshing such expressions of gratitude are. Even when we are most disinterested, a word of appreciation and gratitude gives added joy to us. Instead of being exalted we are humbled as we prepare ourselves for other service. By the joy we have, we ought to learn how much we can give by grateful appreciation. If someone has done you service do not be afraid to express your gratitude.

Let gratitude be a real part of your piety. You cannot miss our Lord's joy in the gratitude of this stranger who returned to give thanks. Of all givers, He gives simply and not in hope of some return, but it is in our power to gladden His heart by remembering His mercy and bringing our thanks. There is a fair story told of the Venerable Bede. His brother monks, knowing his weakness, and the many claims upon his time, urged him not always to attend the singing of the canonical hours in church. "I know," he answered, "that the angels are with us in those hours, what if they find me not there among the brethren? Will they not ask 'where is Bede'?"

I almost despair of getting people to the service of praise as a matter of wisdom and of duty. People will let the most trivial things stand in the way. But when the heart is filled with adoring gratitude for the great things God has done our greatest joy will be to enter His gates with praise and His courts with thankfulness.

Are you with the one or the nine? Do you take God's gifts for granted or with gratitude? For God has done great things for us all and given for everyone the "unspeakable gift." Let us add to the grateful ministry which one day will have grown into a great multitude which no one can number whose song shall be, "Salvation to our God which sitteth upon the throne, and unto the Lamb."

"CHRIST LIFTED UP"
—John 12.32

(Preached eleven times from Fentiman Road to Bishop St., dated only on 3/19/39 at Spring Head Mission)

John 12.32 "And I, if I be lifted up from the earth, will draw all men unto me."

THE REFERENCE IS UNDOUBTEDLY to the death of Jesus on the cross. This we infer, not only from the interjected explanation of the evangelist, but also from the setting of the text. In the seeking Greeks, Jesus saw great possibilities of service. How he would have loved to proclaim the Good News in other lands. But the cross loomed before Him and turning His back on the service that would have been an unspeakable joy. He went to it. And went to it with the conviction that it was in tune with His Father's will and the surest way, the only way, to triumph. It was not by sparing Himself but by sacrificing Himself that He would draw and win the world. History proves that he took the right way. It is not because of His peerless character and priceless teaching, but because of His sacrificial death that He wins the world. Men have been astonished at His doctrine, have marveled at His sinless life, but it is as "Christ crucified" that He has been the center of attention. It is to the "green hill," on which stands a cross that men have come in adoring gratitude and love.

The Moravian missionaries labored in Greenland for many years without apparent fruit. When they spoke of the attributes of God, the sin of man, the excellence of holiness, the horrors of hell, and the glory of heaven, their hearers talked of seal catching and said they did not understand these things. But one day one of the missionaries described the sufferings and the death of Jesus, when one of the Greenlanders stepped forward and said, "How was that? Tell me it again." That was the beginning of a new method by the missionaries and a new response by their hearers.

In his book *Confronting Young Men with Jesus*, J. R. Mott says, "When in my work with students and other young men, other arguments have failed, I have lifted up the cross of Christ, and it has never failed to move men." That has happened on a wider scale. It is Christ lifted up who draws men unto Himself.

LUMINESCENCE

THE SOLITARINESS OF CHRIST IN HIS REDEEMING WORK

He is unique in the acts of His High Priesthood. He does suffer with men but in the deepest sense He suffered for them. There was no other good enough. In our text, speaking of the death He should die, He was speaking for Himself alone. He is the magnet and we are drawn to Him. What He did and suffered has no parallel in our experience. He is the King of Glory and His pierced hand opened the door by which people pass into the kingdom. And yet, while we adoringly confess that, we cannot discuss the text as though there were no other application for us. It does yield a truth which applies to the members as well as the Head, to the church as well as to Christ. It is not ours to be lifted up as He was, but it is ours to lift up the crucified.

TELLING THE OLD, OLD STORY

One thing at least we can do, we can make it known what our Lord has done and give Him the chance of drawing men. "For all, for all, my Saviour died." But how shall they know it unless someone tells them. Many would be drawn in if they heard the story. The great need is that people should see Jesus. Some are conscious of their need and cry out for Him. More are unconscious of their need, but they do need Him and it is our duty and privilege to tell the old, old story of His love.

Think of the thousands at home who do not know that He loved them and gave Himself for them, and ask yourself what you are doing about it. Can you not tell one? Think of the millions abroad who have never heard of Jesus and remember that He is counting on us to see that they hear of a Savior's love. That is what constitutes our obligation to non-Christian lands. He died for all. It is His purpose to draw all men unto Himself. To us He gives the unspeakable privilege of commending our Savior to others. Then this saying of our Lord has something to say to us concerning—

THE ATTRACTIVENESS OF RELIGION

What our Lord proposed was something that should be the great attraction. He knew and we know that in this matter people must be drawn and not driven. Mohammed may offer people his faith or the sword. This is not the way of Jesus and is not the right way. It may add numbers, but it does not win hearts. Our religion must have the same quality as our Lord's. It has to be attractive and winsome. That is where many Christians fail. "Their religion," says Geo Matheson, "is a weapon in the hand, not a magnet in the heart."[1] It repels and drives away instead of drawing and winning.

We have to make religion attractive, but how? Even when our motives have been sincere we have sometimes failed. To make religion attractive we have lowered its demands, come down to the level of unspiritual desires, pandered to worldly demands,

---

1. This is taken from a sermon entitled "The Attractiveness of the Cross."

and have thought to win people by making our services bright, brief, and breezy. That is not our Lord's way, and it is the way of ultimate failure for us.

The real and lasting attractiveness is in lives that are lifted above the world. Crucifixion does not mean for us what it meant for Jesus, but there is a cross for us. Paul spoke of himself as "crucified unto the world and the world unto me." That represents an experience there is for us to share. We are to be as indifferent as dead men to its standards, its prizes, its smiles or its favors. Literally we are to be above it. In a book on *The Weapons of Our Warfare*, the first chapter is titled "The Weapon of Aloofness." There is an aloofness of pride and indifference that wins no one.[2] But there is an aloofness which means being in the world but not of it, a noble indifference, living on higher levels, having exalted thoughts and ideals. People may sneer at such lives as other worldly, but they are the real attraction. In our hearts, we know that if we lived such lives people would feel an influence, want to know our secret, and listen to our story.

THE POWER OF SACRIFICIAL LIVES

It is when we yield ourselves most fully to the drawing of our Lord, when we are so near to the cross that we catch its spirit, that we make religion attractive. We cannot save people, but we can make it easier for them to be saved. When we who profess and call ourselves Christian are unspiritual, selfish, and vain, the world decides our claims for our Lord and the cross is made of none effect.

But when a St. Vincent de Paul lives with galley slaves, in sight of wretchedness no tongue can utter, in contact with all that is foul, abject, and repulsive, that he may win people; when Father Damien shares the leper's lot that he may ease it; when Florence Nightingale sacrifices comfort and luxury and endures darkness, cold, and misery that she may bring comfort and healing to others, then it is that the world understands and feels the attraction of the Christ who inspires these people to sacrificial living.

It is not given to all of us to sacrifice ourselves in such dramatic ways, but it is given to us all to live lives of self-denial and sacrifice that will give Christ a chance. There is a place for speech and argument but Christianity is most helped by those whose lives proclaim it.

OUR LORD'S SERENE OUTLOOK

We speak of the church's dark days and some of them are dark enough. But we have never had a day so dark as was the day in which our Lord uttered this triumphant saying. The clouds being dark and heavy, evil appeared victorious, the men making a cross for the Holy One and the Just. But He "knew what was in person," was aware of

---

2. This is a reference to the book by John A. Hutton published in 1912.

the inherent weakness of wickedness, and also what finally wins people. So, he went calmly and serenely to the cross with the conviction that right and love would be victorious and that all people would be drawn to this.

It is not easy to maintain that faith, but it is not possible for those who know Him to think that He was mistaken. "I will draw all people unto Me," said Jesus, and faith, to use Donald Hankey's phrase, is betting your life. He was right. That really is faith and believing that in spite of all that shrieks again it, that Jesus shall reign.

Let us have done with fretting and fussing, worrying and unbelief, let us trust our Lord's magnetic power. People can never be dragooned into faith and goodness. Tell the story of His love for the sinful and His sufferings for the unworthy. Set Him forth as the Son of God who loved people and gave Himself for them. Let your lives be copies of His—unworldly, pure, and sacrificial. For a while, absorbed in its immediate pleasures, greedy of gain, people may pay little heed to the holy appeal of the cross. It may be that they will, like the men who made the cross, sneer, stop their ears and harden their hearts. But the day will come when tired of its worldliness, sick of its sin, convinced of its folly, they would, like the prodigal of the parable, arise from its degradation, come to their senses, and go home.

∽

"HIS MISSION AND OURS"
—John 17.18; 20.21

(Preached three times from Spring Head Mission 3/26/39, Pleck and Holyhead Rd. 12/1/40)

John 17.18 "As Thou hast sent Me into the world, even so have I also sent them into the world."

John 20.21 "As My Father hath sent Me, even so send I you."

Here, in clear and definite terms that cannot be mistaken, is stated the mission of the church. There is no room for doubt or misunderstanding.

THE TRUTH IS GIVEN A SOLEMN SETTING

On the eve of the Passion, in holy communion with His Father, praying for His friends, Jesus declared that He was sending them into the world as He had Himself been sent. After His resurrection, as the disciples waited and watched and wondered, Jesus came to them, showed them His hands and side, bestowed on them His peace, breathed into them His Spirit, and gave them their commission, "As my Father hath sent Me, even so send I you."

IT COMMITS THE CHURCH TO A SOLEMN MISSION

"As Thou didst send Me." That takes us deep into the Father's mind and still deeper into His heart. It links the mission of the church with the eternal thought and purpose of God. Jesus commissions His disciples, His church, as He was commissioned by God, "Even so, send I you." Many things are implied in joining the church, and not one is without significance, but the most solemn thought of all is that when we join the church, we are to live in God's eternal purpose, we are committed to carrying on what God began when He sent His only begotten Son to be the world's Savior. You will agree that so solemn a truth demands and deserves our sermon's attention. The definition of Christ's mission is the declaration of our own. The two are so closely identified as to be identical. So we consider—

LUMINESCENCE

THE MISSION OF CHRIST AND HIS CHURCH

To sum up briefly we may use two great words. *It is a mission of revelation.* Jesus came, he lived, taught, and died, to reveal the fact and the measure of God's love. There had been guesses and hunches before, Jesus came to make it clear that God loves people through all their sins and struggles and sorrows. His central message was, "God so loved the world." After His coming no man could think He was overlooked or forgotten, too small or too sinful. God was revealed as Father and His love revealed as reaching all. In the revelation of that love was a revelation of what life might be.

A mission of restoration. The word is chosen deliberately, though redemption might seem to be the better word. I am not likely to forget Christ's redeeming work or how necessary it was to restoration. Jesus looked upon human beings as children of God, some of them prodigals, some rebels, some foolish and wayward. It was His mission to lead them back and restore them to fellowship with their Father. He came "to seek and to save that which was lost."

As we have seen, in the definition of Christ's mission is the declaration of our own. As He came to reveal the Father and restore His children to fellowship with Him, so are we sent into the world. It is our task to reveal the love of God and restore men and women to Him. Now let us turn to what is of supreme importance to us.

THE METHOD OF FULFILLING THE MISSION

How can we reveal the love of God? The answer to that question depends on the answer to another. How did Jesus reveal that love? Well, He revealed it by talking about it. In many a homely phrase, in lovely parables, He talked to people about the Father's love and care. To little groups, to individuals, He told in gracious speech the story of God's love. And that is one of the ways in which we can reveal the love. Talking is not everything, is not the greatest way of revealing, but there is a revelation in speech. And for the commending of Christianity to our age few things are needed more than wise, gracious, and persuasive speech. If the love of God is the greatest thing in the world, why are we so reluctant to speak of it? Tell the story, tell it again and again, that God loves people. Especially tell it as you know it, and what it means to you.

But He did more than talk about it. There was what has been called "the transformation of language into life." In Him the divine love was incarnate. The Father was in Him. And it is as He is in us that people will see love and believe in it. He and the Father were so utterly one that seeing Him men saw the Father. And we are to be so one with Him that people will see the beauty of Jesus in us. I can put it all in some words of Marcus Dods. "It was not by telling men about God that Christ convinced men that somewhere there existed a holy God who cared for them, but by showing

God's holiness and love present to them in His own person. So, our words may fail to accomplish much if our lives do not reveal a presence men recognize as Divine."[1] In a world of people at arms against God we are to be witnesses by lip and life.

What of the mission of restoration? Here again Christ's method must be ours. He sought the lost with infinite patience and tenderness. He went where they were and mingles freely with them. He did not wait until they came to Him. He pleaded with them and shewed them what they were missing and losing. And when they were weak and weary and afraid, He helped them to God. And He is our pattern. "As Thou hast sought, so let me seek." We must go where they are and not wait until they come where we are.

"Where is my wandering boy tonight?" Well, where are you sons and daughters, the men and women who were brought up in this school and who once attended the services of this church? Some of them are in the far country, some are just turning aside. If our mission is like Christ's, and it is, we must go after that which is going astray. The lost sheep, the Father's wandering children, are the concern of the church. As Jesus sought us, we must seek them. And we must go in His Spirit. The word that was in Christ Jesus must be in us. No arrogant pride and no lordly condescension. It was because He was what He was that He got a chance with people. The Spirit of the Lord God was upon Him and His Spirit must be upon us.

WE SHALL BE INVOLVED IN THE SAME EXPERIENCE

That will mean, as St. Paul says, "knowing . . . the fellowship of His sufferings." He Himself said, "If they have persecuted Me they will persecute you." The mission will involve us in meanness, discouragement, and pain. It may mean for us what it meant for Him, misunderstanding, rejection, crucifixion. We need no more than His blood, but He may ask for ours. Before the bitter cup, He said, "Father, not my will but thine be done." And we must be prepared to say, "Savior, not my will but Thine be done." For our sakes, He sanctified Himself and we must sanctify ourselves for the sake of others.

But there is a further parallel. The missions are identical, and the experiences. But further, all that the Father was to Jesus He will be to us. "As the Father knoweth me, so know I you." "As I live by the Father, ye shall live by Me." "As the Father hath loved Me so love I you." In the commission is strength. The Father sent me and I send you. To know that we are His and about His work. To know that our work is linked with His. Here surely is seen the source of sustaining strength. What a parallel! What a mission! To reveal the love of God and to bring people home to God! "O

---

1. Marcus Dods was a Scottish theologian and biblical scholar of the nineteenth century, and a somewhat controversial one. This quotation seems to come from his exegesis of John 17 in the old edition of *The Expositor's Bible Commentary*.

come let us go and find them, in the paths of death they roam. At the end of the day, twill be sweet to say, I have brought some lost one home."[2]

⁓

---

[2]. This is from a poem by Robert Lowry entitled "The Straying Sheep." He was an American minister, a professor of literature, and a writer of hymns in the second half of the nineteenth century.

"THE GARDEN BY THE CROSS"
—John 19.41

(Preached five times from Fentiman Road to Brandon, undated; an Easter Sermon)

John 19.41 "Now in the place where He was crucified, there was a garden."

THE CROSS OF OUR Lord stood close up against the radiant joy of a Syrian summer and it was set in an oriental garden. From that we generally deduce the lesson that a cross mars our gardens, that death lurks near the beautiful, and that all our roses have thorns. Then we sigh sadly and conclude that we had better not set our affections too closely on what has the symbol of death so near it. Really the emphasis ought to be on the other side. It is not that there was a cross in the garden as that there was a garden by the cross. Tragedy is not unrelieved. Beauty and order and fragrance are around life's sorrows. Look at the literal fact.

IT WAS THE TRIUMPH HOUR OF EVIL

The Son of God died on a cross made for Him by the people He came to save. It would not have been surprising to find a desert there. Nature might have made a black hall for the sepulcher. But it was not so. Not a desert but a garden was by the cross. The sun shone, the birds sang, and the flowers He loved bloomed beautiful and fragrant. The place of a skull was "embosomed in beauty and nature smiled in the tragedy." *It is ever thus*. The garden not only bloomed by the cross of Jesus, it is by our own sorrows and tragedies. The birds sing and the flowers shed their fragrance even while we dig our graves. More than once I have returned "earth to earth" to the accompaniment of a thrush's song in the summer sky. Nature seems indifferent to our crosses and our graves. In one of his almost perfect stanzas Burns says what we all feel: "Ye banks and braes o' Bonny Doon, how can ye bloom so fresh so fair? Ye little birds, how can ye sing, and I so weary, fu' o' care?"[1] I never understood those words so well as I did when a young woman came to ask me to conduct the funeral service of her brother who had died under tragic circumstances. "As I came down the road," she said, "someone was

---

1. This is from Burns's poem "The Banks O' Doon," which was turned into a song.

playing a piano, and I wanted to rush in and say, 'how can you play the piano when my brother lies dead?'"

So our heart's cry out. How could the garden bloom by the cross where the king suffered? How can things go on as usual when our hearts are heavy with sorrow and breaking with pain? But they do. Watching a child suffer and bidding him goodbye we resent the rising of the sun, the world should be in mourning. But the sun rises and reveals the gay gardens, the world goes on as usual. Our own cemeteries become gardens.

It looks like indifference and we resent it. The pagan sees behind it all a malignant demon mocking our pain and pouring scorn on our sorrow. We do not put it that way, but it does seem cruel that nature should seem so indifferent as it breathes music and scatters flowers over our lost loves and our broken promises, and on our newly dug graves. It is not indifference, it is a—

PART OF GOD'S GRACIOUS MINISTRY

He will not let nature bewail our calamities as if they were irreparable and the last word. Pain and storm, strife and anguish, the travail of birth and the agony of death, these are for a time, order, beauty, music, life, are for eternity. God sees the end toward which all our sorrows are working. He knows that the stroke we think crushing is a benediction. People only see the blackness and shame and cruelty of the cross, but it was the blossom as a tree the leaves and fruit of which were for the healing of the nations. The flowers that bloom while we suffer are part of the "far off interest of tears" to be gathered.

Why should the beautiful process be stayed? He who makes the flowers grow and the birds sing sees through the glower that gathers round Calvary the gleam of glory of the resurrection. And if we have faith we shall see in the gardens by our crosses a sacred memorial of the Paradise we are to enter. Now leaving the literal fact let us turn to a—

PIECE OF SUGGESTIVE SYMBOLISM

It is no mere coincidence that we are told there was a garden by the cross. To John's mystical and poetical eye it was a parable. Jesus was giving Himself for people, pouring out His life in service for others. Around the cross, and because of the cross, there was a garden. Our own poets have caught the idea and set us singing: "Round his pierced feet, fair flowers of Paradise extend, their fragrance ever sent."[2] It is in the garden by the cross, made by the cross, we gather the fruits of His passion. It is by His cross that

---

2. This is from Matthew Bridges's famous nineteenth-century hymn "Crown Him with Many Crowns."

"THE GARDEN BY THE CROSS"—JOHN 19.41

we find forgiveness for our sins, healing for our wounds, strength for our weakness, and victory over death. All the fruits of the spirit grow in the garden by the cross.

THAT WAS TRUE FOR HIM, AND IT MAY BE TRUE FOR US

To most of us there comes a cross of pain and suffering. Resent it, refuse it, rebel against it and it will make a wilderness. Accept it by faith, submit in love, in the spirit in which Jesus went to the cross, and by your cross as by His there will be a garden. And in it there will bloom the lovely fragrant flowers of patience, sympathy, love. No chastening for the present seems joyous but grievous, nevertheless afterward it yielded the peaceable fruits of righteousness. But go deeper still. We are not only asked to bear with patience the ills that flesh is heir to—we are asked to voluntarily accept and willingly take up a cross. When we take Jesus Christ seriously He asks us to deny ourselves, take up our cross, and give ourselves as living sacrifices. He bids us measure our lives by loss and not gain, by the bloodshed rather than by the wine drunk. The heart of the Christian religion is being crucified with Christ. We want to follow the sun, live for self, and do as we like. To follow Christ seems the way to the wilderness where no passion flowers grow. The amazing thing is that the way that seems to lead to a wilderness is the only way to the garden. Wordsworth, in his "Ode to Duty," says of the man who does his duty, "Flowers laugh before thee on their beds." They do, and when we go further, make the great surrender, accept the way the master went, then the flowers bloom, the birds sing, and life becomes a melody of love. Self-denial and self-surrender are the way to joy and beauty.

See the truth from the other side. Live for self—you live in vain. The life of self-seeking, self-pleasing, the life that turns its back on self-surrender and self-sacrifice, makes no garden for itself in others, it makes for a desert. See the truth embodied in living examples. It is true of some great lives. It is as true of humbler lives: self-sacrificing parents and Christian workers. These make a garden for themselves and others. One of my friends who is no mean musician only found out in his manhood what sacrifices his parents had made that he might have lessons on the organ. When he did find out he sent to his mother, "You shouldn't have done it." To which she replied, "My boy I got it all back the first time I heard you play the organ and lead the people in the worship of God." Of Jesus and all who have lived sacrificially it is true: "I lay in dust life's glory dead, and from the ground there blossomed life that shall endless be."[3]

---

3. This is from George Matheson's nineteenth-century hymn "O Love That Wilt Not Let Me Go."

"THE MAN WHO MISSED THE MEETING"
—John 20.24

(Preached four times from Katherine Road 4/3/32 to Spring Head Mission 9/13/36)

John 20.24 "Thomas, one of the twelve . . . was not with them when Jesus came."

AND THE SUBJECT IS, the man who missed the meeting—and the blessing. No explanation is given for his absence and perhaps he could have given good excuses for it. The eclipse of his faith is linked with the fact that he was not there and probably there was a connection between the two. The fact remains that, when the risen Lord came to the upper room and met the disciples, Thomas was not there. He missed the great occasion and He missed a large blessing.

The first thing I want to say about his absence is that *he ought to have been there*. Whatever reason is given for his absence there are overwhelming reasons why he should have been present. He was a man of peculiar temperament, rather easily depressed, and a lover of solitude. Leo Mathesin describes him as "the man under the Cypress tree." He expected the worst and steeled himself to "grin and bear it." Sorrow affects people differently. Some cannot bear to be alone. Others cannot endure company. We touch here a reason for some people's absence. They are not in a mood for a meeting and don't feel like going. But moods ought to be mastered and not masters. The fact that you do not feel like going is no reason for staying away. John Wesley frequently warned his people against the snare of waiting for the mood to do good. If you are depressed and in no mood for joining the fellowship of those who worship and pray you, like Thomas, are the very one who ought to be in your place.

But we are taken deeper than the question of personal preference or profit. Thomas ought to have been there because he was "one of the twelve." Do not miss the significance of that phrase. He belonged to them. It was a time of stress and strain and danger and there was need for everyone to stand by and take his share. The present danger made absence disloyalty. And here is the need for saying some straight things about church attendance. Association carries with it claims of identification and co-operation. It creates obligations. Membership is voluntary but once accepted it brings responsibility and involves obligations. The large trouble of the church is not with the

"THE MAN WHO MISSED THE MEETING"—JOHN 20.24

outsiders but with those who belong to it. There would be few complaints about half-empty churches if all who belong were present. In many cases the congregation is less than the membership and I wonder how the attendance at our Communion Service will compare with the number on our church roll. No one forced you to be a member of the church, a teacher in Sunday School, a singer in the choir. You joined yourself and you belong.

You created the obligation when you joined. Other churches may be better attended, have a finer preacher, afford you a greater inspiration, but your duty is where you belong. If you are bright and cheery and the services are dull that is not a reason for your staying away—it is the reason for your coming to lighten and brighten them. If the fellowship is stale you can easily remedy that by bringing into it a fresh experience and a new witness. If the Sunday morning service is thin and uninspiring you don't make it any better by staying away, do you? If you are counted you ought to be present. "Thomas, *one of the twelve*, was not there."

Missing the meeting he missed the blessing. He was the loser by his absence. He missed the manifestation of the Risen Savior. And he was of all people the man who could not afford that loss. He got the blessing eight days later but you may be sure it was tempered with reproach and regret. At the risk of seeming narrow I am going to say that the man who is absent when he ought to be present misses what he cannot afford to lose. I know most of what is to be said about being nearer to God's heart in a garden and hearing better sermons over the wireless. But I assert that no one can stand aloof from the fellowship of Christ's people without leanness coming into his soul. That is why so many lose their spirituality as their income tax assessment increases. Not even Christian service can make up for Christian communion. We are striking a false note when we sneer at the culture of the soul and the salvation of the people and talk as if social service were the first thing. To put service before devotion is to reverse God's order.

Christ is jealous for His church. He loves it, died for it, and where two or three meet He is always present. It is to our great loss that we forsake the assembling of ourselves together. One of the amazing things about the ministry of preaching is the way God gives the preacher a special message for someone's need. What if the one for whom the message is given is not present? If the Lord Christ thinks it worth His while to come, do our excuses excuse us? If He is present and we are not whose is the loss? Can we really afford to miss the fellowship of Christ and His people? Let us get right down to bedrock. Tell me—no, don't tell me—but search your soul—are you a better man, I don't say, "better off," more spiritually minded, more like Christ, more used in His service, since you took lightly attendance at meetings for Christian fellowship?

Happily, there is a happy ending to the story of the man who missed the meeting. We meet him as *the man who came back.* Listen to this—"After eight days, again His disciples where within, and Thomas was with them." He still believed they were wrong and he was right, but he stuck to them. When he came, no one challenged his right to be there. It was a brave thing to do and a gracious act on the part of the disciples. It's not easy for the man who has stayed away to come back. It means saying he was wrong to stay away and risking criticism. The hardest thing some people have to do is to admit they were wrong and come back to where they were. When they do, those who have stuck ought to be careful how they treat the returning one. Let him know he is welcome but in the name of common sense don't remind him how long it is since he was present or question his sincerity!

But let one repeat and finish the passage just quoted, "After eight days, again His disciples were within, and Thomas was with them: then came Jesus." The Risen Lord came again when Thomas came back. Did he come because Thomas was there? I think so. The man who came back found the blessing he had missed. His doubts were resolved, his heart was assured. What he had missed in solitude he found in fellowship. And from his grateful, adoring, and believing heart there came the great word of witness, "My Lord and my God." So, there is blessing for the man who comes back still. I've heard people say, "I'd give all I have to get back the old joy and peace." You need not do anything so dramatic. Just go back to the place in the fellowship you left.

But what I want specially to emphasize is that the man who had been absent brought a blessing when he came back. Jesus came again when Thomas returned, for us that means this—there are people in every church who could bring a revival if they went back to where they belong. Christ would come again if they came. You say you have not left the church—no, not outwardly, but are you in its inner fellowship where you rightly belong? I tell you, and with a dire sense of responsibility, that your staying away may mean the delay of revival. I could strengthen my argument by numerous well authenticated incidents.

There was a church where a man had quarreled with his brother-in-law. He did what many do, he vented his temper on God and sulked outside the church. One night he came back and confessed his sin, and that night a revival started in that church. A Methodist in the West Riding of Yorkshire got rich. He was too long to go to a fellowship meeting, and too tired to go to church more than once on Sunday. One day a poor, old woman asked him when he was coming back to class and wept as she told him how she missed him. He was touched by her concern. He came back and Christ came the very night he returned, and immediately the church was in a revival.

It may happen in less dramatic ways. This is one of the things you can test and prove. We have tried a good many ways to get things many ways to get things moving and they have none of them achieved striking success. Do we really want a revival? I mean a real revival—a revival of interest in God's House, of passionate love for Christ, of joy and zeal in his service—a revival that will make a prayer meeting more attractive than a whist drive and a service more thrilling than a dance—a revival of the power of God in the work of saving souls?

Such revivals are God given but they wait on human conditions. You cannot get one up but you may help to bring one down. Be in your place, the place of worship,

"THE MAN WHO MISSED THE MEETING"—JOHN 20.24

prayer, fellowship. If you have missed the central things come back again. Christ came again when Thomas was present. That was a week after Easter and this is the anniversary of the very day.

"FROM BAD TO WORSE"
—Acts 12.2, 3

(Preached at Spring Head Mission 11/3/40; rewritten for Bishop Street 7/23/50)

Acts 12.2, 3 "And he (Herod) killed James the brother of John with the sword, and because he saw it pleased the Jews he proceeded further to take Peter also."

WE HAVE OFTEN READ the story of *The Pilgrim's Progress*. Here is a very few words in the story of a reverse progress. Herod the king "killed James the brother of John." He did a base thing, a bad thing. And because judgment did not at once fall upon him, and because the bad thing increased his popularity, he proceeded further to do another base and bad thing. He went from bad to worse!

My point is that life is often like that. A man does a wrong thing, commits a sin against truth and honor. As we say, "he gets away with it." Instead of being punished, he finds the sin profitable and he is encouraged to proceed further. He goes from bad to worse. He thinks himself clever, and other people think him clever. His head becomes swelled as his conscience shrivels. Flattered by his cronies he thinks he can disregard God's judgment. His friends think, and he thinks, that he is a little god. Then one day he reaches the limit. He is made to realize what he really is and what God thinks of him. He discovers that the pathway he took was what has been called "a path to perdition." It is a serious note I must strike for this subject. It works out in a series of warnings.

BEWARE THE BEGINNINGS OF EVIL

An old proverb says that the first step is the difficult step. The danger of the first step in evil is, not that it might be found out, but that it may succeed. The best thing that could happen to some of us is that we should be found out the first time we do wrong. When the first step is taken, it is almost inevitable that the sinner should proceed further. Wickedness is self-compelling. It gathers momentum as it goes, and one sin leads to another.

You can see that happening on a large scale in Europe today. I have tried to keep my utterances free from fear and ill will. I do not conceive it the duty of a minister of Christ to say bitter and bloodthirsty things. But over the wireless a speaker, who probably had no thought of this scripture in mind, said that because it paid to take Czechoslovakia, Poland followed, and then Denmark and Norway, Holland and Belgium, and now comes the turn to Greece.

You can see the same thing in the story of outstanding criminals. Some years ago, a man who had lived large in the financial world was found guilty of robbery on a colossal scale. Part of his defense was that he had taken money to retrieve himself and in the hope of repaying people whose money he had appropriated. "Yes," said the learned judge, "the old excuse of every criminal who has taken money from a till and taken more to put things right."

The same thing works out in less dramatic settings. The first step in evil is both difficult and dangerous. Having taken the first glass, it is easier to take the second. Make one bet and, if you win, you will want to win more, if you lose, you will want to recover your loss. Yield to a lustful look and it will probably lead to a lustful deed. Having taken the first step on any sinful course it is easier to proceed further. Let your minister beg of you not to yield to the first temptation. Every time you yield to temptation the power of evil is strengthened and your own power of resistance lessened and you are playing into the hands of the enemy. But each victory will help you some other to win.

BEWARE OF SINNING TO WIN POPULARITY

It was "because he saw that it pleased the Jews," that Herod "proceeded further." Here again is an old-time setting of a murderous peril. Many a person has sinned to win a smile and has proceeded further to retain and increase his popularity. Let us be fair, there is a popularity that is worth winning and there are good people who stand well with their fellows. But you know what I mean.

Sometimes a good person finds himself in evil company. At first, he is paused by their conversation and acts. He feels he might express his disapproval, but that would mean he would be marked and perhaps persecuted. So, he is silent, and because he doesn't condemn, they say he is broad-minded and approving. And because it pleases, he proceeds further. He pretends to be worse than he is and does things he knows are evil. Here is a temptation that avails us all and of which we need to beware. It avails persons in public positions, it avails in common, everyday life. And we shall be in danger of pursuing the path to perdition unless we settle it first of all that the approval that needs to be desired is the approval of conscience; unless we settle it that we must do right whether people applaud of sneer. It's a punishment to have men sing, "He's a jolly good fellow," if we have been bad fellows to win the applause.

LUMINESCENCE
BEWARE OF PROCEEDING IN SIN

Beware of proceeding in sin because judgment does not speedily follow. Herod killed James, murdered an apostle. Nothing happened in the way of judgment, so he proceeded further. There is an applicable sentence in the book of Ecclesiastes 8.11: "Because sentence against an evil work is not executed speedily, therefore the heart of the sons of human beings is fully set in them to do evil." Tremblingly, fearfully, a person does a wrong thing. He is almost afraid a thunderbolt will fall on him. He is afraid of the consequences. But the thunderbolt does not fall, he is not found out. He thinks that because he has fooled people his action has escaped the notice of God. So, he proceeds further, and again "gets away with it."

Continue the story of Herod. Read the description of this character. For all his sins, Herod stood out in his glory and the people said he was a god. He believed them. And then came the judgment. He died in agony. That is a dramatic setting of the truth. Sometimes it works out that way still. In my time, I have seen clever rascals, who thought they had fooled both humankind and God, brought to judgment and disaster. It doesn't always work out that way. The mills of God grind slowly but they do grind. Judgment comes slowly and often along lines of natural retribution. But it comes. It comes in deterioration of character. It comes in the hour when you have to face yourself and the wrong you have done. And it comes when you have to face the Lord of Life.

I can take a break now of the serious words I have spoken, but I cannot finish without preaching the gospel. Listen! Judgment has not fallen on you. That is not because you have hoodwinked God. It is because "the Lord is long-suffering." As Peter says, "The long-suffering of God is our salvation." Let it lead you to repentance, to turning around. Instead of proceeding further, retrace your steps, and instead of treading the path to perdition, travel the road that leads back to God.

∽

"MIDNIGHT MUSIC"
—Acts 16.25

(Preached twice at Bishop St. 10/19/52 and Spring Head Mission 10/26/52)

Acts 16.25 "At midnight Paul and Silas prayed and sang praises to God and the prisoners heard them."

THE FACT THAT PAUL and Silas prayed does not greatly surprise us, though I seriously question whether, in their plight, we would have got as far as that. I fancy we would have been too busy, attending to our wounds, bemoaning our lot, and cursing our enemies to pray. Still, one can understand their praying if only to ask for justice, strength, and release.

The really surprising thing is that they not only prayed, they sang. They had been unjustly condemned, cast into an inner and loathsome dungeon, their backs were bleeding and sore, but they sang. And their prison melody was not a dirge or woe, but a song of praise. A song in the sunshine, a song of minstrels with whom all is well, we can understand. But here is music at midnight, with stocks for choir-stalls, and prisoners for choristers. That is a miracle only the grace of God can account for.

"And the prisoners heard them." They couldn't help it. But there is a deeper meaning here. The word carries the sense of listening, hearkening. The prisoners were straining these ears to hear the strange strains. They were giving their attention to the song. They had no song themselves, and it was something very different they usually heard from that cell. You may be sure they were both surprised and interested.

You can be sure, as well, that a careful writer like Luke, in his account of an earthquake and a great spiritual upheaval, puts in the reference to the minstrels and the listening prisoners for a very special reason. He wanted to do something more than kindle admiration for the courage of the brave singers—though we cannot help admiring them. He wanted his readers to learn their secret and catch their spirit.

THE REASON AND PURPOSE OF THIS SERMON

I have a growing feeling, deepening into a strong conviction, that one of our supreme and imperative needs is the need for Christian men and women who have the victorious faith that can sing, not only when the day is bright, but through the darkest night, not only when things are going well, but when they are going ill.

Some years ago, Mr. Wade Robinson said what I mean, and said it better than I can ever hope to. "O we want for the world a great exhibition of men happy in God! We have our Exhibition of Science and Art and Industry. But we want a great Exhibition of men strong in service, and pure in enjoyment, and calm in trouble, and tender in sympathy, and large in love, and joyful always."

This incident supplies and illustrates what I think Luke meant and what I know I mean when I read, "At midnight Paul and Silas prayed and sang praises to God, and the prisoners were listening." That is the conduit we need as we plan and go forth campaigning for Christ, and for which the world wants and listens. I hope I am mistaken, but I greatly fear that we have lost the faith that has a song in the night, and that the world waits in vain for such faith. One of the prayers we need to offer is that great prayer of David's, "Restore unto me the joy of Thy salvation, then shall sinners be converted unto Thee."

I am not sure that we think it matters as much as all that. We say we do. We sing heartily enough, "Hell's foundation quivers at the shout of praise." Do we really believe that the kingdom of darkness is shaken to its very foundations when Christians shout their praises?

THE SONG IN THE NIGHT AND THE LISTENING PRISONERS IN THE LIFE TODAY

Let us bring this incident close to our own life and times. As I have said, it is easy enough to sing the song when the sun shines and all goes well. I do not want to put on the black paint with too heavy a brush, but it is true that few who sing it will be in a prison and at midnight. If we are, they will not be the same as Paul's. Your midnight will be a reason of sorrow, loss, suffering, and trial. Your prison will not be a literal jail, it may be a sick room, a limited life, an exacting and wearying task, irritating and trying circumstances, the approach of death. Does any song of praise sound out from your prison at midnight?

It ought to. For you have an audience. Like that of Paul and Silas it may be unseen, but it is listening. And it would help if we remembered that the members of that audience are fellow prisoners. I think it is a good thing for ourselves to sing in the darkest night and as we travel weary roads. "Though the road may be long, in the lift of a song, I forget I was weary before." "When the heart is weary, sing a happy song."

Bishop Chavasse of Liverpool had a saying which was a guiding principle of his life, "Praise and service are great healers."

But I am still surer that we ought to sing for the sake of others. I wonder how much the Philippian jailer's conversion is owed to the singing of Paul and Silas. The world has no helpful song for the prisoners. The song of faith is the only song for them. You sing it and you will find that praise is contagious and that the song will pour from heart to heart and from lip to lip. Forgive a simple illustration. Someone who has passed through one of life's greatest sorrows said to me, "It was not your words that helped one most, it was the fact that when you faced your great sorrow you found grace and strength to carry on."

I do solemnly believe and declare that if only we had a faith and a song in direst of circumstances men and women everywhere would want to know the secret. Men and women are not going to be argued into goodness. They are not going to be called into it by the brain. They will be won by infectious joy of brave and believing Christians. Now we come to the crux of the whole matter. I will be borrowing the words of the Jews in captivity to show it. How can we sing the Lord's song in a strange land? To that question someone answered, "But what might have happened if they had tried?" It is not easy, that I freely admit. But Paul and Silas did, and from them I want us to learn—

THE SECRET OF THE MIDNIGHT MUSIC

Which is to say the secret of a brave, vanquishing, infectious joy? *Sheer courage had something to do with it.* I mean the sheer courage of men who are not easily downed. Men who stand up to life with all its perils, hardships, and trials. Like that of men who marched through mud and rain singing, "Pack up your troubles in your old kit-bag." Or better still, like R. F. S. who made a "task of happiness," in spite of his continued fight with ill health. He turned his danger into a lighthouse from which the light shone out for others. Stand up to life, put a cheerful courage on, and fight your way out and through.

It is a matter of right selection. This may sound prosaic, but it is important. The trouble with many of us is that we fix our eyes first on the miseries instead of the mercies. We total the hardships and forget to count our blessings. To select only the pains and distresses is bad physically, psychologically, and spiritually. I have admitted that there are times when the way is rough, and when the fight is fierce and long because the hosts are against us. But when you feel the downward pull, say to yourself, "Bless the Lord, O my soul, and forget not all His benefits." Count your allies as well as your foes, number your mercies as well as your hardships. You will always find inspiration for a song if you count your blessings, and count them first.

Faith is the inspiration of the song. Let me put it this way. Paul and Silas "prayed and sang praises." They praised because they prayed. For prayer is more than just asking God for something, it is first of all the realization that God is with you. You will pray because you believe someone is there to listen. It is the presence of God that chases away the gloom and inspires the song. If God is for you and with you, you need not fear what man can do unto you. It became as natural for Paul to say, "Notwithstanding, the Lord stood by me," as for him to say, "Timothy is with me and Titus stood by me." It was their faith in an ever-present Lord that inspired their song.

And you, too, have the promise, "I am with you always," and you may add "in everyplace." You know what His presence means. I have heard you sing, "Sun of my soul, Thou Savior dear, it is not night, if Thou be near."[1] And again, "In darkest shades, if Thou appear, my dawning is begun."[2] The song languishes on our lips because faith in our hearts burns low. Faith gives substance to things hoped for, gives us vision and assurance, and tunes our hearts and our lips for midnight music. What a great word of Charles Wesley this is, "Faith lends its realizing light, the clouds disperse, and the shadows flee. The invisible appears in sight, and God is seen by mortal eyes."[3]

A PLEA FOR THE SONG

So, for your own sake, and still more for the sake of others, I plead for a song in the heart that shall rise to the lips. I am not pleading for some rollicking and sentimental singing. I am pleading that though the night be dark and the way steep and hard, you shall set your trust in God's love into a song. It will do you good and your song will sound sweetly through the night to hearts that do not know or have forgotten that love.

It can be done. Paul and Silas did it. Men and women who have been through a darker night and into a deeper dungeon than yours have done it. In the night, you can mourn like a dove, hoot like an owl, or sing like a nightingale. They turned suffering into a music academy and sorrow into a singing master. And through faith, and by God's grace you can do it, too. So sing your old hymns in a new spirit and with fresh power, "Come, ye that love the Lord and let your joys be known."[4]

---

1. This is also the title of the nineteenth-century hymn by John Keble.

2. This is a line from Isaac Watt's hymn "My God, the Spring of All My Joys."

3. This citation is significant for several reasons. For one thing this is the very last thing that John Wesley said in his very last sermon, entitled "Faith," preached in 1791. It is a quotation of his brother's hymn "Author of Faith, Eternal Word."

4. This is from the famous Isaac Watts hymn which was later entitled "Marching to Zion."

"THE GRACE OF CONTINUANCE"
—Acts 26.22

(Preached fourteen times from Spring Head Mission 11/14/34 to Walking Ford 6/41)

Acts 26.22 "Having, therefore, obtained help of God, I continue unto this day."

BEHIND THESE WORDS IS a life story which began with obedience to a heavenly vision. The story was nearing its end. Paul has been retelling it, and it is very little he has to say. Years before he had heard the call of Christ and responded to it, had seen the vision and obeyed it, started out in the appointed way, and then he had just continued, he had just kept going. At first, we are disposed to disappointment. We expected more, a prouder, more triumphant note, a glowing story of great achievements. All we get is, "I continue unto this day." The person who accepts the world's standard of judgment sees no triumph in that, and probably writes down Paul as a failure, a man who has not made good. Even Christian people may miss the glory. The halo is there but it is vulgarly displayed. The words are few and quiet, but there is a story of battle and conquest. In Paul's words we may mark—

THE ABSENCE OF PRIDE

Or, the absence of anything approaching pride. This man might have told stories at which the ears of all who heard would tingle. He had made journeys that were a triumph of endurance. He had suffered persecution that would have killed a lesser man. By trenchant argument and powerful preaching, he had subdued stalwart opponents and won them for his Lord. There were men and women everywhere who owed him their very souls. He had preached the gospel and established churches in strategic places in the empire. But this man was no publisher! He is sparing in his use of red paint. He is one of the plain heroic breed who do their deeds and scorn to blot it with fame. His silence is more eloquent than a rhetorical recital of his deeds. All he says is, "I continue." Even what he did claim he refused credit for. Having "obtained help of God, I continue." In this, he followed the example of his Lord who did not lift up His voice and cry aloud in the street to call attention to Himself.

It is one of our temptations, as Christian workers, to boast of our achievements and glory in our records of conquest. And alas! We lay to our souls the flattering unction that we are doing it to the glory of God. Believe me, Christ would revise some of our newspaper reports and cast out some paragraphs from church magazines. Pride is bad anywhere, in Christians it is an abomination to the Lord and an offense to honest folk. And when we talk glibly about giving the devil a bad time, I'm sure he smiles in his sleeve and goes on his way rejoicing, for he is even the master of a braggart saint. As a general rule, it is a good thing to be silent about our achievements, content to know that our deeds are recorded in heaven and our names in the Lamb's Book of Life. And when success and victory come our way, let us remember that we have triumphed having obtained help of God. But what I want specially to emphasize is—

THE TRIUMPH OF CONTINUANCE

The apostle modestly said, "I continue unto this day." But that is a hero's utterance. You do not see it! Well, all is not gold that glitters, and all gold does not glitter! Let me try an illustration in a modern setting. Here is a man who is appointed to some lowly Christian task in a very lowly sphere. Maybe he is a teacher in a village Sunday School or a pastor of a variety of churches. Or, perhaps it is a woman left to care for her aged parents or younger brothers and sisters. Others strike out in life, go to up-to-date cities in flourishing colonies. They retire having made their pile and done great things. They find their friend growing grey in service, and still at the old post. While they tell of their doings they compassionately contrast their lot with that of the stay-at-home. Of course, he's a good old sort, but a bit of a stick in the mud, and they cannot keep back a smile from which contempt is not absent. The man also may be inclined to feel sorry for himself and think he has failed.

But what if the stay-at-home has achieved the real triumph? It may be that it took more courage and endurance to stay than to go. To "continue" when one would fain strike one's tent and away to serve in wider fields is not the achievement of a coward or a weakling. The fact is that the triumph of Christian life is continuance in the appointed way. It is "through patient continuance in well doing" that men win "glory, honor, and a deathless name." The climax is not in mounting up with wings as eagles, or in running without wearying, but in walking without fainting. The glory is in going on when you have no song to sing of great achievements and daring exploits. Can you say, "By the help of God, I continue unto this day"?

For a person to live his life and come through the struggle with head erect and an unconquered soul is the real triumph. Of all such, Sir Henry Newbolt's words on the sea-kings are peculiarly true: "Though all the world forbade them, they counted not nor cared: They weighed not help or hindrance, they did the thing they dared."[1]

---

1. This is from a poem by Newbolt entitled "The Sailing of the Longships." He was a poet and a novelist, but also a British governmental adviser who died in 1938.

"THE GRACE OF CONTINUANCE"—ACTS 26.22

THE GREATNESS OF THE TRIUMPH

I really mean that to continue, in itself, is to achieve a great triumph. Consider what is against patient continuance. I will borrow Paul's words to make it clear. For one thing, Paul knew that arrayed against him were the forces of evil. He saw them as a marshalled host under a personal head. "We wrestle not against flesh and blood, but against principalities and powers, against the rulers of the darkness of their world, against spiritual wickedness in high places." We do not describe the powers of evil in the same way or meet them in the same forms. But we know them and they are just as obstinate and vicious in their opposition. We have to continue in the teeth of clenched antagonism and against the powers of ill. To be able to say, after years of Christian profession, "I continue unto this day" is to say that neither the wiles of the devil, nor the pleasures of sin, nor the threats and bribes of the enemy have been able to conquer our trust and love.

Further, Paul had to meet his foes and pursue his way with the consciousness that the "outward person" was decaying. We know what that means. We are not as young as we once were. The years have taken something from us. The calls on our faith and courage take something out of us. We tire more easily. Even the youths faint and are weary. How could we ever think it a small thing to continue when every step of the way has to be contested and has to be made with weakening limbs and an outward strength that decays? Again, Paul knew what it was to be wearied by the length of the way and because the victory of his cause was so long delayed. He was not in doubt about the final issue, but the time appointed was long. He knew the temptation to be weary in well doing. We know the weariness of waiting, too. Evil is hard to destroy and faith has to learn to wait. Thank God if in spite of all discouragements, we continue in the faith and service of our Lord.

These things, I affirm, make the greatness of the triumph of continuance. I want to urge this word of cheer in those who, looking back across the years, are able humbly to say, "I continue unto this day." As we face the future, let us remember our debt to—

THE HELP OF GOD

"By God's help." The phrase falls glibly from our lips, but it is a great phrase for all that. Paul would not have been where he was, nor should we be where we are, but that His grace has been sufficient. Let us put the praise where it rightly belongs. It is by the Lord's mercies and by His help that we have maintained our Christian walk and witness. He has done great things for you in enabling you to continue. Have you thought it worthwhile to give Him your heart's gratitude for keeping you in the paths of righteousness?

And, if we are to reach the goal, if we are to the end to endure, it will be because the help of God does not fail. Do not be unmindful of the source of your strength.

LUMINESCENCE

Neither be fearful of the future. The way may be long, the road wind uphill all the way. Your foes may be persistent, unrelenting, and fierce, but God will not fail us. Hither by His help we are come, by His good Spirit we shall continue. "Even the youths shall faint and be weary . . . but they that wait upon the Lord shall renew their strength . . . they shall walk and not faint."

∼

"A GREAT TRIAL SCENE"
—Acts 26.29

(Preached twelve times from Katherine Road 4/22/34 to Vicar St. 1/23/44)

Acts 26.29 "I would to God, that not only them, but also all that hear me this day, were both almost, and altogether such as I am, except these bonds."

THERE ARE SOME INCIDENTS in the Bible which awe our souls by their moral grandeur. Men stand out with sudden brightness like men inspired. The light of God gleans in their eye and the courage of heaven sits upon their brow. The daring of Elijah as he confronts the 450 prophets of Baal, the courage of Daniel as, in face of imperial threats, he kneels in prayer by his open window. The moral grandeur of John the Baptist in the presence of the guilty Herod, the calm confidence of Stephen as the stones crash on his fair, young face. These and other scenes leap to mind as illustrations of what is meant. But for sheer moral power, the scene our text brings before us surpasses them all. There is only one trial scene in the world's history that surpasses it, and that is the one where the Son of Man stands silent, serene, and majestic before Pilate. Next to the great hour in which Pilate faced the question, "what shall I do with Jesus?" I know none to surpass the august hour when Paul stood at the bar of Agrippa in defense of the gospel it was his life to preach. What we need is the genius of a great artist to portray the scene. What we have to be content with is—

AN ATTEMPT AT A WORD PICTURE OF THE SCENE

At first, we are impressed by the splendor and magnificence of the scene. The gay and glittering ladies of the court. The haughty Festus, one of the shining lights of the imperial court. And Agrippa the king, the spoiled darling of Caesar, loaded with riches and flattered by thousands. On the other side, and standing at the bar, was a little man in rough and much worn garments. He was as poor as His master, Jesus Christ, had been and as friendless. His face was thin and scarred with the marks of privation and ill-usage on it. He belonged to a little sect spoken of with contempt and hatred. He was pleading for his life, and defending the gospel he preached, and speaking well of the

Master he served, and he had been submitted to the ridicule of the court, the taunt of Festus, the superfluous and cynical speech of Agrippa.

And yet, and yet, the longer we look at this scene, the more impressed by the moral grandeur and the spiritual passion of that lonely little man. He hardly seems to see the pomp, the glitter, the crown. He sees only immortal beings with souls to be saved and brought out of darkness into light, out of bondage into freedom. His great heart swelled with compassion, he forgot his own sufferings and the insults heaped on him, and lifting his manacled hand, he said, "Would to God you were all as I am, except these bonds." That is the scene, and I am profoundly sorry for the person who is not moved to admiration of the central figure in it.

TO ADMIRE IS NOT ENOUGH

The Bible does not set before us a galley of noble men and women to be admired. The things written are, in oft-quoted words, "written for our learning." They are intended to teach and inspire, admiration is to beget emulation. This is indeed a moving scene, and is intended not simply to move us to sentimental tears, but to like morality of action. Mark what is worthy of our admiration and our imitation. There is what has been called—

THE MAGNANIMITY OF PAUL

Look again and steadily at the scene. There stands the lonely, defenseless man in defense of the faith. He makes his calmly reasoned appeal. Then Festus flings at him the taunt, "Thou art beside thyself, much learning doth make thee mad." Agrippa smiles and says, "Would you with that little persuasion make me a Christian?" Here was provocation enough, and some of us would have answered fools according to their folly. Paul had power to make a quick and crushing retort. Who would have blamed him if he had wished for his oppressors a taste of the bitterness they were causing him? But Paul had a greater power, the power to keep back the bitter invective he might have used. Instead of wishing his tormentors ill, he prayed that they might know nothing of the pain they were causing him. He lifted his fettered hand as he said "except these chains," and the clang of the chain tore the silence of the court.

Is there any need to extol such magnanimity? Does not Paul stand out as a greater man than the man for whom we have a sneaking regard, the man who is strong and quick, smart at repartee, and able to give tit for tat and a Roland for an Oliver? That, I tell you, is the sign of greatness, to hold yourself in reserve, to suffer wrongfully, to endure such for your persecutor's exemption from what they make you suffer, to set yourself not to the little patterns of men, but to the excellent glory of Him who on the cross prayed, "Father forgive them." That lesson we must learn, that enrichment of character we must seek, if we are to win men for our Lord.

"A GREAT TRIAL SCENE"—ACTS 26.29
PAUL'S EVANGELISTIC PASSION

Barring the bonds, he wished that gay and glittering crowd were like him. I fortify myself with the comment of one of our greatest biblical scholars, Professor Foakes Jackson, "Paul's reply is a model of Christian zeal for the conversion of all present, and of consideration."[1]

If he had said, "I wish I were as you are," we could have understood it. That is what we often say as we look at the opulent and outwardly happy. What he said was, "I wish you were as I am, the chains excepted." He said that because he was one of the great souls who had realized what it is to be a Christian. In spite of poverty, contempt, and chains, his life was strong with a sense of the Divine Presence and protection, uplifted and glorified by a great and solemn purpose, raptured in an unsurpassed love. He was filled with serenity as untroubled as God's throne, with a quenchless hope, and a joy unspeakable and full of glory. He knew, not only that he need not envy Agrippa and his glittering court, but that he had something infinitely better than they had found. And we know it now, know that Paul with his rags and chain was greater than Agrippa with his riches and his crown.

We know it was true for Paul, but are we as sure that it is true for ourselves? Do we really believe that it is better to be a Christian than anything else in the world? In our hearts I think we do, but we do not always put the true estimate on our privileges, and then we envy the wise, the rich, and the favored. But look at it this way. Suppose some Mephistopheles were to come to you and offer you the wisdom of a Solomon, the fame of a Caesar, the wealth of a Midas, in exchange for your faith in Christ, your hope in God, the heavenly light by which you walk. What would you say? I am sure I know hundreds who would turn away with anger and pain. Not for all that the world has to offer would they make such a sacrifice. Put this way we can all see that the Christian life is worth more than all else.

And yet, we do not always realize how much our faith means or surely we should be more in earnest in commending it to others. That is why I bring you this picture of the man who knew what he had in Christ, and who longed with passionate fervor to share it even with those who treated him ill—"I would you were all such as I am, except these chains." That is the evangelism we commend.

The preacher would be false to his own sermon and to his deepest convictions if he did not, with earnest entreaty and loving solicitude say to the unconverted, "I would that you knew my Savior and I pray from my heart that you will open your hearts to receive Him."

~

---

1. He is doubtless citing from the famous volumes on Acts entitled *The Beginnings of Christianity*, of which F. J. Foakes Jackson was one of the authors, along with Kirsopp Lake.

"CHRIST CRUCIFIED AND RISEN"
—Romans 8.34

(Preached twice at Katherine Road 4/12/36 and Spring Head Mission 4/17/38)

Romans 8.34 "It is Christ that died, yea rather, that is risen again."

THE TEXT IS TAKEN from Paul's great argument in one of his sublimest chapters. Beginning with the grand affirmation that "there is now therefore no condemnation to them that are in Christ Jesus," he moves into the magnificent climax that neither here or hereafter, in height or in depth, in death or in life, nothing can separate believers from the love of God which is in Christ Jesus.

No one can understand that argument apart from Paul's terrific experience. The concluding verses of chapter 7 reveal him as a man under condemnation and in bondage. Then with a shout of triumph he realized his freedom in Christ Jesus. Compare Charles Wesley's bold setting of a similar experience, "Long my imprisoned spirit, etc.," and its glorious ending, "No condemnation now I dread." Arguing for this "no condemnation," Paul asks, "Who shall lay anything to the charge of God's elect?" "Who is he that condemneth?" God might, but then in love He gave His Son for us. Jesus Christ might, but He won't, for He is the One who died and is risen again for us. You can see how great the truth is in its setting, but for our immediate purpose, I want to treat only the statement of the text.

THE HEART OF THE GOSPEL

Christ died and rose again! That is the heart of the gospel. Writing to the Corinthians Paul said, "I delivered unto you first of all . . . Christ died for our sins . . . that He rose again." Apart from those great facts he had no gospel, with them he had the best news of all. Christ died. That must never be forgotten. Paul's glory was in the cross and the deliberate theme of his preaching was Christ crucified. No one will charge him with minimizing the cross and all that it symbolized. But as he utters the words, "It is Christ that died," an upper thought comes into his mind and he amends his expression, "yea rather, that is risen again." That is not to set one over against the other, or magnify one above the other.

CRUCIFIXION AND RESURRECTION

It is rather to show one each needs and completes the other. It is Christ that died, God forbid that we should ever forget that. The cross and all that it symbolizes is the place where we see the light, lose our burdens, and are assured of pardon. It is when we survey the wondrous cross that Christ becomes real to us, that we pour contempt on our pride, and see in our biggest sacrifices a reasonable service. One rejoices at a growing regard for the sacramental service as a memorial of His death, and at all things that remind us that "He died that we may be forgiven." Even so, Calvary does not stand alone. It is Christ that died, yea rather that is risen again. The man whose glory was in the cross said, "If Christ be not raised then is our faith vain."

One asks if there is not a real point in Michelangelo's indignant protest to his fellow painters, "Why do you keep filling gallery after gallery with endless pictures of the one ever reiterated theme, of Christ in weakness, Christ dying, most of all of Christ hanging dead?" The symbol of our faith is not a crucifix, and certainly not one with a dead man on it. Paul's Christ, cried Michelangelo is not dead but risen. Paint Him as the conqueror of death! Paint Him as the Lord of life! Paint Him as what He is, the irresistible Victor who, tested to the uttermost has proved Himself in very deed mighty to save.

There is a real danger in our failure to remember that Easter follows Good Friday and in making the crucifix our symbol. Gazing at the cross alone and too long tends to kindle a queer inferiority complex in our minds that often leads to shrinking from the powers that are arrayed against us as against Him, and that breeds a cowardice in which we lose heart and fling away our weapons. Bring in the upper thought that He conquered in death and we gain courage and become sure of the triumph of the good and true.

In some cases, and with some types of piety, continued meditation on the cross has led only to the luxury of grief, to vapid, lachrymose sentimentalism. By all means remember that He died for you and that will bring you to your knees in grief and gratitude. Remember that He rose again and is abroad in the world, then you will get up from your knees and follow His footsteps as He goes forth to seek and save. You will keep coming back to the cross for inspiration, but you will not seek the living among the dead. At the Sacramental Service, you will take reverently and often the symbols of His broken body and shed blood. You will say with adoring wonder, "He loved me and gave Himself for me," and you will add, "Now I must love Him and give myself for Him."

We need both, and must have them. "It is Christ that died, yea rather that is risen again." Our Lord is He that was dead, but He is above forevermore. He is above, saving, redeeming still and our place is at His side. It is not simply the cross of Jesus that is "going on before." It is Christ our joyful and living Master. After that, anything else must be in nature of an anticlimax. But there is an application that must be made.

THE LAST WORD IN THE GOSPEL IS LIFE AND NOT DEATH

It was so in the experience of Jesus and it is so in our lives. The gospel comes to us with its call to death to sin, the sacrifice of much that is dear to us, the binding of our wills with His. Too often we stop there and then Christian life seems a maimed, if not a dead, thing. But always our own Good Fridays are followed by Easters. We die, yea rather, we live. "I am crucified with Christ, nevertheless I live." We know "the fellowship of Christ's sufferings" and "the power of His resurrection." We die to self, sin, pride, but we live unto God. Matheson summed it up in his great verse, "I lay in dust life's glory dead, and from the ground there blossomed life." Yes, life is the last word. Christ came, lived and died, that we might have life with a capital L.

So it is too with these lives of ours. Our loved ones have their day and there comes what we call the end. We say they are dead. Tenderly and lovingly we tend their graves. But to the believer, death can never be the last word in the grave the last resting place. When we mortals say, a man is dead, angels say a child is born. Where we speak of death they talk of life forevermore. Lift your eyes from the brown earth to the blue sky and know that the sky, not the grave, is our goal, that the soul's resting place is the Father's House. Life is ever lord of death and love can never lose its own. It is Christ that died, yea rather, that is risen again. And His resurrection is the pledge that for the Christian, life and not death is the last word.

"THE FULL-ORBED GOSPEL"
—Romans 15.29

(Preached at Spring Head Mission 9/8/43 and Bishop St. 9/1/46)

Romans 15.29 "I am sure that, when I come unto you, I shall come in the fullness of the blessing of the Gospel of Christ."

THE APOSTLE PAUL WAS one of the world's greatest travelers. But he was never merely a tourist, he was always a missionary. He wanted to visit, and did visit, the world's important and strategic places, but it was not their historic or artistic interest that appealed to him, it was the opportunity of preaching the gospel they presented. His anxiety was to plant the standard of the cross where it had not floated, to preach the gospel where it had not been preached. Of course, he wanted to see Rome, the metropolis of the world. It was one of his crowning ambitions. "I must see Rome," he says, "I am coming to you." And he tells them why he is coming: not that he may see the sights of the Eternal City, but for one thing and one thing only, and that one thing is expressed in the crowded words of our text.

When I was casting about in my mind for some word of God's grace with which to begin a new year of ministry I came upon these words, not first in my Bible, but at the head of a chapter in a book by one of the great masters of the Scottish pulpit. My heart took fire as I saw them and for weeks I have known what my message would be. The suggestion is James S. Stewart's, the sermon is mine. I am coming to you this year, if God gives me grace. I am coming with the fullness of the blessing of the gospel of Christ. Anyone of you, with Stewart's suggestion could preach on this text you have only to take the great words of this text, work through them backwards, and you have matter enough for half a dozen sermons.

Allow me to follow my own counsel, *I am coming to you with Christ*. If that does not mean that Christ is coming with me then I had better not come at all. Without Him I can do nothing. But the preacher's blessed privilege is to be a worker with Christ. And the more Fred Barrett sinks into insignificance and out of sight that ye may see Jesus only, the better it will be for preacher and people. But that is not the first meaning here. Paul meant, and I mean, I am coming to you bringing Christ. He is my theme, in Him is summed up my message. "I determined," said Paul concerning another great, historic city, Corinth, "not to know anything among you except Jesus Christ and Him crucified." That is the preacher's one subject, and the definition is not a limitation, it is a concentration. Again he declares, "The Jews require a sign and the Greeks seek after wisdom, but we preach Christ." Still the pragmatists are asking for signs and the philosophical for arguments. But still the preacher replies, "We preach Christ." And the marvel is that with such a subject any man can preach anything else. The preacher takes an intelligent man's interest in literature, philosophy, economics, and history. But I was not endowed to teach English literature or lecture in natural science. I was endowed to preach the Word of God, for me the last Word of God is the Word made flesh. I am coming to you with Christ and as God helps me that is my main and only subject.

Take the next word, *I am coming with the gospel of Christ*. That means not new, but news. I am not coming to you with some homespun news of my own about Jesus. I am coming with the evangel, the good news. I am a herald, my assignment is to declare, "Behold your God coming in Jesus Christ to save you." I have to declare that God loves you and that Christ Jesus came into the world to save sinners like you and me. I bring you: The joyful news of sins forgiven, of hell subdued, and peace with heaven. You are all eager for news and glad when it is good news. There is what Tennyson said was "old news, good news, and new news." Time was when man thrilled at this news. It set them singing and sent them through the world with a light in their eye and a song in their heart.

The trouble now is that you can listen and wonder why the preacher wants to get so excited about such an old, old story. That may be the preacher's fault in the telling of it. In a book I have just read there was a story of a little girl who was used to the wireless and was taken to church for the first time. When she got home she said, "I liked the music but I did not care for the news." God forgive us that we can preach the greatest love story in the world in such a way that people will want to go to sleep!

But it is not always the preacher's fault. Some of you are not interested. You are more interested in the girl you took to the pictures or the bargain you made or the money you banked. If you are not interested I do not know what I can do but pray for you, and so preach the Word that you may be awakened and aroused. I know you need the news I bring you and my responsibility is to bring it to you and say again and again the good news that God loves you, that Christ died for you, and that He loves and wants to save you.

Consider the next word, *the blessing of the gospel of Christ*. That suggests the reaction of the gospel on everyday life. The good news received and believed makes life good and glad. It makes life blessed. It fills the soul with joy and peace. Every reception of the good news, every revival has meant a new beginning. It has set people singing for sheer joy. Think of the exultation of the early church, and joyfulness of St. Francis, or the "nest of singing birds" in the early Methodist Church. I have just read

Harold Begbie's two-volume story of General Booth and the Salvation Army. There is no mistaking the secret of the success of the Salvation Army in the days of bitter and violent persecution, it was the radiant joy of the new converts. And though you may not believe me when I come to you with the gospel of Christ I am bringing you the secret of a joy that abounds and abides in peace that passes understanding.

I cannot finish without the last word, *the fullness of the blessing of the gospel of Christ*. I cannot be content with less. Some of you have the blessing but have not received all the fullness. I will not judge you, but I know the reason why in my own life. I have not wholly believed, I am not fully surrendered. It is still "some of self and some of Thee." Ah, the secret sins, the door that is not opened to Christ. I sing, "My all is on the altar," but there is something I am keeping back. The fullness of the blessing only comes when we give up on all and claim by faith the fullness of the blessing. Swing the heart's door widely open, hand over the keys, bid Him welcome to every part of your life, and all the fullness you will then forever have.

Seven years ago, to this night I opened my communion and preaching to you in the words, "That which we have seen, that which we have heard, that which we have handled of the word of life, declare we unto you." I am coming to you at the beginning of the eighth year with the same old story. I go further back than that. Thirty-seven years ago, I began my ministry with the same message. I have and want no other. "E'er since by faith I saw the stream, thy flowing wounds supply, redeeming love has been my theme and shall be till I die."[1] And you who are my people, make it easy for your minister to preach this gospel by surrounding his preaching with your prayers and the persistent logic of Christ's redeeming love.

---

1. This is from William Cowper's famous eighteenth-century hymn "There Is a Fountain Filled with Blood."

"RUFUS—A CHOICE CHRISTIAN"
—Romans 16.13

(Preached nineteen times from Fentiman Road, undated, to Horden, undated)

Romans 16.13 "Salute Rufus chosen in the Lord."

THE SIXTEENTH CHAPTER OF Romans is a roll of honor on which are inscribed the names of some lesser known witnesses and workers of the early church. Their deeds are not so striking and outstanding as those recorded in the eleventh of Hebrews, but they are not less worthy of consideration. Most of those named are mentioned only here. Theirs is just a passing significance and then they drop out of the story. The chapter is little known and seldom read, though it ought to be a favorite with those who know themselves to be of the rank and file of the churches. To them it ought to be a continual reminder that we all may be faithful if not famous. In this "page of names," as a recent writer entitles the chapter, occurs the name of Rufus.

Of the man who bore it we know latter tradition says he was the son of Simon of Cyrene, the man who was compelled to carry the cross of Jesus, and probably the tradition is truth. However that may be, this little known man wore for himself a splendid name. That may not appear from the ordinary rendering of the text where he is described as "chosen in the Lord." Frankly, it was another translation of the text that gave it grit. "Salute that choice Christian, Rufus," I read in Dr. Moffatt's translation. That at once arrested attention. It lifts the man above the crowd and stamps him as eminent on piety, makes him a distinguished Christian. It is here that we may begin to apply the lessons of his brief mention.

THE DISTINCTION IS BETWEEN COMMON AND CHOICE

In the garden, there are many flowers of common quality and average beauty, but the pride of the gardener is in a few choice specimens. There are many singers, artists, preachers, but only here and there one who is outstanding, eminent, choice. So there are many Christians, but few who are choice. We do not question or belittle the Christianity of many, they do trust, love, and serve, but it is to be deplored that so many are ordinary, average, common, and so few choice. Far too many are content if they are up to the average and will pass in a crowd. Few things are more to be desired than that Christians shall be fired with a desire to emulate Rufus and become choice Christians. We badly need more Christians and just as badly do we need better Christians.

ALL CHRISTIANS MAY BE CHOICE

In some spheres, most of us must be content to be average or even commonplace. We shall never be outstanding as artists, musicians, orators. We lack the artistic eye, the musical ear, the orator's gift. That is our misfortune and not our fault. But choice Christianity is not a matter of genius or gift, it is a question of ardent desire, earnest effort, and persistent faith. "This honor have all His saints." We are all called to eminence of character if not of service. Christ introduced a new order of aristocracy and you may belong to it. In the realm of purity and piety we may all be aristocrats. Potentially we are all choice Christians and we may be actually. A wonderful fashion of teaching our Master has and no matter how dull the scholar He takes into His school, He makes them wise to salvation.

THE HIGHEST LIFE IS NOT EASY OF ATTAINMENT

It is no use pretending that we easily become an eminent and choice Christian. The path is not easily trodden or the goal cheaply won. The Master made the way clear but He never made it easy. Indeed, distinction and perfection in any sphere are not easy. Ask your sons and daughters who are trying to win distinction in math or a place among the choice musicians. Someone asked a famous violinist how long it would take to learn to play the violin. He replied, "Twelve hours a day for twenty years." Of course, you can become an ordinary performer in less and play this sonata and that cantata so that your friends and admirers say, "Isn't it wonderful?" But it takes time, pain, and patience to become a real choice player. And let me ask you this, "Which is harder, to play like Kreisler or to live like Jesus?"

The moment you turn from your sins and trust Christ you become a Christian, but to become a choice Christian means pain, patience, and prayer. It means submitting to discipline and going to school with the Master. It calls for devotion, study, the daily renewing of vows, and the counting of many things as loss that we may win Christ and be found in Him. It is difficult, but it is possible. Given an earnest desire and a strong intent all the means are available for the perfecting of Christian character. Are you prepared to give the time and pay the price?

THE LORD HAS SPECIAL NEED OF THE CHOICE

That is why He challenged His disciples with such questions as, "What do ye more than others?" "Lovest thou me more than these?" There is work for all Christians, but there is fine, delicate, and difficult work that is for the choice and impossible to the commonplace. God had to reduce Gideon's army and it was by the three hundred picked men that deliverance was wrought out.

During one of his campaigns, William Wallace had to capture the fortress which stood in Dumbarton Rock. The situation was such that the whole army could not be used. The valiant captain chose a few picked men and detailed them for the attack. By choice souls God wins His greatest victories. He counts on a holy remnant. Are we the sort of Christians Christ can count on for special work? We can do the ordinary work of the church. But for eminent work in the cause of the kingdom, He asks, "Are ye able to drink of the cup I drink of and to be baptized with my baptism?" It is when we are able to say, "We can," that He replies, "Ye shall."

Most of us have to confess that we are commonplace and not choice. We are content if we are as good as the rest. Let us have done with our cheap satisfaction and our easy complacence. Of course, choice souls are always unconscious of their eminence. Humility and modesty are part of their fine character. So let us face it this way. Are we striving to rise above the average and fit ourselves for the highest service? It was one of the choicest of Christians, one ready for every call of his Lord, who said, "I count not myself to have apprehended . . . but I follow after . . . I press toward the goal." So let us keep the goal before us, ever press towards it, and remember that the goal is, "Be ye perfect even as your Father in Heaven is perfect."

"THE CHRISTIAN OPTIMIST"
—1 Corinthians 1.4

(Preached at Katherine Road 2/3/35, Spring Head Mission 6/7/42, and rewritten for Bishop St. 8/14/49)

---

1 Corinthians 1.4 "I thank my God always on your behalf, for the grace of God, which is given you by Christ Jesus."

Nearly all of St. Paul's epistles begin on this note of thanksgiving for the reality of the Christian life in those he addresses. Romans, Corinthians, Philippians, Colossians, Thessalonians—he has a word of praise and thanksgiving for them all. Later on, come rebukes, expositions, and exhortations, but the epistles begin with praise and thankfulness. Knowing Paul, we are quite sure that these commendatory words are not simply fulsome flattery. They do more than reveal the tact of a man who has sense to see that the right way of approach to people he wants to win is that of courteous reference to the good already in them.

No, the words reveal his sheer gladness at goodness and the hope and confidence kindled in him by the earnest and sincere Christian life in his friends. Their goodness made him thankful and sent him on his way encouraged and hopeful.

THE DIFFICULT WORK

From Paul's thankful spirit of hope let us turn to the tendency to despair which besets us today. I am thinking of Christian workers. There are so many things that tend to drive us to despair. In the thought of today there is a strong undercurrent of pessimism and gloom. There is a feeling that life's problems are unsolvable and salvation impossible. If we are high-brow we find it in the writings of Schopenhauer and his disciples and ordinary readers find it in the books of Thomas Hardy and some modern novel writers. The suggestion is that man is the creation and slave of heredity and circumstances and that moral responsibility does not exist. The only thing to do under these circumstances is to settle down in gloom and despair, or else let things slide and simply have as good a time as we can for as long as we may.

Perhaps the more potent factor is the fact that in recent year's Christian work has become increasingly difficult. The changed intellectual outlook, the modern craze for amusement and the opportunities for gratifying it, the economic struggle for existence, have left little time for the culture of the soul. The church seems to make little progress and indeed seems to be losing ground. Our witness and our work seem so ineffective that we are in danger of losing faith and hope, sinking into despair. And despair paralyzes. Dante placed doubters and deniers next to the slothful. There is indeed a close connection. Despair leads to inaction. If our work is hopeless what is the use of doing it? If pessimism and gloom have settled on us are we qualified for service?

When our faith is weak and our convictions pale, we are afraid to say our supreme need is men courageous, hopeful, and strong. Against our despair let us set Paul's cheerful courage and shining hope. He was emphatically a Christian optimist and not of the rose-water variety either. Nor did things seem more smoothly for him than for us. The intellectual atmosphere of his time was discouraging. His was an age of disillusion and disappointment. Much in which people had trusted had turned out to be vanity and vexation. People were either forcing themselves to be Stoics, or giving themselves up to be Epicureans. Paul must have listened to many a gloomy account of the prospects before humanity, and he was too sensitive to be untouched by the thought movements of his time.

The practical difficulties and discouragements of his ministry were tremendous. His day-to-day work was arduous and involving him in wearisome travels, serious discomforts, and real risks. He had to preach, organize churches, exercise disciples, and confirm saints. He had to face the opposition of the Jews and the persecution of the official powers. His converts were many from the degraded classes, sometimes they fell back into their old ways and often their factions, their misunderstandings, their littleness.

Yet he went on, and we see him making those journeys, preaching the gospel, building up the churches, often in perils, in weariness, in pain, in the teeth of opposition, and yet never in despair! Through all the dangers, in the midst of all the perils and perplexities, he carried himself with unflinching courage, and with an unconquerable hope for himself and the church.

THE SECRET OF OPTIMISM

The text puts us on the track of his secret. As we have seen he begins his letters to the churches with words of thankfulness and praise. In them, under all that was unworthy, he saw a real work of grace. He commended their work of faith, labor of love, and patience of hope, in these graces he saw what conquered the tendency to despair and filled him with hope. What he saw was God at work saving, sanctifying, and reforming their lives. It was God's grace that was giving them the victory and so he always linked his commendation with thanks to God. He did great things for those little communities, but they did great things for him too. They provided the evidence that God Himself was at work. Paul was a laborer not only for God but with God. There could be no doubt and despair when the work was not so much his as God's. If God was for him, and in the lives of those people he saw that God was for him, what mattered opposition and foes? So, he went on his way, often perplexed, sometimes troubled, always suffering, but never wholly cast down and never despairing.

And have not we the same evidence? It is a minister's great privilege, as it is his heavy responsibility, to go in and out of the homes of his people and especially in times of sickness and sorrow. He is permitted to share sorrow and see wounds that are hidden from the world. For thirty years that has been my privilege and it gives me some right to speak. Let me tell you what has impressed me most—the sure courage, the secret graces, the chivalrous loyalties of lovely Christian people. Here are some of the things that have cheered me.

Last Sunday morning it was wintry, snow everywhere, streets slippery and dangerous. I had no condemnation for any who did not turn up at service. But looking up at me with a shining face was an old man of eighty-two who had braved the elements because he loved God's house and the word of God's grace. Someone once missed the services and someone wondered why. It was the minister's privilege to know that not indifference, but an unselfish and loving ministry was the cause. Into a home of suffering and weakness the minister went and heard the invalid murmur, "Can I doubt His tender mercy who through life has been my guide." Into another such room the minister goes and the patient's anxiety is to give him her offering that the church's finances may not suffer by her absence. I have to write a letter to one who has suffered a staggering blow and who writes, "I am trying to be brave and, God helping me, I will carry on."

That is the secret, "God helping me." In their graces, I see God's grace. In their courage and goodness, I see God at work, as I sing to myself: "And every virtue we possess and every victory win, and every thought of holiness, and His alone."[1] How can we despair when we know that God is with us? It was the assurance of the Divine presence that kept faith and hope alive in Paul. As John Wesley lay dying he was heard to murmur, "The best of all is God is with us." That was the assurance that had borne him through eighty years of wanderings and labors not unlike those of Paul. That is what will save us from despair and keep courage and hope alive. And He is with us, and the evidence of His presence is not in some dramatic and miraculous appearance, but in the saved and disciplined lives of those for whose labors of love we thank our God.

---

1. This is from a nineteenth-century hymn by Harriet Auber entitled "Our Blest Redeemer Ere He Breathed."

"CHRIST'S FAITH IN US"
—1 Corinthians 13.7

(Preached seven times from Fentiman Road to Bishop St. dated only on 7/4/37 at Spring Head Mission)

---

1 Corinthians 13.7 "Love believeth all things, hopeth all things."

THE FIRST REFERENCE IS to human love and its faith and hope. Paul was urging the Corinthians to possess the love which, instead of thinking evil and expecting the worst, would believe and expect the best of people. But the subject is, Christ's faith in us, and it is justifiable from the text. For God does not ask of us what is not in Himself. Our Lord is love incarnate and the ideal towards which we move. It has been suggested that we might substitute "Christ" for "charity" in this great chapter and it would make suggestive reading. Anyhow, it is with perfect love in him that we are concerned. His is supremely the love which believes the best and hopes the best for us. Let us work out the truth in this way—

WE ARE HEAVILY IN DEBT TO THOSE WHO BELIEVE IN US

It is not only our own faith which saves. Many of us only arrive at personal faith after someone has believed in us and for us. Many a lad has been surprised into doing larger things than seemed possible because some teacher expressed faith in his possibilities. Most of us have friends who believed in us and we feel that we must justify their faith. They count on us, expect us to do things, their faith and hope kindle our own and we go out to attempt and accomplish the things of which they think we are capable. On the other hand, we are chilled, repressed, discouraged, when no one believes in us or expects anything of us.

It is here that we owe a debt to Jesus that we do not always recognize. We speak often, never too often, about our faith in Him, but we do not think or speak often enough about His faith in us. "We are saved by hope," says St. Paul, and the hope that saves is ultimately Christ's hope in us. If He had despaired our case would have been hopeless. We sometimes say of people that they are past praying for. When we say that of anyone, it is not long before we cease all efforts to save them and leave them to their fate. God did not think individuals were past praying for, living for, dying for, that is why Christ visited His people to redeem them.

CHRIST BELIEVES IN HUMAN BEINGS AS HUMAN BEINGS

There was once a cynical philosopher who said he could believe in humanity if it were not for people. Well, Christ came into closest contacts with people, talked with them, lived with them, was sometimes disappointed in them, but believed in humanity. He was not blind to their defects and weakness, their sin and shame, but He believed in them and hoped the best for them. When others saw "sons of perdition," "children of the devil," He saw "sons of Abraham," and potential "children of God." Others put the emphasis in the prodigal, He emphasized the son. Anyone who knows people does not find it difficult to believe in original sin. Jesus found our original goodness, a spark of the Divine, a possibility and power of repentance underneath all the growths of selfishness and sin. He believed in people again and again, and they came to believe in His belief and rose to His hope.

Put it this way. In the central doctrine of Christianity is the supreme illustration of the love that believes all things. The heart of Christianity is in the cross of Christ. The amazing fact we have to preach is that God came in Christ to our world, lived in it, suffered in it, agonized in a garden and died on a cross. The purpose of it all is in a child's hymn—"He died to make us good." That is the heart of Christianity. And the great assumptions of it are: That people are worth saving, that people can be saved, that there is in people a desire for goodness and power of response to the attraction of goodness.

Christ believes in us at our worst, in our worth, in our ability to trust and aspire, in the possibility of our full redemption. He does not go all the lengths and depths of the cross for an impossible vision. The cross inspires self-respect and faith in ourselves. What is a human being? It would be easy to give a cold, critical, and even damning answer. But the cross reveals the divine estimate of humankind, His faith in humanity and possibilities beyond our wildest dreams. Never forget that and you will never despair of yourself or anyone.

CHRIST'S FAITH IN HIS OWN

Out of the world of humanity in general, our Lord chose a battle company of persons that they "might be with Him and that He might send them forth." Honesty compels the admission that they were in many ways a sorry lot. They were often proud, selfish, and ill tempered. They argued over first places and often misunderstood His teaching. But He said to them, "I have chosen you, you are my fellow workers and my friends. I will reveal to you my purposes, and you shall help me in this great work of saving the world." Nothing amazes me more than the way Christ trusted His friends and counted on their loyalty, unless it be their splendid response to His faith.

And still He loves and trusts His own. In many ways, we are a sorrier company than that first company. We are often little and mean, proud and selfish, bad tempered and quarrelsome. Yet He did choose us. Sometimes a person in an open-air crowd challenges me with, "Well, if you are the chosen of the Lord, the Lord chose a sorry lot." I do not argue with him, I agree. It is simply amazing that He chose us and trusts us. I can understand Paul saying, "Unto me who am less than the least, of this grace (of service) I have been given."

I cannot understand why He chose me, I only know He did. I am not your minister simply because you invited me, but because He called me. He appointed me to the care of souls. He sent me to go in and out among His people, cheering them in their loneliness, comforting them in their sadness. He sent me to join your hands in the bonds of holy matrimony, to baptize your precious babies, to bury your beloved dead. He sent me to preach the gospel of the grace of God.

But His call is not only to ministers. To some of you He has said, "Take these children and nurse them for me. Give them their first ideas of Me. Guard them against evil and teach them to love Me. Be to them as I have been to you." Do you parents and teachers realize how He trust's you? To others He is saying, "You do the work of My church, run it on right-lines, maintain its financial position, order its services, lead in its councils." It is not easy in these days to get men to accept responsibility, but I can recall the days when to have a place in a leader's meeting was counted a great honor.

The fact that He puts these tasks into our hands is the evidence of His faith in us. Don't whine that the task is exacting and hard, but rather rejoice that He trusts you with it. And O! See to it that you do not let Him down. Don't fail Him for He has faith in you and is expecting great things of you. Perhaps faith rises to its sublimest height in—

CHRIST'S TRUST OF THOSE WHO HAVE FAILED

Not always have we risen to His faith in us, and sometimes we have let Him down badly. There must be many who feel that they have failed Him and so forfeited His friendship. He hoped such great things for us, and what poor things we are. He committed to us a task and we deserted our post. Our record is stained and our sword dishonored. Think of the scene with Peter by the lake. What a ghastly failure Peter had made of things. But undismayed and unafraid Jesus put a great trust in his hands, saying, "Feed my lambs."

Mr. A. J. Gossip, in *From the Edge of the Crowd*, p. 107, relates the following: There was a splendid lad at the front who, through illness, made a serious slip and was court-martialed and punished. When he returned from leave, His colonel insisted that he was too good a boy to be allowed to break, that his fault, being paid for, was now wiped out and ought not to be mentioned. So he, the colonel, slipped at once into the old friendly relations, till the lad, who had sat whited-faced expecting the storm, being dismissed, asked what it meant. "He says you are too good a lad to allow sack," said the padre, "and that it is now everyone's business to let you see that you are absolutely trusted." On which the lad's pale face turned whiter and he turned abruptly away. A few weeks after, placed in a position of danger and authority, the same in which he had failed, he carried himself with such daring and distinction as to be promoted for gallantry in the field, and other honors, too. "What could I do?" was his quiet summing up, "I failed Him, and he trusted me."

Even if you and I have failed Him—and some of us have—He does not lose faith in us. He gives us another chance. He will deal faithfully with us, but even now he is bending over us saying, "Up again, old heart, for we shall win yet, you and I. Bring your dishonored sword and we will redeem and use it." How can we despair? That would be almost the last agony to Him.

THE CALL TO HONOR IN LOVE'S FAITH

There are human loves of ours who love us and believe in us. Can we fail them? There are men and women looking on you lads and lasses, seeing in you what no one else sees, believing and expecting great things of you. They are banking on you, you won't let them down, will you? There are women who kiss some of us good morning as we start our day's tasks, and they think we are wonderful men. God pity and forgive us if we let them down. There are little children who look up into the eyes of parents and think them the best people in the world. They trust you absolutely. You won't let them down, will you?

And above all, there is the Lord Christ, believing in you enough to die to make this possible for you, trusting you with His love and service, giving you a chance after you have let Him down. Can you, will you, betray such a trust? I believe your whole humanity will rise in protest against such a dread possibility. You will pledge yourself to what He believes you can be and died to make you.

"CHRIST'S CAPTIVE"
—2 Corinthians 2.14

(Preached at Katherine Road 1/24/35 and Spring Head Mission 2/21/43)

---

2 Corinthians 2.14 "Thanks be unto God, which always leadeth us in triumph in Christ, and maketh manifest through us the savor of His knowledge in every place. For we are a sweet savor of Christ unto God."

THAT IS THE RENDERING of the Revised Version and if you read from the Authorized Version you will notice a striking difference. For "leadeth us in triumph," you will read, "causeth us to triumph," and the difference is that between a conqueror and a captive! The whole question turns on whether the verb in the sentence is taken transitively or intransitively, and most scholars are agreed that in treating it transitively, the Revisers were right.

At first, there may be some disappointment that the newer version is to be accepted. "Causeth us to triumph" sounds so much better than "leadeth us in triumph," as to be a conqueror sounds better than to be a captive. But let us suspend our judgment. We shall see that what Paul said is a greater thing than what men thought he said. And we shall find that if the supreme glory is for the Conqueror, there is glory for us in being captives. And, after all, what we pray is not "my kingdom come," but "Thy Kingdom come." It is in God's victory that we find our own and understand the paradox in the words: "Make me a captive, Lord, and then I shall be free: Force me to render up my sword and I shall conqueror be."[1]

PROCESSION OF TRIUMPH

Coming to our text, let us remember that we are dealing with the figure of a triumphal procession. It was the custom of Roman captains and Caesars on returning from victorious campaigns to march in triumph at the head of a procession which included their captives in chains. One of the early heroes and kings of Britain, Caratacus, was thus dragged through the streets of Rome to celebrate the victory of Claudius. Paul

---

1. This is from George Matheson's hymn "Make Me a Captive Lord" (1890).

does not press the figure, nor must we, but it was obviously in his mind. He was thinking of God's victory over human beings and regarded himself as one of the captives in God's train.

It is here that we must not press the figure. The captives who were dragged in the train of their Roman conquerors had no share in the triumph. A poet has given us a picture of Caratacus marching slowly, sadly in the train of Claudius, thinking of his home, his freedom, the days when he was a king among people. But when God wins a victory over a person and leads His captive in triumph, the captive has an interest in what happens and finds his joy in being where he is.

Take the case of Paul. He had been the enemy of God in Christ, had fought Him in his own soul and had wasted the church. The battle was long and fierce, but on the Damascus Road it was won and by God. There the mighty man fell, laid down his arms, and surrendered to God. His pride, his self-righteousness, his sense of superiority collapsed. He rose from the ground saying humbly to his Conqueror, "Lord, what wilt Thou have me to do?" That was the sound of God's triumph over Paul and from there Paul's honor was to be the bond-slave of the Lord he had fought. God led him in triumph and Paul shared the triumph and marched proudly as the captive of Christ, exclaiming, "Thanks be unto God which always leadeth us in triumph."

Our deepest cause for thanksgiving is if we have a like experience. The thanksgiving to God may well be a test. We rejoice when we have triumphed, when we have got our own way, achieved success, and out-distanced others, won wealth or fame or honor. But can we say, "Thanks be unto God for it"? No, the real cause of praise to God is when God's love has triumphed in us, when it has broken down our pride, cleansed our hearts from impurity and falsehood, conquered our selfishness and our lusts, and made us Christ's willing slaves. When we speak and sing of "The Triumphs of His Grace," we are usually thinking of striking cases of conversion outside ourselves, but the real triumph of His grace is when it has subdued us to His will, brought us willing captives to His feet. Not when we sing about our victories, but when we sing, "I sunk by dying here compelled, come Thee conqueror."[2] Then it is that we too are glad, proud, and thankful to march in the train of those who our Christ is their conquering Lord, "led in triumph by Him."

Let us proceed to the second thought and it will help to make the first clearer. The captive reveals the conqueror's power. Come back to the figure of the triumphal procession. The captives who were dragged in chains behind a Roman chariot made manifest the knowledge of their conqueror. They proclaimed to all spectators his power and his pitilessness.

Now look at Paul's words again. God leads us in triumph and makes manifest through us the savor of His knowledge. What he means is that, in him and his fellow captives, men everywhere came to a knowledge of God's gracious power, they say the king of victories God wins and his love by which He wins them. Christ's captives are

---

2. This is from a hymn of Charles Wesley, one title for which is "The Resignation."

His trophies. Wherever Paul and his friends went, people saw in them the evidences of Christ's conquering power. They saw lust conquered by love, pride mastered by grace, peace taking the place of restlessness. It was not so much what these people said as what they were that bore witness to their Lord's power.

I ask you in all simplicity and earnestness, are we, in this way, revealing the knowledge of our Lord? I greatly fear, and I am thinking of myself, that what the world sees in us is only half surrendered men and women. We have not yielded ourselves unconditionally to the Divine Conqueror: we have not suffered His grace to fully triumph over our pride and our selfishness. And the world may be pardoned for saying, "If you are samples of what Christ does we do not think much of His work." If only we were fully and wholly conquered by grace, our pride utterly slain, every idol cast out of our heart, and our whole life gladly, grandly, gratefully surrendered to Christ, the world would have its most convincing evidence of the glory of His grace. For still, men and women who are glad to be His slaves are His trophies.

GOD'S SWEET REDEEMING LOVE

We cannot even stop there for Paul introduces a word that suggests, not only the power but the sweetness of God's redeeming love. He speaks of the "savor of His knowledge" and the phrase suggests sweetness and fragrance. Once more, we have to return to the triumphal procession. As the Roman conqueror went on his way with his captives behind him, incense smoked on every altar and the fragrant smoke floated over the procession, a silent proclamation of victory and joy. Fragrance, the fragrance of violets, of lavender—you cannot define it, but you know how pleasing and pervasive it is.

What Paul means is that the proclamation of the knowledge of God in Christ is to be a fragrant and pervasive thing. We have seen that the captive behind the Roman chariot proclaimed the power and the pitilessness of the conqueror. But in His captives the power and the salvation of God's redeeming love are proclaimed. Our constraint is of love and to conquering grace we are ourselves debtors. There is nothing freed and fierce about the captives, they are Christ's willing slaves. They move in an atmosphere of grace, charm, and love. The atmosphere in which they move is performed with the love of Christ.

That is always so ideally. To be constrained by the love of Christ, to willing bondage and utter surrender is to diffuse the knowledge of Christ as Savior. But actually, the fragrance is often the missing thing. Sometimes it is missing when we proclaim the gospel in our sermons. Winsomeness, sweetness, attractiveness are absent. It is not always there when we personally try to command Christ's power to others. And because Christ's triumph in us is not complete it is not always evident in our relations with others. Is there not a sting in the sneer that Christians are often awkward and angular and unattractive?

The explanation too often is that we are not fully surrendered, that we have not suffered the Lord to lead us unresistingly in triumph that we have not yet got to the point where we say, "None of self, all of Christ." When we get there, the sweet savor will go forth. And let this be added in a word it will not only be fragrant to men, but also to God. For we are, says the apostle, a sweet savor unto God. There you are, whatever people think of you, when you are Christ's willing and fully surrendered captives, you are a joy to God. For saints are lovely in His sight.

"GRACE ABOUNDING"
—2 Corinthians 9.8

(Preached four times from Katherine Road 1/3/32 to Spring Head Mission 1/38)

---

2 Corinthians 9.8 "God is able to make all grace abound toward you; that ye, always having all sufficiency in all things, may abound unto every good work."

THAT IS ONE OF the wealthiest texts in the richest book in the world. Its riches are the preacher's embarrassment. New translators, instead of detracting from its affluence, only enhance and illustrate it. Let me read the text to you as it is variously translated.

"God is able to bless you with ample means, so that you may always have quite enough for any emergency of your own and ample besides for any kind act to others." Dr. Moffatt.

"God is able to bestow every blessing on you in abundance, so that richly enjoying all sufficiency at all times, you may have ample means for all good works." Dr. Weymouth.

And this which I like best of all: "God has power to shower all kinds of blessings upon you so that having, under all circumstances and on all occasions, all that you can need, you may be able to shower all kinds of benefits upon others." Twentieth Century New Testament.

What can a preacher add to that? His only fear is lest he puts false limits upon it and impoverishes by preaching on it. But, for today, let us come back to the rendering in the Authorized Version.

THE GREATNESS OF GOD'S GRACE

"God is able to make all grace abound toward you." That introduces the word that is in itself a kind of wealth. The word grace appears less frequently in modern religious language than it did in the language of our fathers. And it must be admitted that sometimes the word has been soiled by unclean hands and tainted by contact with corrupt and pernicious forms of religious thought. But the word is too precious to be surrendered. Early Christianity took the word over from the Greeks, and among them it stood for all that is most winning in personal liveliness, for the nameless fascination that is irresistibly attractive and charming. It was also used for that warm, free-handed, spontaneous generosity which is kind where there is no claim or merit, and kind without hope of return. I say Christianity took over this word and exalted and transfigured it. Jesus was full of grace, and the manifestation of Divine grace and the means of its coming in fullness to humankind.

I can give you no definition of grace. There is no adequate definition. But you never can define the biggest and best things. Fancy taking a dictionary down to discover the meaning of being in love! And grace transcends love. It is love, but it is love which, after fulfilling the obligations infused by law, has an unexhausted wealth of kindness. Grace transcends mercy. Mercy forgives sin, grace floods with affection the sinner. "Grace," said a little girl with that might children often have, "is getting everything for nothing." It is that and more. It is the getting of everything good by those who deserve the bad. "Grace is the pulsations of the heart of God pouring a tide of gracious love in sinful humans, who do not deserve one drop of it to fall on them." It is the love of the lofty for the low, of the holy for the unholy, of the sinned-against for the sinner. It is the love of God coming out towards humans and meeting every need of theirs on all occasions and under all circumstances. It is not only love for the sinful, it is power for the weak, sufficiency for the tempted and tried, a victorious strength for the oft vanquished. It is, as I once heard Dr. Jowett say in an unforgettable phrase, "the river of God's love, with love gifts in its bosom, flowing out to men."

GRACE ABOUNDING

Whenever people have meditated on the grace of God, still more when they have known themselves to be recipients of it, their hearts have been warmed, and their minds have glowed, and their tongues have been loosed to speak of its magnificence, its abundance you hardly even find. Paul, speaking of it without talking of "the riches of his grace," is saying that "where sin abounded, grace did much more abound." When John Bunyan wanted to tell of God's amazing goodness to him, he called the book in which the story was told *Grace Abounding to the Chief of Sinners*. When the hearts of the Wesley's were warmed by the memory of God's love, they went through the length and breadth of one band singing: "O that the world might taste and see the riches of His grace."[1]

In days which some of you remember when William Booth and his first helpers went with a message of love to the sinners of the Mile End Waste, they set it to the strains of: "Grace there is my every debt to pay."[2] And squeamish as some of us tend to become, we can still get at the heart of a people with "plenteous grace with Thee is found," and "grace is flowing like a river." At a time of great strain and need in his life,

1. This is from Charles Wesley's hymn "Jesus the Name High Over All."
2. This is from a Salvationist hymn by Herbert Booth.

Paul had this message from God, "my grace is sufficient for thee." The truth our text brings to us is that God's grace meets every need of ours. God is able to make all grace abound towards us that is in all occasions and under all circumstances we may have sufficiency of all things.

What is your need as you face the future? Forgiveness for your sins? In God's grace, there is forgiveness for the sins that are colossal in magnitude and crimson in color. Pardons are multiplied to the penitent soul and the angels of God sing and welcome him into God's house and heart. Victory over besetting sins and strong temptations? His grace is sufficient to make you conqueror, ay, more than conqueror. Strength to bear up under trials and difficulties? Why the grace of God weaves blessings out of trials and turns difficulties into stepping stones by which you climb to a higher life. Are you afraid as you face the future, afraid of the battle of life, of the struggle for existence, of breaking down, of crossing the river? Here is the promise of grace, Divine help, and God's love for you.

Oh, it's a wonderful message. I never craved more for an eloquent tongue to give it a worthy setting. Take it as it stands, let it sink into your hearts, keep it by you for all the days to come. "God is able, and is willing, to make all grace abound towards you, that you, having all sufficiency in all things, may abound unto every good work."

That last phrase introduces a thought you must give me just a minute or two to emphasize. *The pointed and practical purpose.* It will seem like an anticlimax, but it isn't. Like so many of Paul's greatest passages it is harnessed to a practical purpose. It is part of an appeal for a collection for the poor. The apostle wanted the Corinthians to be generous toward poor saints, and he reminded them of God's amazing generosity. God had made all grace abound to them, they ought not to be niggardly in their considerations of others. The purpose of the Divine generosity and grace was that they should "abound unto every good work."

Our own strong condemnations are for those who, having been generously dealt with, are mean in their treatment of others. It is not unworthy to relate God's abounding grace to the question of our gifts to God's work. When we think of God's goodness to us, can we make our first "cut" in our subscriptions to the church? But the principle rises far beyond our gifts of money. See God's grace in forgiveness, and can you grudge forgiveness to those who have done some petty injury? Consider God's grace meeting every need of ours and can we be inconsiderate of the needs of others? We are to shower all kinds of benefits upon others, to abound unto every good work. We have ample means for it that is part of the provision of God's grace. Let something of the magnificence of God's grace characterize our service. Don't be content with one good deed or with one kind of service. There is no stint in God's grace, let there be no stint in our service. Rather, as the grace abounds toward us, let us abound in every good work.

∼

"GOD'S UNSPEAKABLE GIFT"
—2 Corinthians 9.15

(Preached six times from Katherine Road 12/4/32 to Bishop St. 12/12/48)

---

2 Corinthians 9.15 "Thanks be to God for His unspeakable gift."

THE APOSTLE WAS WRITING to the Corinthians about gifts and urging them to abound in the grace of generosity. He was pleading for kindly consideration of the poor and needy. That reminded him of God's grace to the spiritually impoverished and of God's great gift to humans in need. At that his heart caught fire and he burnt into a song of praise. Praise leapt to his lips from a grateful heart. In Paul's reckoning Jesus Christ was the crowning gift to the race, the greatest Gift of the greatest Giver. Far beyond all the good and perfect gifts of the material world was the preciousness of Jesus Christ. The unspeakable gift. That does not reveal the poverty of his vocabulary. He was a master of great words, but he had one word to ascribe the greatness of this Gift. It was, as Mr. Way's translation, "precious beyond description." For the moment, all else was forgotten in an ecstasy of praise at the grace of the Giver and the wonder of the Gift.

THE WONDER OF GOD'S GIFT

Here you strike something characteristic of the Apostle Paul. The love of God and His gift of the Savior was ever a source of wonder and amazement to him. As I have said, as excellent with words as he was, he was never able to adequately describe all he felt. He could only speak of unsearchable riches, unfathomable wisdom, measureless power, and love that passes knowledge. He could not keep back the song of exuberant prayer, and he did not try to.

The same thing is true of the early church in general. God not sparing His only Son, but giving him as a love gift for sinful humanity filled them with adoring wonder and rapturous praise. That is why the Magnificat is, not only the song of Mary, but became the song of the church. The soul of the church magnifies the Lord and its spirit rejoices in God its Savior.

The same thing has been repeated in every new manifestation of God's love in the gift of Jesus. No tongue nor pen could ever tell or show the wonder of the heart when God's greatest Gift was realized. Of Christ, people have made their loftiest songs and even then, felt that they did not do justice to the theme. In the Evangelical Revival with its new emphasis of God's grace, people wanted "a thousand tongues to sing their great Redeemer's praise." The Oxford Movement gave us "praise to the Holiest in the height and in the depth of praise."[1] Say what you will of the Moody and Sankey movement. It did give men new songs of redeeming love.

Perhaps you have noticed that I never announce, "The choir will now render the anthem." You owe that to a man, Richard Blackmore, who was the conductor of one of the best church choirs I have ever heard. When I was preaching at the church at Bideford, he came to me and said, "Please do not say, 'the choir will render the anthem.' It sounds like announcing a performance." He was a musician of high order and he once said to me, "Men may say what they will of Moody and Sankey hymns, but I shall never forget seeing Sankey at his little American organ, singing in his rich bass voice, 'Behold what love, what boundless love, the Father hath bestowed on sinners lost.'" Men who have seen the vision have always been "lost in wonder, love, and praise." There was nothing left to say but, hallelujah!

HAS THE UNSPEAKABLE GIFT BECOME COMMONPLACE?

A proverbial saying declares that "things grown common lose their dear delight."[2] We have lived through an age of such wonderful discoveries that we have almost lost the power of being thrilled and amazed. What once moved us to gratitude and praise now leaves us cold and thankless. We do not even value our health until we lose it. Civil and religious liberties, won for us at tremendous cost we are reluctant to care. The open Bible is neglected and the freedom to assemble according to conscience is spurned.

Or, let us make the thought seasonable. We have entered the Advent season and we know Christmas is on the way. But to some blasé folk even the outward accompaniments of the season mean nothing. One of my little extravagances is "Christmas Numbers," and I note that some writers ask if there is anything in it, and are inclined to say with Scrooge, "Christmas! Bah, humbug!" We need another Dickens to teach us how to spend Christmas. Though we are not unmindful of cheery souls who joyfully and thankfully anticipate the gladness and good cheer.

But the heart of Christmas is this—"God so loved the world that He gave His only begotten Son." Does that thrill and amaze us? It ought to beyond all else. But we

---

1. This is from a hymn that John Henry Newman himself wrote whose title is the first half of the phrase cited above.

2. Actually, this is a line from one of Shakespeare's sonnets, Sonnet 110, and the line actually is "sweets grown common, loose their dear delight."

are so familiar with the story that it is in danger of becoming commonplace. Other gifts we plan to give and those we receive stir us to gratitude. But the "unspeakable gift" too often knocks upon our thankless hearts in vain. What people once marveled at as a gift whose worth was beyond all telling leaves us with unmoved and unappreciative hearts. No hallelujah comes from thankful hearts through happy lips. These are days of great and varied needs, and not least among them is that of renewing in our hearts the sense of wonder and gratitude, enthusiasm of faith, and ecstasy of love, at God's amazing gift of love.

How can we renew in our hearts, and in the hearts of others, a due sense of the greatness of God's gift, and so kindle and quicken our gratitude and praise? Believe me, that is a supremely important question and the answer to it calls for the most serious consideration. If we can get the right answers, our hearts and the church may again ring with hallelujahs.

CLEARER AND WIDER KNOWLEDGE WOULD ENHANCE OUR VALUE OF THE GIFT

Our knowledge of Jesus, God's gift, is so scant, carnal, secondhand. And the source of knowledge lies close at hand in the pages of the New Testament. Our ignorance is colossal and almost criminal and yet the gospel written in blood is unread. In its pages the portrait of Jesus is to be found. We can watch the glorious figure and listen to His teaching. His mind is revealed, His cross and passion speak. Read your New Testament, read it with the intelligence and devotion that you bring to other books. Read a Gospel at a sitting. Do not neglect the help of experts, they, too, are God's gift to you. Books like Glover's *Jesus of History* or John Watson's *Life of the Master* would help you to a vision of Jesus that would touch the depths of your soul and lead you to see in Him God's unspeakable gift.

CONSIDER THE DIFFERENCE HIS COMING HAS MADE TO THE WORLD IN WHICH WE LIVE

That will help you to realize the greatness of God's gift. There are two great divisions of the world's history, the world BC and the world AD, and the dividing line runs hard by the manger cradle of Christ. To grasp the tremendous difference between the two is to realize how tremendous our debt to Christ is. His coming created a new world. He enriched people's thoughts of God, taught the true worth of humanity, and inspired our kindliest philanthropies. He has been and is in the world remolding and remaking it. He is the light of the world, a quickening, redeeming force to nations, communities, and individuals. What sort of response does such a gift call for?

LISTEN TO THE TESTIMONY OF OTHERS AS EVIDENCE OF THE GREATNESS OF THE GIFT

Do not neglect great Christian devotional books. Men like à Kempis, Law, Rutherford, Wesley, and Bunyan wrote of what God's wondrous gift has meant to them and for the one reason that Jesus was so ineffably dear to them. Their books are their testimony to the pearl of great price they had found. And men and women who are neither poets nor prose writers have testimonies to give concerning the preciousness of Jesus Christ. Listen to what they have to say, especially when they say, "Come see a man who told me all that ever I did, is not this the Christ." It may be that, like the men of the Samaritan village, you will come to say, "Now we believe, not because of this saying, for we have heard Him ourselves and know that this is indeed the Christ."

WE SHALL NEVER KNOW THE UNSPEAKABLE WORTH OF GOD'S GIFT UNTIL WE RECEIVE IT

The testimony of others may lead us to the threshold, but to know all the value of Jesus, we must enter the circle of the believing disciples. "The love of Jesus, and the worth of Jesus, none but His loved ones know." To know the real value of the gift you must receive it. Too many of us leave Jesus in the background. We are glad to know He is there and in the crises of life we call for him. We pray to Him in our deep and dark troubles and it is an added tribute to His grace that He does not refuse our call. But receive Him in all His glorious fullness, give Him a chance to redeem your life from littleness and use it for noble purposes. Open your heart to the incoming of His power, peace, and joy. Let him walk beside you all the way and bring you the comfort of His friendship. And from a wondering and adoring heart will spring the song, "Thanks be to God for His unspeakable gift."

IT IS NOT AN ANTICLIMAX TO RETURN TO THE IMMEDIATE LESSON OF THE TEXT

The theme of the chapter is that of ministering to the saints and making gifts. The inspiration of our generosity in giving is surely in God's most gracious gift to us. But there is more than that in it. What Paul is arguing is this—your gifts will not only relieve the wants of the poor, they will turn their thoughts and their thanksgivings to God. Your gift may prepare people to receive God's gift. General Booth used to tell of a man in a London slum who unexpectedly befriended him when he thought all friendliness had departed and he exclaimed, "Love and kindness! Then there really is a God." Receive God's gift in all its fullness, and then help others to believe it is for them by giving your love gift in the Spirit of Christ.

"SERMON ON THE MOTTO FOR 1937"
—2 Corinthians 13.11

(Preached at Spring Head, New Year 1937)

---

2 Corinthians 13.11 "Be perfected, be comforted, be of the same mind, live in peace, and the God of love and peace shall be with you."

WHEN WE THINK OF the earliest churches of our Lord we are apt to idealize them, to think of them as perfect in life and devotion. And, especially remembering that they were the earliest churches, there was much in their zeal and devotion to admire and emulate. But they were by no means perfect as a reading of the Pauline epistles reveals. Take the Church at Corinth as an example. In it there were painful divisions, jealousies, and unworthy members. Even in this affectionate farewell at the close of the letter, there is a reminiscence of their faults as well as a desire for their good. Dr. Denney, in his commentary, says: "There was much among them to rectify, much that was inevitably disheartening to overcome, much dissension to compose, and much friction to alloy."

It is here that the text touches our modern church life. For in modern church life there is much to be condemned. And the criticizing should be done by lovers of the church. We can recognize the good in it and at the same time acknowledge that there is much that is contrary to the mind of Christ. We do not make the House of God a "den of thieves," but it is often a place of bitterness, pride, jealousy, and quarrels.

Not until the church is perfected is it an effective instrument in world redemption. The real attraction of the church is in its pure, peaceful, and Christ-like life. Frankly, if I were an outsider I wouldn't go into a church where there was constant place-seeking and bitterness and strife. I should want a church where I could find relief from that kind of thing. Let us be clear on that. The church will not win the world until it lives in purity and peace. Let us bring that nearer home. Spring Head will not unite with Wednesbury until its own life is Christ-like. The perfecting of the church involves the perfecting of the individual members. We talk about the church as if it were something abstract, but the church is you! What we are we help to make the church, and "if every church member were just like me, what sort of a church would our church be?" What you know the church ought to be, you, as an individual member ought to strive to become.

GREAT IMPERATIVES

So, the apostle introduces great imperatives. For our present purpose, we dwell on the first two only briefly. Be perfected. There is something active as well as passive about that. The Lord will perfect that which concerns us. Without His word and work we shall never be complete. But we must work out our own salvation. See where you can work. Confess your failings. Aim at perfection and do not be content until you are perfect in faith, love, and hope. Be comforted. This again is active as well as passive. Be comforted in your sorrows and pains by God's comfort. But you know that comfort is akin to strength and courage. A possible translation of this imperative is "take courage," or even, "stimulate one another." The idea is that of Christian people being of good courage themselves and stimulating their fellow Christians to strength and courage. The lesson is summed up in these words: "Help us to help each other, Lord, each other's cross to bear, let each his friendly aid afford, and feel a brother's care."

But the main imperative is the twofold one: Be of the same mind, live in peace. That is a call to unity in the church. The translation I like best is, "live in harmony." Think of the word in musical terms. Simply put, it doesn't mean all playing the same instrument or sounding the same note. It is "a combination of different tones, according to the law of modulation." Of course, in a church array—where people are of different temperament, hold different views on many things, adopt different methods—if each plays his part, and all don't want to play first fiddle or blow their own trumpets too loudly, you can still have harmony. The way into that harmony is to have the same mind, the mind of Christ. If we were all keen on the coming of the kingdom of God we shouldn't care whether we played first or second fiddle. Instead of being jealous of another's success we should rejoice in it. We should never dream of quarreling with a fellow worker. It is our divided minds, our lack of the mind of Christ that causes disharmony and dissension. Be of the same mind, think not of self but of the coming of the kingdom, and you will bring in peace.

THE CHURCH OF MY DREAMS

I am not much of a dreamer, but sometimes I have daydreams of the church as it should be. Here it is described for me. All the members striving after perfection—"in the stretch for it" as the old Bible Christians used to say—comforting one another and exhorting each other to love and good works, having the mind of Christ so fully that there are no quarrels, but all living together happily and harmoniously. In such a church, Christ would see of the travail of His soul, and in it the world would see the ideal society.

"SERMON ON THE MOTTO FOR 1937"—2 CORINTHIANS 13.11

What makes the ideal possible? It all seems dreary, far away, and impossible of attainment. There are those who say that human nature being what it is we shall never see such a church. If human nature were the only factor I should share the despair. But listen to the full message—be perfected, etc., "and the God of love and peace shall be with you." Love and peace are Divine attributes and God is the inexhaustible source of them. Our desiring these things brings God near to us, makes it possible for Him to impart them. He cannot give Himself unless we are willing to receive, but if and when we are He will impart His best gifts to us and we shall see established the church of our noblest dreams.

"THE CHRISTIAN'S CREDENTIALS"
—Galatians 6.17

(Preached once at Spring Head Mission 8/15/37)

Galatians 6.17 "From henceforth let no man trouble me, for I bear branded in my body the marks of Jesus."

You will have noticed in reading the story of Paul's missionary journeys, as related in the Acts of the Apostles, that wherever he went he was followed and hindered in his work by certain Judaizers. These men could not or would not see the glory and liberty of the gospel Paul preached. They insisted that only through the gate of the old Law could men enter the kingdom of Christ, and that "they must obtain a Jewish passport for the New Jerusalem." Paul would have none of this. He stood for the freedom of the faith and would not have it that a man must needs go to Sinai before he could kneel at the cross, or be circumcised before becoming a Christian. For him, in Christ, there was neither Jew nor Greek.

Not content with contradicting his teaching, these men questioned Paul's apostolic authority, assailed his character, undermined his influence, and did all they could to hinder his work. They declared that he had not seen the Lord, had no authority to preach, and was simply a self-appointed apostle. They caused trouble wherever he went and nowhere more than in Galatia.

Paul vigorously defended his position. He was not a whit behind the other apostles. He had seen the Lord and received his commission to preach from on high. Still his opponents haggled. And then sick of the endless controversy and pettifogging and paltry rejections, Paul rapped out his last word in our text. "Let no man trouble me further. I have proof of my apostleship that brooks no denial. I have branded in my body the stigmata of my Lord." The honorable scars he carried were the final proof that he was no self-appointed and self-glorifying apostle, but a sincere, earnest crusader in the Cause of Christ. In applying the text, we may begin with something that is implicit rather than explicit in the declaration. It is—

"THE CHRISTIAN'S CREDENTIALS"—GALATIANS 6.17

A SLAVE'S GLORYING IN HIS BONDAGE

The reference is to the branding in some part of a slave's body, generally the hand, of some mark which denoted his owner. Wherever he went it denoted that he was a slave and whose slave he was. Paul was a slave and gloried in the fact. He signed himself the bond slave of Jesus Christ. That was the underlying and imperative fact of his life. He was not his own. He gave himself and his service without stint to another. And we shall get no further along the line I am thinking of until we have a similar conviction and consecration. No one bears the marks of Christ unless he is Christ's. That is the essence of the Christian life. "Ye are not your own." "Whose I am and whom I serve?"

Where the Lord puts His hand, he says, "That is mine." As Christ entered the temple, he said, "It is my Father's House." So, He puts His hand on us and says, "You are mine." Real Christianity is recognizing and revealing that ownership. It means holding all you have at the Master's service and glorying in being a slave. Paul glories in his bondage and going further declares that he carries—

THE STIGMATA OF CHRIST

He was thinking of the weals left by the lector's lash, of the scars left by the stones that had been hurled. His emaciated form witnessed to the hardships he had endured. He needed no outward authorization or commendation from human beings. His sufferings were sufficient proof that he was aimed and used by Christ. Do we know anything of this? Do we carry the stigmata? If we are wholeheartedly Christ's, it will be given us, not only to believe in Him, but to suffer for Him. We shall not now be called to endure stripes or stonings or shipwrecks, but no one can give himself wholly to Christ and not know pain and weariness, headache and heartache, for Him.

We read of the sufferings of some for Christ's sake. Of Livingstone, who, in one of his missionary journeys, slept every night for seventy-four months on a stretch of the floor. The prospect of a breakfast under civilized conditions almost gave him wings so that the last eight miles of the journey seemed but a few steps. Of Spurgeon, so exhausted after his services that he could only fling himself on a rug at his wife's feet while she read softly to him. I say we read of these men and cannot keep back our admiration. But it is not enough merely to admire them and their sufferings for their Lord and our lives be without any such tokens. We, too, must bear in our body the brand marks.

THE MARKS OF SUFFERING ARE THE CHRISTIAN'S CREDENTIALS

They are evidence to the Christian himself that he is Christ's. "Let no one trouble me," said Paul. Those lines and scars were the final proof that Christ owned him and used him. Thereafter no man could shake his confidence or disturb his peace. And when our service has cost us something, when we have endured pain and carry the marks of suffering, then, and not till then, shall we know the depths of peace and the heights of joy. All uncertainty and doubt will end and we shall know the content of assurance. David Hill spoke quietly once of the unutterable joy he experienced when a Chinaman struck him, though the blow left a pain the missionary felt for hours. And let me add as quietly that seldom have I felt such elation and joy as when struck by a "missile thrown by an opponent of the gospel when I was leading a mission band in the open air." It is worth a great deal to have in your own soul the peace which springs from the assurance that, beyond all question, you are Christ's.

Still more are the marks of suffering the Christian's credentials before the world. Without them it is of little use to face the world with our witness. The world has taken up the challenge of Thomas, which says, "Except I see the print of the nails I will believe." A man's patriotism is measured, not by what he gets out of it, but by what he gives to it and for it. And the world's test of our Christianity is in what we are prepared to suffer for it. It is said that a philosopher once brought a new gospel to a saintly hermit. After carefully and confidently expounding his scheme for restoring the world to happiness and comfort, he asked the hermit what he should do to get men to accept it. "There is only one way," was the answer, "go and get yourself crucified for it and then people will believe."

Always it is the marks that carry conviction. It is by His pierced hands and feet and side that we know Jesus is the Savior of men. Who could doubt the sincerity of the apostle or the reality of his message when he stood and preached with the weals in his back and the scars on his face? Scarred warriors make good evangelists. The marks of sufferings endured and sacrifices made give point and power to our testimony.

On the other hand, how can we expect people to believe or even take us seriously if they see no signs of suffering or sacrifice? And too often we are unwilling to suffer the slightest inconvenience in the name of our religion. We will not even give an extra half hour to the Communion Service and we resign when the work becomes difficult and makes demands. Not until the world sees the "stigmata" of Christ received and gloried in will it believe.

At heaven's gate, too, the marks are our credentials. We have our little jokes, not always in good taste, about Peter and entrance to heaven. There is only one passport there. Professions and talk are useless there. Not even the fact that you are a church member and can produce your class tickets for years will admit you. Only those who bear the brand marks will be welcome and accorded "well done." If you have these you need not fear, though you are unknown among humanity, the Master will know you and His pierced hand will open the gate. Do not worry that you have not been able to do great and striking deeds. The humblest of us can carry the same marks as did Paul. The simple and homely poem makes clear what I mean—I think of many a toiling servant, or self-denying mother, or unselfish brother or sister, who will be able to do no more than "show Him their hands," hands scarred and shapeless through sacrificed toil. But it will be enough. When I was a young and enthusiastic evangelist we used to sing, "I shall know Him by the print of the nails in His hand."[1] And He will know us by His own brand marks in our hands.

~

---

1. This is from a Fanny Crosby hymn, "My Savior First of All" (1891).

"THE UNSEARCHABLE RICHES"
—Ephesians 3.8

(Preached once at Spring Head Mission 12/4/38)

Ephesians 3.8 "The unsearchable riches of Christ."

This morning our meditation was on "The Unspeakable Gift." We noted that whenever Paul came within sight of the gifts and the grace of God, he was amazed—flabbergasted, we should say—by their vastness. He had not the words for description or definition. He could only speak of them as measureless, fathomless, surpassing knowledge, unspeakable. They defied definition. There is a great sermon for someone to preach on the "O's of the Pauline Epistles." "O the depth of the riches."

Almost before I had finished the sermon on "The Unspeakable Gift" I was busy with this sermon on "The Unsearchable Riches." I was haunted by the saying before I had written a word. It is a lovely saying, and it seems almost like sacrilege to analyze it for the purpose of exposition. It seems like taking a rose to pieces to discover the secret of its beauty. I only make the attempt with the desire to get you into touch with the riches, to put into your hands a cheque so that you will be able to draw on the unfathomed wealth. This is my first point. The unsearchable riches are not simply the subject of meditation, they are—

OBJECTS OF APPROPRIATION

Paul did, and we ought to contemplate them with wonder and reverence. Here is a theme worthy of profoundest thought—that in Him dwells all the fullness of the Godhead, that God was in Christ. The faithful will always come and adore Him and we ought to find time to adore and worship the new born king.

But it is not simply utilitarian to regard the unsearchable riches as available wealth. Indeed, that is what makes riches richer. No one but a fool or miser wants to hoard wealth for the sake of gloating over it. Its value is in its power to meet and satisfy needs. The possession of it gives security, provides comfort, and gives the opportunity for fuller life. There was a time when Paul saw neither beauty nor use in Jesus. He came to find both. Bringing his needs to Jesus he found rich supplies for every one of them. Out of his own experience he could say to his friends at Philippi, "My God shall supply every need of yours according to His riches in glory by Christ Jesus." Let us go a step further and consider—

PAUL'S NEED AND OURS

There was need created by the fact of sin. Paul knew its guilt, power, defilement. He knew that he stood in need of pardon, purity, power. Sin had made life all wrong. He needed to be set right with men and with God. He needed peace, joy, victory. And He found his needs met in the unsearchable riches.

That suggests the poverty of our sin. We too have to face the fact of sin and its defilement and debasement, in our own lives. Like the prodigal in the far country we are in want and no one gives to us. There is plenteous grace, grace to cover all our sins. There is power, power to make and keep us pure within.

Our growing needs are met by the same wealth. An illustration will make clear what I mean. At the Methodist Vision Meeting in Hyde Park, Mr. Gray said that as he grew older almost everything in life dwindled and was dwarfed. But, he declared, "Christ grew bigger and bigger and equal to every need. He was all I needed when a Sunday School teacher told me, as a little chap, of the Good Shepherd. He was all I needed as a young man, in middle life, and now that I am old He is all I want." You cannot get to the end of the unsearchable riches. All you need for all time is there. The wealth has always been there. But the world knew it not. Christ's coming revealed it, threw open the treasure store. Put in your claim, every need will be supplied. "His grace and power are such, none can ever ask too much."

PAUL'S EXPERIENCE MADE HIM A PREACHER

In Christ he found, as we have seen, his deepest needs met. The slave was made free and become a new creature. He was made right with God and his fellows. He was constantly discovering some new power and glory in Christ Jesus. That is why he speaks of the unsearchable riches. "Fathomless wealth," says Dr. Moffatt, "boundless wealth," says the Twentieth Century New Testament, and Dr. Rendell Harris, trying to find a word to set forth the riches, exclaimed, "Inexplorable!" No wonder Paul counted it a duty and an honor to proclaim such good tidings. He exclaims, "Unto me, who are less than the least of the saints was this grace given that I should preach among the Gentiles the unsearchable riches of Christ."

LUMINESCENCE

It is always the experience that makes the preacher. Paul's gospel was learned and praised in the school of experience. He could not but speak of the riches he had found. And whenever people have discovered the wealth they have proclaim the glad tidings. "Tis mercy all, immense and free, for O my God it found out me," say Wesley and his helpers. And then they went out with their gospel set to the music of, "O that the world might taste and see the riches of His grace."[1] Let your need and his great fullness meet and you will be constrained to proclaim the riches of His grace. You must, you simply must proclaim the wealth you have found. That is why I finish with my own proclamation. I can humbly and honestly say, "Thou O Christ art all I want, more than all in Him I find."[2] And out of all I have found in Him I must commend my Savior to you.

∼

---

1. The hymn "Jesus the Name High Over All" by Charles Wesley is quoted here.
2. This is from Charles Wesley's hymn "Jesus Lover of My Soul."

"THE MIND OF CHRIST"
—Philippians 2.5

(Preached seven times from Patricroft 5/3/36 to Bishop St. 12/10/50)

Philippians 2.5 "Let this mind be in you, which was also in Christ Jesus."

THE PASSAGE FROM WHICH the text is taken has been the ground of endless theological writing and controversy. Paul used a Greek word—ἐκένωσεν—which is translated, or rather paraphrased, in the Authorized Version, "made Himself of no reputation," or in the Revised Version, "emptied Himself." This has given rise to what is known as the "Kenotic Theology" and every theologian of note has expressed his views in the sense in which the Son of God could empty Himself of His Divine glory. The subject is worthy of all the discussion and it is heartening to think that good people have brought great minds to the consideration of it. I am not vain enough to think that I have found the solution. All I want to do is to point out that the apostle was contending not for a kenotic theory, but—

APPEALING FOR KENOTIC PRACTICE

It is only by accommodation that the passage can be used for theological purposes. It is a practical exhortation and not merely a disquisition. Paul was neither rebutting heresy nor arguing a point. There is no evidence that the Philippians were unsound in the faith. All the evidence is on the other side. The apostle was making a practical appeal, and making it as he always did in a large way. He was supplying one of those great motives without which you cannot have great Christian living. It is in that light that we interpret the passage, and our first business is to consider—

THE SITUATION PAUL ADDRESSED

In the main, the Church at Philippi gives Paul less trouble and more joy than any of his churches. It was sound in the faith and free from the evils which stained other churches. It was considerate of his standing and in a very generous way ministered to his comfort. Incidental phrases, however, reveal the fact that there was a danger of disharmony within its ranks and also show the cause. Paul had to beseech Euodia and Syntyche that they be of the same mind. He put in a passionate plea for unity and concord in a solemn warning against faction and doing things through vain glory. He appealed to his friends to consider others and count them better persons than themselves. He urged them to have an eye for the interests of others. These things indicate the danger zone members of the church were in if activated by wrong motives. They were vain of their power and service and standing too much in their dignity. They were thinking too much of "glory for me" and grasping too eagerly at their Christian prizes. In a word, they were getting proud.

We know where that kind of thing was bound to lead for we know where it leads to now. Pride always goes before a fall. Pride makes peace impossible, contention is ever the front of pride. No growth in grace is possible where pride is. The proud are self-satisfied and complacent. God resists the proud, it is to the humble He gives grace. We can understand how anxious Paul would be to save the church he loved from so subtle a danger and so real a peril. Of the many ways he might have taken to warn and exhort them, he thought of—

URGING THEM TO HAVE THE MIND OF CHRIST

He might have rebuked and condemned them, pointed out the littleness and meanness of their attitude and action. Instead, he lifted their thoughts and pointed them to the example of their Lord. Usually by "mind" we mean the intellectual faculty, the power by which man conceives a thought, weighs it, and arrives at conclusions. Paul uses the word in a more comprehensive way. He uses it to include the intellect, the aim, the spirit and temper. Applied to Christ it means, not only His thought and vision, but His motives, the expression of His thought. It is better understood as Mr. A. S. Way translates it, "Let the same purpose inspire you as was in Jesus." Simply put, Paul means, "Be like Jesus in your thinking, your actions, and your spirit."

PAUL WAS THINKING CHIEFLY OF CHRIST'S HUMILITY AND COMPASSION

He was thinking, not only of the humility of Christ's life, but of His coming to earth at all. He was in "the essential form of God," yet He took upon Him "the essential form of a human being." He did not grasp at equality with God, He stooped to the form of a servant. He came to earth to be a man and die. He "made Himself of no reputation" sums it all up in an unforgettable phrase. Now think of how that worked itself out in His life upon earth, of the lovely surroundings, of His lowly bearing before the people He had come to save, before Pilate and Herod, and on the cross.

"THE MIND OF CHRIST"—PHILIPPIANS 2.5

Read again Paul's passage, ponder it, and think what the effect would be on those Philippians. Read it yet again and think what its effect ought to be on you. Think, think, how in uttermost humility He sacrificed and suffered even to that last indignity where men spat upon Him, and then say to yourself, "Let this mind be in me which was in Christ Jesus."

THE ABSENCE OF PRIDE

For us this mind means, first of all, the absence of pride. That needs to be said for often we not only have not the mind of Christ, we have its opposite. We are vainglorious, self-assertive, and proud. We stand on our dignity, demand our rights, and claim preeminence. To use a New Testament phrase, "we are puffed up." And that is the root of or trouble. As we have seen, that makes impossible every grace, even the giving of more grace. It is our pride that makes us discontented and unthankful, for humility knows it has more blessings than it deserves. Our pride is at the root of every quarrel I have known in church life. Some man or woman was touchy and easily offended and that was too proud to own it and make friendly approaches.

Lowly though essential duties are, they are neglected because of someone's pomp and pride. Literally it is pride that goes before our falls. That is true, as Dean Church has point out, of a great empire like Rome, and of a great church like the Jewish. Almost the most pathetic words is our language are put into mouth of one who fell from great heights to the lowest depths, and who in his fall said to his friend, "Cromwell, I charge thee, fling away ambition." Can England, our church, we ourselves, afford to neglect the warning? On the positive side, having the mind of Christ means—

REVEALING THE HUMILITY CHARACTERISTIC OF JESUS

He looked down on people. You know what that phrase generally means. But Jesus looked down on people not with contempt but compassion. He not only looked down, He came down. Instead of grasping at privilege as a robber clutches at loot. He surrendered all in His passion to help. He did not insist on being a King, He consented to be a servant. Instead of standing up for His rights He laid down His life for other people's wrongs. He thought not of His reputation, but of our salvation.

And we are to have His mind. We are to look down on people in His sense, to come down to their level that we may lift them. To give up, not only wrong things, but many a prized possession that we may serve our fellows. You know what His mind was and what He did. You are not only to praise Him, in compassion and humility, you are to emulate Him. Pay the price, and though you pay it in investments, pay it to the full.

Let all your pride go and in utter humility reveal the mind of Christ in service even for the unworthy and unthankful.

OUR REAL FAILURE IS FAILURE TO REVEAL HIS MIND

We hear much about the failure of the churches and it is idle to deny our poverty. We are sadly lacking in money. We are deserted by our former members. Preachers are not so eloquent as once they were. But our real poverty is in the realm of the Spirit. We are positively afraid to be poor and ashamed to be humble though our Lord was born in another man's stable and was humble all His days. Our pride masquerades as dignity and we are very jealous of our reputations. We back the spirit that gives itself generously, royally, and without reserve. We could win the world yet if we had the mind that was in Christ Jesus. We are worldly minded, high minded, half minded, and thus we love the world and betray our Lord.

You tell me this is mystical, unreal, other worldly. I tell you it is entirely practical. Before you can have the mind of Christ, you must know it. If you want to know the mind and catch the spirit of Shakespeare or Browning you study their works. Well, here is the book of His life, endowed with His presence, rich in faith, and containing the revelation of His mind. Read it, study it. Search the Scriptures for they testify of Him. Some of my friends want to catch and perpetuate the spirit of Dickens and they join a Dickens fellowship. Every great, creative movement in Christian history began in a fellowship—the Jesus Circle—Wesley and the Methodists. He bids in each, to each, to be restored together and seek His face. If we are to have the mind of Christ, we shall find it in fellowship with each other and with Him.

In the *Idylls of the King* a young knight meets a holy woman and, says Tennyson, "As she spake, she sent the deathless passion in her eyes, through him, and he believed in her belief."[1] If we would meet our Lord like that, and let Him bury His word in us, and send His deathless passion through us, all would be well for us and His church.

---

1. This is a paraphrase from Tennyson's "The Holy Grail."

"THE GRACE OF CONTENTMENT"
—Philippians 4.11–13

(Preached once at Spring Head Mission 11/12/39)

Philippians 4.11–13 "I have learned, in whatsoever state I am, therewith to be content. I know both how to be abased, and I know how to abound: everywhere and in all things I am instructed both to be full and to be hungry, both to abound and to suffer need. I can do all things through Christ who strengtheneth me."

THERE SPEAKS A MAN who has mastered one of the most difficult of arts and who reveals one of the most charming of graces. Under all circumstances and in all conditions, he has learned to be content and mark the fact that this virtue was not native to him, he had to learn the secret and cultivate the grace. Nor was his contentment an easy complacency. Contentment with one's lot is not inconsistent with an earnest endeavor to improve it. The apostle, as you know, was always pressing toward unreached goals, but meanwhile he had learned not to complain but to be content. It was not an easy lesson to learn.

THE LIFE-STORY TOLD IN THE TEXT

It is easy to fill in the details of "I know how to be abased and how to abound, to be full and to be hungry." The words tell of real experiences. Paul began his apostolic ministry with a heavenly vision and the assurance that he was "a chosen vessel," but it was not long before his ministry was challenged and his apostleship questioned. He knew both honor and dishonor. He had friends who honored and appreciated him and would have "plucked out their eyes" for him, but he had also enemies and false friends. He knew what it was to be feted and he knew the inside of a prison. He was caught up into the seventh heaven, but he suffered from a thorn in the flesh, a messenger from Satan.

On his lips the large language of the text was not mere rhetoric. He had a wide range of experiences. His life was full of ups and downs. To be content in such circumstances was a veritable triumph. And we who are so often full of complaints over little things, or who have to face the visitations of life, may well seek Paul's secret.

THE SECRET OF SUCH CONTENTMENT

For, let us admit that there is something in the charge that the Englishman is a grumbler. It is our privilege to complain. The word "grouses" has passed into our common speech. Even those who profess and call themselves Christians are not exempt. Even when in the main things are going well with us some "fly in the ointment" silences our praise and we murmur against God and men—and women. And, like Jonah, we think we do well to be angry and to utter our complaints. Yet it is quite clear that contentment is a Christian grace, and when we see it revealed as it is in Paul's case we know it for one of the shining virtues. We know, too, that this virtue brings its own reward.

What then is the secret of it? Let me reiterate that it was something learned. Paul was schooled into it. It was in the school of Christ Paul had learned it. He had sat at the feet of Jesus. Who, when He was reviled, reviled not again but committed Himself to a faithful Creator. But the school master was more than a teacher, or rather He was a teacher who could and did impart power. The secret is in the thirteenth verse, "I can do all things—am equal to all things—in Christ who strengtheneth—enableth me."

THE PROCESS BY WHICH THE SOUL IS SCHOOLED AND DISCIPLINED INTO CONTENTMENT

First of all, let us frankly recognize that the secret of contentment has to be learned, the art has to be mastered. There is no royal road to the contented life. Part of it can be learned by the school of experience. There we learn how useless our discontent is and how unworthy our murmuring and grumbling. There we see men and women, far worse off than we are, enduring pain and privation without a murmur. We learn, too, the value of a cheerful and thankful spirit.

But supremely the lesson is learned in the school of Christ. We learn the lesson of the great Teacher, see in Him the supreme example. "For even in Thy burdened heart, weight of sorrow hung, yet no ungentle murmuring word escaped Thy silent tongue." In this school, we learn a new scale of values. The supreme things are spiritual and why should we complain of what is developing our character and fitting us for our eternal destiny? It is in this school that we learn to sing, "Whatever my lot, Thou hast taught me to know, it is well, it is well, with my soul."[1]

---

1. Horatio Spofford wrote these lyrics for a hymn entitled "It Is Well," but the story behind it is remarkable, as he lost his daughters at sea when they were to join him in England. Only his wife survived. Later, he and his remaining family became missionaries in Israel. There are to this day pictures

"THE GRACE OF CONTENTMENT"—PHILIPPIANS 4.11–13

But here is something more than a lesson to be learned, here is a duty for which we need to be empowered. "I am equal to all things in Him who enableth me," said Paul. That is what we need and what Christ supplies. Instead of a cheap complacency, the apostle desires to live in the best style, to move among the best society, and he found strength to do it. Christ gave him ample means and that is His work still.

He makes us strong enough to bear up when things go wrong and we suffer loss, and strong enough to remain humble when we possess worldly things. Equal to every demand. It is the weak person who gives way to discontent and murmuring. He strengthens us by putting within us the sources of contentedness and peace. Contentedness is really containedness. "The water that I shall give him shall be in him." The man who trust's Christ has within him a spring of gladness. He can bear any loss for his heart is garnered by a peace the world cannot give and is powerless to take away. Let us abide "in Him" and His strength will enable us to live a life of quiet content and deep peace.

∽

---

in the American Colony Hotel, where I have stayed, of the family. Despite losing two children to scarlet fever, and three more at sea, they went and did the work anyway.

"THE PREACHER'S PLEA FOR THE PEOPLE'S PRAYERS"
—2 Thessalonians 3.1

(Preached seven times from Fentiman Road to Bishop St, dated only on 2/6/38 at Spring Head Mission)

---

2 Thessalonians 3.1 "Bretheren, pray for us, that the Word of the Lord may have free course, and be glorified."

"Himself had prayed for them," says St. Chrysostom, "now he asks them to pray for him." This is not the only occasion in which Paul appealed for the prayers of his friends. In at least five other epistles the same request is made. Nor is it an appeal for occasional, ejaculatory prayer. Rather the apostle is pleading for earnest and sustained intercession. Mr. A. S. Way translates the text, "Pray, pray on brothers mine, for me. Pray that the message of the Lord may speed untrammeled, that its glory may be recognized everywhere."

Mark, it is not for his personal safety and comfort that he asks their prayers, though he did not think that beneath him. His primary concern is the progress of the gospel and the spread of Christian truth. Borrowing a figure from the stadium, he urges his friends to pray that the word of the Lord may speed as a racer without impediment, a chariot with no drag on its wheels. In plain words, he asks the Thessalonians to pray that the gospel may be speedily communicated to all people, may be cordially received, may produce the promised results, and be universally acknowledged as worthy of all acceptation. The suggestion behind the text is that the progress of the gospel depends not alone on the gift and powers, nor even the sincerity and zeal of the preacher, but on the power released by the prayers of the people. It will be wise for us to recognize that there were and there are—

SERIOUS HINDRANCES TO THE SPREAD OF THE GOSPEL

Paul had to face, as many preachers since have faced, determined and organized opposition. Men refused to bear the message and stoned the messenger. And Wednesbury bears

"THE PREACHER'S PLEA FOR THE PEOPLE'S PRAYERS"—2 THESSALONIANS 3.1

witness that since Paul's day preachers have had hostile receptions. But sticks and stones, hostile demonstrations and organized opposition, are not the most serious hindrances.

Our Lord made it clear from the beginning that the preacher of the gospel like the sower of the seed would have to contend with more serious antagonistic forces—the counteracting word of some, the lack of comprehension and apprehension, the want of depth and feeling, the cares of this world and the deceitfulness of riches, the pleasures of this world. All these impede the progress of the Word. People are absorbed in the things of this world, skeptical concerning the message, indifferent to the claims and calls of religion. Their ears are too full of the words of people for them to care much for the Word of God. And the point is that, to overcome the obstacles and secure success—

PRAYER MUST COOPERATE WITH PREACHING

It is vain to expect the preacher to succeed alone. He may be as earnest as Paul, as impassioned as Stephen, as eloquent as Apollos, but without the prayers of the people, he is doomed to failure. Prayer and preaching are different but they must work together. Preaching speaks to human beings for God. Prayer speaks to God for humankind. Preaching casts in the seed, prayer brings the sunshine and rain. Preaching is what humans can do, prayer asks for what God only can do. There, if anywhere, it is true that, "Not by might, nor by power, but by God's Spirit," and it is in answer to prayer that the Spirit is given.

What we have to realize is that the spread of the gospel, the acceptance of the Word, depends on the united effort of the church. The preacher is needed but he can no more do without praying people than the eye can manage without the hand or the foot. That is what Paul was proclaiming. He was acknowledging and claiming a common brotherhood. He would have his people think of themselves as one with him. He needed their support and depended on their prayers. We are "members one of another," and upon us all rests responsibility for the progress of the gospel. You do not discharge your responsibility by calling and maintaining a minister. It is only as you cooperate with him, pray while he preaches, that success comes and the Word has free course.

EVIDENCE IN EXPERIENCE

Paul knew how preaching was reinforced by prayer. If he, with all his tremendous powers felt the need of the prayers of God's people, it is not surprising that ordinary preachers do. Illustrations could be multiplied and quotations given to show how preachers have depended, and not in vain, on the prayers of the people. Perhaps William Carey did not actually use the words "you must hold the ropes," but he made it clear that in going to preach in India he was depending on the prayers of the people at home. It is well known that the silver-tongued Spurgeon attributed any powers he had to the prayers of his people.

At a critical time in the history of missions, Mr. J. R. Mott gave an address on "Intercessors—the Primary Need." In it, he says, "For many years, it has been my practice in travelling among the nations to make a study of the sources of the spiritual movements which are doing most to vitalize and transform individuals and communities. At times, it has been difficult to discover the hidden spring, but invariably when I have had the time and patience to do so, I have found it in an intercessory prayer life of great reality." Revivals begin in prayer meetings. The person in the pulpit depends on the person on his knees. The word is with power when it is backed by prayer. Prayerless people make powerless preachers. The reason for some empty pews is to be found in the pew and not in the pulpit. The blame for some weak churches rests not on the preachers but on the people.

Here is a mighty ministry for the coming of the kingdom and in it we may all have a part. People who cannot preach in public can pray in private. The aged, invalids, and the shyest can pray. Pray for us. How we need your prayers! And we are strengthened when we know we have them. If we have faults—and we have—don't only criticize, pray that we may be cleansed and perfected. Pray that in our studies we may be guided into all truth. Ask God to wing our words that they may reach the hidden depths of many hearts. Pray, pray for us, for "more things are wrought by prayer than this world dreams of."[1] Let us make a compact that preaching and prayer shall cooperate, and though those who pray have their part in secret, God knows whence the power comes.

Adelaide Proctor puts the truth in these words: "The monk was preaching: strong his earnest word. From the abundance of his heart he spoke, and the flame spread—in every soul that heard. Sorrow and love and good resolve awoke: The poor lay brother, ignorant and old, thanked God that he had heard such words of gold. 'Still let the glory, Lord, be Thine alone.' So prayed the monk, his heart absorbed in prayer. 'O Lord, I thank Thee that my feeble strength Has been so blessed, that sinful hearts and cold were melted at my pleading, knew at length how sweet Thy service and how safe Thy fold: While souls that love Thee saw before them rise still holier heights of loving sacrifice. So prayed the monk, when suddenly he heard an angel speaking thus: 'Know, O my son, thy words had been in vain, but hearts were stirred, and saints were edified and sinners won by this, the poor lay brother's humble aid who sat upon the pulpit's steps and prayed.'"[2]

---

1. This is from Tennyson's famous poem on prayer.
2. Adelaide Proctor was a nineteenth-century feminist who worked on behalf of women and the homeless. She was also a writer, in particular a poet and philanthropist. Her poems were published in Charles Dickens's periodicals. She studied with Charles Kingsley at Queens College in 1850. She eventually converted to Catholicism. She published several volumes of poems and reflections, but I could not discover which one contains this story.

"OUR ENJOYMENT OF GOD'S GIFTS"
—1 Timothy 6.17

(Preached at Spring Head Mission 7/19/42 and Great Croft St H. F. 9/12/43)

---

1 Timothy 6.17 "God, who giveth us richly all things to enjoy."

HERE, IN AN ASIDE, is the apostle's repudiation of the idea that God is niggardly in His giving or jealous of His people's enjoyment of life's good things. The main purpose of this passage is to utter a warning to people who are rich. They are not to be high-minded and arrogant, nor are they to put their trust in anything so uncertain as riches. They are to be rich in good works and ready to share their wealth with their less fortunate neighbors. Their trust is to be in God; and here he slips in the aside, "Who giveth us richly all things to enjoy." It is with the aside rather than the main argument that we are here concerned.

We enter the apostolic aside as a protest against the notion that the life of faith is poverty stricken and joyless. In earlier days Christians were so suspicious that they excluded many legitimate things. They were leery about laughter and learning, about beauty and adornment of the person, the home, the church. John Bunyan turned a woman out of church because she wore a silk dress. John Wesley tells us that he would no more dare to affect a fine style in writing than wear a fine coat. Angelico would paint no secular subject and Miss Havergal would sing nothing but sacred songs. In even later years they felt that anything like joy was foreign to God's way. A gentleman brought up in Scotland says that if he had sung anything like a joyous song on the Sabbath he would be chastened. So, as he felt he must sing somewhere he went into the country where the birds sang and the brooks made music.

The idea has largely passed away. Our danger is in another and opposite direction. Only here and there a few Christians and particular sects deny themselves interests and pleasures God has not banned. They think the depth of a man's piety is indicated by the length of his face and that he estimates his joy hereafter by his denial now. But in the main it is only outsiders who regard the Christian life as being a joyless, mendicant kind of life and think of Christians as having a very lean time. And there are those who shrink from following Christ because they think He has nothing for them but a set of prohibitions and restrictions.

COMPREHENSIVE CHRISTIAN LIFE

As I say, we set against this idea the comprehensiveness and catholicity of the Christian life. God gives with a generous hand and His desire is that His people shall rejoice in His gifts. This ought always to have been clear: when God made the world, He did not leave it bleak and barren. He might have made the earth bring forth enough for food, medicine, and shelter, and yet have made no flowers. But he made everything beautiful in its season, and He intended for human beings to enjoy what He had given. In the garden story, we put the emphasis on the forbidden tree and forget that God said of every other tree, "Thou mayest eat thereof." When God led the people of His choice to their home it was to a land flowing with milk and honey and He bade them to eat and drink to the fill (Deut 8.7–10).

What is even more to the point is that when Jesus came He declared as the heart of His message, "I came that they might have life and have it abundantly." He set Himself against the thieves and robbers who artificially tried to steal from life what God intended to make it rich, full, and free. His great interpreter declared, "All things are yours. The beauty of the earth and the glory of the sky. Science, literature, and art are yours and yours to enjoy and revel in." God gives richly and gives that we may enjoy. Nothing should blind us to the truth of the text!

FULLNESS OF GOD'S GIFTS

(1) Fullness of life and joy can only be realized through choosing the best of God's gifts. Too often when we talk of good things our thoughts do not rise above the material. We think of the larder and the dining room. Our standard of well-being is plenty to eat and drink, nice clothes to wear, comfortable homes to live in, and plenty of money to spend. We are like people who judge a holiday by the ability of the landlady as a cook.

There is no need to despise these. If a person is a soul he has a body and much of his happiness is bound up with physical pleasure and comfort. There is no virtue in voluntary starvation or poverty. The luxuries of life may be put to good uses and are. Many serve God by feasting as well as fasting. "Better a dinner of herbs where love is," says the proverb, "than a stalled ox and hatred therewith." But we might have love where a stalled ox is and that is better still. Dainties and delicacies of the table, fine clothes, beautifully bound books, music and art, material comforts, are God's gifts and are to be richly enjoyed. But they are not the greatest gifts. He offers us our pardon and peace, high fellowship and noble service, glorious hopes and radiant anticipations. More than that: He offers Himself in friendship, redemption, and sanctification. What

"OUR ENJOYMENT OF GOD'S GIFTS"—1 TIMOTHY 6.17

sort of men and women, or rather foolish children are we if, when He gives so richly all things to enjoy we choose only the second or third rate things?

(2) To enjoy the lesser gifts to the full we must conform to the law of limitation. The text gives no sanction to those who resent everything in the nature of restriction or limitation. Not all lawful things are expedient. Some understand enjoying things as having anything they like and in such quantities as they like. Gratify to the full your appetite for food and you will pay for your folly in the dyspepsia that allows you a very restricted menu! Gratify all your passions and you will become their slave. It is only as you discipline your corporeal life and learn to live temperately that you will enjoy the fullness of your temporal life. Jesus did mean something when He called for the denial of self. The finest things, the deepest peace, the truest satisfaction are for those who deny themselves and discipline their bodies. Again, as Jesus said, "He that loseth his life shall save it."

(3) We shall only fully enjoy what God richly bestows if we share it. That is what Paul is urging. If people try to hold all they have they will get conceited and vain. The opulent must be ready to distribute and willing to communicate. That is the way to fully possess your possessions and perfectly enjoy them. Help yourself to the luxury of doing good and you will help others to happiness and yourself to the joy that never fails. Share what God has given you to enjoy and you will enjoy it all the more. Try to hog and hound it and you will lose it. The heart grows rich in giving, its wealth is living grain. Don't be a miser when God has given you all things, even his own Son, richly to enjoy.

∼

"THE SPIRIT'S THREEFOLD GIFT"
—2 Timothy 1.7

(Preached five times from Fentiman Road, undated, to Spring Head Mission 5/24/42)

---

2 Timothy 1.7 "For God hath not given us the spirit of fear; but of power, and of love, and of a sound mind."

ULTIMATELY EVERY SYSTEM, POLITICAL, social, religious, is judged not by the ideal it cherishes, but by the sort of person it produces. It is not enough that the ideal is high and worthy, there must be sufficient dynamic to make its attainment possible. The religion of Jesus Christ cannot escape that test. Indeed, it has always desired to be brought to the touchstone and tested by it. It has not been found wanting. It has cherished the loftiest ideal and has supplied the power that helped men and women to attain it. Its final evidence is not in its sublime teaching, but in lives transformed by its power; not in its standard of ethics, but its ethical followers. Its saints are its apologetic. "Ye men and women of my spirit, ye are my witnesses," said our Lord and Master.

In our text, Paul gives an illuminating sketch both of the ideal cherished and the person produced. Look at it as it hangs here for our admiration and encouragement. The centuries have failed to present or produce a more perfect person. Power, love, and sound mind! Ability, benevolence, self-criticism! Energy, sympathy, discipline! What more can you add? What less would satisfy the demand?

QUALITIES OF THE PERFECT PERSON

Power is the essence of a mature person. To be a weakling is to be pitied or despised. What we desire for ourselves and admire in our friends is strength. Strength to do, to suffer, to conquer. But power alone does not make the perfect person. It may make a tyrant. Power may be used for personal ends and work havoc in other lives. A Napoleon striding across Europe may commend admiration but can never be an ideal person. To strength must be added love, power must be joined with pity. It is only when might is moved by mercy that it proves a blessing. When love rules, power never upturns, strength is never selfish, and might is used to serve rather than command.

Add to power and love the regulative quality of self-control, discipline, prudence—the word leaves either interpretation—and surely you have the perfect man, a man in whom liberty never descends to license, strong to resist and achieve yet tender to sense and help, a person who does not use his strength to tyrannize and oppress and whose love does not run to mere sentiment.

We have the right to ask of any system seeking our suffrages that it shall prove its power to produce such people. Leaving other systems, we ask can the religion of Jesus produce such people? Paul claims that it can and does. Summarized his claim is this. The perfect person appeared in Jesus. He is more than a perfect man, He is the Son of God and He is reproducing, by His Spirit, His own character in the lives of those who put their trust in Him. The life of Jesus is being made manifest in all who believe. The Pentecostal Gift is the gift of the Holy Spirit, the Spirit of God and the God revealed in Jesus. To the humblest believer is given the Spirit of Jesus, the Spirit of power, of love, and a sound mind. How true is Paul's claim can be proved by anyone who will take the trouble to read the Gospels and the Acts of the Apostles. There is the story of men and women delivered from weakness and cowardice and filled with power, love, and a healthy and sound mind.

HOLY GHOST POWER

Filled with the Holy Ghost and with power. The gift of the Spirit is always associated with power. The promise of Jesus to His disciples was, "Ye shall receive power after the Holy Ghost is come upon you." Pentecost saw the promise fulfilled and abundant power came to the disciples. That was the very quality they had been deficient in. In earlier days, they had been as reeds shaken with the wind, timid and pliable. In the courses of the Master's life they had failed often. They were about the last person fitted for world conquest. How could such weaklings face and endure the opposition and persecution meeting them and the kingdom?

The coming of the Spirit endowed them with power. The timid and shrinking became positive and affirmative. Shaking reeds became sturdy oaks. Spirit filled persons had power to think, to witness, to suffer, to die, to conquer. The spirit of craven fear gave place to the courage which shook the kingdoms of darkness and set up the kingdom of God. That is always the result of the coming of the Spirit. The baptism of the Holy Ghost is a baptism of power which make the recipients wax valiant in fight, turning to flight the armies of the aliens. Time fails to tell of the heroes of the past in whose lives the truth is illustrated, people who were weaklings, slaves to their own passions or the conventions of their day, afraid of great tasks and with no strength to carry them through, until they opened their hearts to the meaning of God's Spirit and are transformed into strong, reliable, and victorious persons.

A Spirit-filled church is the only strong church. It may be high or low, established or free, but if it be not a spiritual church it will be a weak church. The church that is established in the power of the Spirit stands before all opportunities, overcomes all difficulties, and adds its foes to the kingdom of its Lord.

THE FRUIT OF THE SPIRIT IS LOVE

Turn again to the Apostolic Days and see how the coming of the Spirit meant the birth of love. The Pentecostal gift was the gift of love as well as power. Spirit filled people loved God with all their strength, loved Jesus with a passion the world has never seen equaled, and loved one another and their neighbors as themselves. The spirit of power delivered them from fear and the spirit of love delivered them from selfishness. The coming of the Spirit meant the outgoing of generous love. It was their love that attracted and won men. They loved one another and they loved unloving and unlovely people. The ones who sought first places in the kingdom and wanted to call down fire on those who opposed them lavished their love on those who scorned them and they prayed for their persecutors. The springs of such love were not in themselves. Love was a fruit of the indwelling Spirit of Jesus.

The same indwelling Spirit still delivers from the selfishness to which humans are prone. Nothing else will make us persistently love the outcast, the unloving, and the sinful. With his Spirit within we all love as he has loved, forgive as he forgave. We shall over leap all bounds and pour forth our lives in healing ministries. Baptized with His Spirit we too shall love God with our heart, mind, and strength, and our neighbors as ourselves. The spirit of love is given to all who pray: "Holy Spirit, Love Divine! Glow within this heart of mine. Kindle every high desire. Perish self in Thy pure fire."[1]

SPIRIT FILLED

Not drunk with wine, but filled with the Spirit. Lastly, the Spirit God gives is the Spirit of sobriety, self-control, discipline. Back once more to the day of Pentecost. "These men are full of new wine: they are drunk," said the onlookers. "No," said Peter, "they are not full of wine but filled with the Spirit." Some of the surface manifestation of these two experiences are similar. Dr. Black calls the Spirit filled, "God's drunken men." Paul links the two in the words, "Be not drunk with wine, but be filled with the Spirit." In essence the two experiences are diametrically opposed. Wine means riot, it gives the room to all kinds of foolish and sinful thoughts, passions, actions. The Spirit brings control and discipline, creates a sound mind.

We speak of a disordered mind, an undisciplined mind, and diseased mind. A "sound mind" is the opposite. It means an ordered, informed, and healthy mind. Prior to Pentecost the disciples were always acting and speaking foolishly. Someone has said that the disciples are only mentioned in the Gospels for the mistakes they made. They

---

1. This is from a nineteenth-century hymn by Samuel Longfellow entitled "Holy Spirit, Truth Divine."

"THE SPIRIT'S THREEFOLD GIFT"—2 TIMOTHY 1.7

ran into all kinds of experiences and acted like the imprudent and foolish. In the Acts of the Apostles you see the same persons in possession of new power, love, and at the same time revealing balanced minds, controlled passions, and well-ordered minds. It was the Spirit of Jesus that possessed them, and we know how balanced and ordered His life was. He knew just when to use His power to unmask hypocrites and tyrannies, and how to love bruised reeds and dimly burning wicks.

The same Spirit is promised to us and His presence in us would teach us wisdom, sanctify our passions, and refine our lives. So often we act foolishly, allow our passions and our enthusiasms to run away with us, and we say and do things which cause needless trouble and injure our cause. We need power, and we need love, and we need no less wisdom, poise, and discipline; all that is meant by a "sound mind." And all we need is supplied by the Spirit. Here, then, is the ideal Christianity cherishes and the person it produces. A strong person whose power moves at the dictation of love, whose power and love are controlled by a healthy and disciplined mind. Such people are twice-born persons, born of the flesh and born of the Spirit. The excellence of their lives is the fruit of the indwelling Spirit of the God Jesus revealed and was. Such people we may all be for the gift of the Spirit is for everyone who asks and opens his heart to receive.

~

"THE SECOND CHANCE"
—2 Timothy 4.11

(Preached at Bishop St. 2/20/49)

---

2 Timothy 4.11 "Take Mark, and bring him with thee: for he is profitable to me for the ministry."

CONCERNING MARK

The second chance in life implies that the first has been missed. And Mark, the man about whom we are to think, had had a grand first chance. He came from a home which had played an outstanding part in the life of the early church. His mother, Mary, had put her home in Jerusalem at the disposal of the first Christians. It was in the upper room of her house that they met for weekly worship. When Peter was dramatically released from prison it was to that house he made his way. There is a reasonable probability that it was in that upper room that the Last Supper was held before Calvary, and that it was there the disciples were gathered on the Day of Pentecost. Further, Mark was a cousin to the generous-hearted Barnabas, one of the pillars of the early church. A still greater honor was his. When Paul and Barnabas were chosen by the Holy Spirit and sent by the church on the very first Christian missionary enterprise, Mark was appointed as the junior minister to accompany them. A great honor and a great chance!

FAILURE TO TAKE THE FIRST CHANCE

It does not require much imagination to picture Mark setting out with Barnabas and Paul. There would be the sense of exaltation that he had been chosen for such a task and to accompany such men. There would be the novelty and glamour of adventure in the new enterprise. But it is not long before we come to the tragic words, "John departing from them, returned to Jerusalem." He went home. We are not told why, but it is easy to conjecture. The eager heart of Paul was planning journeys far beyond what had been in Mark's mind. He was pushing on into strange, unknown, and dangerous places. They were getting a long way from their home and one day he packed up, turned back, and went home and he left the two older men to go forward without him.

So, Mark missed his first chance and has, at this stage, to be written down a failure. It looked, too, as if the chance had gone by forever. A little later, in Acts 15.36, 37, we read that Paul and Barnabas planned a second missionary journey. Barnabas was minded to take Mark with them again. But Paul would not have it. He evidently felt the man who had left them the first time was not to be trusted a second time. The two old friends parted on the issue. And as I say, it looked as if so far as Paul was concerned, there was no further chance for Mark.

THE STORY AND THE PROBLEM TODAY

The story of Mark is modern as well as ancient. It may be the story of our own life. Our problem is not only that of gaining people, it is that of retaining them. We all know these people, and some older ones, who had a splendid start. They set out with high hopes in their hearts and in ours. They had a great chance to make good and do heroic service for Christ. But they failed. Some made a shipwreck of their faith. Others grew weary or afraid. They could not endure the hardships or stand the ridicule or make the sacrifices involved. They just went back home. And it looks as if they had lost their chance and must be written down as failures if not renegades. Few of us dare cast stones at Mark. We live in glass houses.

So much was necessary to say about the first chance, but our main theme is the second chance. Sixteen years elapse, years of remorse for Mark, but more, years of rehabilitation. In the light of what had happened, look at our text, Paul, the man who had refused to take Mark back, was in prison, lonely and hard-pressed. Paul writes to Timothy, "Take Mark, and bring him with thee, for he is profitable to me in the ministry." I wish I could make these words known for the person who needs to know there is a second chance for the one who missed the first. Mark had been a failure and now he was profitable.

That has a vital and heartening message for the failure. The world gives little chance to them. It is too eager to say, "You have had your chance and must make way for a better man." Many a person knows that in the world's eyes there is no second chance for him, and sinks into remorse and despair. More people than we imagine are singing Cowper's lines: "What peaceful hours I once enjoyed! How sweet their memory still! But they have left an aching void, the world can never fill."[1] As I wrote I prayed God to give me a word for all such.

But first let me say a word about giving the first chance. I am not blaming Paul for his attitude at the first. At that time, the work could only be done by strong and courageous persons. With Paul, the work came first and he could not trust it to a person

---

1. This is from Cowper's eighteenth-century hymn "O for a Closer Walk with God."

who had left it once. But even he came to see that a person who had failed could be recovered and be trusted. And I am sure that his later attitude is the one we must adopt. Are we, any of us, so perfect that we can be too hard on others? Where should our lives be if there had been no second chances? Let us deal with others as Christ has dealt with us, and in patience and love give them a second chance. Think of the joy in Mark's heart when Paul sent him that message.

My main message is for those who have missed the first chance. I can understand their remorse and shame for I have shared it. Perhaps you are tempted to say, "It is no more, and I had my chance and threw it away." I cannot let you say that or yield to that temptation. "Take Mark, and bring him with thee, for he is profitable." The one-time renegade may yet become a brave soldier of the cross. You can find your way back and be the companion of heroes and martyrs. The person with his name on the blacklist may yet have it marked in the roll of honor. In the days of war one sometimes reads in the papers, "Reported missing, now rejoined." You must believe in the redeeming grace of God and repent if you fail. There will always be a tinge of regret in your life. But I say as solemnly as I know how, as surely as God is God, if you repent of your failures and put your trust in God, you will get your second chance.

CHRIST AND THE SECOND CHANCE

I say that, not on my own authority, but on that of Jesus Christ. It is His glory to give people another chance. He knows our weakness and frailty, knows too what He can do with persons who were once failures. To Peter who had failed Him badly He committed the shepherding of His lambs and feeding of His sheep. However badly we who are his friends fail Him, He never does. He does not break the bruised reed nor quench the smoking flax. For Mark, he had an even greater honor than that of becoming again Paul's friend and comrade. You read the Gospel according to St. Mark, but do not always realize what that means. It means this: Mark became the close friend of the Apostle Peter. Perhaps the two had many a tearful talk about their respective failures. Peter knew better than any man the intimate things of the life of Jesus, but he was no scholar and could not set them down. So, he told them to Mark, who wrote them down in what was the first gospel. When you read that gospel remember you are reading the words of the man to whom Christ gave a second chance, and a man who took it.

It would be a great thing if the gospel were only for those who had fought a good fight, finished their course and kept the faith. But the evangelist has the gladdest and most thrilling task in the world. He has to preach good news of hope to the hopeless, love for the loveless, courage for the cowardly, strength for the weak, and a second chance for the failures. In the mercy of God, I have to preach this gospel to you. Christ can do for you what He did for John Mark—make you profitable for the ministry, to proclaim His gospel.

"THE SECOND CHANCE"—2 TIMOTHY 4.11

You say, "I could never do that!" In a word, no. But you could proclaim it in a life, so that people who never read the Gospel of St. Mark can read in your life what Christ has done for those who trust Him. Give him a chance and He will give you yours. We are coming presently to the Lord's Table. I have been coming for over fifty years, and more than ever the words thrill me, "This is my body broken for you." I answer, "But Lord, I have failed and forsaken you, turned back because I was afraid of the ridicule and persecution, and reduced by eager voices and the promise of pleasure and gain." And again, comes the voice, "This is my blood that was shed for you." And I can only answer, "Here, Lord, I give myself away, tis all that I can do." In His name, I bid you welcome to His table and ask you to renew your vow of allegiance.

"THE STORY OF A SLAVE"
—Philemon 10, 11

(Preached three times from Fentiman Road 3/22/25 to Forest Hill 3/17/26)

Philemon 10, 11 "I beseech thee for my child, whom I have begotten in my bonds, Onesimus, who was aforetime unprofitable to thee, but now is profitable to thee and to me."

A GREATLY GIFTED WRITER has pointed out that the Epistle to Philemon has not escaped the ill fortune that threatens all things of people of small stature: it has been very much neglected. So much so that it would not be surprising, and it would be no reflection on your piety or early training, if you could not at this moment turn up the epistle in the New Testament without reference to the index. But just as "good stuff goes into little room," as wisdom often dwells with small and obscure people, so this much-neglected epistle is a great little book.

It is of value if only for the fact that it is the only strictly private letter of Paul preserved for us in the canon of Scripture. All the other epistles are either letters to churches or pastoral epistles of authoritative direction. Here we have Paul presented in a new light. Apostolic dignity and fatherly authority are thrown off and the apostle writes simply as one Christian gentleman to another. Perhaps we shall best gather up the lessons of this precious letter if we look first at the—

OUTSTANDING FIGURES INTRODUCED TO US

We have an early saint, Philemon. He was evidently a converted Colossian merchant. His circumstances must have been comfortable for he was able to keep slaves and to entertain the traveling preacher when he was that way. His wife, Apphia, and his son Archippus, were with him in the service of the Lord. Philemon had opened his house for prayer and we read of "the church in thy house." His affluent means were used for the easing of the burdens of others and his generosity was a proverb in the churches. "We have," writes Paul, "great joy and consolation in thy love, because the bowels of the saints are refreshed by thee, brother."

Then Onesimus comes to the front—a vastly different figure. He was a Phrygian slave in Philemon's household. From the apostle, we gather that he had stolen some of his master's money and fled with it to Rome, hoping to be lost in the crowds thronging the metropolis. But he was not to escape. While there, *he met Paul.* The apostle was awaiting his trial. As we know from the Acts of the Apostles, he was free to receive his friends and at liberty to preach the gospel to such as came to him.

The Phrygian slave came and was convicted and converted. It was not long before the story of the slave's sin was told. Paul had to counsel return and confession. But Paul would not leave Onesimus to shift for himself. He must return, and Paul would write a letter to his friend, the slave's master. And what a letter it was! Read sympathetically through it and you will almost feel the throbbing of the writer's heart. Read the letter in Way's translation! We have no direct evidence as to what was the result of this noble appeal: but we need be in little doubt. Picture Philemon receiving the letter, reading it with moist eyes, and welcoming the runaway slave. What we know of the actors in this little drama makes us fairly confident that Onesimus was received into the household of Philemon and loved as a brother. Tradition says that he became bishop of Berea.

A LESSON IN CHRISTIAN TACT, DELICACY, AND COURTESY

There is nothing hard and driving in Paul's approach to Philemon. "I might command as an Apostle," he says, "but rather for love's sake I beseech." How much better it would be, how much more we might achieve, if we had more of this spirit and less of the bull-at-a-gate spirit that so often characterizes our approach to people. They tell me that at Land's End is a rock called Logan Rock. From most angles a dozen persons try in vain to move it: from one particular point, one person can set it "logging" quite easily. You must find the spot. Queer, isn't it? But in the north, we have a saying, "There's nowt so queer as folk." Approach them from the north and you bluster and blow in vain: come to them from the sunny south, take pains to find the spot and you can do as you will with them. That is worthwhile considering in the ordinary give and take of life. Still more if you are trying to win men and women to the higher life.

PAUL IDENTIFIED HIMSELF WITH ONESIMUS

Paul made the slave's cause his own. "Receive him as you would receive me: if he has wronged you or owes you ought, I will pay it with my own hand." "We see," says Luther, "how Paul layeth himself out for poor Onesimus and with all his means, pleadeth his cause with his master, and so setteth himself as if he were Onesimus and had himself done wrong to Philemon." The noblest apostle stood with a slave of the lowest order. That was what saved Onesimus. You can only save moral lepers by dealing with them as Jesus did the actual leper and as Paul did with this one. You must put your hand on them: you must stand with them, and not in a lordly condescension either. A doctor has no squeamish scruples with loathsome diseases. If you would be physicians to sin-sick souls you must be willing to come into close contact with ugly and repulsive sins. A squeamish, kid gloved, put me in a glass case kind of Christianity will never save men and women.

Take this incident as illustrating this point and my previous one too. In the days when condemned men were more get-at-able than now, there was a man under condemnation. He was visited by many people who tried to bring him to a repentant frame of mind, and they all failed. At last a saint of good repute took up the task. With a deal more tact and delicacy than the others had shown, he told the story of Jesus in much the same way as you can read it in the Gospels—how that He was merciful and forgiving, and had a kind word for the fallen. Then in a quiet way he ended with, "This friend died for sinners like you and me." The effect on the prisoner was instantaneous. Tears came at once, and he kept on saying to himself, "To think that he should class himself with such as I am, when all men know him for his goodness."

Is that our attitude? Do we stand by the side of sinners and put our hands in sympathy on the sin-sick? Someone said of a very respectable free church that it was the cream of nonconformity. Someone quickly replied, "Yes, but it's the ice cream." That is what I am afraid is the trouble with many of us. Our danger is that of getting smug and self-satisfied, comfortable and conceited. The cream of the churches consists of those who are likest to Jesus and Paul in willingness to give themselves for the salvation of others.

THE ATONEMENT IN PRACTICE

There is only time to touch on this one other thing, and that very inadequately. With quiet play upon the slave's name Paul says, "He was unprofitable, but now is profitable." The gospel had touched and changed the heart and life of Onesimus. He went out a robber and returned an Apostle's friend. The gospel discovered a possible bishop in a Phrygian slave. That is the unique power of the gospel. That is how the atonement works out in practice. Sinners it transforms into saints: persons who are unprofitable it makes into profitable citizens and helpers of every good cause.

God sees gardens in deserts and it is His glory to make the wilderness blossom as a rose. Yielding heart and life to Him, glorious possibilities are discovered, helpful powers are realized, and men who aforetime were unprofitable are profitable to God and men.

"THE SACRIFICE OF PRAISE"
—Hebrews 13.15

(Preached five times from Katherine Road 4/5/36 to Bishop St. 9/22/46)

Hebrews 13.15 "Let us offer the sacrifice of praise to God continually, that is the fruit of our lips giving thanks to His name."

NO APOSTOLIC INJUNCTION TO Christian people stands in greater need of emphasis than this one. The sacrifice of praise is most acceptable to God, yet it is often the one sacrifice the altar lacks. "Praise waiteth for Thee in Zion," said the psalmist, but it is often something else that awaits God in our modern Zions. The "fruit of our lips" is as often grumblings as grateful expression. There are far too many Christians who rail at the world and murmur at their lot. They are disappointed, discouraged, and inclined to be cynical and bitter. In vain we call them, in words that are not classic, to a duty to "count their blessings." They see only the sordid and underside of things. Many of us come sulkily to the Throne of Grace and with our unspoken grudge against the Almighty in our hearts.

It would be ungracious and untrue not to say there are others—and thanks be to God for these—who surprise us with their delight in offering the sacrifice of praise. Men and women who rejoice in their lot, find beauty everywhere, love in the darkest spots, and who even rejoice that their joy is touched with pain. They bless the Lord at all times and His praise is continually in their mouths.

This is not to suggest that praise consists only in the singing of sacred words to the glory of God. There is the silent praise of the heart and there is a praise of the life as well as of the lips. "Fill Thou my life, O Lord, my God in every part with praise." But the context makes it clear that it is the praise of the lips that the writer has in mind. The Bible generally associates praise with "psalms, hymns, and spiritual songs." In the canon of Sacred Scripture one of the greatest books is the collection of poems intended to be sung at the service of the temple and the festivals of the people of God. In our own day, hymns and anthems fill a large place in the services of the sanctuary. That fact justifies a consideration of the place of praise in our worship service.

PRAISE THAT IS SPONTANEOUS

This is the song that leaps unbidden from heart to lips. There are times when we feel like singing. We have witnessed some new glory, received some new gift, experienced some great deliverance, shared some new joy and we break forth into singing as did the people at the end of the Thirty Years War when Martin Rinkart led them in "Now thank we all our God, with hearts and hands and voices." Such praise is comely and acceptable to God. There must always be a place for it. When the Lord turns again to the captivity of Zion the hearts of the people will be filled with gratitude and they will break forth in song together, and with their praise God will be well pleased.

PRAISE SET FORTH AS DUTY

Going deeper still, we find that praise is a duty. It is not to be at the mercy of our fickle moods. We do not feel like singing all the time. There are days when praise languishes on our lips and the songs die down to a whisper. We say we are not in the mood for praise. But the writer says praise is to be offered continually. "Ye shall praise the Lord," is a duty and is not left to our whim and fancy. Even sorrow is not to silence the song. Praise is our response to God's goodness and no one suggests that in our trouble God has forgotten to be gracious. Tender take the task as a duty and it will deepen into delight. Literally the statute will become a song. Oft, "though the way may be long, in the lilt of a song, I forget I was weary before." Often the light surprises the Christian while he sings. Therefore, it is our duty to answer streams of mercy with songs of loudest praise. This takes us deeper yet and speaks of—

THE SACRIFICE OF PRAISE

The two main words are not often linked and it was the association that suggested the sermon. The writer speaks of the altar and praise is to be laid on it as a sacrifice. The offering for the altar was always the best, the first fruits. Is our praise worthy to be mentioned in this way? What if every soloist laid her solo as an offering on the altar? The choir the anthem, the organist the voluntary, the congregation the praise? What an atmosphere that would make for preaching! The grace of God reaches us through the Lamb slain from the foundation of the world. We are to come to the Throne of Grace, not only to obtain mercy, but bringing our offering. At the altar in Golgotha we learn what sacrificial giving means and our praise is to be the response of sacrifice.

The sacrifice we are to lay on the altar continually. The emphasis is on the last word and as I have said, there are moods in which we feel like singing. But there are

"THE SACRIFICE OF PRAISE"—HEBREWS 13.15

times when we think we do well to be silent if not sulky. Let us face some of the things that silence the song and set over against them its inspirations.

SAVED BY GRACE

The world has not been an easy place for some. Life has been anything but a bed of roses. Much that we desired has been denied. But, and it is a mighty large *but*, in this world we have found Jesus Christ. Life's greatest good has not eluded us. Whatever has been denied the grace that saves is ours. "Saved by the power divine! Saved to new life sublime!"[1] Think of what that means. An old woman said to Bishop Burnett as she held up her crust, "All this—and Christ." A Crust and Christ made El Dorado. Though I have not risen to that, I will not rail at a world in which I have found Christ. I have had my disappointments and denials, but I will not murmur and complain as I remember the grace I have that sought and found me and the grace that saves me. While God continues to be gracious we must lay on the altar a sacrifice of praise.

THE VOTE OF THANKS

Turn to our work as Christians. Often, we murmur at its location and its lowly nature. No one seems to appreciate it and often we are discouraged. We want for the usual vote of thanks and are disappointed and sometimes resign because it doesn't come. Why instead of waiting for it we ought to move it. Think of Paul and of what service meant to him. He was often weary and sometimes beaten and put into prison, but he never failed in gratitude that he was counted worthy to serve and to suffer. His one fear was that he might prove unworthy and be dropped. Give up grumbling about "the toil of the traces" and thank God you are in. God has honored you in giving you a place, the more difficult it is, the greater the honor. While God counts you worthy and puts you into a ministry, let the fruit of your lips be a song of praise.

THE WAY AND THE GUIDE

The fear of the future is often the foe of praise. Life is uncertain. The way is dark before us and we know not what awaits. There is no inspiration for a song in that—but there is in this: if we do not know the way we know the Guide. I do not see my way, I do not wish to see it: it is enough for me that He sees His and that I see Him. "He goeth before you." "He leadeth them out." Thank God for that, and for this: the grace of God is pledged to us and that is all sufficient. "My grace is sufficient for thee." So, for the

---

1. Here is the one exception to the rule that Fred only cites eighteenth- and nineteenth-century hymns. This one comes from 1911, from the pen of J. P. Scholfield, and is entitled "Saved, Saved."

Guide and the Grace, for the certainties that outweigh all the uncertainty, let us offer the sacrifice of praise continually.

BATTLE AND VICTORY

The best things of life only come to us through struggle and strife. It is "through much tribulation" that we enter the kingdom. We win our way by strife. For all of us there is many a battle with the world, the flesh, and the devil. Can we go into the fight with a song? We can, for the victory is not in doubt. Like the Patriarch we may "hold upon our thigh," but like him we can become princes with power to prevail. As one says, "We came with steps that falter, but we came." And as a greater said, "In all these things we are more than conquerors through Him that loves us." Even when we face the last enemy there is no need to fear. We can say with Browning: "I go to prove my soul, I see my way as birds their trackless way. I shall arrive! What time, what circuit first, I ask not, but unless God sends His hail, or blinding fireballs, sleet or stifling snow, in good time, His good time, I shall arrive, He guides me and the bird. In His good time."[2]

Through grace even death is swallowed up in victory. It is grace all the way. Grace first, last, and midway through, and: "Grace all thy work shall crown, through everlasting days, it lays in heaven the topmost stone and well deserves the praise."[3] Why should we murmur and complain, or be bitter in spirit? Why should the song of praise languish on our lips or the altar lack the sacrifice? We have received grace. We know Christ as our Savior and friend. We have a place in the ranks of His servants. Our victory is assured. Come with a smile as well as with boldness to the Throne of Grace, and bring your offering. Let the fruit of your lips be ever praise. "So shalt thou, Lord, from me, even me, receive the glory due, and so shall I begin on earth the song forever new."[4]

---

2. This comes from a lengthy dialogical poem by Browning entitled "Paracelsus."
3. This is from a hymn written by P. Doddridge entitled "Grace Tis a Charming Sound."
4. This is from Horatio Bonar's hymn "Fill Thou My Life, O Lord My God."

"GOD WILLING"
—James 4.15

(Preached twice at Spring Head Mission 10/5/41 and Bishop St. 10/6/47)

James 4.15 "Ye ought to say, if the Lord will, we shall live and do this or that."

IT WAS A WIDELY observed custom, not so many years ago, for good people to include in their letters and print in their bills the letters D. V.—the initials of two Latin words, *Deo Volente*. And the words mean, "If God will," or "God willing." These good people meant that they would visit such a place, do this or that, hold certain meetings if the Lord willed. The custom has largely passed out of use and we are inclined to smile superciliously at the few people who persist in it.

    I can be quite frank and admit that the use of the letters is rather smug and the tone in which they are uttered is irritating to robust and happy spirits. Personally, I do not often use them in letters I write or in posters for which I am responsible. Yet the smile need not become a sneer. And it hardly becomes us to criticize if we have come to believe that things happen by fate, or if we are forgetting God and the part He plays in everyday life. These simple folk are not all guilty of superstition, and it is true that we only live and do the things we plan if God wills them. They have the New Testament on their side, for it was one of the sanest and most practical of its writers who used the words of our text.

IT IS THE INWARD UTTERANCE OF D. V. THAT COUNTS

In order to do the apostolic injunction, it is not necessary to be constantly writing or quoting, God willing, any more than it is necessary to carry a Bible or hymnbook to show that you spend Sunday by going to church. If you live in the spirit of subjection to God's will, if you realize all the time that only as God wills can you perform the things you propose, you are keeping the truth of the text in spirit and that counts for more than keeping the letter of it.

But I have to add this—if we feel and say D. V. in our hearts, it will find outward expression oftener than it does. It is not necessary for a man who loves his wife to be always saying "dear" or "darling," but if his love is deep and sincere he will say it sometimes. And if a man is truly and deeply loving his life in utter dependence upon God, the fact will surely find some outward expression. There is a real danger of our religious life becoming dumb. There is no need for a parade but there is need for a confession. And confession can be frank and manly. Besides, it is one of the principles of modern psychology that expression deepens impression. And we all know that what finds no expression often becomes atrophied. The more sincerely you are worshipping in a believing heart, "If God wills," the more should and will the words find expression in your speech and letters. But it is with the inward utterance I am mainly concerned.

THE TEST OF LIFE

What I mean is this—the utterance of the inward D. V. means that, when you are in doubt about certain courses of conduct, when you are faced with different propositions, you will say, "I shall take the way, accept the proposition that is in harmony with God's will." What a difference that would make to our lives! What an elevation it would give them. There are some things we should never do, some courses we should never follow, for we know He does not will them. It would settle many doubtful questions for us and it would give our lives the strength and dignity which His will gives. That, I know, is a high and severe test. But it is the Christian standard. We are followers of Jesus Christ and the motto of His life was, "Not my will, but Thine be done." He could and did say, "My meat is to do the will of Him that sent me." The acceptance of what is God's will is the test and standard of Christian living. If we are afraid of carrying everything to that searching test, let me remind you of what we often forget.

GOD'S WILL IS ALWAYS GOOD WILL

I want to stress that because so often we associate God's will with what is somber and dark. We sing, "The way, not mine, O Lord, however dark it be."[1] And if we say or sing, "Thy will be done," it is in a spirit of regretful and almost resentful resignation. As I wrote the earlier part of this sermon, I was feeling for an alternative phrase to "God's will," so as not unduly to repeat one phrase. "God's good pleasure" suggested itself. That pulled me up. It is more than an alternative phrase, it is exhortatory. Jesus used it and meant it. He said, "It is your Father's good pleasure to give you the Kingdom." That is, it is your Father's will. Never forget that God's will is the Father's will and it is good will. Whatever is His will, is well.

---

1. This too is from a hymn by Horatio Bonar, entitled "Thy Way Not Mine O Lord."

It is something the Father finds joy in because it is for His children's good. Why even you earthly parents would have no pleasure in what is ill for your children. How much more your Father in heaven! So, when you inwardly say of every way you take, I am taking it because it is God's will, you are taking the surest way to good that an all-wise and all-loving Father can devise. Again, I say, what a difference it would make to our choices in life if we always remembered that God's will is only and always our good, and so we called God's will the Father's good pleasure.

THE SIGN OF GRACE AND GROWTH

We ought to ask ourselves if it is becoming more and more a habit with us to bring everything to the test of God's will and to pass the test. If we are getting into the way of doing as we like, consulting only our own will and pleasure, and resenting any interference with our own plans, then, camouflage it as we may, we are forgetting God and falling from grace.

But if as the years go by, we find ourselves appealing more and more to God's will, ordering our lives according to it, if we know that His will is good will and accept it even when it crosses our dearest plans, we do well. In a word, if we say in our hearts D. V. then we may be sure that our sanctification is proceeding and that we are growing in grace. For it is the prayer our Lord would have us all pray, "Thy will be done on earth as it is done in heaven."

"THE GRACE OF CHARITY"
—1 Peter 4.8

(Preached once at Spring Head Mission 4/3/38)

---

1 Peter 4.8 "Charity shall cover the multitude of sins."

IN DR. WEYMOUTH'S TRANSLATION of the New Testament the text reads, "Love throws a veil over a multitude of faults." This rendering—

CORRECTS A DOUBLE FALLACY

First, it corrects the idea that brotherly love is "a kind of secondary atonement." Sometimes a person's charities have been regarded as a setoff against his sins, as when those many outlaws of Sherwood Forest, after robbing a fat Abbott sought to cover their own sins by distributing a very small portion of their ill-gotten gains to widows and orphans. In more modern days, some gay young spark thinks to cover his follies and plundering by certain acts of kindness. In a sermon on charity it ill becomes the preacher to be uncharitable: but is it not a fact that many imagine they can cover a lifetime of selfishness and greed by leaving their money, when they can no longer use it to the church or some orphanage? This is not simply a verbal inaccuracy that needs correcting by textual criticism, it is a vital fallacy that needs correcting by stern facts. And the fact is that Peter meant, and the truth is, what is stated in the new translation, that love throws a veil over the faults and failings of others.

Second, there is no suggestion here that we must always be silent in the presence of sins or that all exposure of evil is wrong. In some circumstances, to hold our peace would be to become partakers of other men's sins. Where would thousands of trusting people be if the official and competent accountant were to cover up the defalcations of a rascally company promoter? Besides, that would be no real kindness to the wrong doer, for he would then simply go on his way to damnation. As one who speaks in parables says, "There are cases where duty demands public censure. The sore must not be covered lest it prove deadly. It must be lanced or it cannot be cured. But," he adds, "the lancing is done with exquisite tenderness. The wrong doer is repaired, rebuked, exhorted, but with all long-suffering."[1] Exposure is sometimes a public duty, and many of us fail because we are too lax to think out our duty, too fearful of consequences to do it.

The reference in the text is not to public, but private concerns, to those faults and wrongs for which our charity can and should find a veil. There are many cases in which we are neither judge nor juror. Peter is thinking not of the realm of the legal but that of private relationships. Here our duty is clear and we may begin by saying that—

LOVE TAKES NO DELIGHT IN EXPOSING SINS

That is elementary, but it needs to be said. Every person has his faults and failings. The loving person is skilled in that gliding tact which avoids unnecessary exposure. A very nervous individual at a public diner made a stain on a cloth. The man seated next to him, being much more at home at such functions, quietly moved a vase of flowers and covered the stain. That was a gracious thing to do. It would have been vulgar to call attention to the stain. Yet, when a person has stained his character many are eager to be first with the spicy gossip. If it is not necessary, why call attention to moral delinquencies? Love is never anxious to expose sins, but to cover them. Further, love covers sins by putting some—

GENEROUS CONSTRUCTION UPON FAULTS

Archbishop Leighton, the seventeenth-century divine, puts the truth delightfully: "Love is witty in finding out the fairest construction of things doubtful." "Love covers sins," says F. W. Robertson, "by making large allowances." Love is mute at the balance because, "what's done we partly may compute, but know not what's resisted." Love looks for the best and says it. A person may be slow and awkward, love covers that by pointing out that he is reliable and trustworthy. If a person is irritable and abrupt, love remembers that he is worried or is not well. When the worst is proved, love makes what allowances it can. It is not for the sinner himself to make these excuses, but lovable men and women make a principle of always putting good qualities in the foreground. Did not Jesus pray for His murderers, "Father forgive them for they know not what they do"? We even cover sins this way at death, why not in life? Again, love covers sins by—

---

1. This is from a sermon by F. B. Meyers entitled "Love Covers Sins."

LUMINESCENCE

A WISE AND KINDLY FORGETFULNESS

We all have more to do with the fashioning of our memory. We cannot determine the number of things we remember or the length of time we can remember them, but we can determine the kind of things we remember. It is a hard saying but necessary. Cultivate a memory that remembers the wrongs you have done and forgets the wrongs done to you. Keep a list of your creditors, but not of your debtors.

When a wrongdoer turns over a new leaf, do not keep turning up the back pages: cast a veil over the past and try to unveil the possibilities of the future. How terrible it would be if God were continually recalling and casting up at us our transgressions! He "blots out" our transgressions and love does the same with the faults of others.

THE LOVE THAT COVERS SINS SHELTERS THE SINNER

I am not sure that Peter meant it in the text, but I am certain it is true. There are men whose duty it is to bring transgressors to book and in the interests of society to punish them for their sins. Their duty must often be painful and disagreeable. Sometimes, as we have seen, public morality demands that we expose the evil doer. But there are many cases, personal cases, where love can throw around the wrong doer, sometimes when he has paid the penalty, the mantle of protecting prayers, influence, and service. We are never nearer Christ than when we, in love and charity, throw a veil over sins and shelter a sinner.

PETER COUNSELS THE ACTION HE HAD SEEN IN JESUS

Indeed, quite deliberately, this is my last word. You remember Peter's awful fall. When Peter met the Lord, he had denied there was no unveiling of his sin and no harsh condemnation. He knew that divine love had covered his sin and trusted him again. There was no hint at his failure. In the light of that we must read, "Love covers sins."

How much we have in our lives that we are glad is covered! What if those who know us best were to reveal all they know? How much God has covered or blotted out! So, in our turn let us have that fervent charity which throws a veil over the sins of others and forgiveness as we have been forgiven. And let any who are afraid of their past, and have been harshly treated by people, be quite sure that God does not ask of others what He does not grant. "There is mercy for the sinner, and more graces for the good, there is mercy with the Saviour, there is healing in His blood."[2]

∼

---

2. This is from F. W. Faber's hymn "There's a Wideness in God's Mercy."

"THE ADDITIONS OF GRACE"
—2 Peter 1.5

(Preached twice at Katherine Road 3/15/36 and Bishop Street, undated)

---

2 Peter 1.5 "Giving all diligence, add to your faith."

I AM NOT VAIN enough to think that my experiences are of special value to others or that special interest attaches to the origin of my sermons. But, to one's own intimate folk and friends, there may, at very occasional times be kindled some interest and some help afforded by a relating of the personal experience out of which a sermon comes.

It is very, very seldom that I use my personal devotional reading for sermonic purposes. Long ago I learned from Dr. Jowett the value of a preacher having literally a Bible never used for homiletical purposes, but reserved for the culture of his own soul. But a few weeks ago, our home Bible reading and the notes in it inspired a thought which I simply must pass on in the hope that it may mean to you something of what it meant to me.

The daily reading was on the passage in which our text is set. The writer of the notes pointed out what we all accept, the fact that the Bible is concerned not with what a person has, but with what he is. It puts far greater emphasis upon character than it does upon opinions or even action. Starting from that accepted principle he pointed out that what the writer of this epistle is here pleading for is—

A FULL-ORBED BEAUTY OF CHARACTER

That is a phrase that fascinates and challenges. Especially when it is set in the light of the fact that the virtues of many of us are incomplete and partial. There are too many "buts" in life and too few "ands." Let me illustrate. Working out a similar theme, that great bookman, Robertson Nicoll, tells of a plain-spoken, old Englishman who said of a lady: "She has beautiful hair, but I think of the head beneath the hair." "Why should he not think about both," asks Nicoll, "there is no reason why a pretty woman should be uncultivated any more than why a learned woman should be untidy. Surely beauty and accomplishment were meant to go together."[1]

Often, we have to say of one person, he is capable but not honest, and of another, he is honest but not very capable. You say of a preacher, he has good thoughts but he has not learned how to express them. We have known a few persons of genius and some of them had not learned good manners. Now apply this in the realm of Christian character.

We have this virtue but not that, one or two graces but not the other. A man is generous but he is rude. A woman has charm but she is indolent. "Father is a good man," said a lady to me, "but he is so hard." And a man confessed to me that the grandparents who brought him up were good, straight people, but their religion was somber and sad. Against such partial and incomplete character, we are called to full-orbed beauty. We should be just and generous, have charm and activity, be straight and true as steel, but not as cold and hard. That is why we are called to—

THE ADDITIONS OF GRACE

Here is no discouragement for humble souls who feel their poverty in spiritual things. It is well that we have any grace or graces at all. They are the signs that God's Spirit is working within us. For "every virtue we possess, and every victory won, and every thought of holiness, are His alone."[2] But we must not be content with passing one or two tests, content with the possession of lonely virtues. We must ever be adding and never content until all the graces are ours.

There are some literary examinations where the candidate is allowed to specialize and if he passes in one or two subjects he is accepted. There are other examinations in which the candidate is examined in a variety of subjects and must reach a certain standard in each and every one, or he fails. Skill in mathematics is not accepted for incompetence in classics, a good paper in philosophy does not balance a bad one in science. The candidate must prove himself an "all-round person." God's tests are of the second order. We are expected to attain proficiency in all the lore of heavenly wisdom.

How much most of us have to learn! How many graces and virtues to add! That is where the call comes to introduce the word the apostle uses—"giving all diligence." True graces and complete Christian character do not come of themselves. Ask your young people what is the price they have to pay if they are to pass their tests. It is only by diligent use of their powers, strengthening themselves when they know they are

---

1. This is from *The Key of the Blue Closet* (1906). The original, however, reads, "Why should he not think about both? There is no reason why a pretty woman should be uncultivated and stupid. There is no reason why a learned woman should be untidy and frowsy. Beauty and accomplishment were mean to go together..."

2. This is from Harriet Auber's hymn "Our Blessed Redeemer ere He Breathed."

"THE ADDITIONS OF GRACE"—2 PETER 1.5

weak, and continually adding to their store of knowledge, that they win their certificates and degrees. And not without diligence and strong handling shall one pass God's test. It will mean earnest endeavor, lonely vigils, strong crying and prayers. It will mean taking ourselves to task, facing our weaknesses and vices.

One sin begets another, provokes another and facilitates another. Sin is not done with when it is done. Wrong done requires a lie to cover it, and the lie demands deception. The connection between the virtues is just as real. Each victory helps you some other to win. I want to emphasize that because I want you to see that if the task we are set is difficult, it is not impossible. Start cultivating some virtue you lack and perfecting some grace you know is weak. The presence of a perfected grace will make you long for everything to match—like a new carpet in your room makes you want new furniture. Victory at one point will make you long for an all-round triumph, and will help you to believe in it. Winning at one point, you can at another. Every virtue attained will raise the whole tone of your life. One golden link will draw another until the chain of Christian graces is complete.

I come back to where I started. The Bible puts the emphasis, not on what a person has, but what he is, upon character and not on opinions or action. But as a person grows and increases in grace and virtue he is saved from the pathetic fatalities of life. "If these things be in you and abound," says the apostle, "they make you that ye shall be neither barren not unfruitful." Every added grace to character is an enrichment of its power, and our best continuation to the goodness of the world is the power of a life of full-orbed beauty of character.

∼

"THE WAY OF BALAAM"
—2 Peter 2.15

(Preached twice at Spring Head Mission 10/13/40 and Bishop St. 11/14/50)

---

2 Peter 2.15 "Which have forsaken the right way, and are gone astray, following the way of Balaam the son of Bosor, who loved the wages of unrighteousness."

BALAAM IS REMEMBERED, IF at all, simply as the man who was rebuked by an ass. Yet his character is one of the most difficult studies in the Bible. You can read his life story—and you might read it—in the book of Numbers, chapters 22, 23, and 24. His best known saying is, "Let me die the death of the righteous." Actually, he was slain as a corrupter of the words of God's people. "Balaam they slew with the sword," Numbers 31.8. The epitaph of the man who wished to die the death of the righteous is, "Balaam . . . who loved the wages of unrighteousness."

Between his prayer and his end is a life of strange inconsistency. He talks like a saint and acts like a sinner. He seldom says a foolish thing and seldom does a wise one. He is always asking for Divine guidance and yet goes his own way. He declares that untold wealth cannot tempt him and yet he pockets a bribe and yields to temptation. He charms us with his noble sentiments and disgusts us with his vulgar actions. He prays that he may die the death of the righteous and actually dies the death of a sinner. That is why I say his life is so curious and difficult to study. But it is more than that. It is a solemn and imperishable warning. Peter found it necessary to warn the people of his day against following the way of Balaam, and the warning is never out of date.

THE WAY OF BALAAM INDICATED BY GOD

There is no time to go into all the details, but look at the heart of it. Balak, king of Moab, was alarmed at the approach of the hosts of Israel and by the stories he had heard of their conquests. He lived in the days when it was believed that certain persons had power to impose a curse. Balaam was such a man. So Balak sent to Balaam offering him a reward if he would curse the Israelites. Quite rightly Balaam inquired of the Lord, and the answer came to him in words that no one can mistake. Listen to them, "Thou shalt not go with them (Balak's messengers); thou shalt not curse the people, for they are blessed." Could anything be more unmistakable and clear? The right way for Balaam was as straight as a rule could make it. Balaam knew it and said to the king's messengers, "Get you into your land: for the Lord refuseth to give me leave to go with you." So far so good.

THE WAY BALAAM TOOK

Not satisfied with the reply, Balak sent more honorable messengers and the offer of an even greater reward to Balaam. "Let nothing hinder thee from coming to me . . . I will promote thee unto very great honor" was the message. And instead of repeating God's orders and keeping to God's way, Balaam ultimately went with the men. When he got within sight of Israel he could not curse, but had to bless them. So, he went to another place. All the time one has the feeling that here was a man who knew the right and did the wrong. He "loved the wages of unrighteousness" and wanted the reward that Balak offered. His covetousness got in the way of his judgment, his conscience, and his actions. So, he failed miserably and died in his folly.

WARNING AGAINST THE WAY OF BALAAM

Dr. Moffatt's translation puts Peter's warning in admirable words. He says of some in his day that "they have gone wrong by leaving the straight road, by following the road of Balaam." That puts it exactly. Balaam did not deliberately take the wrong road. Few people do. He left the straight road and took a crooked one. That is how most of us go wrong. We may break this warning up into some practical advice.

SELF-MADE TEMPTATION

The way of Balaam was the way of self-made temptation. We need not have been tempted as he was. If only he had stood by the clear word of God and kept to the straight road there would have been no difficulty. But he put himself in the way of temptation. That is where many of us fail. "I was tempted and the temptation was too strong for me," we say. Well, temptation can be strong and one sympathizes with the tempted. Just because it is so strong, and because there are some temptations you cannot avoid, for God's sake and your own, don't encourage them! Don't put yourself into positions where you know they will come. Remember that every time you yield you give evil an advantage. New temptations come out of every yielding. Remember that every time you yield to the devil you are putting yourselves into his power.

TRIFLING WITH CONSCIENCE

It is only putting this another way to say that the way of Balaam was of parleying and trifling with conscience. As we have seen, Balaam saw the right road clearly and at first said he would walk in it. Then he began to parley with his conscience. Perhaps he could affect a compromise and still get those rewards. What a familiar story! What an old road! We know the right and we mean to do it. Then the old argument begins. Why not compromise a little. The sin to which we are tempted is not so bad. Lots of people do it. No one will find out. We will make up for our defection by devotion in other directions. So we travel the old crooked road. There is not a person here who does not know where this parleying and trifling leads to. We begin by telling fibs and white lies, but sin is in the telling and lies are as black as hell and inspired by the father of lies. There is only one thing to do, and it is to "exercise ourselves to have a conscience void of offense towards God and humankind." Let your refusal of the beginnings of evil be a thunderous *no!* Where the right way is clear, there is no need for second thoughts. When God, through your conscience says, "This is the way, walk ye in it" you walk.

WAY OF COVETOUSNESS

The way of Balaam was the way of covetousness. The way of unrighteousness, the profits of evil doing, were always in his mind and they led him astray. He did not want to do wrong but he did want the reward that wrong doing would bring. Sometimes it is money, sometimes it is pleasure and the gratification of the appetite. The love of money is a root of all kinds of evil and for pleasures we often sacrifice duty. Then the road that seems profitable turns out to be a way of destruction and death. Thinking of wages, never forget that other grave truth, "The wages of sin is death." What did it profit Balaam? What will it profit you, if you gain riches, honor, and pleasure, and lose your soul? For never, never forget that the way of Balaam ends in death.

The story of Balaam ends there but the sermon does not. I have tried to utter a solemn warning and I can take no word of it back. But I have to preach a gospel as well as utter a warning. What is to be said to a person who has taken the way of Balaam? There is no mistaking the first word. It is "repent." A soldier's definition of that may well serve—"Halt. Right about turn. Quick march!" No more parleying and trifling. The crooked way must be left and honest confession of the wrong doing is required. The consequences of wrongdoing must be faced and accepted. The word of Jesus to a paralyzed man was, "Wilt thou be made whole?" His word to us is, "Do you will to go straight?" If you do, here is the gospel for you, "The crooked shall be made straight and the rough places plain." And Christ will walk with you the steep, rough road that leads to life eternal.

"FELLOWSHIP WITH GOD"
—1 John 1.3

(Preached twice at Fentiman Road 10/28/28 and Sheatham 11/4/28)

---

1 John 1.3 "It is of what we heard and saw that we bring you word, so that you may share our fellowship, and our fellowship is with the Father and with His Son Jesus Christ."

THE GREAT WORD OF this passage is the word "fellowship." The word grabs our attention at once, and we feel that it is rich and spacious, so full of suggestiveness that it is almost impossible of full and final translation. That fact is borne out by this—in the New Testament there are six translations of the original word. For "fellowship," you may substitute communion, communication, distribution, contribution, partnership, or comradeship. All the great facts suggested are within the meaning of the word. They are different notes combining to make a perfect harmony, or they are the different facets of the diamond.

If you want a definition, the best I know is Henry Ward Beecher's. "Fellowship is more than sympathy, although that is the core of it. It is sympathy expressed or manifested in such a way as to draw others towards you in the bonds of brotherhood. Fellowship is making men feel that they are fellows with you, that they are your brethren, that they are related to you, that they are part of your person, as it were."[1] Fellowship is oneness of spirit as well as oneness of aim, it includes community of life as well as unity of purpose.

Perhaps illustration is better here than definition. Take the case I know best—a ministerial fellowship—people keen about the same things and meeting to quicken a common faith and devotion. The Fellowship of Reconciliation affords an admirable illustration. The ideal church is a fellowship and we are using the word more than ever. In the church, we meet to help each other and we sing "and if our fellowship below in Jesus be so sweet, what height of rapture shall we know when round His throne we meet."[2]

---

1. This is from Beecher's sermon "Christian Fellowship," delivered June 22, 1879, and subsequently published in *The Christian Union* vol. XX, no. 1 (July 2, 1879).

2. This is from Charles Wesley's hymn "All Praise to Our Redeeming Lord."

FELLOWSHIP WITH THE FATHER

It is of such fellowship that the text speaks. Earthly illustrations are only used to help us to understand the higher fellowship. Look at the context. This epistle opens with a reference to the fellowship the writer and his friends had had with the historical Jesus. He had gone from them but they still lived in fellowship with Him and with the Father He had revealed. The human comradeship had been transformed into a Divine communion. The "transient" intimacy was a parable of an abiding fellowship. What Jesus had been to them for a while, God was to them forever. They were God's friends, sharing in His purposes and His life, even as they had been the friends of Jesus. As George MacDonald makes David Elgin quaintly and beautifully say, "The Lord took Himself from the sight of them that lo'ed him well, that instead o' being visible afore their eyes, He might hide Himself in their hearts."[3] The abiding fellowship John and his friends could and would share with these who had never known the transient intimacy.

This is where we come in. Fellowship with the Jesus of history was limited, by geographical and temporal boundaries, to a few. We can understand how precious that was and may be pardoned if sometimes we sing, "I should like to have been with him then." But it was Jesus Himself who said, "It is expedient that I go away." His going away opened the door into fellowship with the Father, and the door is open for us. There are no boundaries and limitations here. All that Jesus was to His disciples, God can and will be to us. As the Master called people to be with Him so we are invited into fellowship with the Father.

IT IS INTO FELLOWSHIP THAT WE ARE INVITED

Remember all that fellowship is. That is, it is a real communion. Some of us are content with a mere acquaintance. One day, in Paris, a religious procession with a crucifix at its head passed Voltaire and a friend. Voltaire, who was generally regarded as an atheist, lifted his hat. "What!" exclaimed his friend, "are you reconciled with God?" Voltaire, with fine irony, replied, "We salute but we do not speak."[4] That is the attitude of many who are theists. We have only a nodding acquaintance with God. Maybe we recognize His claims and regard certain days and places as more or less His, but we go no further.

But He invites us to constant communion, to a mind-to-mind and heart-to-heart relation with Him. To the opening of all the inlets of our being to His influence. He wants you to live with Him in the same frank, full fellowship that existed between Jesus and His disciples.

---

3. This is from MacDonald's first realistic novel, *David Elginbrod* (1863). The original reads, "the Lord took himsel' frae the sicht o' them 'at lo'ed him weel, that instead o' bein' veesible afore their een, he micht hide himsel' in their verra herts."

4. This can be found in Voltaire's *Letters on England*.

"FELLOWSHIP WITH GOD"—1 JOHN 1.3

THE INESTIMABLE PRIVILEGE OF HIS FELLOWSHIP

To be counted one of God's friends is surely as great an honor as can be ours. He means so much to us. We can pour out our heart before our friend in perfect confidence. We can bring to him our fears and our sorrows, our doubts and our difficulties, our weaknesses and our sins. He will not fail in understanding or in sympathy, or in anything that belongs to friendship. We need keep nothing back and in turn He will lavish upon us all that Divine friendship suggests. We can have such a friend as the disciples had in Jesus—condescending, patient, kind, loving us enough to deal honestly with us, and wise enough to guide us aright. "O blest communion, fellowship divine!"

FELLOWSHIP AS TERMS OF RESPONSIBILITY

For fellowship on the side of privilege I have suggested the word "communion." Now let us borrow a word from the realm of business and call fellowship a "partnership." On the one side, God makes our interests His and puts His resources at our disposal. The other side of the same fellowship is making His interests ours, and putting ourselves and our resources at His disposal. Here our fellowship means an active partnership with Him in accomplishing the ends for which Jesus was sent into the world. That might be put in many ways, but as I wrote, some words we sang last Sunday leaped to my mind as stating the mission in which God sent his Son into the world. "Jesus the Saviour the Gospel to tell, joyfully came—came with the helpless and hopeless to dwell, sharing their sorrow and shame. Seeking the lost, saving, redeeming, at measureless cost."[5]

If we are really in fellowship, if we are partners with Him. We shall share with Him the toil and the pain, the service and the cost, by which the helpless and hopeless are redeemed and saved. We shall be wholeheartedly with Him in the endeavor to carry the knowledge of redeeming love even to the ends of the earth. We shall keep with Him at the high and holy task of evangelizing and uplifting people near and far until the purpose for which God was manifest in the flesh is realized. Nothing short of that is sufficient.

Phillips Brooks once finely said, "The foreign missionary idea is the necessary completion of the Christian life. It is the apex to which all the lives of the pyramid lead up. The Christian life without it is an imperfect, mangled thing."[6] Yes, our fellowship is with the Father and His Son, and it is through the Holy Spirit. That fellowship works out into God's gracious condescending and our glad and full responding. It is a communion and it is a partnership.

~

5. This nineteenth-century hymn is by Robert Walmsley, and is titled "Come Let Us Sing of a Wonderful Love."

6. This is from a sermon Brooks published as "The Heroism of Foreign Missions," in *Preachers' Monthly* 1.1 (July 1884) 24–29.

"THE GRACE OF PATIENCE"
—Revelation 1.9

(Preached once at Spring Head Mission 7/9/39)

Revelation 1.9 "I John, who also am your brother, and companion in tribulation, and in the kingdom and patience of Jesus Christ."

I SET OUT TO prepare a sermon on the Grace of Patience. I wanted to urge on you and myself the exercise of this virtue in view of the slow progress and retarded triumph of the church and the kingdom. It was not until I had started that this text, which sets patience in a larger frame, gripped me. The subject is still patience, but I am going to give it a wider setting. Let us set ourselves the task of closely examining the text. Mark first the strange conjunction of terms.

TRIBULATION, KINGDOM, PATIENCE

Tribulation and patience, and the two together, we understand. But kingdom and kingship we associate with exemption from tribulation and the need for patience. Well, there is both a conjunction and a connection. For the moment, I state the fact and will return to it presently.

Notice, too, that the three words are reminiscent of great sayings of Jesus. "In the world you shall have tribulation." "It is your Father's good pleasure to give you the kingdom." "In patience ye shall win your souls." So, we are in harmony with our Lord's teaching and have evidence of the deep impression it made on those who heard it.

Now turn to the context. The writer was counseling patience to his already suffering friends. He could not tell them that their sufferings were nearly over. Indeed, he had to tell them that they must prepare for still greater hardships. They were on the eve of the great tribulation, the fiery trial. There was the paramount need of a more patient endurance than had as yet been revealed. If such an appeal had come from one who had only trodden an easy and rosy path it would have irritated. We all object when pampered favorites preach patience to sorrow's sons. So, this man begins by reminding his readers that he was their companion in tribulation and partner with them in suffering. He had endured the sorrow of exile, the pain of imprisonment, and sweated and toiled in the quarries of lonely Patmos. He had taken his share of hardship and that gave him the right to speak and made it their duty to listen. It is worth our while to remember that, when we listen to counsels of patience and endurance coming to us from the pages of the New Testament, we are listening to men who have the right to speak. Before their sufferings, ours pale and they ask for us more than they revealed.

The writer, having stated his authority to speak, is going on to urge his comrades to patient endurance of the pain and persecution coming upon them. But before he does that, with a masterly touch, he reminds them that their fellowship in suffering is not their only experience in Christ. They are sharers in the pain and travail, they have suffered and are about to suffer more for Christ. But they are partners too in the kingdom of Christ. The world holds them in little esteem, even casts them out and puts them to shame. Let them never forget that if they are sharers in Christ's sufferings they are sharers in His glory too. It is well for us to remember that. Our discipleship involves suffering but it brings glory. Partners in tribulation we are sharers of honor also. That is the significance of the strange conjunction of terms here—tribulation, kingdom, patience.

THE COMING KINGDOM

It is only fair to say that the first reference here is to a coming kingdom, and the way to it leads through much tribulation. The glory is to be revealed and meanwhile the path of pain must be walked. In fact, the writer sees his friends entering the great tribulation, in vision he sees them coming out. "These are they which are coming out of the great tribulation, etc." Call that other worldly if you will, to me it is true to the sayings of Jesus and the facts of life. Jesus had to tell His followers that in the world they would have tribulation but it was the Father's good pleasure to give them the kingdom.

Certain it is that in the world at present Christians have need of patience. I can see no justification of their patient endurance except in the coming of the kingdom for which they suffer and labor. There is a noble way of thinking of the sufferings that have to be endured in view of the coming kingdom. You cannot call Paul ignoble and yet he said, "I reckon that the sufferings of this present time are not worthy to be compared with the glory that shall be revealed." Pain and grief must be endured before the kingdom comes and they prepare for and hasten its coming. As John Newton sings, "Why should I complain of want or distress, temptation or pain? He told me no less. The heirs of salvation, I know from the word, through much tribulation must follow their Lord."

THE KINGDOM ALREADY HERE

But it is no contradiction to say that there is a real sense in which the kingdom is already here and we are in it. This very writer has already spoken of Christ loosing people from their sins and making them priests and kings. We are in the kingdom of which Christ is the King and Christ-ruled men are rulers. "Lord of themselves, though not lands, and having nothing yet have all."[1] We are too fond of pampering ourselves and giving the impression that sorrows and trials are our only experience in Christ. That is not true. It is true that in Him we are in the kingdom and sharers in all its joys and hopes. Say that to yourselves—partners in the tribulation and in the kingdom. Just now the helmet may be more prominent and more becoming than the crown, but every Christian carries the crown of life.

PATIENCE AND THE KINGDOM

It is to the kingdom and the kinghood that the virtue of patience is related. That suggests on the surface an incongruous conjunction. We think of patience as meek acceptance of tribulation and our murmuring acquiescence in whatever affliction God or man like to inflict on us. We picture a meek, little woman who suffers in silence, never complains, and is a kind of doormat. There seems nothing kingly about that. We think of kings as men who will accept neither hindrance nor objection to their will.

The patience of the New Testament is much more than passive acquiescence. It is positive, the patient endurance which springs from self-control and strength. It is the virtue which inspires bearing up and pressing on in the path and duty even when the burden is heavy and the road rough and steep and long. The patient spirit is the real kingly spirit. Majesty lies not in fiery haste or arrogant banter. That man is a slave whatever his social position who cannot control his impatient and wayward spirit. The true ruler is the man who has himself in hand and all his powers under control. Patience expresses itself in uncompromising fidelity to the highest standards of truth and duty. Craven souls lower the standard. Kings are they who nail their colors to the mast and stand unmoved and unafraid. That is the patient endurance of the kingdom. "Who patient bear His cross below, they follow in His train."[2]

Patience learns to labor and to wait. The kings of great achievement have won their victories by sustained and patient effort. We are beginning to have greater respect for the person who can hold on there than for the person who can strike out. Can we prove our kinghood by holding in and out though the battle seems to going against us and the victory long delayed? The true king, as Carlyle taught long ago, is the man who can. And when we prove that we can control our fiery spirits, bear our cross, and carry on, we are proving our kingship.

1. This quote is from Harry Wotton's tract "The Character of a Happy Life" (1614).
2. This is from Reginald Heber's nineteenth-century hymn "The Son of God Goes Forth to War."

"THE GRACE OF PATIENCE"—REVELATION 1.9

In this, as in all things, Jesus is the ideal and our example. By the side of the haughty Pilate looked so little like a king that that haughty ruler asked, "Art Thou a king then?" He did not look it, but He was. Think of His majestic and kingly demeanor in all the circumstances of life. He never gave way to petulant impatience or allowed Himself to be driven by the passions of human beings. He bore the worst that people could hold with unflinching loyalty to truth. And how He could wait—for His disciples to learn and for people to accept the truth, for the slow growth of the seed of the kingdom. He is the sublimest example of patience in all time and He stands out as the King. We are called to be partners in the tribulation, and in the kingdom, and in patient endurance.

"CHRIST AT THE DOOR"
—Revelation 3.20

(Preached twenty-seven times from Gateshead to Chester-le-Street, dated only for Bishop St. 11/14/48)

Revelation 3.20 "Behold, I stand at the door and knock: if any one hear my voice, and opens the door, I will come in to Him, and will sup with him, and he with Me."

IN EARLIER DAYS, THAT was one of the red-letter texts in the evangelists New Testament. I seriously question whether any passage of Scripture has been more greatly used to lead people to Christ. It is still one of the great texts of the Bible, simple and sublime. No preacher worthy of the name takes it without trembling. It demands a preacher's best. I can only pray that God will help me to treat it as it deserves and you to give it the hearing of which it is worthy.

THE SERMON IN ART

Perhaps the greatest sermon on this text is not in homiletics but in art. Copies of Holman Hunt's picture hang in many homes. The true setting of it is the original in St. Paul's Cathedral, in London. Many a time I have stood before it. Everything is suggestive, the patient, pleading, thorn-crowned Savior, the door without a handle and overgrown verdure, the pierced hand on the knocker. That is the real sermon. The wounded Christ waiting outside the door of a man's life. The tense of the words adds to the effectiveness. "I am now standing at the door and knocking."

FIGURE AND FACT

For some of you that means little or nothing. The figure is too daring, too anthropomorphic. You cannot or do not visualize God as coming in the likeness of a guest. You do not think of your life as a house with a door you can open or shut. God is not so real or personal to you. I cannot understand that. It may be my fault, but to me, a Deity without personality is almost meaningless. The God who made me must be greater

"CHRIST AT THE DOOR"—REVELATION 3.20

than I am, must be able to think and feel and will more than I can. For me, God is the personal Spirit. It may be your fault, your lack of imagination, poetry, or faith.

For the moment let that pass. If at first you cannot hear it as a fact, it is at heart a suggestive figure. It you cannot think of the Word of God coming to your life in the person of Jesus, think of ways in which the Word does come—in condemnation of your indifference, your indolence, your selfishness. In the appeal of some higher ideal, in some call to service. Think of Him as coming in the poor and needy. God is always coming, knocking to arouse you, calling you to listen, pleading for room in your busy, crowded life. You cannot escape Him. As Browning says, "Just when we fancy we're safest." Whether you interpret the text as fact or figure, it has some vital things to say, and the first is that—

GOD TAKES THE INITIATIVE

The stranger at the door is an uninvited guest. His standing and waiting signifies his desire to enter. If that does not mean much to you, let me remind you that no other great religion will let you say that. They set you climbing the "great world's altar stairs that slope through darkness up to God." Or they send you on long pilgrimages in search for Him. To Christianity belongs the distinctive glory of declaring that God is seeking humankind. The incarnation declares that the Son of Man is come to seek and to save, and reveals the lengths to which He will go in the search. And still He is the world's best seeker. And though we have kept Him outside and rejected, He advances. He is still coming near to us, coming so near that it was once said that only an inch and a half represents the difference. Sankey's hymn has finely caught the idea. "The pilgrim, strange and kingly stops to ask for room in the hearts of men."[1]

MAN'S HIGHEST ENDOWMENT—HIS CAPACITY TO RECEIVE THE DIVINE

Human beings may be the host of the Incarnate. God can and will be the guest of a human heart. The lowliest life may be a temple of the Holy Ghost. That is your distinctive endowment and your supreme capacity. That puts you in a different order to that of the highest animals. It is in your power to think God's thoughts after Him, to speak

---

1. Though Ira Sankey wrote several hymns and composed music for several more, this quotation is apparently a reference to Harriet Beecher Stowe's hymn, "Knocking, knocking, who is there?" which contains the line "'Tis a Pilgrim, strange and kingly," but not the second half of what's quoted here. Instead, while not containing the words of the second half of the quotation, the entire hymn can be seen as a plea for people to make room in their hearts for the pilgrim, "Of thy Saviour waiting there." The reference to Sankey likely comes from the fact that the hymn was published in *Sacred Songs and Solos* (1877), which was compiled by Ira Sankey and Dwight Lyman Moody but contained mostly tunes and lyrics by other authors. The hymnbook was popularly referred to as Sankey and Moody's Songs or The Sankey-Moody Hymnbook.

heavenly words, to do divine works. When the Divine knocks and seeks admission, He is calling you to find a place for the Highest. That is the privilege of the lowliest and most sinful heart.

Think of the coming of Jesus. He was born in a stable, cradled in a manger. One of our hymns makes a parable that every Christmas we sing. "Evil things are there before Thee, in the heart when they have fed, wilt thou pitifully enter, Son of Man, and lay Thy head? Enter, then, O Christ most Holy, make a Christmas in my heart, make a heaven of my manger, it is heaven where Thou art."[2]

The call is for you to find a place in your life for the Highest. It is surely your honor to find room even if something else is crowded out. There is real tragedy expressed in the lines, "Room for pleasure, room for business, but for Christ the crucified, not a place that He can enter in the heart for which He died."

THE COURTESY OF GOD

St. Francis has an exquisite saying, "God is always courteous and does not invade the privacy of the human soul."[3] That is the truth expressed in the text. He knocks and asks admission. The Divine wants the human. Everything depends on the faithful "if." As Holman Hunt said of his picture, "The latch is on the inside." God knocks and pleads, but does not invade. He is a wooer, but not a house breaker. He would have us, not His puppets and pawns, but His children, subject to His persuasion and discipline. You can keep Him outside if you so wish.

Though it is aside from my main thought, notice that it is outside a church that Christ is represented as standing. That adds to the pathos of the figure. Christ crowded out of His own church! It is a repetition of, "He came into His own and His own received Him not." But "if any man will open the door." That does mean that you can open the door and let Him into the church. But it means also that whatever others do, you can open the door of your life. Do not condemn the church if you are not letting Christ into your own life. You at least can bid Him welcome and give Him the satisfaction He seeks.

That is the picture, and a beautiful picture it is. Christ is now knocking at the door. He is coming to us in the strain and business of life, in our crowded days and nights of pleasure, in the cares and anxieties of life. One would think we should fling the heart's door widely open and bid the King of Glory enter. But we keep Him outside.

---

2. This is from George P. Rowe's nineteenth-century hymn "Cradled in a Manger Meanly."

3. The original location of this quote from St. Francis has proven elusive. It is often quoted. See, for instance, George Arthur Buttrick, ed., *The Interpreter's Bible*, (New York: Abingdon, 1952) 8:323.

"CHRIST AT THE DOOR"—REVELATION 3.20
WHY MEN DO NOT LET HIM IN

Some do not hear the knocking. They are preoccupied, do not give time to listen. There is a story of a boy at the Milton Keynes Mission seeing Holman Hunt's picture and who said, "They must be in the back."

Some are afraid of what would have to go if he came in. Some things would go and with our full consent. There would not be room for Him. You do not have to put them out before He comes in! For me, one of the greatest verses Charles Wesley ever wrote, the one that gives me hope of full salvation is, "When Jesus makes my heart His home, my sin shall all depart. And lo, He saith, 'I quickly come, to fill and rule thy heart.'"[4]

For some, the door is hard to open. They hear the knocking and know who is at the door, are inclined to open. Old habits, though, block the door. You try opening the door and you will see what I mean.

So, I leave you with the figure and the fact. Christ is now standing at the door of your life, knocking and seeking admission. If any man or woman will open the door He will come in. He will be your guest. And then he will be host, for He brings you joy from heaven above, pardon, peace, and love. You are afraid of what would go, it is not to be compared with what would come.

I bear testimony. I think I have always been a happy Christian, but just over twenty years ago I went to Newcastle to share in an Evangelistic Campaign. For the first time I heard people singing, "Floods of joy o'er my soul like the sea billows roll, since Jesus came into my heart."[5] Up to then I had thought of "sorrows like sea billows" rolling. Sometime my heart got more widely open and the floods of joy came in. I want no one's pity, I envy no one's future. I know what happens when Jesus comes. And it is out of a great love and an earnest longing that I ask, "Have you any room for Jesus?"

~

---

4. This is from Wesley's hymn "What Is Our Calling's Glorious Hope?"
5. This is from Rufus Daniel's 1914 hymn "Since Jesus Came Into My Heart."

"KNIGHTS OF THE CROSS"
—Revelation 14.4,5

(Preached eleven times from Katherine Road 2/4/34 to Oakengates 4/13/43)

Revelation 14.4, 5 "These are they which follow the Lamb whithersoever He goeth. These were redeemed from among men, to be the first fruits unto God and to the Lamb. And in their mouth was found no guile, for they are without fault before the throne of God."

It is not easy to determine whether the striking scene from which our text is taken is set in heaven or on earth. Commentators differ and when experts are divided the ordinary man finds it difficult to arrive at a satisfactory conclusion. Perhaps it will be safest and truest to say that we have the mingling of the two worlds. Certainly, John seems to hear a voice from heaven and just as certainly the people he is speaking of seem to be on earth. The fullness of the ideal may be realized only in the life to come, but certainly its beginnings are here and now. The fullness of the vision of life belongs to the future, we see the outlines in the present. Even if the vision is wholly heavenly, it sets a pattern for everyday striving on earth. Let us notice at the outset that—

THE VISION IS GIVEN TO CORRECT AND COMFORT

The previous chapter records one of the most depressing and disheartening of visions. It is concerned with the activities of the Beast and his followers. There seems no end to his dirty and devilish works. It looks as if none could escape his craft and cruelty. He seems destined to have all his own way and to win the world to his sway.

But the point of our vision is that the Beast is not having it all his own way. If there are those who bear his mark, there are those who bear on their foreheads the Divine seal. They have never bended a knee to him and they openly avow their allegiance to the Lamb. The Lamb is in the midst of their faithful band and they are sworn to make war against the Beast until all his works are destroyed. I want you to mark that. They were not simply concerned about coming out of the great tribulation and getting to heaven. They were warriors of the Lamb, fighters for the kingdom. They were sealed for service and equipped for warfare.

It is here we may begin our application. It is impossible for us to escape the vision of the evils of our own days, our danger is that of being obsessed by it. There are moods and moments in which, like Elijah under the Juniper tree, the enemies of the faith looms so large that we overlook the thousands who have not bowed the knee to any false god. It would be foolish not to recognize the forces of evil and their activities in the world, it is just as foolish to ignore the forces of the good. Do let us remember the hosts of godly people, earnest preachers and Sunday School teachers, men and women who are untainted by the corruption and idolatry of the world, and who gladly bear the brand marks of the Lord Jesus. Let us remember too that their leader is in the midst of them, and that all heaven is interested in them, and that they march to the music of the eternal world. Frankly, our purpose is to win—

RECRUITS FOR THE ARMY

Our purpose is to recruit for the army men and women sealed with the sign of Christ. Understand what I am pleading for—it is not men and women who are fairly good and who will one day do to heaven. It is not for me to condemn such people. At the moment, I am not concerned about people getting to heaven. I believe lots of people will get there by the skin of their teeth and be more than a lot ashamed when they arrive. I want men and women who are not ashamed to boldly confess Christ and who ask, "Lord, what would Thou have me to do?" And who, when the answer comes will obey without reserve and without delay. I want men and women who will match and more than match the activities and zeal of the workers of iniquity, men and women who are ever more concerned about being fit for the fight and following their leader than they are ever about getting to heaven. I am pleading for Knights of the Cross who regard themselves as "sent forth upon the field of life to war with evil." And this text, as well as any I know, sets forth the qualities of life and character such men and women need.

KNIGHTS OF THE CROSS ARE THE REDEEMED OF THE LORD

"Redeemed from among men"—Authorized Version. "Purchased from among men"—Revised Version. "Ransomed from among men"—Moffatt. That makes us think of the atonement. There is no need to think of the ransom as something legal and mechanical. The same word is used here as in "Ye are not your own, ye are bought with a price." Men are redeemed by goodness, by love, by the infinite grace of Christ. The whole glory of this book is "unto Him that loved us and loosed us from our sins in His own blood." We know enough about the early church to be sure that many of those who made up its membership were once of the earth, earthy. Speaking of sinners guilty of awful evil, Paul wrote, "Such were some of you, but ye are washed, ye are sanctified" (1 Cor 6.11). The very phrase "redeemed from among men" means that these men and women had once been as others, but now they were the "redeemed of the Lord" and they knew it.

All the rest of my appeal will fail and you will never be true Knights of the Cross unless you begin there. New life and service begin when we "survey the wondrous cross" and see in it the grace of Him "who loved us and gave Himself for us," when we realize that we were redeemed with the precious blood of our Lord Jesus Christ. For it is then that we realize that whatever the past has been, and just because it has not been what it might have been, we are henceforth His and He is ours. As the old African Americans used to sing in one of their spirituals, "I've been redeemed! I've been redeemed!"

THE CHARACTER OF THE REDEEMED—THEY WERE TRUE AND STAINLESS

Once they had been false and sinful. Now as Dr. Moffatt translates it, "On their lips no lie was ever detected, they are stainless." You have to remember that they were living in days when there was little regard for the majesty of truth, when lying was exalted into a fine art. Often, they might have saved themselves from persecution by compromise and hypocrisy. But no lie was detected on their lips. The foulness of their times was a proverb but they kept their garments unspotted and their souls unsullied.

Even the first business of a Knight of the Cross is to "love pure, and speak true." The trouble in the days of old when knights were bold was that the knights ceased to be bold against themselves. They carried the name, "Knights of the Cross," when they had lost the spirit of it. On the other hand, it was said of that chivalrous soul, Charles Kingsley, that, "to do a knight's work he lived a knight's life." Here, if my own experience is any guide, is our hardest task. In a world of lies and deception to keep our tongues from evil and our lips from speaking guile, in a world corruption to keep ourselves unspotted from the world. This is the leader's prayers for His followers, not that they should be taken out of the world, but kept from the evil that is in it. Let us make it our aim, not only to be true as steel but true as stainless steel.

THE WHOLE-HEARTED ALLEGIANCE OF THESE KNIGHTS OF THE CROSS

What a magnificent tribute. "These are they which follow the Lamb whithersoever He goeth." He is there to lead and they are there to follow. "There's not to make reply, there's not to reason why," there's only to follow where He leads. Think of all that means. For one man, it means a lonely outpost in China, for some sensitive woman it means a difficult sphere in Africa. If you ask them why they are there they will reply,

"Because He led me here." For some it means staying at home with humdrum duties and tasks, often it is easier to go than stay. But for all of us who would be Knights of the Cross it means not what others are doing and what I would like to do, but what does he want me to do. It means following Him when the way is hard and long, the fire fierce and eager, and the victory long delayed. Here we are at the heart of things and you know now what I meant when I said that I was not pleading simply for nice, respectable people who would go to heaven. On lion-hearted followers of the Lamb, Silvester Horne once wrote a hymn beginning, "O Thee, o'er all exalted far. Out of the depths to Thee I cry, lend but Thy gleam, O Morning Star, and I will follow till I die."[1]

It is easy to write and sing hymns about it, but Silvester Horne followed, served, and loved, until he dropped dead in his tracks. Whatsoever He says unto you, do it. Wherever He leads, you follow. That is the only thing possible to a true Knight of the Cross. And in every crisis, and in every ordinary day, all you have to ask is, "where is He leading," and all you have to do is follow.

THE JOYOUS SETTING OF THE TEXT

Go back to the beginning of the chapter. Here is the band of knights setting out in their brave adventure and the unseen world is interested in them. What I want you specially to mark is their joy. They were threatened with danger, their foes abounded and were fierce and cruel. But they neither complained nor feared. They marched to heavenly music and they had learned for themselves a new song. They were a happy band of fighters. I want you to mark that because I know what many are fearing if not saying. They fear that a life as has been urged, a life of stainless truthfulness and absolute devotion to Christ, will mean a life devoid of joy. Not a bit of it. John's vision is true to the facts of life.

Think of all the joy associated with redemption—the joy of sins forgiven, of fellowship with God. "Ransomed, healed, restored forgiven, who like thee His praise should sing? Hallelujah!" what joy there always is in a pure heart a true spirit! Those who have escaped the corruption of this world can sing as none else can. And, oh the joy of having come completely under the spell of Christ and following Him without reserve. I sometimes ask myself why we are less happy in our religion than Christians of a former generation. Few we are. We have a great many more opportunities for joy rides and joy days, but we have not the same radiant gladness in our religion. It pleases us to pity them for what we think were their long, dull, and weary Sabbaths. Don't waste your pity. To them, Sunday was a day of supreme delight and worship was not so much a duty as a privilege. Why, they were so happy that when they thought of heaven they thought of it as a vast sanctuary, and they sang with fervor, "O when,

---

1. Horne was a late nineteenth-century Congregationalist preacher who took over Whitfield's church and wrote a well-received book on the *Romance of Preaching*. The source for this hymn, however, could not be located.

thou City of my God, shall I thy courts ascend when congregations never breakup and Sabbaths have no end."[2]

That is a sentiment we can hardly understand, and which some people have the bad taste to ridicule. Some of us began with that joy but we have drifted and are seeking pleasures in other things. We sing, "Where is the blessedness I knew?" I can't tell you. It is just where you left it. For all of us the secret, not only of joy, but of joy unspeakable and full of glory, is in ceasing to be half-halfers and becoming non-actors. Follow the Lamb, not where and when you please, but "whithersoever He goeth," and you will learn and sing the heavenly song.

---

[2]. The original author of this hymn is unknown, as it is very ancient and originally in Latin, and it went through various revisions over the centuries. The common title is "Jerusalem My Happy Home," and perhaps William Burkitt's 1693 version is the most common one in English.

"No More Sea"
—Revelation 21.1

(Preached at Fentiman Road 7/13/30, Katherine Road 7/5/36, and Spring Head Mission 3/28/43)

Revelation 21.1 "And there was no more sea."

You are not, of course, to think John was speaking literally. This is one of his many visions of spiritual things. We are dealing with apocalyptic and with symbols. He was thinking of and picturing for us the golden age, the good time coming, what was at least in part to be realized here and perfected in heaven. It all represents the ideal toward which God is working and wants us to work, the ideal which will be the actual when God's will is done on earth as it is in heaven. There is to be a new earth as well as a new heaven and we have to help God create it. That is the value of these visions. They reveal God's mind and call us to the task of living and working for their realization.

Even when we remember we are dealing with symbols, it is surprising to us that John has no use for the sea. To us it represents health and adventure, challenge and joy. It is our boast that we are the sons of the sea and that the "silver streak" is our best protection. Our children play on its beach and puddle gleefully in its waters. Most of us think it ideal for holidays and long for at least one day in the year by the silver sea.

Why, then, had John no use for the sea, and even picture the ideal as having none of it? For one thing, he was a Jew. The Jews were an agricultural people and loved not the sea. Almost every reference in the Bible is to it as a symbol of unrest, terror, a destructive force. Rivers? Yes they were gladdening rivers of value to fields and crops, but the sea? No. It was barren and unfriendly. It had robbed the Jews of their ships, their merchandise their loved ones. In the book of Revelation, the sea was the abode of the beasts. They rose up "out of the sea." It was the source of wicked powers and the home of evil things. He puts in his vision the river flowing by the throne of God.

But the strongest reason is to be found in John's experience. There he was in the rocky isle in the open sea, surrounded by its waters and cut off by them from all he held dear. The sea made him a prisoner, held him in solitude, and limited his eager activities. It was a barrier and not a highway to him. So, as he looked across the barren and friendless waste he felt that there was no place for the sea in the ideal times which were coming. We must look at the subject from John's prison on the rocky, lonely island if we would catch the spiritual meaning of the sea-less heaven and earth.

NO MORE SEPARATION

Then it suggests that there will be no more separation. John was longing for the fellowship of worship, wanting to see and talk with well-loved friends, anxious to talk with them of his Lord and theirs. He couldn't get to them. He was lonely and heart-hungry. As he envisioned the new heaven and earth it came to him, there would be no more sea, and he meant "no more separation." Now, how that picture answers the heart-cry of many. Oh! The pain and the tears of life's separations! Where is now the merry party I remember long ago? They are scattered far and wide, homes are broken up, brothers and sisters who played and quarreled together are living far apart, friends have emigrated, the little folk we cuddled and caressed are grown up now and have gone their several ways. In many a home father and mother sit alone and soon strangers will take their place. There are others, and we have to look away and across another sea for them, sometimes it seems so wide.

Now do you see the meaning and value of John's words, "there shall be no more sea?" Nothing shall separate us from the love of God in Christ Jesus and nothing shall separate us from those who are in that love. Even now the more we know of dwelling in Him, the more we know of the spot where spirits blend independently of distance. We can wait with patience and in hope for the meeting when no seas separate us form those whom we "have loved and lost awhile."

NO MORE LIMITATION

And, John means, no more limitation. Without doubt, John was thinking of all that needed to be done. The cause he loved was wanting every loyal heart and every faithful mind, yet he was shut in, limited, could do nothing. He wanted to shepherd his flock, extend his Master's kingdom, and carry the light to those who sat in darkness. And that sea which shut him in and held him prisoner became the symbol of cruel limitation that must be done away before he could attain his heart's desire.

Here again the vision touches us closely. Often, we speak of those who are low minded, sadly contented with a show of things. But there are many who have noble ambitions, earnest longing, great and pure desires. They would fain do great things but are shut in to narrow and small achievements. Some are limited by weak bodies, others are crippled in mind, and others are hedged in by circumstances they cannot control. They have felt and thought as have others, but for them the dream has never become a deed. They have planned in marble, but have had to build in common stone. In heart they have given gold, but actually only copper.

What a message this is for all such. A message of freedom, spaciousness, and in a word, freedom for cruel limitations. This mortal is to put on immortality. There shall be no more sea. There shall be perfect health, freedom from all mental limitations, liberty to become all that it is in our hearts to be. All we have wished and willed shall be, not its semblance, but itself. Say it to yourself. I shall be so healthy and well that I shall mount up with the wings like eagles, run and not be weary, walk and not faint.

NO MORE UNREST

It has already been said that the sea represents unrest. John's promise is of no more unrest. To Jews in general and to John in particular the sea was troubled and never at rest. That heaving and tossing sea was the symbol of the unrest in the world and in our own heart. Why this separation and limitation? What so much mystery and trouble? Then there are surging unrests of his own spirit, conflicting longings, and heart-hunger for other things. His very words have passed into our common speech. We, talking of "tossing seas." "Sorrows like sea billows roll," and the sea for us too is a symbol of unrest. This "no more sea" message is for us, too. There was one who bids the waves be still, and He is at work creating the place in which there shall be no more sea, no unrest. We shall be stayed in His tranquility, every restless longing satisfied, all our weariness forgotten, all our questions answered. "On Jesus' bosom naught but calm is found." There shall be no more sea.

NO MORE SIN

And you must give time for the last and greatest word. There shall be no more sin. Professor Milligan insists that the main reference is to the sea as the place whence evil arises. The Hebrews looked upon the sea as the symbol of evil. "The wicked are like a troubled sea" which casts up its mire and dirt. They looked upon it as the home of all manner of evil, evil thoughts, desires, and ways. We, too, so think and speak of storms of passion and self-will, of making shipwreck of faith and a good conscience. We know that the real separation, the inflictor of limitations, the causes of unrest, is sin. John meant and the message for us is, there shall be no more sin. What a glorious message, the message of deliverance form the thing that separates, limits, and troubles. Many a person's sins are not of his will, but of his body. He is kept down, enslaved, by a coarse nature and fleshly hands of sensuality, so that he misses God's "awful rose of dawn." Here is the promise that this crippling, shaming, damning thing is to be no more. That deep troublous sea, wherein is all manner of evil, and which is forever hurling itself against the character we are seeking to build, is to be dried up. Then the symbol will be not a sea representing unrest, but a river typifying peace.

Brethren, our Lord is doing these things now. The true message is, "I am making all things new." And you and I are helping or hindering Him. He is working as

He always does, through human agents. We can do something to lessen the sense of separation and solitude, we can clear away some limiting barriers, we can tell troubled men and women of the rest given, we can point crippled sinners to the Savior, and we can have our share in building the New Jerusalem. For we are meant to be builders of that city and workers together with Christ in the holy task. Let us do our best, and make sure it is our best. Then, though we die in faith without seeing the glorious dream fully realized, we shall have brought it nearer, and all shall pass into the perfect fellowship, freedom, peace, and purity of that heaven where there is no more sea.

www.ingramcontent.com/pod-product-compliance
Lightning Source LLC
Chambersburg PA
CBHW060454300426
44113CB00016B/2583